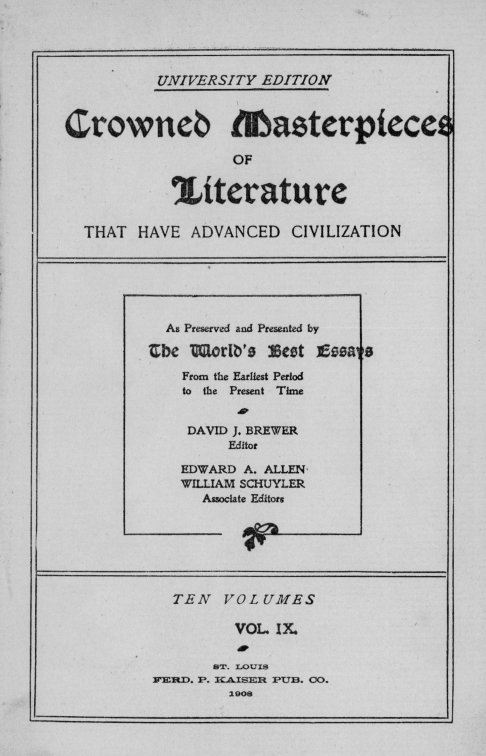

UNIVERSITY EDITION

Crowned Masterpieces

OF

Literature

THAT HAVE ADVANCED CIVILIZATION

As Preserved and Presented by

The World's Best Essays

From the Earliest Period
to the Present Time

DAVID J. BREWER
Editor

EDWARD A. ALLEN
WILLIAM SCHUYLER
Associate Editors

TEN VOLUMES

VOL. IX.

ST. LOUIS
FERD. P. KAISER PUB. CO.
1908

University Edition

SPECIAL TESTIMONIAL SET

Copyright, 1908

BY

FERD. P. KAISER PUB. CO.

THE ADVISORY COUNCIL

16397

TABLE OF CONTENTS

VOLUME IX

—

vii

ix

FULL-PAGE ILLUSTRATIONS

VOLUME IX

———

MADAME ROLAND

(Manon Jeanne Phlipon Roland de la Platière)

(1754–1793)

N INTELLECT, Madame Roland was one of the most remarkable women of the eighteenth century, and in the romantic interest of her life, she is second among the heroines of the French Revolution only to Charlotte Corday. Her "Philosophical and Literary Essays," published soon after her death and republished in London in 1800, fully sustain the historical and traditional theory of her ability. It was the remarkable power of her intellect which energized her husband and enabled the Girondist party to keep a foothold in the stormy politics of the Revolution at a time when to be accused of moderation was almost equivalent to a conviction of capital crime. Gratien Phlipon, Madame Roland's father, was an engraver by profession and it is from him that she seems to have received the speculative impulses which enabled her to break away from the political conventionality of her time and become a leader in revolution. Her earliest reading was of the great classical writers from whom she imbibed the republican principles which animated her work for the overthrow of the royalty in France. In M. Roland, whom she married in 1781, she found a kindred spirit. He was nearly twenty-two years her senior and no doubt greatly her superior in thoroughness, but he lacked her quickness of intellect and was always ready to rely rather upon the intuitions of her genius than on his own common sense. When they appeared together at Paris in 1791, they soon became one of the potent influences against royalty. Roland became a member of the Jacobin Club and acted with them until their radicalism resulted in the formation of a more conservative party,—the Girondists,—which in the crisis of 1792 made him Minister of the Interior. He used this position to force issues with the king. A letter written by Madame Roland, and addressed by her husband to the king, led to a Cabinet crisis and to the dismissal of Roland. This was the prelude to the overthrow of royalty, but instead of being the Aspasia of a great and world-reforming republic as she had hoped, Madame Roland found herself at first the sport and then the victim of forces too violent to be checked or directed by any power of intellect or of combination. After the death of the king and the September massacres, the Girondists fearlessly devoted themselves to inevitable destruction.   Hated alike by Royalists and Jacobins, they had no refuge except in honorable death; and this, with Vergniaud and Roland at their head, they challenged by impeaching Robespierre when he was at the height of his power.   On June 1st, 1793, Madame Roland was arrested, and on November 8th, 1793, was carried to the guillotine in the Place de la Revolution, where the scaffold was overlooked by a statue of Liberty, which she addressed in her celebrated apostrophe, "O Liberty, what crimes are committed in thy name!" On hearing of her death, her husband, then at Rouen, pinned on his breast a paper declaring his unwillingness to survive her, and killed himself by falling on the point of the stiletto he carried in his walking cane.

LIBERTY—ITS MEANING AND ITS COST

INSULATED and tranquil, in the stillness of the night and in that of the passions, I dare think, I dare write, without presumption and without fear.   Silence, son of repose, it is in thy profound bosom that my wandering ideas are heaped up and collected.   The shades spread on the theatre of illusion stop its prestiges; all is confounded; all is silent . . . even to my heart: this is the moment when victorious reason commands, and acts with liberty.   What have I said?   What implies that great name, whose imposing and confused object by turns astonishes, misleads, and inflames the imagination?   What is liberty?*

I cannot consider it so generally; I distinguish, liberty of the will, that of the mind.   I doubt whether the first exists; the second appears to me very uncommon, and the third belongs but to sages.   Metaphysical liberty is a problem on which I endeavor to exercise my ideas; political liberty is a blessing the image and utility of which I love to recall to mind; philosophical liberty, the only liberty, perhaps, that it is my province to know, is a treasure which I wish to acquire.

Political liberty, for each individual of a society, consists in doing everything that he judges proper for his own happiness, in what does not injure others.   It is the power of being happy, without doing harm to any one.   Is there an advantage that can be compared to it?   Nothing in the world can supply its place: delicious fruit of the laws, it gives the human soul all the energy of which it is susceptible.

* This paragraph follows exactly the text of 1800 as do all the articles by Madame Roland here given.

The reign of the general will is the only reign that maintains public felicity; from the moment when power secures independence to some parts of the state, corruption introduces itself, and soon becomes manifest by the misery of the oppressed.

Slavery and virtue are incompatible. Slavery breaks all the ties that connect man with his fellow-creature; it relaxes and destroys the two springs that contribute most to the development of our faculties, the esteem of ourselves, and glory, which is only the result of public esteem; it suffers nothing to subsist but odious force and degrading fear.

Tyranny equally debases him who exercises it and those whom it enslaves; with it all lose the sentiment of truth, the idea of justice, and the taste of good.

It is to him who knows the extent and the limits of his rights, that we may look for a respect for those of others, a generous intrepidity in their defense, and the noble care of their preservation.

True courage belongs only to the free man. Of what can those be capable who are nothing except by the will of the master? And to what obligations would he believe himself restricted, who must fancy himself of a nature superior to that of the people he commands?

The enjoyment and the inviolability of the first rights of social man,— personal safety and property,— with the power of claiming them in case of an accidental injury, properly constitute the essence of liberty. This is the masterpiece of legislation; but so many things prevent its being carried into execution, or counteract its being brought to perfection and concur in its ruin, that very seldom is it seen to subsist, even for a short time, unimpaired.

All nations are not capable of enjoying liberty; the same nation cannot support it equally at all times.

The climate, the soil, and the species of its productions, the situation of the places, their extent, etc., pave the way to it or estrange it from its inhabitants, according to the spirit, the wants, and the resources which it affords them. Liberty is for the most part the companion of poverty; the fertility of a country abounding in superfluities, stifles it in a manner by its richness. And, indeed, it is pretty generally true, that the finest countries are those which have the worst governments.

Bare competence, or comfort acquired by labor, makes men honest and the state happy; in this, it is with the nation as with the individual, too many wants excite cupidity and engender corruption.

The English are said to be free, and I believe they are so more than their neighbors,—more than most of the nations of Europe, except the Swiss; but commerce and the love of gain, riches, and luxury, by weakening their morals, insensibly sap their constitution, or render useless a great part of its effects.

People are often mistaken respecting the word liberty. I give not this name to the anarchy into which fell again, certain republics; such, for instance, as Syracuse, after the death or expulsion of the tyrants who had governed them by intrigue or by violence, and whom they had given themselves through weakness. Liberty suits none but simple men, who have few wants. When we consider the infinite care, the continual vigilance, which the maintenance of the laws demand in a free state, the time required for the acts of sovereignty which regard each of the citizens, we are sensible how few of them remain for other occupations. If we reflect, besides, that industry and the arts open the first door to inequality, insulate those who profess them by affording them extraordinary means of acquiring property, and offering them resources independent of the common good, we shall perceive how great was the wisdom of the legislators who banished them from their states.

The Lacedæmonians were nothing else than husbandmen and soldiers; but they had helots? It would be very astonishing if, in the same government, the slavery of one part of the species should be absolutely necessary to the perfect happiness of the other. This idea makes me shudder; I dare not investigate it.

I hasten to arrive at what suits me much better; I leave metaphysical reveries and political speculations to the more able; I prefer what more nearly concerns action, and I think that is my element. I understand by liberty of mind, not only that sound view of an enlightened judgment which is not disturbed by prejudices or by passions, but also that firm and tranquil temper of a strong soul, superior to events. I call it philosophy, because it is the fruit of wisdom and one of its most unequivocal proofs; it is under these titles that I regard it as a treasure. I add that I am determined to labor to acquire it; nothing is more true nor more easy. With reason sufficient to appreciate things at what they are worth, we may suffer ourselves to be affected too warmly by some of them, for want of having contracted the habit of conquering ourselves by courageous and daily exercise. The same vivacity of feeling which on many occasions elevates us above ourselves, often sinks us again below our level by the frequent revolutions of which it renders us the sport.

The empire over ourselves is the finest of empires, that of which the conquest costs us most, and the possession of which is the sweetest. We think we have done much when we have familiarized ourselves with austerity,— let us speak more correctly, with grief; it seems that it is it which, acting on our organs in the most immediate manner, must principally disturb the liberty of the mind. Yet if it be true that the value which we attach to things makes almost their whole importance, and that the force of ideas and the power of imagination are capable of diverting us from the actual impressions which they make on our senses, it must be acknowledged that physical evils are not the most dangerous for an elevated and delicate soul. It is not precisely in undergoing such and such trials that our courage is manifested, but it is in supporting the loss of what is dearest to us, and this, too, is where it generally fails. Alas! we are so constituted for pain, that all the efforts employed to bear us up against it, serve only to render it more acute in certain parts. The better we have known the variety of those things which fix the desires of the misled vulgar, and the more we have diminished the objects of our esteem, the more, too, do we remain violently attached to those which we preserve and which we think we ought to distinguish. Reason, virtue, everything draws these ties the closer; if cruel necessity chance to break them, what dreadful torments! the disorder of the body is nothing; the rigors of fate scarcely deserved to be mentioned; but in the pains which proceed from the heart, or which strike at it, I can do no more than wrap up my head and waste away in silence. O sensibility! delight and torment of our days, how much do thy sacrifices exercise and fatigue our philosophy! it is with the greatest justice that has been established, as the first principle of happiness, that secret enjoyment of virtue, which consists in the recollection of having done well, and in the resolution of continuing to do so; beyond that, every thing is full of illusions and falsehoods, and the sweetest accessories to this first pleasure are crossed by poignant and bitter afflictions. Where is the man who has learned to content himself **with** this satisfaction and dispense with every other? His felicity is independent and unchangeable; that is the true sage and my hero; he alone can preserve perfect liberty of mind.

We have so perverted the use of the blessings bestowed on us by nature, that we have reduced ourselves no longer to find, but in their voluntary privation, the peace that ought to accompany them.

We must love mankind sufficiently to concern ourselves about their welfare, and esteem them so little as not to expect any return on their part.

Judgment appears to me to consist in discovering that we can accomplish our own happiness only in laboring at that of others; reason seems to me the firm resolution of acting always agreeably to this principle; the highest degree of virtue is to do good with enthusiasm, because it is honorable and delightful. Sublime delirium, by which the exalted soul finds unheard-of strength, and puts itself on a footing with the gods! Happy he who knows its transports and renders himself worthy of ever enjoying them! Exact calculation and cold reasoning never make us capable of doing so; it belongs to feelings alone to inspire us with them. Reflection sometimes damps the ardor of our efforts, as repose cools courage; in point of morals, as soon as we are certain of having adopted the best, we must follow them blindfold. But it is to the fascination, to the enchantment of virtue alone, that it is allowable to subject the liberty of the mind.

I touch lightly on these subjects; how many things concerning each of them do I perceive confusedly in my mind, and which a little application would draw forth! But I will not labor: I rapidly sketch the most prominent ideas, and I wait for the others to become clear.

Complete.   From the works of Mme. Roland.
London, 1800.

PENSÉES

On Happiness

HAPPINESS! . . . every one talks of it, few know it, and those who feel it, waste not their time in describing it. I, who am meditating on it I enjoy it not at this moment.

Feeling fills the soul; every enjoyment absorbs profound reflections; he, whose mind discusses matters coolly, is certainly not affected in a warm and touching manner. Such never wrote but from the want of something to divert his mind: how many others would have thought little had not active grief unfolded their faculties?

Complete.

DOING GOOD

BENEFICENCE has this peculiarity, that the more we exercise it, the more pleasure we find in its exercise. We attach our-selves to the unfortunate object that we relieve, and the assistance we give him becomes a want to those by whom it is administered.

He who has once caused the tears of gratitude to flow, and who can afterwards seek a pleasure sweeter than that, is not worthy of feeling all the charm of doing good.

Complete.

BORROWED IDEAS

IT is useful to borrow the ideas of others; but the habit of con-sulting them, makes the mind contract a sort of sloth and dullness, which renders it incapable of ever determining by its own powers. Reading extends the judgment; to form it, is the province of meditation.

There are some people who are stupid from dint of science; so many names, facts, and experiences are heaped up in their head, that natural genius has been smothered by them; their con-versation is a repertory of what they have read, without ever being the expression of what they have reasoned upon; it does very well to make use of them as of a dictionary, but the think-ing, contemplative being must be sought for elsewhere.

Too much reading overloads the memory, and dulls the imag-ination; meditation, on the contrary, carried to excess, heats, exalts, and leads to madness.

Complete.

The Gift of Silence

I HAVE often remarked, that the persons who passed for the most discreet were not the most happy in the choice of their confidants.

There is a strength of mind, by no means common, in burying in silence what strongly affects us. Yet prudence imposes on us a law almost equal, to conceal the secrets of others and our own violent feelings; the passions mislead us to such a degree, that, blushing, after their crisis is over, at the blindness into which they have plunged us, we almost always regret our having communicated the opinions with which they inspired us. Besides, an excessive reserve, at least with friends, bespeaks a mistrust of ourselves, and a fear of examination, which are not very honorable to him who entertains them. Honest souls are unreserved; dissimulation, on the contrary, serves as a mask to bad intentions; it is the cloak of the courtier and the virtue of intrigue.

In affairs, there must be inviolable secrecy; in the ordinary commerce of life, a prudent reserve; and in the connections of the heart, an unlimited confidence.

The last part of my precept is not without inconvenience, I know; but for myself, I rather choose to run the risk of its observation, than to deprive myself of the pleasures that must thence result.

Complete.

Virtue an Inspiration

VIRTUE is not to be demonstrated, it is calculated to be felt; we must inspire it, and not preach it up; it is by far the best thing in the world, but it is for those who love it. Some one has said, with a deal of justness, that we attach ourselves still less to virtue from the charms that we find in it, than from the sacrifices that we make to it. I like this idea; it touches, flatters, and penetrates me.

In a constitution of things where natural order is perverted, where consequence, esteem, distinctions,—exterior advantages, in short,—are the reward of factitious merit, it would be a very improper idea to wish to cause virtue to be adopted because it is useful; we must cause it to be cherished, because it is amiable;

it belongs to those who possess it, to know all its utility, and to congratulate themselves on their choice.

Our morals are such, that it amounts almost to audacity, to undertake to rear new citizens; we must hope for many circumstances, and rely still more on the example that we feel ourselves capable of affording.

Complete.

Character and Association

THE commerce of the world affords us the facility of expressing ourselves readily and gracefully concerning the objects which present themselves; but it cannot contribute to improve the judgment, except of those who have theirs already well formed.

Men, in general, lose part of their natural character by being in continual company, and we are never less ourselves than in living much with others. It is hardly anywhere but in solitude that we learn to think strongly; there it is that the mind is improved and enlightened, that the ideas are extended and strengthened, that the feelings become refined and fortified, that the moral man acquires a consistency, and assumes those qualities which he afterwards exercises among his fellows.

There are persons who cannot endure solitude; and it is so much the worse for them; I know some of these; I see only the more reason to pity them.

We may cherish solitude without becoming misanthropes; none are less susceptible of attachment than dissipated people; feeling souls withdraw from the crowd.

I am tired of those amphibious beings whom we cannot define, who do not know themselves, and whom we find everywhere dragging their incapacity; they make me impatient for retirement.

Complete.

Intellect and Progress

IF WE understand by thinking, the action of the mind, inasmuch as it considers its own ideas, combines and rectifies them, I state it as a fact that the most contemplative man has not thought the quarter of his life.

Our wants are so numerous, the necessity of satisfying them occurs so frequently, engages so much of our attention,— continued sensations occupying us in such a manner, by the mere images of objects, or tyrannizing over us so much by their presence, that it is still surprising that we can employ ourselves about so many things. What a considerable portion of time lost to the mind! In representing to ourselves the species as a great individual being, ought we to be astonished at the slowness of its progress in every way, and at the almost eternal infancy in which it seems to remain? I am frightened at the immensity of time that has been required to bring us only where we are.

Enter into details: see every man, always confused by varied and successive impressions,— he acquires without enjoying, adopts without examining, and judges mechanically. Inattention and habit maintain and encourage ignorance and error; every thing counteracts the discovery of truth, and dilatory experience cannot cause it to be admitted but in the process of time.

Complete.

JEAN JACQUES ROUSSEAU

(1712–1778)

ERHAPS if an impartial jury were called upon to decide on the evidence what thousand words of modern prose have made the most history, the verdict would be for (or against!) the sixth chapter of Rousseau's first book on the "Social Contract." It is the most definite formulation made, prior to 1776, of the idea that "all men are created equal; that they are endowed by the Creator with certain unalienable rights; that among these are Life, Liberty, and the Pursuit of Happiness; that to secure these rights governments are instituted among men, deriving their just powers from the consent of the governed." The problem of government, as Rousseau stated it, is "to find a form of association which may defend and protect with the whole force of the community the person and property of every associate, and by means of which each, coalescing with all, may, nevertheless, obey only himself and remain as free as before."

John Locke in England and Rousseau in France, gave the intellectual impulse to the movement which resulted in the two great revolutions of the eighteenth century. The Republic of America and the Republic of France might have come without them through evolution, had it been possible for evolution to do its work against the obstructive forces of eighteenth-century "Toryism." With the eighteenth century as it was, however, nothing might have been accomplished except through the power of great intellects moved to radicalism by such uncompromising analyses of fundamental principles as those in which Rousseau swept away the claim that one class of men can rightly assert a title from Heaven to rule. Since the "Social Contract" appeared, "Divine Right," as a title to govern, has been abandoned by all publicists who make any serious pretension to logic. When "Higher Civilization" is substituted for "Divine Right" in later times, Rousseau's definition is evaded rather than combated. Indeed, the corollary from his definition, "that governments are instituted to secure rights rather than to support privilege," and that "they derive their just powers from the governed," has not been met with any other logic than that of the *status quo ante*, in the presence of which it remains still to the minds of many practical-minded men what it was called by Rufus Choate,—"a glittering generality." It is one of those definitions, however, which, when once formulated, become to thousands who do not possess the power of analysis in their own intellectual right, as sacred as a religious creed. The American Revolution of 1776, the French Revolution which followed it, and the American Civil War, alike testify the terrible power of a definition which first and finally reduces a great, world-moving idea to its simplest terms. Had Rousseau not impregnated the mind of civilization with the idea that "just government" must be representative in order to be just, the plea that American slavery made the slave contented and happy might have been accepted by the public opinion of the world,— which, however, could not entertain it when Rousseau was represented in the nineteenth century by Garrison and Lincoln, as he had been in the eighteenth by Jefferson, Danton, and Wilberforce. It is singular that this remarkable man should not only dominate thus the politics of the eighteenth and nineteenth centuries, but that the theories of education which he formulated in his "Émile" should, at the opening of the twentieth century, still remain the governing impulse in all that is most distinctively modern in the training of youth for citizenship. He inspired Fröbel in Germany, as he did the founders of the public school system in America. It is hard to find in history any one who, by purely intellectual force, has exerted a power over the course of events which can be compared to that attributable with certainty to Rousseau. It is impossible to account for his possession of it on any other theory than that his genuine benevolence overcame weaknesses and vices which otherwise would have vitiated his influence and nullified his work. No life was ever more unequal to the demand of a great intellect than his. The highest benevolence seemed not incompatible in him with moral weakness verging close on depravity.— as when, while writing on Virtue and Philosophy, he sent his own children one after another to the foundling asylum. Perhaps what often verges on "moral idiocy" in him may be accounted for to a very great extent by the circumstances of his birth and early education. At Geneva, where he was born (June 28th, 1712), his father was without social standing, and, as his mother died in giving him birth, he was left without the training which gives intellectual power its stimulus and complement of moral force. His father "mended watches and taught dancing" for a living, and Jean Jacques himself "was successively an engraver's apprentice, a lackey, a student in a seminary, a clerk, a private tutor, and a music copyist," before he became a great author. Where the least said about his morals is the soonest mended, this, perhaps, is sufficient to suggest the lack of stability of character which seems to be the radical infirmity of his nature. The astonishing versatility of his genius, the powerful analytical faculty which characterized his intellect, and the incessant activity of his mind,—these are rather to be wondered at than accounted for. Of the scores of books and pamphlets he left behind, his "Confessions" and the "New Héloïse" are the most generally read, while the "Social Contract" and the "Émile" are the most influential. Of the great power both these works have exerted for progress there can be no question. There is a reasonable question, however, if writing in the spirit which comes only of a virtuous life, Rousseau might not have accomplished far greater results through the same intellectual energy exerted in modes which would have made those he influenced more willing to trust the power of demonstrated truth, than to triumph suddenly and violently at the expense of those whose weakness or selfishness made them its opponents.

W. V. B.

THAT MEN ARE BORN FREE

MAN is born free, and everywhere he is in chains. Many a one believes himself the master of others, and yet he is a greater slave than they. How has this change come about? I do not know. What can render it legitimate? I believe that I can settle this question.

If I considered only force and the results that proceed from it, I should say that so long as a people is compelled to obey and does obey, it does well; but that, so soon as it can shake off the yoke and does shake it off, it does better; for, if men recover their freedom by virtue of the same right by which it was taken away, either they are justified in resuming it, or there was no justification for depriving them of it. But the social order is a sacred right which serves as a foundation for all others. This right, however, does not come from nature. It is, therefore, based on conventions. The question is to know what these conventions are.

"Social Contract," Book I., Chap. i.

THE SOCIAL CONTRACT

I ASSUME that men have reached a point at which the obstacles that endanger their preservation in the state of nature overcome by their resistance the forces which each individual can exert with a view to maintaining himself in that state. Then this primitive condition can no longer subsist, and the human race would perish unless it changed its mode of existence.

Now, as men cannot create any new forces, but only combine and direct those that exist, they have no other means of self-preservation than to form by aggregation a sum of forces which may overcome the resistance, to put them in action by a single motive power, and to make them work in concert.

The sum of forces can be produced only by the combination of many; but the strength and freedom of each man being the chief instruments of his preservation, how can he pledge them without injuring himself, and without neglecting the cares which he owes to himself? This difficulty, applied to my subject, may be expressed in these terms: —

"To find a form of association which may defend and protect, with the whole force of the community, the person and property of every associate, and by means of which each, coalescing with all, may, nevertheless, obey only himself, and remain as free as before." Such is the fundamental problem of which the social contract furnishes the solution.

The clauses of this contract are so determined by the nature of the act that the slightest modification would render them vain and ineffectual; so that, although they have never perhaps been formally enunciated, they are everywhere the same, everywhere tacitly admitted and recognized, until, the social pact being violated, each man regains his original rights and recovers his natural liberty, whilst losing the conventional liberty for which he renounced it.

These clauses, rightly understood, are reducible to one only, viz., the total alienation to the whole community of each associate with all his rights; for, in the first place, since each gives himself up entirely, the conditions are equal for all; and, the conditions being equal for all, no one has any interest in making them burdensome to others.

Further, the alienation being made without reserve, the union is as perfect as it can be, and an individual associate can no longer claim anything; for, if rights were left to individuals, since there would be no common superior who could judge between them and the public, each, being on some point his own judge, would soon claim to be so on all; the state of nature would still subsist, and the association would necessarily become tyrannical or useless.

In short, each giving himself to all, gives himself to nobody; and as there is not one associate over whom we do not acquire the same rights which we concede to him over ourselves, we gain the equivalent of all that we lose, and more power to preserve what we have.

If, then, we set aside what is not of the essence of the social contract, we shall find that it is reducible to the following terms: "Each of us puts in common his person and his whole power under the supreme direction of the general will; and in return we receive every member as an indivisible part of the whole."

Forthwith, instead of the individual personalities of all the contracting parties, this act of association produces a moral and collective body, which is composed of as many members as the assembly has voices, and which receives from this same act its unity, its common self (*moi*), its life, and its will. This public person, which is thus formed by the union of all the individual members, formerly took the name of city, and now takes that of republic or body politic, which is called by its members state when it is passive, sovereign when it is active, power when it is compared to similar bodies. With regard to the associates, they take collectively the name of people, and are called individually citizens, as participating in the sovereign power, and subjects, as subjected to the laws of the state. But these terms are often confused and are mistaken for one another; it is sufficient to know how to distinguish them when they are used with complete precision.

Complete. "Social Contract,"
Book I., Chap. vi.

NATURE AND EDUCATION

EVERYTHING is perfect, coming from the hands of the Creator; everything degenerates in the hands of man. He forces a spot of ground to nourish the productions of a foreign soil; or a tree to bear fruit by the insition of another; he mixes and confounds climates, elements, seasons; he mutilates his dog, his horse, his slave; he inverts the nature of things, only to disfigure them; he is fond of deformity and monstrous productions; he is pleased with nothing, as it is framed by nature, not even with man; we must break him to his mind, like a managed horse; we must fashion him to his taste, like the trees or plants of his garden.

Were it not for this culture, things would still be worse; for our species will not bear being fashioned by halves. In the present constitution of things, man abandoned from his birth to his own guidance among the rest of society, would be a monstrous animal. Prejudices, authority, necessity, example, and all the social institutions with which we are surrounded, would stifle the voice of nature, and substitute nothing else in its place. Nature would be to him like a plant or shrub, that shoots up spontaneously in the highway, but is soon trodden down and destroyed by travelers.

To thee do I therefore address my discourse, O fond and careful mother, whose sense has led thee out of the common tract, and taught thee to preserve the tender plant from the injurious blast of human opinions! Be sure to water the young sprig before it dies; it will one day yield such fruit as must afford thee infinite delight. Take care to erect an early enclosure around the infant's mind; others may mark out the circumference, but to thee alone it belongs to fix the barrier.

Plants are fashioned by culture, and men by education. Were man to be born of full size and strength, these would avail him nought, till he learnt to make use of them; nay, they would rather resound to his prejudice, by preventing others from lending him assistance; so that, being left to himself, he would die miserably before he knew his wants. We are apt to complain of the state of infancy; not reflecting, that if man had not commenced an infant, the human species must have perished.

We are all brought into the world feeble and weak, yet we stand in need of strength; we are destitute of everything, yet we want assistance; we are senseless and stupid, yet we have occasion for judgment. All that we have not at our birth, and that we stand in need of at the years of maturity, is the gift of education.

Education is either from nature, from men, or from things. The developing of our faculties and organs, is the education of nature; that of men, is the application we learn to make of this very developing; and that of things is the experience we acquire in regard to the different objects by which we are affected.

Mankind are all formed by three sorts of masters. The pupil, in whom their instructions contradict each other, is ill-educated, and will never be self-consistent. He, in whom they all coincide on the same point, and tend to the same end, he alone may be said to hit his aim, and to live consistently. In short, he alone is well educated.

Now, of those three different educations, that of nature is independent in us; that of things depends on us only in particular respects, and this in a hypothetical sense; for who can pretend to direct every word and action of those who have the care of an infant?

No sooner, therefore, does education become an art, than it is almost impossible it should succeed; since the concurrence of circumstances necessary for its success is in no man's power. All that we can possibly do, by dint of care, is to come near the mark, more or less; but he must be very fortunate indeed who hits it.

But what mark is this? you will say; the very same that nature has in view. This we have just now proved; for since the concurrence of the three educations is necessary for their completion, the other two must be directed towards that which is no way subject to our control. But, perhaps, the word nature may bear, on this occasion, to indeterminate a sense; we shall, therefore, endeavor to fix it.

Nature, you will say, is nothing more than a habit. But what do you mean by that? Are not habits contracted by mere force, which cannot be said, however, to stifle nature? Such, for instance, is the habit of plants, constrained in their vertical direction. Restored to their liberty, they still retain the direction they have been forced to assume; yet the sap has not changed its original impression; and if the plant continues to vegetate, its prolongation once more becomes vertical. It is the same in regard to human inclinations. So long as we continue in the same state, we may retain such inclinations as result from habit, and are least natural to us; but as soon as the situation changes, the habit ceases, and nature revives. Education surely is nothing more than habit. And yet are there not some people who altogether forget, and others who retain, their education? Whence this difference? If we are to confine the word nature to habits conformable to nature, surely we may spare ourselves the trouble of this nonsensical expression.

We are all born with a certain degree of sensibility, and from the very first instant of our existence we are differently affected

by the objects that surround us. As soon as we acquire, if I
may so speak, a consciousness of our sensations, we are disposed
either to pursue or to flee from the objects that produce them;
at first, as they are agreeable or displeasing to us; in the next
place, in proportion to the agreement or disagreement we find
between ourselves and the objects; and lastly, pursuant to the
judgment we form of them, from the idea of happiness or perfection acquired by reason. These dispositions are enlarged and
strengthened, in proportion as we become more sensible and intelligent; but restrained by habit, they are altered more or less
by opinion. Before this alteration, they are what I distinguish
in man by the name of nature.

To these primitive dispositions every thing must, therefore, be
referred; and this might easily be done, were the three sorts of
education no more than different; but what are we to do, when
they happen to be opposite? When, instead of educating a man
for himself, you want to educate him for others, the harmony or
agreement is then impossible. Being obliged either to combat
nature or social institutions, you must make your option, whether
you are to form the man or the citizen; for you cannot do both.

Every partial society, when it is close and compact, deviates
greatly from the general link; great lovers of their country are
rude and uncivil to strangers; they look upon them only in the
common light as men, and as unworthy of their regard. This
inconveniency is inevitable, but of no great consequence. The
point is, to behave kindly towards our fellow-subjects. Abroad,
the Spartans were ambitious, avaricious, and unjust; while disinterestedness, equity, and concord reigned within their walls. Be-
ware of those cosmopolites who pore over old books in search of
duties, which they neglect to fulfill within their own communi-
ties. Thus you will see a philosopher admiring the Tartars, in
order to be excused from loving his neighbors.

Man in his natural state is all for himself; he is the numer-
ical unit or the absolute integer, that refers only to himself, or to
his likeness. Man in the civil state is a fractionary unit, who
depends on the denominator, and whose value consists in his relation to the integer, namely, the body politic. Among social
institutions, those are the best, which are best adapted for divest-
ing man of his natural state; for depriving him of his absolute,
to give him a relative, existence; in short, for transferring self
to a common unit; to the end, that each individual may no

longer consider himself as one, but as part of a unit, and have no sense or feeling but in conjunction with the whole. A Roman citizen was neither Caius nor Lucius,—he was a Roman; but he loved his country exclusive of himself. Regulus pretended to be a Carthaginian, as he was become the property of his masters. In the quality of a stranger, he refused to take his seat in the Roman senate; and before he would comply, he insisted upon receiving orders from a Carthaginian. With indignation he beheld the endeavors used to save his life. He carried his point, and returned triumphant to Carthage, to resign his last breath amidst the most exquisite tortures. Here we behold a man of quite a different stamp from those of the present age.

From « Émile.» Translated by N. Nugent.

CHRIST AND SOCRATES

I WILL confess that the majesty of the Scriptures strikes me with admiration, as the purity of the Gospel hath its influence on my heart. Peruse the works of our philosophers with all their pomp of diction: how mean, how contemptible are they compared with the Scriptures! Is it possible that a book, at once so simple and sublime, should be merely the work of man? Is it possible that the sacred personage, whose history it contains, should be himself a mere man? Do we find that he assumed the tone of an enthusiast or ambitious sectary? What sweetness, what purity in his manner! What an affecting gracefulness in his delivery! What sublimity in his maxims! what profound wisdom in his discourses! What presence of mind, what subtlety, what truth in his replies! How great the command over his passions! Where is the man, where the philosopher, who could so live, and so die, without weakness, and without ostentation? When Plato described his imaginary good man loaded with all the shame of guilt, yet meriting the highest rewards of virtue, he describes exactly the character of Jesus Christ: the resemblance was so striking, that all the Fathers perceived it.

What prepossession, what blindness must it be to compare the son of Sophronicus to the son of Mary! What an infinite disproportion there is between them! Socrates dying without pain or ignominy, easily supported his character to the last; and if his death, however easy, had not crowned his life, it might have been doubted whether Socrates, with all his wisdom, was anything more than a vain sophist. He invented, it is said, the theory of morals. Others, however, had before put them in practice; he had only to say, therefore, what they had done, and to reduce their examples to precepts. Aristides had been just before Socrates defined justice; Leonidas had given up his life for his country before Socrates declared patriotism to be a duty; the Spartans were a sober people before Socrates recommended sobriety; before he had even defined virtue, Greece abounded in virtuous men. But where could Jesus learn, among his competitors, that pure and sublime morality, of which he only hath given us both precept and example? The greatest wisdom was made known amongst the most bigoted fanaticism, and the simplicity of the most heroic virtues did honor to the vilest people on earth. The death of Socrates, peaceably philosophizing with his friends, appears the most agreeable that could be wished for; that of Jesus, expiring in the midst of agonizing pains, abused, insulted, and accused by a whole nation, is the most horrible that could be feared. Socrates, in receiving the cup of poison, blessed, indeed, the weeping executioner who administered it; but Jesus, in the midst of excruciating torments, prayed for his merciless tormentors. Yes, if the life and death of Socrates were those of a sage, the life and death of Jesus are those of a God. Shall we suppose the evangelic history a mere fiction? Indeed, my friend, it bears not the marks of fiction; on the contrary, the history of Socrates, which nobody presumes to doubt, is not so well attested as that of Jesus Christ. Such a supposition, in fact, only shifts the difficulty without obviating it: it is more inconceivable that a number of persons should agree to write such a history, than that one only should furnish the subject of it. The Jewish authors were incapable of the diction, and strangers to the morality, contained in the Gospel, the marks of whose truth are so striking and inimitable, that the inventor would be a more astonishing character than the hero.

JOHN RUSKIN

(1819–1900)

AMONG English prose writers of the second half of the nineteenth century, John Ruskin was scarcely equaled in the attractiveness of his style, and he was not equaled at all in the range of his thought and the variety of his productions. He is peculiarly identified with the second half of the century, for, with the exception of the first and minor edition of his "Modern Painters," nearly all his great works were published between 1849 and 1900. As an "art critic," he 'has had no equal among English writers. But it is with "art" as the expression of the whole idea impressed on humanity by nature that he deals, rather than with art in the limited sense in which it is generally understood. Students of any single art, as of painting or sculpture, are apt to dissent from his conclusions and to question the practical usefulness of his methods; and in the sense in which a professional painter criticizes technique, Ruskin is hardly to be classed as an art critic at all. He represents in England more nearly than any one else the larger view of art which Hegel in Germany did so much to make possible. It was from Carlyle, however, rather than from any German master, that Ruskin received his most potent inspiration. He may be called Carlyle's greatest pupil. Indeed in many things he is Carlyle's superior. His prose style shows traces of Carlyle's mannerisms, but it is more fluent, more melodious, and more persuasive, than that of Carlyle, whose intensity of expression is often more apt to excite admiration than to carry conviction. Like Carlyle, Ruskin was, in his political views, distrustful of freedom as a mode of progress. He defined his distrust in the assertion that men are only fit for freedom in the inverse ratio of their desire for it. In his later life, he developed an ideal of æsthetic culture for the masses, depending on socialism as a mode of aristocratic control and tutelage. He was deeply moved by beauty in art and nature. The old Greek "beauty worship" has had no greater disciple than he. He himself looked on beauty as a revelation of divine goodness. And his message was one of reverence for the good and true not less than for the beautiful. He seems not to have considered, however, that physiological laws which made the Greeks what they were, operate against substituting the Greek for the Puritan ideal among "Anglo-Saxons." Pericles and Aspasia, listening to a recitation from Homer with an "ear" which enabled

them to co-ordinate perfectly the relation of every vowel to every
other in a period of melody as easily as a trained composer does in
listening to his own opera,— such finely-organized beings as these
were not fitted to serve as saints of progress for the race which
produced John Milton and John Bunyan,— which in their spirit
must seek its salvation by pressing through the "Valley of the
Shadow of Death," with the smoke of hell coming up through the
grass-roots and a leather-winged Apollyon hovering over it. "Sin"
was something the Greeks knew nothing about, and when Phidias
worked, the self-consciousness of the world had not advanced far
enough to make possible the conception of a Devil as it is present in
the subconsciousness of English-speaking peoples. The world of the
old Saxons was a "Midgard"—a "middle enclosure," with heaven on
one side and hell on the other. The world of the primitive Greeks
was thronged with genially human gods and demigods. Heaven
was no further away than the top of Mount Olympus, and the idea
of hell, of the progressive and finally climacteric punitive reactions
of evil, was not sufficiently developed to cause alarm. Neither Ruskin
nor any other prophet of art could have transferred to nineteenth-
century England the artistic cult developed by such conditions as
these. But Ruskin in attempting it, achieved all that was possible.

He was born in London, February 8th, 1819. His father was a
wine merchant who had accumulated a large fortune. On his death
it descended to Ruskin, who was thus enabled to gratify without
great sacrifices the desire for the study of art, which early in life
became his ruling passion. After graduating from Christ Church
College, Oxford, in 1842, he studied painting under Copley Fielding,
and Harding, and afterwards spent much of his time in Italy,—
especially in Venice where he found everything he most needed to
inspire him. He held professorships both at Cambridge and Oxford,
and utilized his lectures as material for a number of the remarkable
volumes which during the last twenty-five years of his life he published with such astonishing rapidity. The completion of his "Modern
Painters" established his standing as the leading English authority
on the philosophy of art, and, in consequence, the public demands
on his energies were incessant and remorseless. In endeavoring to
meet them, he wrecked his nervous system and for several years before he died (January 20th, 1900) he was insane. His life was a
tragedy. The beautiful woman whom he loved and married did not
love him. Finding that she did love his friend, the painter, Millais,
Ruskin secured a divorce for her and brought about her marriage to
Millais. Deprived thus of domestic happiness, he devoted himself
wholly to his work, and in it found "every good and perfect gift"
except that consummation and sum of all, without which all is
fruitless — peace.   W. V. B.

THE SKY

IT IS a strange thing how little in general people know about the sky. It is the part of creation in which nature has done more for the sake of pleasing man — more for the sole and evident purpose of talking to him, and teaching him — than in any other of her works; and it is just the part in which we least attend to her. There are not many of her other works in which some more material or essential purpose than the mere pleasing of man is not answered by every part of their organization; but every essential purpose of the sky might, so far as we know, be answered if once in three days, or thereabouts, a great, ugly, black rain cloud were brought up over the blue, and everything well watered, and so all left blue again till next time, with perhaps a film of morning and evening mist for dew — and instead of this, there is not a moment of any day of our lives, when nature is not producing scene after scene, picture after picture, glory after glory, and working still upon such exquisite and constant principles of the most perfect beauty, that it is quite certain * it is all done for us, and intended for our perpetual pleasure. And every man, wherever placed, however far from other sources of interest or of beauty, has this doing for him constantly. The noblest scenes of the earth can be seen and known but by few; it is not intended that man should live always in the midst of them; he injures them by his presence, he ceases to feel them if he is always with them; but the sky is for all: bright as it is, it is not

> « too bright nor good
> For human nature's daily food »;

it is fitted in all its functions for the perpetual comfort and exalting of the heart, — for soothing it, and purifying it from its dross and dust. Sometimes gentle, sometimes capricious, sometimes awful — never the same for two moments together; almost human in its passions, almost spiritual in its tenderness, almost divine in its infinity, its appeal to what is immortal in us is as distinct as its ministry of chastisement or of blessing to what is

---

* At least, I thought so, when I was four-and-twenty. At five-and-twenty I fancy that it is possible there may be other creatures in the universe, to be pleased, or, — it may be, — displeased by the weather.

                                                                    J. R.

mortal is essential. And yet we never attend to it, we never make it a subject of thought, but as it has to do with our animal sensations, we look upon all by which it speaks to us more clearly than to brutes, upon all which bears witness to the intention of the Supreme that we are to receive more from the covering vault than the light and the dew which we share with the weed and the worm, only as a succession of meaningless and monotonous accident, too common and too vain to be worthy of a moment of watchfulness, or a glance of admiration. If in our moments of utter idleness and insipidity, we turn to the sky as a last resource, which of its phenomena do we speak of? One says, it has been wet; and another, it has been windy; and another, it has been warm. Who among the whole chattering crowd can tell me of the forms and the precipices of the chain of tall white mountains that girded the horizon at noon yesterday? Who saw the narrow sunbeam that came out of the south, and smote upon their summits until they melted and moldered away in the dust of blue rain? Who saw the dance of the dead clouds where the sunlight left them last night, and the west wind blew them before it like withered leaves? All has passed unregretted as unseen; or if the apathy be ever shaken off even for an instant, it is only by what is gross, or what is extraordinary. And yet it is not in the broad and fierce manifestations of the elemental energies, nor in the clash of the hail, nor the drift of the whirlwind, that the highest characters of the sublime are developed. God is not in the earthquake, nor in the fire, but in the still small voice. They are but the blunt and the low faculties of our nature, which can only be addressed through lampblack and lightning. It is in quiet and unsubdued passages of unobtrusive majesty, the deep and the calm, and the perpetual; that which must be sought ere it is seen, and loved ere it is understood; things which the angels work out for us daily, and yet vary eternally; which are never wanting, and never repeated, which are to be found always, yet each found but once; it is through these that the lesson of devotion is chiefly taught, and the blessing of beauty given.

We habitually think of the rain cloud only as dark and gray; not knowing that we owe to it perhaps the fairest, though not the most dazzling, of the hues of heaven. Often in our English mornings, the rain clouds in the dawn form soft, level fields, which melt imperceptibly into the blue; or, when of less extent, gather into apparent bars, crossing the sheets of broader clouds above; and all these bathed throughout in an unspeakable light of pure rose-color, and purple, and amber, and blue; not shining, but misty-soft; the barred masses, when seen nearer, composed of clusters or tresses of cloud, like floss silk; looking as if each knot were a little swathe or sheaf of lighted rain.

Aqueous vapor or mist, suspended in the atmosphere, becomes visible exactly as dust does in the air of a room. In the shadows, you not only cannot see the dust itself, because unillumined, but you can see other objects through the dust, without obscurity; the air being thus actually rendered more transparent by a deprivation of light. Where a sunbeam enters, every particle of dust becomes visible, and a palpable interruption to the sight; so that a transverse sunbeam is a real obstacle to the vision — you cannot see things clearly through it. In the same way, wherever vapor is illuminated by transverse rays, there it becomes visible as a whiteness more or less affecting the purity of the blue, and destroying it exactly in proportion to the degree of illumination. But where vapor is in shade, it has very little effect on the sky, perhaps making it a little deeper and grayer than it otherwise would be, but not, itself, unless very dense, distinguishable, or felt as mist.

Has the reader any distinct idea of what clouds are?

That mist which lies in the morning so softly in the valley, level and white, through which the tops of the trees rise as if through an inundation — why is it so heavy, and why does it lie so low, being yet so thin and frail that it will melt away utterly into splendor of morning when the sun has shone on it but a few moments more? Those colossal pyramids, huge and firm, with outlines as of rocks, and strength to bear the beating of the high sun full on their fiery flanks, — why are they so light, their bases high over our heads, high over the heads of Alps? Why will these melt away, not as the sun rises, but as he descends, and leave the stars of twilight clear; while the valley vapor gains again upon the earth, like a shroud? Or that ghost of a cloud, which steals by yonder clump of pines; nay, which does not steal by them, but haunts them, wreathing yet round them, and yet, — and yet, — slowly; now falling in a fair waved line like a woman's veil; now fading, now gone; we look away for an instant, and look back, and it is again there. What has it to do with that clump of pines, that it broods by them, and waves itself among their branches to and fro? Has it hidden a cloudy treasure among the moss at their roots, which it watches thus? Or has some strong enchanter charmed it into fond returning, or bound it fast within those bars of bough? And yonder filmy crescent, bent like an archer's bow above the snowy summit, the highest of all the hills — that white arch which never forms but over the supreme crest, — how it is stayed there, repelled apparently from the snow, — nowhere touching it, the clear sky seen between it and the mountain edge, yet never leaving it — poised as a white bird hovers over its nest! Or those war clouds that gather on the horizon, dragon-crested, tongued with fire, — how is their barbed strength bridled? What bits are those they are champing with their vaporous lips, flinging off flakes of black foam? Leagued leviathans of the Sea of Heaven, — out of their nostrils goeth smoke, and their eyes are like the eyelids of the morning; the sword of him that layeth at them cannot hold the spear, the dart, nor the habergeon. Where ride the captains of their armies? Where are set the measures of their march? Fierce murmurers, answering each other from morning until evening — what rebuke is this which has awed them into peace; — what hand has reined them back by the way in which they came?

I know not if the reader will think at first that questions like these are easily answered. So far from it, I rather believe that some of the mysteries of the clouds never will be understood by us at all. " Knowest thou the balancing of the clouds?" Is the answer ever to be one of pride? The wondrous works of him, which is perfect in knowledge? Is our knowledge ever to be so?

For my own part, I enjoy the mystery, and perhaps the reader may. I think he ought. He should not be less grateful for summer rain, or see less beauty in the clouds of morning, because they come to prove him with hard questions; to which, perhaps, if we look close at the heavenly scroll, we may find also a syllable or two of answer, illuminated here and there.

And though the climates of the south and east may be comparatively clear, they are no more absolutely clear than our own northern air. Intense clearness, whether in the north, after or before rain, or in some moments of twilight in the south, is always, as far as I am acquainted with natural phenomena, a notable thing. Mist of some sort, or mirage, or confusion of light or of cloud, are the general facts; the distance may vary in different climates at which the effects of mist begin, but they are always present; and therefore, in all probability, it is meant that we should enjoy them. . . . We surely need not wonder that mist and all its phenomena have been made delightful to us, since our happiness as thinking beings must depend on our being content to accept only partial knowledge even in those matters which chiefly concern us. If we insist upon perfect intelligibility and complete declaration in every moral subject, we shall instantly fall into misery of unbelief. Our whole happiness and power of energetic action depend upon our being able to breathe and live in the cloud; content to see it opening here, and closing there; rejoicing to catch through the thinnest films of it glimpses of stable and substantial things; but yet perceiving a nobleness even in the concealment, and rejoicing that the kindly veil is spread where the untempered light might have scorched us, or the infinite clearness wearied. And I believe that the resentment of this interference of the mist is one of the forms of proud error which are too easily mistaken for virtues. To be content in utter darkness and ignorance is indeed unmanly, and therefore we think that to love light and find knowledge must always be right. Yet (as in all matters before observed), wherever pride has any share in the work, even knowledge and light may be ill pursued. Knowledge is good, and light is good; yet man perished in seeking knowledge, and moths perish in seeking light; and if we, who are crushed before the moth, will not accept such mystery as is needful to us, we shall perish in like manner. But, accepted in humbleness, it instantly becomes an element of pleasure; and I think that every rightly constituted mind ought to rejoice, not so much in knowing anything clearly, as in feeling that there is infinitely more which it cannot know. None but proud or weak men would mourn over this, for we may always know more if we choose by working on; but the pleasure is, I think, to humble people, in knowing that the journey is endless, the treasure inexhaustible,—watching the cloud still march before them with its summitless pillar, and being sure that, to the end of time, and to the length of eternity, the mysteries of its infinity will still open further and further, their dimness being the sign and necessary adjunct of their inexhaustibleness. I know there are an evil mystery and a deathful dimness,—the mystery of a great Babylon—the dimness of the sealed eye and soul; but do not let us confuse these with the glorious mystery of the things which the angels "desire to look into," or with the dimness which, even before the clear eye and open soul, still rests on sealed pages of the eternal volume.

On some isolated mountain at daybreak,* when the night mists first rise from off the plain, watch their white and lake-like fields, as they float in level bays, and winding gulfs about the islanded summits of the lower hills, untouched yet by more than dawn, colder and more quiet than a windless sea under the moon of midnight; watch when the first sunbeam is sent upon the silver channels, how the foam of their undulating surface parts, and passes away, and down under their depths the glittering city and green pasture lie like Atlantas, between the white paths of winding rivers; the flakes of light falling every moment faster and broader among the starry spires, as the wreathed surges break and vanish above them, and the confused crests and ridges of the dark hills shorten their gray shadows upon the plain. Wait a little longer, and you shall see those scattered mists rallying in the ravines, and floating up towards you, along the winding valleys, till they couch in quiet masses, iridescent with the morning light, upon the broad breasts of the higher hills, whose leagues of massy undulation will melt back, back into that robe of material light, until they fade away, and set in its lustre, to appear again above in the serene heaven like a wild, bright, impossible dream, foundationless, and inaccessible, their very base vanishing in the unsubstantial, and making blue of the deep lake below. Wait yet a little longer, and you shall see those mists gather themselves into white towers, and stand like fortresses along the promontories, massy and motionless, only piled with every instant higher and higher into the sky, and casting longer shadows athwart the rocks; and out of the pale blue of the horizon you will see forming and advancing a troop of narrow, dark, pointed vapors, which will cover the sky, inch by inch, with their gray network, and take the light off the landscape with an eclipse which will stop the singing of the birds, and the motion of the leaves, together;—and then you will see horizontal bars of black shadow forming under them, and lurid

* I forget now what all this is about. It seems to be a recollection of the Rigi, with assumption that the enthusiastic spectator is to stand for a day and night in observation; to suffer the effects of a severe thunder storm, and to get neither breakfast nor dinner. I have seen such a storm on the Rigi, however, and more than one such sunrise; and I much doubt if its present visitors by rail will see more.

J. R.

wreaths create themselves, you know not how, among the shoulders of the hills; you never see them form, but when you look back to a place which was clear an instant ago, there is a cloud on it, hanging by the precipice as a hawk pauses over his prey; — and then you will hear the sudden rush of the awakened wind, and you will see those watchtowers of vapor swept away from their foundations, and waving curtains of opaque rain let down to the valley, swinging from the burdened clouds in black bending fringes, or, pacing in pale columns along the lake level, grazing its surface into foam as they go. And then as the sun sinks you shall see the storm drift for an instant from off the hills, leaving their broad sides smoking and loaded yet with snow-white, torn, steam-like rags of capricious vapor, now gone, now gathered again, — while the smoldering sun, seeming not far away, but burning like a red hot-ball beside you, and as if you could reach it, plunges through the rushing wind and rolling cloud with headlong fall, as if it meant to rise no more, dyeing all the air about it with blood; — and then you shall hear the fainting tempest die in the hollow of the night, and you shall see a green halo kindling on the summit of the eastern hills, brighter, brighter yet, till the large white circle of the slow moon is lifted up among the barred clouds, step by step, line by line; star after star she quenches with her kindling light, setting in their stead an army of pale, penetrable fleecy wreaths in the heaven, to give light upon the earth, which move together hand in hand, company by company, troop by troop, so measured in their unity of motion that the whole heaven seems to roll with them, and the earth to reel under them. And then wait yet for one hour, until the east again becomes purple, and the heaving mountains, rolling against it in darkness, like waves of a wild sea, are drowned one by one in the glory of its burning; watch the white glaciers blaze in their winding paths about the mountains, like mighty serpents with scales of fire; watch the columnar peaks of solitary snow, kindling downwards chasm by chasm, each in itself a new morning — their long avalanches cast down in keen streams brighter than the lightning, sending each his tribute of driven snow, like altar smoke up to heaven, the rose light of their silent domes flushing that heaven about them, and above them, piercing with purer light through its purple lines of lifted cloud, casting a new glory on every wreath, as it passes by. until the whole heaven one scarlet canopy is interwoven with a roof of waving flame, and tossing vault beyond vault, as with the drifted wings of many companies of angels: and then when you can look no more for gladness, and when you are bowed down with fear and love of the Maker and Doer of this, tell me who has best delivered this his message unto men!

*The account given of the stages of creation in the first chapter of Genesis is in every respect clear and intelligible to the simplest reader, except in the statement of the work of the second day. I suppose that this statement is passed over by careless readers without any endeavor to understand it, and contemplated by simple and faithful readers as a sublime mystery which was not intended to be understood. But there is no mystery in any other part of the chapter, and it seems to me unjust to conclude that any was intended here. And the passage ought to be peculiarly interesting to us, as being the first in the Bible in which the heavens are named, and the only one in which the word "heaven," all important as that word is to our understanding of the most precious promises of Scripture, receives a definite explanation. Let us therefore see whether, by a little careful comparison of the verse with other passages in which the word occurs, we may not be able to arrive at as clear an understanding of this portion of the chapter as of the rest. In the first place the English word "firmament" itself is obscure and useless; because we never employ it but as a synonym of heaven, it conveys no other distinct idea to us; and the verse, though from our familiarity with it we imagine that it possesses meaning, has in reality no more point nor value than if it were written, "God said, Let there be a something in the midst of the waters, and God called the something, Heaven." But the marginal reading, "Expansion," has definite value; and the statement that God said, Let there be an expansion in the midst of the waters, and "God called the expansion, Heaven," has an apprehensible meaning. Accepting this expression as the one intended, we have next to ask what expansion there is, between two waters, describable by the term "heaven." Milton adopts the term "expanse," but he understands it of the whole volume of the air which surrounds the earth. Whereas, so far as we can tell, there is no water be-

---

*This passage, to the end of the section, is one of the last, and best, which I wrote in the temper of my youth; and I can still ratify it, thus far, that the texts referred to in it must either be received as it explains them, or neglected altogether.   J. R.

yond the air, in the fields of space; and the whole expression of division of waters from waters is thus rendered valueless. Now with respect to this whole chapter, we must remember always that it is intended for the instruction of all mankind, not for the learned reader only; and that therefore the most simple and natural interruption is the likeliest in general to be the true one. An unscientific reader knows little about the manner in which the volume of the atmosphere surrounds the earth; but I imagine that he could hardly glance at the sky when rain was falling in the distance, and see the level line of the bases of the clouds from which the shower descended, without being able to attach an instant and easy meaning to the words, " expansion in the midst of the waters "; and if, having once seized this idea, he proceeded to examine it more accurately, he would perceive at once, if he had ever noticed anything of the nature of clouds, that the level line of their bases did indeed most severely and stringently divide " waters from waters " — that is to say, divide water in its collective and tangible state, from water in its aërial state; or the waters which fall and flow, from those which rise and float. Next, if we try this interpretation in the theological sense of the word Heaven, and examine whether the clouds are spoken of as God's dwelling place, we find God going before the Israelites in a pillar of cloud; revealing himself in a cloud on the mercy seat, filling the temple of Solomon with the cloud when its dedication is accepted; appearing in a great cloud to Ezekiel; ascending into a cloud before the eyes of the disciples on Mount Olivet; and in like manner returning to judgment: " Behold he cometh with clouds, and every eye shall see him." " Then shall they see the Son of Man coming in the clouds of heaven, with power and great glory." While further the " clouds " and " heavens " are used as interchangeable words in those Psalms which most distinctly set forth the power of God: " He bowed the heavens also, and came down; he made darkness pavilions round about him, dark waters, and thick clouds of the skies." And again, " Thy mercy, O Lord, is in the heavens, and thy faithfulness reacheth unto the clouds." And again, " His excellency is over Israel, and his strength is in the clouds." And again, " The clouds poured out water, the skies sent out a sound, the voice of thy thunder was in the heaven." Again, " Clouds and darkness are round about him, righteousness and judgment are the habitation of his throne; the heavens declare his righteousness, and all the people see his glory." In all these passages the meaning is unmistakable if they possess definite meaning at all. We are too apt to take them merely for sublime and vague imagery, and therefore gradually to lose the apprehension of their life and power. The expression, "He bowed the heavens," for instance, is, I suppose, received by most readers as a magnificent hyperbole, having reference to some peculiar and fearful manifestation of God's power to the writer of the Psalm in which the words occur. But the expression either has plain meaning, or it has no meaning. Understand by the term "heavens" the compass of infinite space around the earth, and the expression "bowed the heavens," however sublime, is wholly without meaning: infinite space cannot be bent or bowed. But understand by the "heavens" the veil of clouds above the earth, and the expression is neither hyperbolical nor obscure; it is pure, plain, accurate truth, and it describes God, not as revealing himself in any peculiar way to David, but doing what he is still doing before our own eyes, day by day. By accepting the words in their simple sense, we are thus lead to apprehend the immediate presence of the Deity, and his purpose of manifesting himself as near us whenever the storm cloud stoops upon its course; while by our vague and inaccurate acceptance of the words, we remove the idea of his presence far from us, into a region which we can neither see nor know: and gradually, from the close realization of a living God, who "maketh the clouds his chariot," we define and explain ourselves into dim and distant suspicion of an inactive God inhabiting inconceivable places, and fading into the multitudinous formalisms of the laws of nature. All errors of this kind — and in the present day we are in constant and grievous danger of falling into them — arise from the originally mistaken idea that man can, "by searching, find out God — find out the Almighty to perfection" — that is to say, by help of courses of reasoning and accumulations of science, apprehend the nature of the Deity, in a more exalted and more accurate manner than in a state of comparative ignorance; whereas it is clearly necessary, from the beginning to the end of time, that God's way of revealing himself to his creatures should be a simple way, which all those creatures may understand. Whether taught or untaught, whether of mean capacity or enlarged, it is necessary that communion with their Creator should be possible to all; and the admission to such communion must be rested, not on their having a knowledge of astronomy, but on their having

a human soul.   In order to render this communion possible, the
Deity has stooped from his throne, and has, not only in the person of the Son, taken upon him the veil of our human flesh,
but, in the person of the Father, taken upon him the veil of our
human thoughts, and permitted us, by his own spoken authority,
to conceive him simply and clearly as a loving father and friend;
a being to be walked with and reasoned with, to be moved by our
entreaties, angered by our rebellion, alienated by our coldness,
pleased by our love, and glorified by our labor; and finally to be
beheld in immediate and active presence in all the powers and
changes of creation.   This conception of God, which is the child's,
is evidently the only one which can be universal, and, therefore,
the only one which for us can be true.   The moment that, in our
pride of heart, we refuse to accept the condescension of the Almighty, and desire him, instead of stooping to hold our hands,
to rise up before us into his glory, we, hoping that, by standing
on a grain of dust or two of human knowledge higher than our
fellows, we may behold the Creator as he rises,— God takes us
at our word.   He rises, into his own invisible and inconceivable
majesty; he goes forth upon the ways which are not our ways,
and retires into the thoughts which are not our thoughts; and
we are left alone.   And presently we say in our vain hearts,
« There is no God.»

I would desire, therefore, to receive God's account of his own
creation as under the ordinary limits of human knowledge and
imagination it would be received by a simple-minded man; and
finding that the « heavens and the earth » are spoken of always
as having something like equal relation to each other (« Thus
the heavens and the earth were finished, and all the host of
them »), I reject at once all idea of the term « heavens » being
intended to signify the infinity of space inhabited by countless
worlds; for between those infinite heavens and the particle of
sand, which not the earth only, but the sun itself, with all the
solar system, is, in relation to them, no relation of equality or
comparison could be inferred.   But I suppose the heavens to
mean that part of creation which holds equal companionship with
our globe; I understand the « rolling of these heavens together
as a scroll,» to be an equal and relative destruction with the
melting of the elements in fervent heat; and I understand the
making of the firmament to signify that, so far as man is concerned, most magnificent ordinance of the clouds;—the ordinance

that as the great plain of waters was formed on the face of the
earth, so also a plain of waters should be stretched along the
height of air, and the face of the cloud answer the face of the
ocean; and that this upper and heavenly plain should be of
waters, as it were, glorified in their nature, no longer quenching
the fire, but now bearing fire in their own bosoms; no longer
murmuring only when the winds raise them or rocks divide, but
answering each other with their own voices, from pole to pole;
no longer restrained by established shores, and guided through
unchanging channels; but going forth at their pleasure like the
armies of the angels, and choosing their encampments upon
the heights of the hills; no longer hurried downwards forever,
moving but to fall, nor lost in the lightless accumulation of the
abyss, but covering the east and west with the waving of their
wings, and robing the gloom of the further infinite with a vesture
of diverse colors, of which the threads are purple and scarlet,
and the embroideries flame.

This, I believe, is the ordinance of the firmament; and it
seems to me that in the midst of the material nearness of these
heavens, God means us to acknowledge his own immediate presence as visiting, judging, and blessing us: " The earth shook, the
heavens also dropped at the presence of God." " He doth set his
bow in the clouds," and thus renews, in the sound of every
drooping swathe of rain, his promises of everlasting love. " In
them he hath set a tabernacle for the sun "; whose burning ball,
which, without the firmament, would be seen but as an intolerable
and scorching circle in blackness of vacuity, is by that firmament
surrounded with gorgeous service, and tempered by mediatorial
ministries: by the firmament of clouds the temple is built, for
his presence to fill with light at noon; by the firmament of
clouds the purple veil is closed at evening, round the sanctuary of
his rest; by the mists of the firmament his implacable light is
divided, and its separated fierceness appeased into the soft blue
that fills the depth of distance with its bloom, and the flush with
which the mountains burn, as they drink the overflowing of the
dayspring.   And in this tabernacling of the unendurable sun
with men, through the shadows of the firmament, God would
seem to set forth the stooping of his own Majesty to men, upon
the throne of the firmament.   As the Creator of all the worlds,
and the Inhabiter of eternity, we cannot behold him; but as the
Judge of the earth and the Preserver of men, those heavens are

indeed his dwelling place: "Swear not, neither by heaven, for it is God's throne; nor by the earth, for it is his footstool!" And all of those passings to and fro of fruitful showers and grateful shade, and all those visions of silver palaces built about the horizon, and voices of moaning winds and threatening thunders, and glories of colored robe and cloven ray, are but to deepen in our hearts the acceptance, and distinctness, and dearness, of the simple words, "Our Father, which art in heaven."

Complete as edited from "Modern Painters"
in "Frondes Agrestes."

PRINCIPLES OF ART

PERFECT taste is the faculty of receiving the greatest possible pleasure from those material sources which are attractive to our moral nature in its purity and perfection; but why we receive pleasure from some forms and colors and not from others is no more to be asked or answered than why we like sugar and dislike wormwood.

The temper by which right taste is formed is characteristically patent. It dwells upon what is submitted to it. It does not trample upon it, — lest it should be pearls, even though it look like husks. It is good ground, penetrable, retentive; it does not send up thorns of unkind thoughts, to choke the weak seed; it is hungry and thirsty too, and drinks all the dew that falls on it. It is an honest and good heart, that shows no too ready springing before the sun be up, but fails not afterwards; it is distrustful of itself, so as to be ready to believe and to try all things, and yet so trustful of itself, that it will neither quit what it has tried, nor take anything without trying. And the pleasure which it has in things that it finds true and good is so great, that it cannot possibly be led aside by any tricks of fashion, or diseases of vanity; it cannot be cramped in its conclusions by partialities and hypocrisies; its visions and its delights are too penetrating, — too living, — for any whitewashed object or shallow fountain long to endure or supply. It clasps all that it loves so hard that it crushes it if it be hollow.

It is the common consent of men that whatever branch of any pursuit ministers to the bodily comforts, and regards material uses, is ignoble, and whatever part is addressed to the mind only, is noble; and that geology does better in reclothing dry bones and revealing lost creations, than in tracing veins of lead and beds of iron; astronomy better in opening to us the houses of heaven than in teaching navigation; botany better in displaying structure than in expressing juices; surgery better in investigating organization than in setting limbs. Only it is ordained that, for our encouragement, every step we make in the more exalted range of science adds something also to its practical applicabilities; that all the great phenomena of nature, the knowledge of which is desired by the angels only, by us partly, as it reveals to further vision the being and the glory of him in whom they rejoice and we live, dispense yet such kind influences and so much of material blessing as to be joyfully felt by all inferior creatures, and to be desired by them with such single desire as the imperfection of their nature may admit; that the strong torrents, which, in their own gladness, fill the hills with hollow thunder, and the vales with winding light, have yet their bounden charge of field to feed, and barge to bear; that the fierce flames to which the Alp owes its upheaval and the volcano its terror, temper for us the metal vein, and warm the quickening spring; and that for our excitement, I say, not our reward,—for knowledge is its own reward,—herbs have their healing, stones their preciousness, and stars their times.

Had it been ordained by the Almighty * that the highest pleasures of sight should be those of most difficult attainment, and that to arrive at them it should be necessary to accumulate gilded palaces, tower over tower, and pile artificial mountains around insinuated lakes, there would never have been a direct contradiction between the unselfish duties and the inherent desires of every individual. But no such contradiction exists in the system of Divine Providence; which, leaving it open to us if we will, as creatures in probation, to abuse this sense like every other, and pamper it with selfish and thoughtless vanities, as we pamper the palate with deadly meats, until the appetite of tasteful cruelty is lost in its sickened satiety, incapable of pleasure, unless, Caligula like, it concentrates the labor of a million of lives into the sensation of an hour, leaves it also open to us,—by hum-

* The reader must observe that, having been thoroughly disciplined in the evangelical schools, I supposed myself, at four-and-twenty, to know all about the ordinances of the Almighty. Nevertheless, the practical contents of the sentence are good if only they are intelligible, which I doubt.

J. R.

ble and loving ways, to make ourselves susceptible of deep de-light, which shall not separate us from our fellows, nor require the sacrifice of any duty or occupation, but which shall bind us closer to men and to God, and be with us always, harmonized with every action, consistent with every claim, unchanging and eternal.

A great idealist never can be egotistic. The whole of his power depends upon his losing sight and feeling of his own ex-istence, and becoming a mere witness and mirror of truth, and a scribe of visions — always passive in sight, passive in utterance, lamenting continually that he cannot completely reflect nor clearly utter all he has seen — not by any means a proud state for a man to be in. But the man who has no invention is al-ways setting things in order,* and putting the world to rights, and mending, and beautifying, and pluming himself on his do-ings, as supreme in all ways.

So far as education does indeed tend to make the senses del-icate, and the perceptions accurate, and thus enables people to be pleased with quiet instead of gaudy color; and with graceful instead of coarse form; and by long acquaintance with the best things, to discern quickly what is fine from what is common — so far acquired taste is an honorable faculty, and it is true praise of anything to say, it is "in good taste." But so far as this higher education has a tendency to narrow the sympathies and harden the heart, diminishing the interest of all beautiful things by familiarity, until even what is best can hardly please, and what is brightest hardly entertain — so far as it fosters pride, and leads men to found the pleasure they take in any-thing, not on the worthiness of the thing, but on the degree in which it indicates some greatness of their own (as people build marble porticoes, and inlay marble floors, not so much because they like the colors of marble, or find it pleasant to the foot, as because such porches and floors are costly, and separated in all human eyes from plain entrances of stone and timber), — so far as it leads people to prefer gracefulness of dress, manner, and aspect, to value of substance and heart, liking a well-said thing better than a true thing, and a well-trained manner better than a sincere one, and a delicately-formed face better than a good-

---

*I am now a comic illustration of this sentence, myself. I have not a ray of invention in all my brains: but am intensely rational and orderly, and have resolutely begun to set the world to rights.

J. R.

natured one — and in all other ways and things setting custom and semblance above everlasting truth — so far, finally, as it induces a sense of inherent distinction between class and class, and causes everything to be more or less despised which has no social rank, so that the affection, pleasure, or grief of a clown are looked upon as of no interest compared with the affection and grief of a well-bred man — just so far in all these several ways, the feeling induced by what is called "a liberal education" is utterly adverse to the understanding of noble art.

He who habituates himself in his daily life to seek for the stern facts in whatever he hears or sees will have these facts again brought before him by the involuntary imaginative power, in their noblest associations; and he who seeks for frivolities and fallacies will have frivolities and fallacies again presented to him in his dreams.*

All the histories of the Bible are yet waiting to be painted. Moses has never been painted; Elijah never; David never (except as a mere ruddy stripling); Deborah never; Gideon never; Isaiah never.† What single example does the reader remember of painting which suggested so much as the faintest shadow of their deeds? Strong men in armor, or aged men with flowing beards, he may remember, who, when he looked at his Louvre or Uffizii catalogue, he found were intended to stand for David or Moses. But does he suppose that, if these pictures had suggested to him the feeblest image of the presence of such men, he would have passed on, as he assuredly did, to the next picture representing, doubtless, Diana and Actæon, or Cupid and the Graces, or a gambling quarrel in a pothouse — with no sense of pain or surprise? Let him meditate over the matter, and he will find ultimately that what I say is true, and that religious art at once complete and sincere never yet has existed.

*Very good. Few people have any idea how much more important the government of the mind is than the force of its exertion. Nearly all the world flog their horses, without ever looking where they are going.

J. R.

† I knew nothing, when I wrote this passage, of Luini, Filippo Lippi, or Sandro Botticelli; and had not capacity to enter into the deeper feelings even of the men whom I was chiefly studying,— Tintoret and Fra Angelico. But the British public is at present as little acquainted with the greater Florentines as I was then, and the passage, for them, remains true.

J. R.

Complete as edited in "Frondes Agrestes" from "Modern Painters." The notes are Ruskin's own.

WORK

WISE work is, briefly, work with God. Foolish work is work against God. And work done with God, which he will help, may be briefly described as " Putting in Order," — that is, enforcing God's law of order, spiritual and material, over men and things. The first thing you have to do, essentially; the real " good work" is, with respect to men, to enforce justice, and, with respect to things, to enforce tidiness and fruitfulness. And against these two great human deeds, justice and order, there are perpetually two great demons contending,— the devil of iniquity, or inequity, and the devil of disorder, or of death; for death is only consummation of disorder. You have to fight these two fiends daily. So far as you don't fight against the fiend of iniquity, you work for him. You " work iniquity," and the judgment upon you, for all your " Lord, Lord's," will be " Depart from me, ye that work iniquity." And so far as you do not resist the fiend of disorder, you work disorder, and you yourself do the work of Death, which is sin, and has for its wages, Death himself.

Observe, then, all wise work is mainly threefold in character. It is honest, useful, and cheerful.

It is honest. I hardly know anything more strange than that you recognize honesty in play, and you do not in work. In your lightest games, you have always some one to see what you call "fair play." In boxing you must hit fair; in racing, start fair. Your English watchword is Fair play; your English hatred, Foul play. Did it ever strike you that you wanted another watchword also, Fair work, and another hatred also, Foul work ? Your prize fighter has some honor in him yet; and so have the men in the ring round him: they will judge him to lose the match, by foul hitting. But your prize merchant gains his match by foul selling, and no one cries out against that. You drive a gambler out of the gambling room who loads dice, but you leave a tradesman in flourishing business who loads scales! For observe, all dishonest dealing is loading scales. What does it matter whether I get short weight, adulterate substance, or dishonest fabric ? The fault in the fabric is incomparably the worst of the two. Give me short measure of food, and I only lose by you; but give me adulterate food, and I die by you. Here, then, is your chief duty, you workmen and tradesmen — to be true to yourselves, and to us who would help you. We can do nothing for you, nor you for yourselves, without honesty. Get that, you get all; without that, your suffrages, your reforms, your free-trade measures, your institutions of science, are all in vain. It is useless to put your heads together, if you can't put your hearts together. Shoulder to shoulder, right hand to right hand, among yourselves, and no wrong hand to anybody else, and you'll win the world yet.

Then, secondly, wise work is useful. No man minds, or ought to mind, its being hard, if only it comes to something: but when it is hard and comes to nothing; when all our bees' business turns to spiders', and for honeycomb we have only resultant cobweb, blown away by the next breeze — that is the cruel thing for the worker. Yet do we ever ask ourselves, personally, or even nationally, whether our work is coming to anything or not? We don't care to keep what has been nobly done; still less do we care to do nobly what others would keep; and, least of all, to make the work itself useful instead of deadly to the doer, so as to use his life indeed, but not to waste it. Of all wastes the greatest waste that you can commit is the waste of labor. If you went down in the morning into your dairy, and you found that your youngest child had got down before you, and that he and the cat were at play together, and that he had poured out all the cream on the floor for the cat to lap up, you would scold the child and be sorry the milk was wasted. But if, instead of wooden bowls with milk in them, there are golden bowls with human life in them, and instead of the cat to play with — the devil to play with; and you yourself the player; and instead of leaving that golden bowl to be broken by God at the fountain, you break it in the dust yourself, and pour the human blood out on the ground for the fiend to lick up — that is no waste! What! you perhaps think, "to waste the labor of men is not to kill them." Is it not? I should like to know how you could kill them more utterly — kill them with second deaths? It is the slightest way of killing to stop a man's breath. Nay, the hunger, and the cold, and the little whistling bullets — our love messengers between nation and nation — have brought pleasant messages from us to many a man before now; orders of sweet release, and leave at last to go where he will be most welcome and most happy. At the worst you do but shorten his life, you do not corrupt his life. But if you put him to base labor, if you bind his thoughts, if you blind his eyes, if you blunt his hopes, if you steal his joys, if you stunt his body, and blast his soul, and at last leave him not so much as to reap the poor fruit of his degradation, but gather that for yourself, and dismiss him to the grave, when you have done with him, having, so far as in you lay, made the walls of that grave everlasting (though, indeed, I fancy the goodly bricks of some of our family vaults will hold closer in the resurrection day than the sod over the laborer's head), this you think is no waste, and no sin!

Then, lastly, wise work is cheerful, as a child's work is. And now I want you to take one thought home with you, and let it stay with you.

Everybody in this room has been taught to pray daily, "Thy kingdom come." Now, if we hear a man swear in the streets, we think it very wrong, and say he "takes God's name in vain." But there's a twenty times worse way of taking his name in vain than that. It is to ask God for what we don't want. He doesn't like that sort of prayer. If you don't want a thing, don't ask for it; such asking is the worst mockery of your King you can mock him with; the soldiers striking him on the head with the reed was nothing to that. If you do not wish for his kingdom, don't pray for it. But if you do, you must do more than pray for it; you must work for it. And, to work for it, you must know what it is: we have all prayed for it many a day without thinking. Observe, it is a kingdom that is to come to us; we are not to go to it. Also, it is not to be a kingdom of the dead, but of the living. Also, it is not to come all at once, but quietly: nobody knows how: "the kingdom of God cometh not with observation." Also, it is not to come outside of us, but in the hearts of us: "the kingdom of God is within you." And being within us, it is not a thing to be seen, but to be felt; and though it brings all substance of good with it, it does not consist in that: "the kingdom of God is not meat and drink, but righteousness. peace, and joy in the Holy Ghost," — joy, that is to say, in the holy, healthful, and helpful Spirit. Now, if we want to work for this kingdom, and to bring it, and enter into it, there's just one condition to be first accepted. You must enter it as children, or not at all: "Whosoever will not receive it as a little child shall not enter therein." And again, "Suffer little children to come unto me, and forbid them not, for of such is the kingdom of heaven."

Of such, observe. Not of children themselves, but of such as children. I believe most mothers who read that text think that all heaven is to be full of babies. But that's not so. There will be children there, but the hoary head is the crown. "Length of days, and long life and peace," that is the blessing, not to die in babyhood. Children die but for their parents' sins; God means them to live, but he can't let them always; then they have their earlier place in heaven, and the little child of David, vainly prayed for; — the little child of Jeroboam, killed by its mother's step on its own threshold, — they will be there. But weary old David, and weary old Barzillai, having learned children's lessons at last, will be there too; and the one question for us all, young or old, is, Have we learned our child's lesson? It is the character of children we want, and must gain at our peril; let us see, briefly, in what it consists.

The first character of right childhood is that it is Modest. A well-bred child does not think it can teach its parents, or that it knows everything. It may think its father and mother know everything, — perhaps that all grown-up people know everything; very certainly it is sure that it does not. And it is always asking questions, and wanting to know more. Well, that is the first character of a good and wise man at his work. To know that he knows very little; — to perceive that there are many above him wiser than he; and to be always asking questions, wanting to learn, not to teach. No one ever teaches well who wants to teach, or governs well who wants to govern; it is an old saying (Plato's, but I know not if his first), and as wise as old.

Then, the second character of right childhood is to be Faithful. Perceiving that its father knows best what is good for it, and having found always, when it has tried its own way against his, that he was right and it was wrong, a noble child trusts him at last wholly, gives him its hand, and will walk blindfold with him, if he bids it. And that is the true character of all good men also, as obedient workers, or soldiers under captains. They must trust their captains; — they are bound for their lives to choose none but those whom they can trust. Then, they are not always to be thinking that what seems strange to them, or wrong in what they are desired to do, is strange or wrong. They know their captain: where he leads they must follow, what he bids they must do; and without this trust and faith, without this captainship and soldiership, no great deed, no great salvation, is possible to man. Among all the nations it is only when this faith is attained by them that they become great; the Jew, the Greek, and the Mahometan agree at least in testifying to this. It was a deed of this absolute trust which made Abraham the father of the faithful; it was the declaration of the power of God as captain over all men, and the acceptance of a leader appointed by him as commander of the faithful, which laid the foundation of whatever national power yet exists in the East; and the deed of the Greeks, which has become the type of unselfish and noble soldiership to all lands, and to all times, was commemorated, on the tomb of those who gave their lives to do it, in the most pathetic, so far as I know, or can feel, of all human utterances: " O stranger, go and tell our people that we are lying here, having obeyed their words. "

Then the third character of right childhood is to be Loving and Generous. Give a little love to a child, and you get a great deal back. It loves everything near it, when it is a right kind of child — would hurt nothing, would give the best it has away, always, if you need it — does not lay plans for getting everything in the house for itself, and delights in helping people; you cannot please it so much as by giving it a chance of being useful, in ever so little a way.

And because of all these characters, lastly, it is Cheerful. Putting its trust in its father, it is careful for nothing — being full of love to every creature, it is happy always, whether in its play or in its duty. Well, that's the great worker's character also. Taking no thought for the morrow; taking thought only for the duty of the day; trusting somebody else to take care of to-morrow; knowing, indeed, what labor is, but not what sorrow is; and always ready for play,— beautiful play,— for lovely human play is like the play of the Sun. There's a worker for you. He, steady to his time, is set as a strong man to run his course, but, also, he rejoiceth as a strong man to run his course. See how he plays in the morning, with the mists below, and the clouds above, with a ray here and a flash there, and a shower of jewels everywhere;— that's the Sun's play; and great human play is like his — all various — all full of light and life, and tender, as the dew of the morning.

So then, you have the child's character in these four things: Humility, Faith, Charity, and Cheerfulness. That's what you have got to be converted to. " Except ye be converted and become as little children " — You hear much of conversion nowa-

days; but people always seem to think you have got to be made
wretched by conversion,—to be converted to long faces. No,
friends, you have got to be converted to short ones; you have
to repent into childhood, to repent into delight, and delightsome-
ness. You can't go into a conventicle but you'll hear plenty of
talk of backsliding. Backsliding, indeed! I can tell you, on the
ways most of us go, the faster we slide back the better. Slide
back into the cradle, if going on is into the grave—back, I tell
you; back—out of your long faces, and into your long clothes.
It is among children only, and as children only, that you will
find medicine for your healing and true wisdom for your teaching. There is poison in the counsels of the man of this world;
the words they speak are all bitterness, "the poison of asps is
under their lips," but "the sucking child shall play by the hole
of the asp." There is death in the looks of men. "Their eyes
are privily set against the poor"; they are as the uncharmable
serpent, the cockatrice, which slew by seeing. But "the weaned
child shall lay his hand on the cockatrice den." There is death
in the steps of men; "their feet are swift to shed blood; they
have compassed us in our steps like the lion that is greedy of
his prey, and the young lion lurking in secret places," but, in
that kingdom, the wolf shall lie down with the lamb, and the
fatling with the lion, and "a little child shall lead them." There
is death in the thoughts of men; the world is one wide riddle to
them, darker and darker as it draws to a close; but the secret of
it is known to the child, and the Lord of heaven and earth is
most to be thanked in that "he has hidden these things from the
wise and prudent, and has revealed them unto babes." Yes, and
there is death—infinitude of death in the principalities and powers of men As far as the east is from the west, so far our
sins are—not set from us, but multiplied around us: the Sun
himself, think you he now "rejoices" to run his course, when he
plunges westward to the horizon, so widely red, not with clouds,
but blood? And it will be red more widely yet. Whatever
drought of the early and latter rain may be, there will be none of
that red rain. You fortify yourselves against it in vain; the enemy
and avenger will be upon you also, unless you learn that it is not
out of the mouths of the knitted gun, or the smoothed rifle, but
"out of the mouths of babes and sucklings" that the strength
is ordained, which shall "still the enemy and avenger."

> From "The Crown of Wild Olives."
> Conclusion of the first lecture.

SIBYLLINE LEAVES

WANT OF SELF-KNOWLEDGE

HALF the evil in this world comes from people not knowing what they do like, not deliberately setting themselves to find out what they really enjoy. All people enjoy giving away money, for instance: they don't know that,—they rather think they like keeping it; and they do keep it under this false impression, often to their great discomfort. Everybody likes to do good; but not one in a hundred finds this out.

THE RESPONSIBILITY OF A RICH MAN

A RICH man ought to be continually examining how he may spend his money for the advantage of others; at present, others are continually plotting how they may beguile him into spending it apparently for his own. The aspect which he presents to the eyes of the world is generally that of a person holding a bag of money with a stanch grasp, and resolved to part with none of it unless he is forced, and all the people about him are plotting how they may force him; that is to say, how they may persuade him that he wants this thing or that; or how they may produce things that he will covet and buy. One man tries to persuade him that he wants perfumes; another that he wants jewelry; another that he wants sugarplums; another that he wants roses at Christmas. Anybody who can invent a new want for him is supposed to be a benefactor to society; and thus the energies of the poorer people about him are continually directed to the production of covetable, instead of serviceable things; and the rich man has the general aspect of a fool, plotted against by all the world. Whereas the real aspect which he ought to have is that of a person wiser than others, intrusted with the management of a larger quantity of capital, which he administers for the profit of all, directing each man to the labor which is most healthy for him, and most serviceable for the community.

ART AND DECADENCE

WE DON'T want either the life or the decorations of the thir-
teenth century back again; and the circumstances with
which you must surround your workmen are those simply
of happy modern English life, because the designs you have now
to ask for from your workmen are such as will make modern
English life beautiful. All that gorgeousness of the Middle Ages,
beautiful as it sounds in description, noble as in many respects
it was in reality, had, nevertheless, for foundation and for end,
nothing but the pride of life — the pride of the so-called superior
classes; a pride which supported itself by violence and robbery,
and led in the end to the destruction both of the arts themselves
and the States in which they flourished.

The great lesson of history is, that all the fine arts hitherto —
having been supported by the selfish power of the nobless, and
never having extended their range to the comfort or the relief
of the mass of the people — the arts, I say, thus practiced, and
thus matured, have only accelerated the ruin of the States they
adorned; and at the moment when, in any kingdom, you point
to the triumphs of its greatest artists, you point also to the
determined hour of the kingdom's decline.

INFINITY

THAT which we foolishly call vastness is, rightly considered, not
more wonderful, not more impressive, than that which we
insolently call littleness, and the infinity of God is not
mysterious, it is only unfathomable, not concealed, but incompre-
hensible; it is a clear infinity, the darkness of the pure unsearch-
able sea.

THE SOCIETY OF NATURE

TO THE mediæval knight, from Scottish moor to Syrian sand,
the world was one great exercise ground, or field of adventure; the stanch pacing of his charger penetrated the
pathlessness of outmost forest, and sustained the sultriness of
the most secret desert. Frequently alone,— or if accompanied,

for the most part only by retainers of lower rank, incapable of entering into complete sympathy with any of his thoughts,— he must have been compelled often to enter into dim companionship with the silent nature around him, and must assuredly sometimes have talked to the wayside flowers of his love, and to the fading clouds of his ambition.

ALL CARVING AND NO MEAT

THE divisions of a church are much like the divisions of a sermon; they are always right so long as they are necessary to edification, and always wrong when they are thrust upon the attention as divisions only. There may be neatness in carving when there is richness in feasting; but I have heard many a discourse, and seen many a church wall, in which it was all carving and no meat.

MODERN GREATNESS

THE simple fact, that we are, in some strange way, different from all the great races that have existed before us, cannot at once be received as the proof of our own greatness; nor can it be granted, without any question, that we have a legitimate subject of complacency in being under the influence of feelings, with which neither Miltiades nor the Black Prince, neither Homer nor Dante, neither Socrates nor St. Francis, could for an instant have sympathized.

Whether, however, this fact be one to excite our pride or not, it is assuredly one to excite our deepest interest. The fact itself is certain. For nearly six thousand years the energies of man have pursued certain beaten paths, manifesting some constancy of feeling throughout all that period, and involving some fellowship at heart, among the various nations who by turns succeeded or surpassed each other in the several aims of art or policy. So that, for these thousands of years, the whole human race might be to some extent described in general terms. Man was a creature separated from all others by his instinctive sense of an Existence superior to his own, invariably manifesting this sense of the being of a God more strongly in proportion to his own perfectness of mind and body; and making enormous and self-denying efforts, in order to obtain some persuasion of the immediate presence or approval of the Divinity.

THE CORONATION OF THE WHIRLWIND

MUCH of the love of mystery in our romances, our poetry, our art, and, above all, in our metaphysics, must come under that definition so long ago given by the great Greek, "speaking ingeniously concerning smoke." And much of the instinct, which, partially developed in painting, may be now seen throughout every mode of exertion of mind,— the easily encouraged doubt, easily excited curiosity, habitual agitation, and delight in the changing and the marvelous, as opposed to the old quiet serenity of social custom and religious faith, is again deeply defined in those few words, the "dethroning of Jupiter," the "coronation of the whirlwind."

SACRIFICES THAT MAKE ASHAMED

THE vain and haughty projects of youth for future life; the giddy reveries of insatiable self-exaltation; the discontented dreams of what might have been or should be, instead of the thankful understanding of what is; the casting about for sources of interest in senseless fiction, instead of the real human histories of the people round us; the prolongation from age to age of romantic historical deceptions instead of sifted truth; the pleasures taken in fanciful portraits of rural or romantic life in poetry and on the stage, without the smallest effort to rescue the living rural population of the world from its ignorance or misery; the excitement of the feelings by labored imagination of spirits, fairies, monsters, and demons, issuing in total blindness of heart and sight to the true presences of beneficent or destructive spiritual powers around us; in fine, the constant abandonment of all the straightforward paths of sense and duty, for fear of losing some of the enticement of ghostly joys, or trampling somewhat " *sopra lor vanità, che par persona* "; all these various forms of false idealism have so entangled the modern mind, often called, I suppose ironically, practical, that truly I believe there never yet was idolatry of stock or staff so utterly unholy as this our idol-

atry of shadows; nor can I think that, of those who burnt
incense under oaks, and poplars, and elms, because "the shadow
thereof was good," it could in any wise be more justly or sternly
declared than of us—"The wind hath bound them up in her
wing, and they shall be ashamed because of their sacrifices."

OPPRESSION UNDER THE SUN

You cannot but have noticed how often in those parts of the
Bible which are likely to be oftenest opened when people
look for guidance, comfort, or help in the affairs of daily life,
namely, the Psalms and Proverbs, mention is made of the guilt
attaching to the Oppression of the poor. Observe: not the neglect of them, but the Oppression of them; the word is as frequent as it is strange. You can hardly open either of those
books, but somewhere in their pages you will find a description
of the wicked man's attempts against the poor, such as, "He
doth ravish the poor when he getteth him into his net."

"His mouth is full of deceit and fraud; in the secret places
doth he murder the innocent."

"They are corrupt, and speak wickedly concerning oppression."

"Their poison is like the poison of a serpent. Ye weigh the
violence of your hands in the earth."

Yes: "Ye weigh the violence of your hands"; weigh these
words as well. The last things we usually think of weighing are
Bible words. We like to dream and dispute over them, but to
weigh them and see what their true contents are—anything but
that! Yet weigh them; for I have purposely taken these
verses, perhaps more strikingly to you read in this connection,
than separately in their places out of the Psalms, because, for all
people belonging to the Established Church of this country these
Psalms are appointed lessons, portioned out to them by their
clergy to be read once through every month. Presumably, therefore, whatever portions of Scripture we may pass by or forget,
these, at all events, must be brought continually to our observance as useful for the direction of daily life. Now, do we ever ask
ourselves what the real meaning of these passages may be, and
who these wicked people are, who are "murdering the innocent"?
You know it is rather singular language this!—rather strong

IX—208

language, we might, perhaps, call it—hearing it for the first time. Murder! and murder of innocent people!—nay, even a sort of cannibalism. Eating people,—yes, and God's people, too —eating my people as if they were bread! swords drawn, bows bent, poison of serpents mixed! violence of hands weighed, measured, and trafficked with as so much coin! where is all this going on? Do you suppose it was only going on in the time of David, and that nobody but Jews ever murder the poor? If so, it would surely be wiser not to mutter and mumble for our daily lessons what does not concern us; but if there be any chance that it may concern us, and if this description, in the Psalms, of human guilt is at all generally applicable, as the descriptions in the Psalms of human sorrow are, may it not be advisable to know wherein this guilt is being committed round about us, or by ourselves? And when we take the words of the Bible into our mouths in a congregational way, to be sure whether we mean sincerely to chant a piece of melodious poetry relating to other people (we know not exactly whom)—or to assert our belief in facts bearing somewhat astringently on ourselves and our daily business. And if you make up your minds to do this no longer, and take pains to examine into the matter, you will find that these strange words, occurring as they do, not in a few places only, but almost in every alternate Psalm, and every alternate chapter of Proverbs or Prophecy, with tremendous reiteration, were not written for one nation or one time only, but for all nations and languages, for all places and all centuries; and it is as true of the wicked man now as ever it was of Nabal or Dives, that "his eyes are set against the poor."

MERCANTILE PANICS

No merchant deserving the name ought to be more liable to a "panic" than a soldier should; for his name should never be on more paper than he could at any instant meet the call of, happen what will. I do not say this without feeling at the same time how difficult it is to mark, in existing commerce, the just limits between the spirit of enterprise and of speculation. Something of the same temper which makes the English soldier do always all that is possible, and attempt more than is possible, joins its influence with that of mere avarice in tempting the

English merchant into risks which he cannot justify, and efforts which he cannot sustain; and the same passion for adventure which our travelers gratify every summer on perilous snow wreaths and cloud-encompassed precipices surrounds with a romantic fascination the glittering of a hollow investment, and gilds the clouds that curl round gulfs of ruin. Nay, a higher and a more serious feeling frequently mingles in the motley temptation; and men apply themselves to the task of growing rich as to a labor of providential appointment, from which they cannot pause without culpability, nor retire without dishonor. Our large trading cities bear to me very nearly the aspect of monastic establishments in which the roar of the mill wheel and the crane takes the place of other devotional music, and in which the worship of Mammon and Moloch is conducted with a tender reverence and an exact propriety: the merchant rising to his Mammon matins with the self-denial of an anchorite, and expiating the frivolities into which he may be beguiled in the course of the day by late attendance at Mammon vespers. But, with every allowance that can be made for these conscientious and romantic persons, the fact remains the same, that by far the greater number of the transactions which lead to these times of commercial embarrassment may be ranged simply under two great heads,—gambling and stealing; and both of these in their most culpable form, namely, gambling with money which is not ours, and stealing from those who trust us. I have sometimes thought a day might come, when the nation would perceive that a well-educated man who steals a hundred thousand pounds, involving the entire means of subsistence of a hundred families, deserves, on the whole, as severe a punishment as an ill-educated man who steals a purse from a pocket, or a mug from a pantry.

IMMORTALITY OF THE BIBLE

You are not philosophers of the kind who suppose that the Bible is a superannuated book; neither are you of those who think the Bible is dishonored by being referred to for judgment in small matters. The very divinity of the Book seems to me, on the contrary, to justify us in referring everything to it, with respect to which any conclusion can be gathered from its pages. Assuming, then, that the Bible is neither superannuated now, nor ever likely to be so, it will follow that the illustrations which the Bible employs are likely to be clear and intelligible illustrations to the end of time. I do not mean that everything spoken of in the Bible histories must continue to endure for all time, but that the things which the Bible uses for illustration of eternal truths are likely to remain eternally intelligible illustrations.

DISSECTORS AND DREAMERS

ALL experience goes to teach us, that among men of average intellect the most useful members of society are the dissectors, not the dreamers. It is not that they love nature or beauty less, but that they love result, effect, and progress more; and when we glance broadly along the starry crowd of benefactors to the human race, and guides of human thought, we shall find that this dreaming love of natural beauty — or at least its expression — has been more or less checked by them all, and subordinated either to hard work or watching of human nature.

THE USE OF BEAUTY

BEAUTY has been appointed by the Deity to be one of the elements by which the human soul is continually sustained; it is therefore to be found more or less in all natural objects, but in order that we may not satiate ourselves with it, and weary of it, it is rarely granted to us in its utmost degrees. When we see it in those utmost degrees, we are attracted to it strongly, and remember it long, as in the case of singularly beautiful scenery, or a beautiful countenance. On the other hand, absolute ugliness is admitted as rarely as perfect beauty; but degrees of it more or less distinct are associated with whatever has the nature of death and sin, just as beauty is associated with what has the nature of virtue and of life.

RESPECTABILITY OF ART

I BELIEVE that there is no chance of art truly flourishing in any country, until you make it a simple and plain business, providing its masters with an easy competence, but rarely with anything more. And I say this, not because I despise the great painter, but because I honor him; and I should no more think of adding to his respectability or happiness by giving him riches, than, if Shakespeare or Milton were alive, I should think we added to their respectability, or were likely to get better work from them, by making them millionaires.

OPINIONS

IN MANY matters of opinion, our first and last coincide, though on different grounds; it is the middle stage which is furthest from the truth. Childhood often holds a truth with its feeble fingers, which the grasp of manhood cannot retain,— which it is the pride of utmost age to recover.

THE NECESSITY OF WORK

BY FAR the greater part of the suffering and crime which exist at this moment in civilized Europe arises simply from people not understanding this truism,— not knowing that produce or wealth is eternally connected by the laws of heaven and earth with resolute labor, but hoping in some way to cheat or abrogate this everlasting law of life, and to feed where they have not furrowed, and be warm where they have not woven.

I repeat, nearly all our misery and crime result from this one misapprehension. The law of nature is, that a certain quantity of work is necessary to produce a certain quantity of good, of any kind whatever. If you want knowledge, you must toil for it; if food, you must toil for it; and if pleasure, you must toil for it. But men do not acknowledge this law, or strive to evade it, hoping to get their knowledge, and food, and pleasure for nothing; and in this effort they either fail of getting them, and remain ignorant and miserable, or they obtain them by making other men work for their benefit; and then they are tyrants and robbers. Yes, and worse than robbers. I am not one who in the least doubts or disputes the progress of this century in many things useful to mankind; but it seems to me a very dark sign respecting us that we look with so much indifference upon dishonesty and cruelty in the pursuit of wealth. In the dream of Nebuchadnezzar it was only the feet that were part of iron and part of clay; but many of us are now getting so cruel in our avarice, that it seems as if, in us, the heart were part of iron, and part of clay.

On War

WHEREVER there is war, there must be injustice on one side or the other, or on both. There have been wars which were little more than trials of strength between friendly nations, and in which the injustice was not to each other, but to the God who gave them life. But in a malignant war of these present ages there is injustice of ignobler kind, at once to God and man, which must be stemmed for both their sakes.

Base Criticism

IT MAY perhaps be said that I attach too much importance to the evil of base criticism; but those who think so have never rightly understood its scope, nor the reach of that stern saying of Johnson's (Idler, No. 3, April 29th, 1758): " Little does he (who assumes the character of a critic) think how many harmless men he involves in his own guilt, by teaching them to be noxious without malignity, and to repeat objections which they do not understand." And truly not in this kind only, but in all things whatsoever, there is not to my mind, a more woeful or wonderful matter of thought than the power of a fool. In the world's affairs there is no design so great or good but it will take twenty wise men to help it forward a few inches, and a single fool can stop it; there is no evil so great or so terrible but that, after a multitude of counselors have taken means to avert it, a single fool will bring it down. Pestilence, famine, and the sword are given into the fool's hand as the arrows into the hand of the giant, and if he were fairly set forth in the right motley, the web of it should be sackcloth and sable; the bells on his cap, the passing bells; his badge, a bear robbed of her welps; and his bauble, a sexton's spade.

EDUCATION

THE most helpless and sacred work which can at present be done for humanity is to teach people (chiefly by example, as all best teaching must be done) not how to "better themselves," but how to "satisfy themselves." It is the curse of every evil nature and creature to eat and not be satisfied. The words of blessing are, that they shall eat and be satisfied; and as there is only one kind of water which quenches all thirst, so there is only one kind of bread which satisfies all hunger,—the bread of justice or righteousness, which, hungering after, men shall always be filled, that being the bread of heaven; but hungering after the bread of wages of unrighteousness shall not be filled, that being the bread of Sodom. And in order to teach men how to be satisfied, it is necessary fully to understand the art of joy and humble life — this, at present, of all arts or sciences, being the one most needing study. Humble life, that is to say, proposing to itself no future exaltation, but only a sweet continuance; not excluding the idea of foresight, but wholly of fore-sorrow, and taking no troublous thought for coming days; so also not excluding the idea of providence or provision, but wholly of accumulation; — the life of domestic affection and domestic peace, full of sensitiveness to all elements of costless and kind pleasure; — therefore, chiefly to the loveliness of the natural world.

CHARLES AUGUSTIN SAINTE-BEUVE

(1804–1869)

HARLES AUGUSTIN SAINTE-BEUVE, one of the most admired critical essayists of France, was born at Boulogne-sur-Mer,
December 23d, 1804. He began life as a physician, but he
had been carefully educated in general literature, and his tastes
drew him away from his profession. He began writing critical essays, chiefly book reviews, which soon brought him reputation. He
became a contributor to La Revue de Paris, La Revue des Deux
Mondes, and other leading periodicals. He published several volumes of poems between 1829 and 1837, and in 1832 "Volupté," a
novel. His "Literary Portraits" and "Portraits of Women" appeared
between 1832 and 1844, and his "Causeries du Lundi" from 1851 to
1857. He was elected to the French Academy in 1845, and to the
Senate in 1865. He interested himself in education as well as in literature and politics. Besides lecturing in the smaller French cities,
he taught in the Collège de France as professor of Latin Poetry, and
from 1857 to 1861 was a lecturer in the École Normale. He died at
Paris, October 13th, 1869.

A TYPICAL MAN OF THE WORLD

EACH epoch has produced its treatise intended for the formation of the polite man, the man of the world, the courtier,
when men only lived for courts, and the accomplished gentleman. In these various treatises on knowledge of life and
politeness, if opened after a lapse of ages, we at once see portions
which are as antiquated as the cut and fashion of our forefathers' coats; the model has evidently changed. But looking
into it carefully as a whole, if the book has been written by a
sensible man with a true knowledge of mankind, we shall still
find profit in studying those models which have been placed before preceding generations. The letters that Lord Chesterfield
wrote to his son, and which contain a whole school of *savoir
vivre* and worldly science, are interesting in this particular, that
there has been no idea of forming a model for imitation, but

they are simply intended to bring up a pupil in the closest intimacy. They are confidential letters, which, suddenly produced in the light of day, have betrayed all the secrets and ingenious artifices of paternal solicitude. If, in reading them nowadays, we are struck with the excessive importance attached to accidental and promiscuous circumstances, with pure details of costume, we are not less struck with the durable part, with that which belongs to human observation in all ages; and this last part is much more considerable than at a superficial glance would be imagined. In applying himself to the formation of his son as a polite man in society, Lord Chesterfield has not given us a treatise on duty as Cicero has; but he has left letters which, by their mixture of justness and lightness, by certain lightsome airs which insensibly mingle with the serious graces, preserve the medium between the "Mémoires of the Chevalier de Grammont" and "Télémaque."

Before going into detail, it will be necessary to know a little about Lord Chesterfield, one of the most brilliant English wits of his time, and one most closely allied to France. Philip Dormer Stanhope, Earl of Chesterfield, was born in London, on the twenty-second of September, 1694, the same year as Voltaire. The descendant of an illustrious race, he knew the value of birth, and wished to sustain its honor; nevertheless, it was difficult for him not to laugh at genealogical pretensions when carried too far. To keep himself from this folly, he had placed amongst the portraits of his ancestors two old figures of a man and woman; beneath one was written, "Adam de Stanhope," and beneath the other, "Eve de Stanhope." Thus, while upholding the honor of race, he put his veto upon chimerical vanities arising from it.

His father paid no attention whatever to his education; he was placed under the care of his grandmother, Lady Halifax. From a very early age he manifested a desire to excel in everything, a desire which later he did his utmost to excite in the breast of his son, and which for good or ill is the principle of all that is great. Like himself in his early youth, he was without guidance, he was deceived more than once in the objects of his emulation, and followed some ridiculous chimera. He confesses that at one period of inexperience he gave himself up to wine, and other excesses, for which he was not at all inclined by nature, but it flattered his vanity to hear himself cited as a man of pleasure. In this way he plunged into play (which he considered a necessary ingredient in the composition of a young man of fashion), at first without passion, but afterwards without being able to withdraw himself from it, and by that means compromised his fortune for years. "Take warning by my conduct," said he to his son, "choose your own pleasures, and do not let others choose them for you."

This desire to excel and to distinguish himself did not always lead him astray, and he often applied it rightly; his first studies were the best. Placed at the University of Cambridge, he studied all that was there taught, civil law and philosophy; he attended the mathematical classes of Saunderson, the blind professor. He read Greek fluently, and sent accounts of his progress in French to his old tutor, M. Jouneau, a French clergyman and refugee. Lord Chesterfield had, when a child, learned our tongue from a Norman nurse who attended him. When he visited Paris the last time, in 1744, M. de Fontenelle having remarked a slight Norman accent in his pronunciation, spoke of it to him, and asked him if he had not first been taught French by a person from Normandy,—which turned out to be the case.

After two years of university life, he made his continental tour, according to the custom of young Englishmen. He visited Holland, Italy, and France. He wrote from Paris to M. Jouneau, on the seventh of December, 1714, as follows:—

"I shall not tell you what I think of the French, because I am being often taken for a Frenchman, and more than one of them has paid me the highest possible compliment, by saying: 'Monsieur, you are quite one of ourselves.' I shall only tell you that I am impudent; that I talk a great deal very loudly, and with an air of authority; that I sing; that I dance in my walk; and, finally, that I spend immense sums in powder, feathers, white gloves, etc."

In this extract one recognizes the mocking, satirical, and slightly insolent wit, who makes his mark for the first time at the expense of the French; he will do justice later to our serious qualities. In his letters to his son, he has pictured himself the first day he made his entrée into good society, still covered with the rust of Cambridge, shamefaced, embarrassed, silent; and, finally, forcing his courage with both hands to say to a beautiful woman near him, "Madame, don't you find it very warm to-day?" But Lord Chesterfield told his son that to encourage him, and to show what it is necessary to pass through. He makes himself an example to enbolden him, and to draw the boy more readily to him. I shall be careful not to take his word for this anecdote. If he was for a moment embarrassed in the world, the moment was assuredly very short, nor was he much concerned with it.

Immediately on the death of Queen Anne, Chesterfield hailed the accession of the House of Hanover, of which he became an avowed champion. He had at first a seat in the House of Commons, and made his début there with fair credit. But a circumstance, in appearance frivolous, kept him, it is said, in check, and in some measure paralyzed his eloquence. One of the members of the House, who was distinguished by no talent of a superior order, had that of imitating and counterfeiting to perfection the orators to whom he replied. Chesterfield was afraid of ridicule: it was one of his weaknesses, and he kept silence more than he otherwise would have done for fear of giving occasion for the exercise of his colleague and opponent's talent. He inherited a large property on the death of his father, and was raised to the Upper House, which was, perhaps, a better setting for the grace, finish, and urbanity of his eloquence. He found no comparison between the two scenes with regard to the importance of the debates and the political influence to be acquired.

" It is surprising," he said later of Pitt, at the time when that great orator consented to enter the Upper House as Lord Chatham, " it is surprising that a man in the plenitude of his power, at the very moment when his ambition has obtained the most complete triumph, should leave the House which procured him that power, and which alone could ensure its maintenance, to retire into that Hospital for Incurables, the House of Lords. "

It is not my intention here to estimate the political career of Lord Chesterfield. Nevertheless, if I hazarded a judgment upon it as a whole, I should say that his ambition was never wholly satisfied, and that the brilliant distinctions with which his public life was filled, covered, at bottom, many lost desires and the decay of many hopes. Twice, in the two decisive circumstances of his political life, he failed. Young, and in the first heat of ambition, he took an early opportunity of staking his odds on the side of the heir presumptive to the throne, who became George II. He was one of those who, at the accession of that prince, counted most surely upon his favor, and upon enjoying a share of power. But this clever man, wishing to turn himself to the rising sun, knew not how to accomplish it with perfect justice; he had played court to the prince's mistress, believing in her destined influence, and he had neglected the legitimate wife, the future queen, who alone had the real power. Queen Caroline never pardoned him, and this was the first check in the political fortune of Lord Chesterfield, then thirty-three years old, and in the full flush of hope. He was in too great a hurry and took the wrong road. Robert Walpole, less active, and with less apparent skill, took his measures and made his calculations better.

Thrown with eclat into the opposition, especially from 1732, the time when he had to cease his court duties, Lord Chesterfield worked with all his might for ten years for the downfall of Walpole, which did not take place until 1742. But even then he inherited none of his power, and he remained out of the new ministries. When two years afterwards, in 1744, he became one of the administration, first as embassador to The Hague and Viceroy of Ireland, then as Secretary of State and member of the Cabinet (1746–48), the honor was more nominal than real. In a word, Lord Chesterfield, at all times a noted politician in his own country, whether as one of the chiefs of the opposition, or as a clever diplomatist, was never a powerful, or even a very influential minister.

In politics he certainly possessed that far-sightedness and those glimpses into the future which belong to very wide intelligence, but he possessed those qualities to a much greater degree than the patient perseverance and constant practical firmness that are so necessary to the members of a government. It may truly be said of him, as of Rochefoucauld, that politics served to make an accomplished moralist of the imperfect man of action.

In 1744, when he was only fifty years of age, his political ambition seemed, in part, to have died out, and the indifferent state of his health left him to choose a private life. And then the object of his secret ideal and his real ambition we know now. Before his marriage he had, about the year 1732, by a French lady (Mdme. du Bouchet) whom he met in Holland, a natural son, to whom he was tenderly attached. He wrote to this son, in all sincerity, "From the first day of your life, the dearest object of mine has been to make you as perfect as the weakness of human nature will allow." Towards the education of this son all his wishes, all his affectionate and worldly predilections tended. And whether Viceroy of Ireland or Secretary of

State in London, he found time to write long letters full of minute details to him to instruct him in small matters and to perfect him in mind and manner.

The Chesterfield, then, that we love especially to study is the
man of wit and experience, who knew all the affairs and passed
through all phases of political and public life only to find out its
smallest resources, and to tell us the last mot; he who from his
youth was the friend of Pope and Bolingbroke, the introducer
into England of Montesquieu and Voltaire, the correspondent of
Fontenelle and Mdme. de Teucin, he whom the Academy of In-
scriptions placed among its members, who united the wit of the
two nations, and who, in more than one intellectual essay, but
particularly in his letters to his son, shows himself to us as a
moralist as amiable as he is consummate, and one of the masters
of life.   It is the Rochefoucauld of England of whom we speak.
Montesquieu, after the publication of L'Esprit des Lois, wrote
to the Abbé de Guasco, who was then in England — "Tell my
Lord Chesterfield that nothing is so flattering to me as his approbation; but that, though he is reading my work for the third
time, he will only be in a better position to point out to me
what wants correcting and rectifying in it; nothing could be
more instructive to me than his observations and his critique."
It was Chesterfield who, speaking to Montesquieu one day of the
readiness of the French for revolutions, and their impatience at
slow reforms, spoke this sentence, which is a résumé of our
whole history: "You French know how to make barricades, but
you never raise barriers."

Lord Chesterfield certainly appreciated Voltaire; he remarked,
à propos of the "Siècle de Louis XIV.," "Lord Bolingbroke had
taught me how to read history, Voltaire teaches me how it
should be written."   But, at the same time, with that practical
sense which rarely abandons men of wit on the other side of the
straits, he felt the imprudences of Voltaire, and disapproved of
them.   When he was old, and living in retirement, he wrote to
a French lady on the subject thus: —

"Your good authors are my principal resource: Voltaire especially
charms me, with the exception of his impiety, with which he cannot
help seasoning all that he writes, and which he would do better carefully to suppress, for one ought not to disturb established order. 'Let
every one think as he will, or rather as he can, but let him not communicate his ideas if they are of a nature to trouble the peace of
society.' "

What he said then, in 1768, Chesterfield had already said more than twenty years previously, writing to the younger Crébillon, a singular correspondent and a singular confidant in point of morality. Voltaire was under consideration, on account of his tragedy of "Mahomet," and the daring ideas it contains:—

"What I do not pardon him for, and that which is not deserving of pardon in him," wrote Chesterfield to Crébillon, "is his desire to propagate a doctrine as pernicious to domestic society as contrary to the common religion of all countries. I strongly doubt whether it is permissible for a man to write against the worship and belief of his country, even if he be fully persuaded of its error, on account of the trouble and disorder it might cause; but I am sure that it is in no wise allowable to attack the foundations of true morality, and to break necessary bonds which are already too weak to keep men in the path of duty."

Chesterfield, in speaking thus, was not mistaken as to the great inconsistency of Voltaire. His inconsistency, in a few words, was this: Voltaire, who looked upon men as fools or children, and who could never laugh at them enough, at the same time put loaded firearms into their hands, without troubling himself as to the use they would put them to.

Lord Chesterfield himself, in the eyes of the Puritans of his country, has been accused, I should state here, of a breach of morality in the letters addressed to his son. The strict Johnson, who was not impartial on the subject, and who thought he had cause of complaint against Chesterfield, said, when the letters were published, that "they taught the morals of a courtesan, and the manners of a dancing master."

Such a judgment is supremely unjust, and if Chesterfield, in particular instances, insists upon graces of manner at any price, it is because he has already provided for the more solid parts of education, and because his pupil is not in the least danger of sinning on the side which makes man respectable, but rather on that which renders him agreeable. Although more than one passage in these letters may seem very strange, coming from a father to a son, the whole is animated with a true spirit of tenderness and wisdom. If Horace had had a son, I imagine he would not have written to him very differently.

The letters begin with the A B C of education and instruction. Chesterfield teaches his son in French the rudiments of **mythology and history**. I do not regret the publication of these

first letters. He lets slip some very excellent advice in those
early pages. The little Stanhope is no more than eight years
old when his father suits a little rhetoric to his juvenile understanding, and tries to show him how to use good language, and
to express himself well. He especially recommends to him attention in all that he does, and he gives the word its full value.
It is attention alone, he says, which fixes objects in the memory.
" There is no surer mark of a mean and meagre intellect in the
world than inattention. All that is worth the trouble of doing
at all deserves to be done well, and nothing can be well done
without attention. " This precept he incessantly repeats, and
varies the application of it as his pupil grows, and is in a condition to comprehend it to its fullest extent. Whether pleasure
or study, everything one does must be well done, done entirely
and at its proper time, without allowing any distraction to intervene. " When you read Horace pay attention to the accuracy of
his thoughts, to the elegance of his diction, and to the beauty
of his poetry, and do not think of the ' De Homine et Cive ' of
Puffendorf; and when you read Puffendorf do not think of
Mdme. de St. Germain; nor of Puffendorf when you speak to
Mdme. de St. Germain. " But this strong and easy subjugation
of the order of thought to the will only belongs to great or very
good intellects. M. Royer-Collard used to say that " what was
most wanting in our day was respect in the moral disposition,
and attention in the intellectual. " Lord Chesterfield, in a less
grave manner, might have said the same thing. He was not
long in finding out what was wanting in this child whom he
wished to bring up; whose bringing up was, indeed, the end
and aim of his life. " On sounding your character to its very
depths, " he said to him, " I have not, thank God, discovered any
vice of heart or weakness of head so far; but I have discovered
idleness, inattention, and indifference, defects which are only
pardonable in the aged, who, in the decline of life, when health
and spirits give way, have a sort of right to that kind of tranquillity. But a young man ought to be ambitious to shine and
excel. " And it is precisely this sacred fire, this lightning, that
makes the Achilles, the Alexanders, and the Cæsars to be the
first in every undertaking, this motto of noble hearts and of eminent men of all kinds, that nature had primarily neglected to
place in the honest but thoroughly mediocre soul of the younger
Stanhope: " You appear to want, " said his father, " that *vivida*

vis animi which excites the majority of young men to please, to strive, and to outdo others." "When I was your age," he says again, "I should have been ashamed for another to know his lesson better, or to have been before me in a game, and I should have had no rest till I had regained the advantage." All this little course of education by letters offers a sort of continuous dramatic interest; we follow the efforts of a fine distinguished energetic nature as Lord Chesterfield's was, engaged in a contest with a disposition honest but indolent, with an easy and dilatory temperament, from which it would, at any expense, form a masterpiece accomplished, amiable, and original, and with which it only succeeded in making a sort of estimable copy. What sustains and almost touches the reader in this strife, where so much art is used, and where the inevitable counsel is the same beneath all metamorphoses, is the true fatherly affection which animates and inspires the delicate and excellent master, as patient as he is full of vigor, lavish in resources and skill, never discouraged, untiring in sowing elegances and graces on this infertile soil. Not that this son, the object of so much culture and zeal, was in any way unworthy of his father. It has been pretended that there could be no one duller or more sullen than he was, and Johnson is quoted in support of the statement. There are caricatures which surpass the truth. It appears from the best authorities, that Mr. Stanhope, without being a model of grace, had the air of a man who had been well brought up, and was polite and agreeable. But do you not think that that is the most grievous part of all? It would have been better worth while, almost, to have totally failed, and to have only succeeded in making an original in the inverse sense, rather than with so much care and expense to have produced nothing more than an ordinary and insignificant man of the world, one of those about whom it suffices to say, there is nothing to be said of them; he had cause to be truly grieved and pity himself for his work, if he were not a father.

Lord Chesterfield had early thought of France to polish his son, and to give him that courtesy which cannot be acquired late in life. In private letters written to a lady at Paris, whom I believe to be Mdme. de Monconseil, we see that he had thought of sending him to France from his childhood.

"I have a boy," he wrote to this friend, "who is now thirteen years old: I freely confess to you that he is not legitimate; but his mother was well born and was kinder to me than I deserved. As to the boy, perhaps it is partiality, but I think him amiable: he has a pretty face; he has much sprightliness, and I think intelligence, for his age. He speaks French perfectly; he knows a good deal of Latin and Greek, and he has ancient and modern history at his fingers' ends. He is at school at present, but as they never dream here of forming the manners of young people and they are almost all foolish, awkward, and unpolished, in short such as you see them when they come to Paris at the age of twenty or twenty-one, I do not wish my boy to remain here to acquire such bad habits; for this reason, when he is fourteen I think of sending him to Paris. As I love the child dearly, and have set myself to make something good of him, as I believe he has the stuff in him, my idea is to unite in him what has never been found in one person before — I mean the best qualities of the two nations."

And he enters into the details of his plan, and the means he thinks of using; a learned Englishman every morning, a French teacher after dinner, but above all the help of the fashionable world and good society. The war which broke out between France and England postponed this plan, and the young man did not make his début in Paris until 1751, when he was nineteen years old, and had finished his tour through Switzerland, Germany, and Italy.

Everything has been arranged by the most attentive of fathers for his success and well-being upon this novel scene. The young man is placed at the Academy with M. de la Guérinière; the morning he devotes to study, and the rest of the time is to be consecrated to the world. "Pleasure is now the last branch of your education," this indulgent father writes; "it will soften and polish your manners, it will incite you to seek and finally to acquire graces." Upon this last point he is exacting, and shows no quarter. Graces! he returns continually to them, for without them all effort is vain. "If they are not natural to you, cultivate them," he cries. He indeed speaks confidently; as if to cultivate graces, it is not necessary to have them already!

Three ladies, friends of his father, are especially charged to watch over and guide the young man at his début; they are his *gouvernantes;* Mdme. de Monconseil, Lady Hervey, and Mdme. du Bocage. But these introducers appear essential for the first time only; the young man must afterwards depend upon himself, and choose some charming and more familiar guide. Upon this delicate subject of woman, Lord Chesterfield breaks the ice: "I shall not talk to you on this subject like a theologian, or a moralist, or a father," he says: "I set aside my age, and only take yours into consideration. I wish to speak to you as one man of pleasure would to another if he has taste and spirit." And he expresses himself in consequence, stimulating the young man as much as possible towards polite arrangements and delicate pleasures, to draw him from common and coarse habits. His principle is that "a polite arrangement becomes a gallant man." All his morality on this point is summed up in a line of Voltaire:—

"*Il n'est jamais de mal en bonne compagnie.*"

It is at these sentences more especially that the modesty of the grave Johnson is put to the blush; ours is content to smile at them.

The serious and frivolous are perpetually mingling in these letters. Marcel, the dancing master, is very often recommended; Montesquieu no less. The Abbé de Guasco, a sort of toady to Montesquieu, is a useful personage for introductions. "Between you and me," writes Chesterfield, "he has more knowledge than genius; but a clever man knows how to make use of everything, and every man is good for something. As to the Président of Montesquieu, he is in all respects a precious acquaintance; he has genius, with the most extensive reading in the world. Drink of this fountain as much as possible."

Of authors, those whom Chesterfield particularly recommends at this time, and those whose names occur most frequently in his counsels, are La Rochefoucauld and La Bruyère. "If you read some of La Rochefoucauld's maxims in the morning, consider them, examine them well, and compare them with the originals you meet in the evening. Read La Bruyère in the morning, and see in the evening if his portraits are correct." But these guides, excellent as they are, have no other use by themselves than that of a map. Without personal observation and experience, they would be useless, and would even be conducive to error, as a map might be if one thought to get from it a complete knowledge of towns and provinces. Better read one man than ten books. "The world is a country that no one has ever known by means of descriptions; each of us must traverse it in person to be thoroughly initiated into its ways."

Here are some precepts or remarks which are worthy of those masters of human morality: —

"The most essential of all knowledge, I mean the knowledge of the world, is never acquired without great attention, and I know a great many aged persons who, after having had an extensive acquaintance, are still mere children in the knowledge of the world."

"Human nature is the same all over the world; but its operations are so varied by education and custom that we ought to see it in all its aspects to get an intimate knowledge of it."

"Almost all men are born with every passion to some extent, but there is hardly a man who has not a dominant passion to which the others are subordinate. Discover this governing passion in every individual; search into the recesses of his heart, and observe the different effects of the same passion in different people. And when you have found the master passion of a man, remember never to trust to him where that passion is concerned."

"If you wish particularly to gain the good graces and affection of certain people, men or women, try to discover their most striking merit, if they have one, and their dominant weakness, for every one has his own, then do justice to the one, and a little more than justice to the other."

"Women, in general, have only one object, which is their beauty, upon which subject hardly any flattery can be too gross to please them."

"The flattery which is most pleasing to really beautiful or decidedly ugly women, is that which is addressed to the intellect."

On the subject of women, again, if he seems disdainful now and then, he makes reparation elsewhere; and, above all, whatever he thinks of them, he never allows his son to slander them too much. "You appear to think that from the days of Eve to the present time they have done much harm: as regards that lady I agree with you; but from her time history teaches you that men have done more harm in the world than women; and to speak truly, I would warn you not to trust either sex more than is absolutely necessary. But what I particularly advise you is this; never to attack whole bodies, whatever they may be."

"Individuals occasionally forgive, but bodies and societies never do."

In general, Chesterfield counsels his son to be circumspect and to preserve a sort of prudent neutrality, even in the case of the knaves and fools with which the world abounds. "After their friendship there is nothing more dangerous than to have them for enemies." It is not the morality of Cato nor of Zeno, but that of Alcibiades, of Aristippus, or Atticus.

Upon religion he shall speak, in reply to some trenchant opinions that his son had expressed: "The reason of every man is and ought to be his guide; and I should have as much right to expect every man to be of my height and temperament as to wish that he should reason precisely as I do."

In everything he is of the opinion that the good and the best should be known and loved, but that it is not necessary to make oneself a champion for or against everything. One must know even in literature how to tolerate the weaknesses of others: "Let them enjoy quietly their errors both in taste and religion." Oh! how far from such wisdom is the bitter trade of criticism, as we do it!

He does not, however, advise lying; he is precise in this particular. His precept always runs thus, do not tell all, but never tell a lie. "I have always observed," he frequently repeats, "that the greatest fools are the greatest liars. For my part, I judge of the truth of a man by the extent of his intellect."

We see how easily he mixes the useful and the agreeable. He is perpetually demanding from the intellect something resolute and subtle, sweetness in the manner, energy at bottom.

Lord Chesterfield thoroughly appreciated the serious state of France and the dread events that the eighteenth century brought to light. According to him, Duclos, in his "Reflections," is right when he says that "a germ of reason is beginning to appear in France." "What I can confidently predict," adds Chesterfield, "is that before the end of this century the trades of king and priest will have lost half their power."

Our revolution has been clearly predicted by him since 1750.

He warned his son from the beginning against the idea that the French are entirely frivolous. "The cold inhabitants of the North look upon the French as a frivolous people who sing and whistle and dance perpetually; this is very far from being the truth, though the army of fops seems to justify it. But these fops, ripened by age and experience, often turn into very able men." The ideal, according to him, would be to unite the merits of the two nations; but in this mixture he still seems to lean towards France: "I have said many times, and I really think,

that a Frenchman who joins to a good foundation of virtue,
learning, and good sense, the manners and politeness of his country, has attained the perfection of human nature." He unites
sufficiently well in himself the advantages of the two nations,
with one characteristic which belongs exclusively to his race,
there is imagination even in his wit. Hamilton himself has this
distinctive characteristic, and introduces it into French wit.
Bacon, the great moralist, is almost a poet by expression, one
cannot say so much of Lord Chesterfield; nevertheless, he has
more imagination in his sallies and in the expression of his wit
than one meets with in St. Evremond and our acute moralists
in general. He resembles his friend Montesquieu in this respect.

If in the letters to his son we can, without being severe, lay
hold of some cases of slightly damaged morality, we should have
to point out, by way of compensation, some very serious and
really admirable passages, where he speaks of the Cardinal de
Retz, of Mazarin, of Bolingbroke, of Marlborough, and of many
others. It is a rich book. One cannot read a page without finding some happy observation worthy of being remembered.

Lord Chesterfield intended this beloved son for a diplomatic
life; he at first found some difficulties in the way on account of
his illegitimacy. To cut short these objections, he sent his son
to parliament; it was the surest method of conquering the scruples of the court. Mr. Stanhope, in his maiden speech, hesitated
a moment, and was obliged to have recourse to notes. He did
not make a second attempt at speaking in public. It appears
that he succeeded better in diplomacy, in those second-rate places
where solid merit is sufficient. He filled the post of embassador
extraordinary to the court of Dresden. But his health, always
delicate, failed before he was old, and his father had the misfortune to see him die before him when he was scarcely thirty-six
years old (1768). Lord Chesterfield at that time lived entirely
retired from the world, on account of his infirmities, the most
painful of which was complete deafness. Montesquieu, whose
sight failed, said to him once, " I know how to be blind." But
he was not able to say as much; he did not know how to be
deaf. He wrote of it to his friends, even to those in France,
thus: " The exchange of letters," he remarked, " is the conversation of deaf people, and the only link which connects them with
society." He found his latest consolations in his pretty country
house at Blackheath, which he had called by the French name

of Babiole. He employed his time there in gardening and cultivating his melons and pineapples; he amused himself by vege-
tating in company with them: —

"I have vegetated here all this year," he wrote to a French
friend (September, 1753), "without pleasures and without troubles;
my age and deafness prevented the first; my philosophy, or rather
my temperament (for one often confounds them), guaranteed me
against the last. I always get as much as I can of the quiet
pleasures of gardening, walking, and reading, and in the meantime
I await death without desiring or fearing it."

He never undertook long works, not feeling himself sufficiently
strong, but he sometimes sent agreeable essays to a periodical
publication, the World. These essays are quite worthy of his
reputation for skill and urbanity. Nevertheless, nothing approaches the work — which was no work to him — of those letters,
which he never imagined any one would read, and which are yet
the foundation of his literary success.

His old age, which was an early one, lasted a long time. His
wit gave a hundred turns to this sad theme. Speaking of himself and of one of his friends, Lord Tyrawley, equally old and
infirm, "Tyrawley and I," he said, "have been dead two years,
but we do not wish it to be known."

Voltaire, who under the pretense of being always dying, had
preserved his youth much better, wrote to him on the twenty-
fourth of October, 1771, this pretty letter, signed, "*Le vieux
malade de Ferney*" : —

"Enjoy an honorable and happy old age, after having passed
through the trials of life. Enjoy your wit and preserve the health
of your body. Of the five senses with which we are provided, you
have only one enfeebled, and Lord Huntingdon assures me that you
have a good stomach, which is worth a pair of ears. It will be perhaps my place to decide which is the most sorrowful, to be deaf or
blind, or have no digestion. I can judge of all these three conditions
with a knowledge of the cause; but it is a long time since I ven-
tured to decide upon trifles, least of all upon things so important. I
confine myself to the belief that, if you have sun in the beautiful
house that you have built, you will spend some tolerable moments;
that is all we can hope for at our age. Cicero wrote a beautiful
treatise upon old age, but he did not verify his words by deeds; his
last years were very unhappy. You have lived longer and more
happily than he did. You have had to do neither with perpetual
dictators nor with triumvirs. Your lot has been, and still is, one of

the most desirable in that great lottery where good tickets are so scarce, and where the Great Prize of continual happiness has never been gained by any one. Your philosophy has never been upset by chimeras which have sometimes perplexed tolerably good brains. You have never been in any sense a charlatan, nor the dupe of charlatans, and that I reckon as a rare merit, which adds something to the shadow of happiness that we are allowed to taste of in this short life."

Lord Chesterfield died on the twenty-fourth of March, 1773. In pointing out his charming course of wordly education, we have not thought it out of place even in a democracy, to take lessons of *savior vivre* and politeness, and to receive them from a man whose name is so closely connected with those of Montesquieu and Voltaire, who, more than any of his countrymen in his own time, showed singular fondness for our nation; who delighted, more than was right, perhaps, in our amiable qualities; who appreciated our solid virtues, and of whom it might be said, as his greatest praise, that he was a French wit, if he had not introduced into the verve and vivacity of his sallies that inexplicable something of imagination and color that bears the impress of his race.

Complete.

GEORGE EDWARD BATEMAN SAINTSBURY

(1845-)

OR nearly two decades past, Saintsbury has been a favorite contributor to the English reviews. Much of his work as an essayist has been in the form of literary biographies and book reviews. As a book reviewer, he is much less aggressive than the slashing critics of the first half of the century. The change of style is as marked as the improvement of literary morality which made it possible. Saintsbury was born at Southampton, England, October 23d, 1845. After graduating from Merton College, Oxford, he taught the Classics at Elizabeth College in Guernsey, and was head master of the Elgin Educational Institute (1874-76). In 1876 he began in London the work as an editor and essayist he has since continued. Among his works are "English Worthies," "History of Elizabethan Literature," and "Essays on English Literature."

ON PARTON'S «VOLTAIRE»

OF NEARLY all the events of this remarkable life Mr. Parton has given an account, sometimes faulty in form, but sufficient and complete in substance. His book, though it may give some new facts, will, of course, not materially alter the idea of Voltaire to those who have previously studied his life and his works; but to those who do not already possess much knowledge of him it furnishes a convenient means of informing themselves. A book of thirteen hundred pages, deformed by American misspelling of the English tongue, and by references to "inflationists" and such-like irrelevances, not to mention constant expressions of the author's sentiments, which are, to say the least, unimportant, may seem a formidable undertaking. But its copiousness of incident and anecdote and its abundant quotations lighten the task of reading very considerably. At the end of it he must be a somewhat thoughtless reader (if, indeed, any such be likely to reach the end) who does not endeavor to make up for himself, assisted by the critical comments of those of Mr. Parton's predecessors to whom Pallas has been more kind, some notion of the singular personality here portrayed. Mr. Parton's own notion of that personality is decided enough. In his own marvelous language he tells us that Voltaire's empty sepulchre "is vocal, it is resonant, it booms and thunders over the earth." The superstition-crusher pushes everything and everybody else aside in his estimate. I think, for my own part, that from such a standpoint it is as difficult to judge Voltaire rightly as from that of my friend who called him a wretch, from that of Johnson, or from that of George III.

The truth seems to be that Voltaire was an extremely complicated character; the wonderful diversity of his literary work only reflects this complexity in part, though the one, no doubt, is the reason of the other. As I can hardly think of any man who displayed so many different forms of the literary faculty, so I can hardly think of any man, whether of letters or of business, who united the capacity and in a way the actual performance of so many different parts. Of his varied ability in practical administrative business there is proof almost as ample as of his varied ability in literary work. If he failed anywhere in what he undertook it was in diplomacy, and it is fair to remember that he had an antagonist to contend with there by whom it was no shame to be beaten. He has not, like Wordsworth, left us explicit intimations that in his own opinion his mission was to be Prime Minister, or Archbishop of Canterbury, or Commander in Chief, or Lord Chancellor, or all of them together. But I have no doubt that if the opportunity of any or all of these posts had come in his way he would have accepted it cheerfully, and would have performed the duties on the whole very well. The complementary defect of the quality of jack of all trades is well known. Voltaire suffered from it less than most people, but he did suffer from it. In no literary style, except in that of satirical prose fiction, or allegory of the social kind, can he be said to have attained the highest mastery. In work requiring research of any kind he was rather rapid than thorough, and he carried to excess the national habit of hasty deduction from insufficiently investigated premises. His moral and intellectual character, with which we are here more specially concerned, shows inconsistencies and blemishes of all kinds. Let us try and sum up what the devil's advocates say against him. He was an unscrupulous liar; he was extraordinarily vain; he was utterly destitute of reverence; he had an impure imagination which was not checked by the slightest sense of even external decency; he was given to filthy lucre; he was spiteful and revengeful in the extreme toward his personal enemies. This is an ugly catalogue, and it is unfortunately true that no single article in it can be struck out entirely by the most uncompromising defender who knows and respects the facts. Mitigating pleas are all that is possible. His lying, which is a very unpleasant feature to English examiners of his character, has to be taken in conjunction with the fact that it was, so to speak, official and professional lying for the most part. The absurd and iniquitous political and social system of the time and country necessitated and in a manner recognized it. It was little more than the conventional "not guilty," not so much as the equally conventional "not at home." The charge of vanity must be admitted *sans phrase*, but it is not a very damning one. The lack of reverence also is not contestable, though there are some circumstances on the other side, notably the mountain-top story, which I have not noticed in Mr. Parton, and his lifelong cult of the starry heavens. This was, however, a distinct and inevitable consequence of his peculiar faculty of ridicule, which must also excuse as far as it can (and that is not very far) the uncleanness of his writings. I shall frankly own that that uncleanness is to me the most unpleasant variety of the disease that I know, with the possible exception of Dryden's. His carrying out of the maxim *non olet* is another blot on his character. There is nothing inexcusable, though perhaps there is something rather undignified, in a poet's making money by stockbroking and money changing; but the Hirsch matter, as to which something has been said already, cannot be defended, and the persistent way in which the author of "L'Homme aux Quarante Ecus" and a hundred other protests against financial mismanagement allowed himself to profit by contracts, loans, and so forth, where the profit was due to corrupt administration, is a still greater blot. With respect to Fréron, Desfontaines, et Cie., perhaps the worst thing that can be said about Voltaire is that in point of malignity there is sometimes nothing and generally very little to choose between himself and his adversaries.

And yet I have not the least intention of admitting that Voltaire was a wretch, or anything of the kind. All the worst of his faults were emphatically the faults of his time and his education. His merits, on the other hand, were personal and his own, a distinction which, however hackneyed it may be, is almost the only one available in this world of ours. These merits Mr. Parton's book ought to make clear to everybody who is not hopelessly prejudiced. One of the chief of them was an extraordinary kindness of heart and affection for his friends, relations, and, indeed, everybody with whom he was not brought into violent collision. Madame du Châtelet and Madame Denis, the feminine plagues of the greater part of his long life, certainly had nothing to complain of in him. Notwithstanding his occasional fits of ill temper, all his servants and dependants were fond of him, and even the passionate Collini did not find those fits intolerable. His friendship for Thieriot, a person of very doubtful merit, and not unfrequently, as in the Desfontaines affair, and in the matter of the employments which Voltaire sought to procure for him from Richelieu, a troublesome and even treacherous friend, was unwearying. No one, even of his enemies, fails to acknowledge his remarkable benevolence to oppressed or unfortunate persons of every degree of merit, from Calas and Lally to La Barre and Desfontaines. Something, perhaps, must be allowed for his love of playing the grand seigneur in estimating his good deeds at Ferney; but even when that allowance is made, a solid amount will remain to his credit. Unscrupulous as he was in some ways in the getting of money, he neither spent it unworthily nor hoarded it for the mere sake of hoarding; his object being, as has been said, the securing of independence, which in his time and country no man, who was neither a priest nor a noble, could hope for without a competent estate. These things are, of course, perfectly well known to students of French literature and French history; but the general reader is less likely to be acquainted with them. Such a reader will find in Mr. Parton's book a good deal to amuse him, and a good deal to correct and heighten his idea of Voltaire as a man. It has been hinted that the merits of the book, as a literary commentary, are hardly equal to its merits as a repository of fact. In the former respect, however, as has also been suggested, more than one *scriptor haud paulo melior quam ego aut*, Mr. Parton has supplied the deficiency in English by anticipation, and it is therefore superfluous to say any more on that score.

From a review of Parton's "Life of Voltaire."

FRIEDRICH WILHELM JOSEPH VON SCHELLING

(1775–1854)

THE "highest relation of Art and Nature," writes Schelling, "is shown in this, that Art makes Nature the medium of manifesting the soul it contains." This strongly suggests, if it does not define, the central thought of the philosophical system he attempted to elaborate, progressively, in a series of works which when collected (1856–61) make fourteen volumes. It is the idea that nature and spirit are both realities, each distinct, but that both are the correlated parts of a whole which cannot exist in its completeness without both. Spirit is not considered in this system as distinct from, but rather as the inspiration of, Nature — as its "reason for existence" (*ratio essendi*). "Art" becomes thus the mode by which the human mind expresses the correlated harmony of the mind in nature. The thought thus developed by the philosophy of Schelling will do much to make intelligible the view of art which inspired Ruskin and his school in England.

Schelling was born in Würtemberg, January 27th, 1775. Receiving his own university education at Tübingen, he became a Professor at Jena (1798) and later at Würzberg, Munich, and Berlin. His university associations brought him into close relations with Hegel and the Schlegels, by whom he was influenced as he was, perhaps to a greater extent, by Fichte. Among his more notable works are "First Plan of a System of the Philosophy of Nature," "Transcendental Idealism," "Exposition of My System of Philosophy," "Philosophy and Religion," and "Human Freedom." He died in Switzerland, August 20th, 1854.

NATURE AND ART

NATURE in her wide circumference ever exhibits the higher with the lower: creating in Man the godlike, she elaborates in all her other productions only its material and foundation, which must exist in order that in contrast with it the Essence as such may appear. And even in the higher world of Man the great mass serves again as the basis upon which the godlike that is preserved pure in the few manifests itself in legislation, government, and the establishment of Religion. So that wherever Art works with more of the complexity of Nature, it may and must display together with the highest measure of Beauty also its groundwork and raw material as it were, in distinct appropriate forms.

Here first prominently unfolds itself the difference in Nature of the forms of Art.

Plastic Art, in the more exact sense of the term, disdains to give Space outwardly to the object, but bears it within itself. This, however, narrows its field; it is compelled, indeed, to display the beauty of the Universe almost in a single point. It must therefore aim immediately at the highest, and can attain complexity only separately and in the strictest exclusion of all conflicting elements. By isolating the purely animal in human nature it succeeds in forming inferior creations too, harmonious and even beautiful, as we are taught by the beauty of numerous Fauns preserved from Antiquity; it can, indeed, parodying itself like the merry spirit of Nature, reverse its own Ideal, and for instance, in the extravagance of the Silenic figures, by light and sportive treatment, appear freed again from the pressure of matter.

But in all cases it is compelled strictly to isolate the work, in order to make it self-consistent and a world in itself; since for this form of Art there is no higher unity, in which the dissonance of particulars should be melted into harmony.

Painting, on the contrary, in the very extent of its sphere, can better measure itself with the Universe, and create with epic profusion. In an "Iliad" there is room even for a Thersites, and what does not find a place in the great epic of Nature and History!

Here the Particular scarcely counts anything by itself; the Universe takes its place, and that, which by itself would not be beautiful, becomes so in the harmony of the whole. If in an extensive painting, uniting forms by the allotted space, by light, by shade, by reflection, the highest measure of Beauty were everywhere employed, the result would be the most unnatural monotony; for, as Winckelmann says, the highest idea of Beauty is everywhere one and the same, and scarce admits of variation. The detail would be preferred to the whole, where, as in every case in which the whole is formed by multiplicity, the detail must be subordinate to it.

In such a work, therefore, a gradation of Beauty must be observed, by which alone the full Beauty concentrated in the focus becomes visible; and from an exaggeration of particulars proceeds an equipoise of the whole. Here, then, the limited and characteristic finds its place; and theory at least should direct the painter, not so much to the narrow space in which the entire Beauty is concentrically collected, as to the characteristic complexity of Nature, through which alone he can impart to an extensive work the full measure of living significance.

Thus thought, among the founders of modern art, the noble Leonardo; thus Raphael, the master of high Beauty, who shunned not to exhibit it in smaller measure rather than to appear monotonous, lifeless, and unreal — though he understood not only how to produce it, but also how to break up uniformity by variety of expression.

For, although Character can show itself also in rest and equilibrium of form, yet it is only in action that it becomes truly alive.

By Character we understand a unity of several forces, operating constantly to produce among them a certain equipoise and determinate proportion, to which, if undisturbed, a like equipoise in the symmetry of the forms corresponds. But if this vital Unity is to display itself in act and operation, this can only be when the forces, excited by some cause to rebellion, forsake their equilibrium. Every one sees that this is the case in the Passions.

But here we are met by the well-known maxim of the theorists, which demands that Passion should be moderated as far as possible, in its actual outburst, that Beauty of Form may not be injured. But we think this maxim should rather be reversed, and read thus: — that Passion should be moderated by Beauty itself. For it is much to be feared that this desired moderation too may be taken in a negative sense — whereas, what is really requisite is, to oppose to Passion a positive force. For as Virtue consists, not in the absence of passions, but in the mastery of the spirit over them, so Beauty is preserved, not by their removal or abatement, but by the mastery of Beauty over them.

The forces of Passion must actually show themselves — it must be seen that they are prepared to rise in mutiny, but are kept down by the power of Character, and break against the forms of firmly founded Beauty, as the waves of a stream that just fills, but cannot overflow its banks.   Otherwise, this striving after moderation would resemble only those shallow moralists, who, the more readily to dispose of Man, prefer to mutilate his nature; and who have so entirely removed every positive element from actions, that the people gloat over the spectacle of great crimes, in order to refresh themselves at last with the view of something positive.

In Nature and Art the Essence strives first after actualization, or exhibition of itself in the Particular.   Thus in each the utmost severity is manifested at the commencement; for without bound, the boundless could not appear; without severity, gentleness could not exist; and if unity is to be perceptible, it can only be through particularity, detachment, and opposition.   In the beginning, therefore, the creative spirit shows itself entirely lost in its form, inaccessibly shut up, and even in its grandeur still harsh. But the more it succeeds in uniting its entire fullness in one product, the more it gradually relaxes from its severity; and where it has fully developed the form, so as to rest contented and self-collected in it, it seems to become cheerful, and begins to move in gentle lines.   This is the period of its fairest maturity and blossom, in which the pure vessel has arrived at perfection; the spirit of Nature becomes free from its bonds, and feels its relationship to the soul.   As by a gentle morning blush stealing over the whole form, the coming soul announces itself; it is not yet present, but everything prepares for its reception, by the delicate play of gentle movements; the rigid outlines melt and temper themselves into flexibility; a lovely essence, neither sensuous nor spiritual, but which cannot be grasped, diffuses itself over the form, and entwines itself with every outline, every vibration of the frame.

This essence, not to be seized, as we have already remarked, but yet perceptible to all, is what the language of the Greeks designated by the name Charis, ours as Grace.

Wherever, in a fully developed form, Grace appears, the work is complete on the side of Nature; nothing more is wanting; all demands are satisfied.   Here, already, soul and body are in complete harmony; Body is Form, Grace is Soul, although not Soul in itself, but the Soul of Form, or the Soul of Nature.

Art may linger, and remain stationary at this point; for, already, on one side at least, its whole task is finished.   The pure image of Beauty arrested at this point is the Goddess of Love.

But the beauty of the Soul in itself, joined to sensuous Grace, is the highest apotheosis of Nature.

The spirit of Nature is only in appearance opposed to the Soul; essentially, it is the instrument of its revelation; it brings about indeed the antagonism that exists in all things, but only that the one essence may come forth, as the utmost benignity, and the reconciliation of all the forces.

All other creatures are driven by the mere force of Nature, and through it maintain their individuality; in Man alone, as the central point, arises the soul, without which the world would be like the natural universe without the sun.

The Soul in Man, therefore, is not the principle of individuality, but that whereby he raises himself above all egoism, whereby he becomes capable of self-sacrifice, and of disinterested love, and (which is the highest) of the contemplation and knowledge of the Essence of things; and thus of Art.

In him it is no longer employed about Matter, nor has to do with it immediately, but only with the spirit (as the life) of things. Even while appearing in the body, it is yet free from the body, the consciousness of which hovers in the Soul in the most beauteous shapes only as a light, undisturbing dream. It is no quality, no faculty, nor anything special of the sort; it knows not, but is Science; it is not good, but Goodness; it is not beautiful, as body even may be, but Beauty itself.

Most readily, or most immediately, indeed, in a work of art, the soul of the artist is seen as invention, in the detail, and in the total result, as the unity that hovers over it in serene stillness. But the Soul must be visible in objective representation, as the primeval energy of thought, in portraitures of human beings, altogether filled by an idea, by a noble contemplation; or as indwelling essential Goodness.

Each of these finds its distinct expression even in the completest repose, but a more living one where the Soul can reveal itself in activity and antagonism; and since it is by the passions mainly that the force of life is interrupted, it is the generally received opinion, that the beauty of the Soul shows itself especially in its quiet supremacy amid the storm of the passions.

But here an important distinction is to be made. For the Soul must not be called upon to moderate those passions which are only an outbreak of the lower spirits of Nature, nor can it be displayed in antithesis with these; for where calm considerateness is still in contention with them, the Soul has not yet appeared: they must be moderated by unassisted Nature in Man, by the might of the Spirit. But there are cases of a higher sort, in which, not a single force alone, but the intelligent Spirit itself, breaks down all barriers; cases, indeed, where the Soul is subjected by the bond that connects it with sensuous existence, to pain, which should be foreign to its divine nature; where Man feels himself invaded and attacked in the root of his existence, not by mere powers of Nature, but by moral forces; where innocent error hurries him into crime, and thus into misery; where deep-felt injustice excites to rebellion the holiest feelings of humanity.

This is the case in all situations, truly, and in a high sense, tragical, such as the Tragedy of the Ancients brings before our eyes. Where blindly passionate forces are aroused, the collected Spirit is present as the guardian of Beauty; but if the Spirit itself be hurried away, as by an irresistible might, what power shall watch over and protect sacred Beauty? Or, if the Soul participate in the struggle, how shall it save itself from pain and from desecration?

Arbitrarily to limit the power of pain, of excited feeling, would be to sin against the very meaning and aim of Art, and would betray a want of feeling and Soul in the artist himself.

Already therein, that Beauty, based on grand and firmly established forms has become Character, Art has provided the means of displaying without injury to symmetry the whole intensity of Feeling. For where Beauty rests on mighty forms, as upon immovable pillars, a slight change in its relations, scarcely touching the form, causes us to infer the great force that was necessary in order to effect it. Still more does Grace sanctify pain. It is the essential nature of Grace that it does not know itself; but not being willfully acquired, it also cannot be willfully lost. When intolerable anguish, when even madness, sent by avenging Gods, takes away consciousness and reflection, Grace stands as a protecting demon by the suffering form, and prevents it from manifesting anything unseemly, anything discordant to Humanity; but if it fall, to fall at least a pure and unspotted victim.

Not yet the Soul itself, but the prophecy of it; Grace accomplishes by natural means, what the Soul does by a divine power, in transforming pain, torpor, even death itself, into Beauty.

IX—210

Yet Grace thus preserved amid the extremest discordance would be dead, without a transfiguration by the Soul. But what expression can belong to the Soul in this situation? It delivers itself from pain, and comes forth conquering, not conquered, by relinquishing its connection with sensuous existence.

It is for the natural Spirit to exert its energies for the preservation of sensuous existence, the Soul enters not into this contest; but its presence moderates even the storms of painfully struggling life. Outward force can take away only outward goods, but not reach the Soul; it can tear asunder a temporal bond, not dissolve the eternal one of a truly divine love. Not hard and unfeeling, nor wanting in love itself, the Soul, on the contrary, displays in pain this alone, as the sentiment that outlasts sensuous existence, and thus raises itself above the ruins of outward life or fortune in divine glory.

It is this expression of the Soul that the creator of the Niobe has shown us in this statue. All the means by which Art tempers even the Terrible, are here made use of. Mightiness of form, sensuous Grace, nay, even the nature of the subject-matter itself, softens the expression, since pain, transcending all expression, annihilates itself, and Beauty, which it seemed impossible to preserve from destruction, is protected from injury by the commencing torpor.

But what would it all be without the Soul, and how shall this manifest itself?

We see on the countenance of the mother, not grief alone for the already prostrated flower of her children; not alone deadly anxiety for the preservation of those yet remaining, and of the youngest daughter, who has fled for safety to her bosom; nor resentment against the cruel deities; least of all, as is pretended, cool defiance: all these we see, indeed, but not these alone, for, through grief, anxiety, and resentment streams, like a divine light, eternal love, as that which alone remains; and in this is preserved the mother, as one who was not, but now is a mother, and who remains united with the beloved ones by an eternal bond.

Every one acknowledges that greatness, purity, and goodness of soul have also their sensuous expressions. But how is this conceivable, unless the principle that acts in Matter be itself cognate and similar to Soul?

For the representation of the Soul there are again gradations in Art according as it is joined with the merely Characteristic, or in visible union with the Charming and Graceful.

Who perceives not, in the tragedies of Æschylus, that lofty morality already predominant, which is at home in the works of Sophocles? But in the former it is enveloped in a bitter rind, and passes less into the whole work, since the bond of sensuous Grace is yet wanting. But out of this severity, and the still terrible charms of earlier Art, could yet proceed the grace of Sophocles, and with it the complete fusion of the two elements, which leaves us doubtful whether it is more moral or sensuous Grace that enchants us in the works of this poet.

The same is true of the plastic productions of the early and severe style, in comparison with the gentleness of the later.

If Grace, besides being the transfiguration of the spirit of Nature, is also the medium of connection between moral Goodness and sensuous Appearance, it is evident how Art must tend from all points towards it as its centre. This Beauty, which results from the perfect interpenetration of moral Goodness and sensuous Grace, seizes and enchants us when we meet it, with the force of a miracle. For, whilst the spirit of Nature shows itself everywhere else independent of the Soul, and, indeed, in a measure opposed to it, here, it seems, as if by voluntary accord, and the inward fire of divine love, to melt into union with it: the remembrance of the fundamental unity of the essence of Nature and the essence of the Soul comes over the beholder with sudden clearness: the conviction that all antagonism is only apparent, that Love is the bond of all things, and pure Goodness the foundation and substance of the whole Creation.

Here Art as it were transcends itself, and becomes means only. On this summit sensuous Grace becomes in turn only the husk and body of a higher life: what was before a whole is treated as a part, and the highest relation of Art and Nature is reached in this, that Art makes Nature the medium of manifesting the soul which it contains.

From «Relations of the Plastic Arts to Nature.»

JOHANN CHRISTOPH FRIEDRICH VON SCHILLER

(1759–1805)

WHEN Goethe wrote "Faust," he left no question of his pre-eminence among German poets, but it can be questioned if even the idea which inspired Faust is as lofty or as deep as Schiller's idea that the "Spieltrieb" is the impulse of higher civilization. As a hypothesis, it begins where the "agnostic" theory of the "survival of the fittest" under pressure of environment ends. The Darwinian theory shows man compelled by necessity to develop so much intelligence as will save him from destruction. The theory of Schiller shows him led by his affections to develop into the Infinity beyond Necessity. The "pressure of environment" may account for the kraal of the Kaffir, and the snow hut of the Eskimo, but Schiller's hypothesis accounts for the Parthenon and the dome of St. Peter's. He saw that men improve most by doing not what they must, but what they love best, and he found his solution of the problem of progress in Liberty and Love. Children who mold the rude image of a man from clay after a rain, or savages who scrawl a drawing into the face of a cliff, are compelled by no other necessity than that of doing their own pleasure — of the "Spieltrieb" or "play impulse," acting under perfect liberty. But in such acts, Schiller saw the beginnings of all those arts which express the higher operations of mind.

As an essayist he is greatly superior to Goethe in the power of connected and sustained statement. Few writers in or out of Germany have equaled him in this. It is as remarkable as in one sense it is regrettable, that a poet who expresses himself through verse in thronging images of sensuous beauty should, in defining in prose the high ideas which animate his verse, become abstract and severe to the last degree. In any ten lines of the essays in which he is stating his conclusions, the strongest intellect can find material for longer meditation than busy readers are generally able to give to ten pages. Hence Schiller has never been popular as an essayist, and he is never likely to become so. But those who will make a serious attempt to respond to the severe demands he makes on all who come to him for instruction are not likely either to forget him as a teacher or to cease to thank him,

He was born at Marbach, Würtemberg, November 10th,* 1759. In 1780, after concluding his studies in medicine, he became regimental surgeon at Stuttgart, where in 1781 he published his first notable work, "The Robbers." Not only was he obliged to publish it at his own expense, but when it appeared, his "suzerain" and military superior, Duke Karl Eugen, of Würtemberg, ordered him as a regimental surgeon to write no more poetry. Seeing no recourse as a poet except to disobey as a military surgeon, Schiller did so. After being sentenced to a fortnight's arrest for his contumacy, he "fled" to Mannheim and afterwards to Darmstadt and Frankfort, living under assumed names until he had made his own so famous that even Duke Karl Eugen concluded it would not be advisable to subject him to further military discipline for writing poetry. Returning to Mannheim in 1783, Schiller left it for Leipsic in 1785. Growing tired successively of Leipsic and Dresden, he removed in 1787 to Weimar, where he made his home for many years and where he died May 9th, 1805. His association with Goethe began in 1794, and it was of great advantage to both. Under the influence of the increased confidence in himself resulting from Goethe's appreciation, Schiller wrote many of his best lyrics, including "The Song of the Bell,"— no doubt the best "ode" in the German language, if the word "ode" be understood in the modern sense. As a writer of odes (*carmina*) in the ancient sense, Schiller is not the equal of Goethe or of Heine. It was not that Schiller failed intellectually of fitness for the highest possible rank in poetry; the greatest poet of any age must be also its greatest musician; and in musical power over language, Schiller, who is second only to Goethe in everything else, is inferior also to Heine. Had it been otherwise he might easily have been the greatest poet, not only of Germany but of modern times, for his power of sustained thought and coherent expression surpasses that of Goethe. It is remarkable that the poems of Schiller should be classical in nearly everything but their melody, while those of Goethe, Teutonic in their spirit, derive their supreme charm from a closer approximation to the classical mode in melody than had been made by any other German poet.

W. V. B.

MAN AND THE UNIVERSE

WHILE man, in his first physical condition, is only passively affected by the world of sense, he is still entirely identified with it; and for this reason the external world, as yet, has no objective existence for him. When he begins in his

---

* The date is also given as November 11th, but the authorities favor the 10th.

æsthetic state of mind to regard the world objectively, then only is his personality severed from it, and the world appears to him an objective reality, for the simple reason that he has ceased to form an identical portion of it.

That which first connects man with the surrounding universe is the power of reflective contemplation. Whereas desire seizes at once its object, reflection removes it to a distance and renders it inalienably her own by saving it from the greed of passion. The necessity of sense which he obeyed during the period of mere sensations, lessens during the period of reflection: the senses are for the time in abeyance; even ever-reflecting time stands still whilst the scattered rays of consciousness are gathering and shape themselves; an image of the infinite is reflected upon the perishable ground. As soon as light dawns in man, there is no longer night outside of him; as soon as there is peace within him the storm lulls throughout the universe, and the contending forces of nature find rest within prescribed limits. Hence we cannot wonder if ancient traditions allude to these great changes in the inner man as to a revolution in surrounding nature, and symbolize thought triumphing over the laws of time, by the figure of Zeus, which terminates the reign of Saturn.

As long as man derives sensations from a contact with Nature, he is her slave; but as soon as he begins to reflect upon her objects and law she becomes her lawgiver. Nature, which previously ruled him as a power, now expands before him as an object. What is objective to him can have no power over him, for in order to become objective it has to experience his own power. As far and as long as he impresses a form upon matter, he cannot be injured by its effect; for a spirit can only be injured by that which deprives it of its freedom. Whereas he proves his own freedom by giving a form to the formless; where the mass rules heavily and without shape, and its undefined outlines are forever fluctuating between uncertain boundaries, fear takes up its abode; but man rises above any natural terror as soon as he knows how to mold it, and transform it into an object of his art. As soon as he upholds his independence towards phenomenal natures he maintains his dignity toward her as a thing of power, and with a noble freedom he rises against his gods. They throw aside the mask with which they had kept him in awe during his infancy, and to his surprise his mind perceives the reflection of his own image. The divine monster of the Oriental, which roams about changing the world with the blind force of a beast of prey, dwindles to the charming outline of humanity in Greek fable; the empire of the Titans is crushed, and boundless force is tamed by infinite form.

But whilst I have been merely searching for an issue from the material world, and a passage into the world of mind, the bold flight of my imagination has already taken me into the very midst of the latter world. The beauty of which we are in search we have left behind by passing from the life of mere sensations to the pure form and to the pure object. Such a leap exceeds the condition of human nature; in order to keep pace with the latter, we must return to the world of sense.

Beauty is indeed the sphere of unfettered contemplation and reflection; beauty conducts us into the world of ideas, without, however, taking us from the world of sense, as occurs when a truth is perceived and acknowledged. This is the pure product of a process of abstraction from everything material and accidental, a pure object free from every subjective barrier, a pure state of self-activity without any admixture of passive sensations. There is, indeed, a way back to sensation from the highest abstraction; for thought teaches the inner sensation, and the idea of logical or moral unity passes into a sensation of sensual accord. But if we delight in knowledge we separate very accurately our own conceptions from our sensations; we look upon the latter as something accidental, which might have been omitted without the knowledge being impaired thereby, without truth being less true. It would, however, be a vain attempt to suppress this connection of the faculty of feeling with the idea of beauty, consequently we shall not succeed in representing to ourselves one as the effect of the other; but we must look upon them both together and reciprocally as cause and effect. In the pleasure which we derive from knowledge we readily distinguish the passage from the active to the passive state, and we clearly perceive that the first ends when the second begins. On the contrary, from the pleasure which we take in beauty, this transition from the active to the passive is not perceivable, and reflection is so intimately blended with feeling that we believe we feel the form immediately. Beauty is then an object to us, it is true, because reflection is the condition of the feeling which we have of it; but it is also a state of our personality (our *ego*) because the feeling is the condition of the idea we conceive of it: beauty is therefore doubtless form, because we contemplate it, but it is equally life, because we feel it. In a word, it is at once our state and our act. And precisely because it is at the same time both a state and an act, it triumphantly proves to us that the passive does not exclude the active, neither matter nor form, neither the finite nor the infinite; and that consequently the physical dependence to which man is necessarily devoted does not in any way destroy his moral liberty. This is the proof of beauty, and I ought to add that this alone can prove it. In fact, as in the possession of truth or of logical unity, feeling is not necessarily one with the thought, but follows it accidentally; it is a fact which only proves that a sensitive nature can succeed a rational nature, and *vice versa;* not that they co-exist, that they exercise a reciprocal action one over the other; and, lastly, that they ought to be united in an absolute and necessary manner. From this exclusion of feeling as long as there is thought, and of thought so long as there is feeling, we should, on the contrary, conclude that the two natures are incompatible, so that in order to demonstrate that pure reason is to be realized in humanity, the best proof given by the analysis is that this realization is demanded. But, as in the realization of beauty or in æsthetic unity, there is a real union, mutual substitution of matter and of form, of passive and of active, by this alone is proved the compatibility of the two natures, the possible realization of the infinite in the finite, and consequently, also, the possibility of the most sublime humanity.

Henceforth we need no longer be embarrassed to find a transition from dependent feeling to moral liberty, because beauty reveals to us the fact that they can perfectly co-exist, and that to show himself a spirit, man need not escape from matter. But if, on one side, he is free, even in his relation with a visible world, as the fact of beauty teaches, and if, on the other side, freedom is something absolute and supersensuous, as its idea necessarily implies, the question is no longer how man succeeds in raising himself from the finite to the absolute, and opposing himself in his thought and will to sensuality, as this has already been produced in the fact of beauty. In a word, we have no longer to ask how he passes from virtue to truth which is already included in the former, but how he opens a way for himself from vulgar reality to æsthetic reality, and from the ordinary feelings of life to the perception of the beautiful.

Complete.

THE IMPULSE TO PLAY AS THE CAUSE OF PROGRESS

I HAVE shown that it is only the æsthetic disposition of the soul that gives birth to liberty. It cannot, therefore, be derived from liberty, nor have a moral origin. It must be a gift of nature; the favor of chance alone can break the bonds of the physical state and bring the savage to duty. The germ of the beautiful will find an equal difficulty in developing itself in countries where a severe nature forbids man to enjoy himself, and in those where a prodigal nature dispenses him from all effort; where the blunted senses experience no want, and where violent desire can never be satisfied. The delightful flower of the beautiful will never unfold itself in the case of the Troglodyte hid in his cavern always alone, and never finding humanity outside himself; nor among nomads, who, traveling in great troops, only consist of a multitude, and have no individual humanity. It will only flourish in places where man converses peacefully with himself in his cottage, and with the whole race when he issues from it. In those climates where a limpid ether opens the senses to the lightest impression, whilst a life-giving warmth develops a luxuriant nature, where even in the inanimate creation the sway of inert matter is overthrown, and the victorious form ennobles even the most abject natures; in this joyful state and fortunate zone, where activity alone leads to enjoyment, and enjoyment to activity, from life itself issues a holy harmony, and the laws of order develop life, a different result takes place. When imagination incessantly escapes from reality, and does not abandon the simplicity of nature in its wanderings, then and there only the mind and the senses, the receptive force and the plastic force, are developed in that happy equilibrium which is the soul of the beautiful and the condition of humanity.

What phenomenon accompanies the initiation of the savage into humanity? However far we look back into history, the phenomenon is identical among all people who have shaken off the slavery of the animal state: the love of appearance, the inclination for dress and for games.

Extreme stupidity and extreme intelligence have a certain affinity in only seeking the real and being completely insensible to mere appearance. The former is only drawn forth by the immediate presence of an object in the senses, and the second is reduced to a quiescent state only by referring conceptions to the

facts of experience.   In short, stupidity cannot rise above reality,
nor the intelligence descend below truth.   Thus, in as far as the
want of reality and attachment to the real are only the consequence of a want and a defect, indifference to the real and an
interest taken in appearances are a real enlargement of humanity
and a decisive step towards culture.   In the first place it is the
proof of an exterior liberty, for as long as necessity commands
and want solicits, the fancy is strictly chained down to the real;
it is only when want is satisfied that it develops without hin-
drance.   But it is also the proof of an internal liberty, because it
reveals to us a force which, independent of an external substra-
tum, sets itself in motion, and has sufficient energy to remove
from itself the solicitations of nature.   The reality of things is
effected by things; the appearance of things is the work of man,
and a soul that takes pleasure in appearance does not take pleasure in what it receives, but in what it makes.

It is self-evident that I am speaking of æsthetical evidence
different from reality and truth, and not of logical appearance
identical with them.   Therefore if it is liked it is because it is
an appearance, and not because it is held to be something better
than it is; the first principle alone is a play, whilst the second
is a deception.   To give a value to the appearance of the first
kind can never injure truth, because it is never to be feared that
it will supplant it — the only way in which truth can be injured.
To despise this appearance is to despise in general all the fine
arts of which it is the essence.   Nevertheless, it happens sometimes that the understanding carries its zeal for reality as far as
this intolerance, and strikes with a sentence of ostracism all the
arts relating to beauty in appearance, because it is only an appearance.   However, the intelligence only shown this vigorous
spirit when it calls to mind the affinity pointed out further back.
I shall find some day the occasion to treat specially of the limits
of beauty in its appearance.

It is Nature herself which raises man from reality to appearance by endowing him with two senses which only lead him to
the knowledge of the real through appearance.   In the eye and
the ear the organs of the senses are already freed from the per-
secutions of nature, and the object with which we are immediately
in contact through the animal senses is remoter from us.   What
we see by the eye differs from what we feel; for the understanding to reach objects overleaps the light which separates us

from them. In truth, we are passive to an object: in sight and hearing the object is a form we create. While still a savage, man only enjoys through touch merely aided by sight and sound. He either does not rise to perception through sight, or does not rest there. As soon as he begins to enjoy through sight, vision has an independent value, he is æsthetically free, and the instinct of play is developed.

The instinct of play likes appearance, and directly it is awakened it is followed by the formal imitative instinct which treats appearance as an independent thing. Directly man has come to distinguish the appearance from the reality, the form from the body, he can analyze; in fact he has already done so. Thus the faculty of the art of imitation is given with the faculty of form in general. The inclination that draws us to it reposes on another tendency I have not to notice here. The exact period when the æsthetic instinct, or that of art, develops, depends entirely on the attraction that mere appearance has for men.

As every real existence proceeds from nature as a foreign power, whilst every appearance comes in the first place from man as a percipient subject, he only uses his absolute sight in separating semblance from essence, and arranging according to subjective law. With an unbridled liberty he can unite what nature has severed, provided he can imagine his union, and he can separate what nature has united, provided this separation can take place in his intelligence. Here nothing can be sacred to him but his own law; the only condition imposed upon him is to respect the border which separates his own sphere from the existence of things or from the realm of nature.

This human right of ruling is exercised by man in the art of appearance, and his success in extending the empire of the beautiful, and guarding the frontiers of truth, will be in proportion with the strictness with which he separates form from substance; for if he frees appearance from reality, he must also do the converse. But man possesses sovereign power only in the world of appearance, in the unsubstantial realm of imagination, only by abstaining from giving being to appearance in theory, and by giving it being in practice It follows that the poet transgresses his proper limits when he attributes being to his ideal, and when he gives this ideal aim as a determined existence. For he can only reach this result by exceeding his right as a poet, that of encroaching by the ideal on the field of experience, and by pretending to determine real existence in virtue of a simple possibility, or else he renounces his right as a poet by letting experience encroach on the sphere of the ideal, and by restricting possibility to the conditions of reality.

It is only by being frank or disclaiming all reality, and by being independent or doing without reality, that the appearance is æsthetical. Directly it apes reality or needs reality for effect, it is nothing more than a vile instrument for material ends, and can prove nothing for the freedom of the mind. Moreover, the object in which we find beauty need not be unreal if our' judgment disregards this reality, for if it regards this the judgment is no longer æsthetical. A beautiful woman, if living, would no doubt please us as much and rather more than an equally beautiful woman seen in painting; but what makes the former please men is not her being an independent appearance, she no longer pleases the pure æsthetic feeling. In the painting, life must only attract as an appearance, and reality as an idea But it is certain that to feel in a living object only the pure appearance requires a greatly higher æsthetic culture than to do without life in the appearance.

When the frank and independent appearance is found in man separately, or in a whole people, it may be inferred they have mind, taste, and all prerogatives connected with them. In this case the ideal will be seen to govern real life, honor triumphing over fortune, thought over enjoyment, the dream of immortality over a transitory existence.

In this case public opinion will no longer be feared, and an olive crown will be more valued than a purple mantle. Impotence and perversity alone have recourse to false and paltry semblance, and individuals as well as nations who lend to reality the support of appearance, or to the æsthetic appearance the support of reality, show their moral unworthiness and their æsthetical impotence. Therefore, a short and conclusive answer can be given to this question — How far will appearance be permitted in the moral world? It will run thus in proportion as this appearance will be æsthetical, that is, an appearance that does not try to make up for reality, nor requires to be made up for by it. The æsthetical appearance can never endanger the truth of morals; wherever it seems to do so the appearance is not æsthetical. Only a stranger to the fashionable world can take the polite assurances, which are only a form, for proofs of affection, and say he has been deceived, but only a clumsy fellow in good society calls in the aid of duplicity and flatters to become amiable

The former lacks the pure sense for independent appearance; therefore he can only give a value to appearance by truth. The second lacks reality, and wishes to replace it by appearance. Nothing is more common than to hear depreciators of the times utter the paltry complaint that all solidity has disappeared from the world, and that essence is neglected for semblance. Though I feel by no means called upon to defend this age against these reproaches, I must say that the wide application of these criticisms shows that they attach blame to the age, not only on the score of the false, but also of the frank appearance. And even the exceptions they admit in favor of the beautiful have, for their object, less the independent appearance than the needy appearance. Not only do they attack the artificial coloring that hides truth and replaces reality, but also the beneficent appearance that fills a vacuum and clothes poverty; and they even attack the ideal appearance that ennobles a vulgar reality. Their strict sense of truth is rightly offended by the falsity of manners; unfortunately, they class politeness in this category. It displeases them that the noisy and showy so often eclipse true merit, but they are no less shocked that appearance is also demanded from merit and that a real substance does not dispense with an agreeable form. They regret the cordiality, the energy, and solidity of ancient times; they would restore with them ancient coarseness, heaviness, and the old Gothic profusion. By judgments of this kind they show an esteem for the matter itself unworthy of humanity, which ought only to value the matter inasmuch as it can receive a form and enlarge the empire of ideas. Accordingly, the taste of the age need not much fear these criticisms if it can clear itself before better judges. Our defect is not to grant a value to æsthetic appearance (we do not do this enough): a severe judge of the beautiful might rather reproach us with not having arrived at pure appearance, with not having separated clearly enough existence from the phenomenon, and thus established their limits. We shall deserve this reproach so long as we cannot enjoy the beautiful in living nature without desiring it; as long as we cannot admire the beautiful in the imitative arts without having an end in view; as long as we do not grant to imagination an absolute legislation of its own; and as long as we do not inspire it with care for its dignity by the esteem we testify for its works.

Complete.

AUGUST WILHELM VON SCHLEGEL

(1767–1845)

AUGUST WILHELM VON SCHLEGEL, celebrated for his essays on art and poetry, as well as for his own verses, was born at Hannover, September 8th, 1767. After studying at Göttingen and teaching in Amsterdam, he became professor of Literature and Æsthetics at Jena in 1798. Leaving this position in 1801, he taught at Berlin and spent several years in travel, remaining for some time in Sweden where he was "ennobled." In 1818 he became professor of Literature and Æsthetics at Bonn and remained there until his death, May 12th, 1845. His "Lectures on Dramatic Literature," delivered in Vienna, were published between 1809 and 1811. His first volume of poems appeared in 1800, and the first of his celebrated translations from Shakespeare in 1797.

THE GREEK THEATRE

WHEN we hear the word Theatre, we naturally think of what with us bears the same name; and yet nothing can be more different from our theatre than the Grecian, in every part of its construction. If in reading the Grecian pieces we associate our own stage with them, the light in which we shall view them must be false in every respect.

The accurate mathematical dimensions of the principal part of it are to be found in Vitruvius, who also distinctly points out the great difference between the Greek and Roman theatres. But these and similar passages of the ancient writers have been most perversely interpreted by architects unacquainted with the ancient dramatists; and the philologists on the other hand, who were altogether ignorant of architecture, have also fallen into egregious errors. The ancient dramatists are still, therefore, altogether in want of that sort of illustration which relates to scenic regulation. In many tragedies I conceive that my ideas on this subject are sufficiently clear; but others again present difficulties which are not so easily solved. We find ourselves most at a loss in figuring to ourselves the representation of the pieces of Aristophanes;

the ingenious poet must have brought his wonderful inventions before the eyes of his audience in a manner equally bold and astonishing. Even Barthelemy's description of the Grecian stage is not a little confused, and the subjoined plan extremely erroneous; in the place which he assigns for the representation of the pieces in Antigone and Ajax, for instance, he is altogether wrong. The following observations will not therefore appear the less superfluous.

The theatres of the Greeks were quite open above, and their dramas were always acted in open day, and beneath the canopy of heaven. The Romans, at an after period, endeavored by a covering to shelter the audience from the rays of the sun; but this degree of luxury was hardly ever enjoyed by the Greeks. Such a state of things appears very inconvenient to us; but the Greeks had nothing of effeminacy about them, and we must not forget, too, the beauty of their climate. When they were overtaken by a storm or a shower, the play was of course interrupted; and they would much rather expose themselves to an accidental inconvenience, than, by shutting themselves up in a close and crowded house, entirely destroy the serenity of a religious solemnity, which their plays certainly were. To have covered in the scene itself, and imprisoned gods and heroes in dark and gloomy apartments with difficulty lighted up, would have appeared still more ridiculous to them. An action which so nobly served to establish the belief of the relations with heaven could only be exhibited under an unobstructed heaven, and under the very eyes of the gods, as it were, for whom, according to Seneca, the sight of a brave man struggling with adversity is a becoming spectacle. With respect to the supposed inconvenience, which, according to the assertion of many modern critics, was felt by the poets from the necessity of always laying the scene of their pieces before houses, a circumstance that often forced them to violate probability, this inconvenience was very little felt by tragedy and the older comedy. The Greeks, like so many southern nations of the present day, lived much more in the open air than we do, and transacted many things in public which usually take place with us in houses. For the theatre did not represent the street, but a place before the house belonging to it, where the altar stood on which sacrifices to the household gods were offered up. Here the women, who lived in so retired a manner among the Greeks, even those who were unmarried, might appear without impropriety. Neither was it impossible for them to give a view of the interior of the houses; and this was effected, as we shall immediately see, by means of the encyclema.

But the principal reason for this observance was that publicity, according to the republican nations of the Greeks, was essential to a grave and important transaction. This is clearly proved by the presence of the chorus, whose remaining on many occasions, when secret transactions were going on, has been judged of according to rules of propriety inapplicable to that country, and most undeservedly censured.

The theatres of the Ancients were, in comparison with the small scale of ours, of a colossal magnitude, partly for the sake of containing the whole of the people, with the concourse of strangers who flocked to the festivals, and partly to correspond with the majesty of the dramas represented in them, which required to be seen at a respectful distance. The seats of the spectators consisted of steps, which rose backwards round the semicircle of the orchestra (called by us the pit), so that they all could see with equal convenience. The effect of distance was remedied by an artificial heightening of the subject represented to the eye and ear, produced by means of masks, and contrivances for increasing the loudness of the voice, and the size of the figures. Vitruvius speaks also of vehicles of sound, distributed throughout the building; but the commentators are very much at variance with respect to them. We may without hesitation venture to assume that the theatres of the Ancients were constructed on excellent acoustical principles.

The lowest step of the amphitheatre was still raised considerably above the orchestra, and the stage was placed opposite to it, at an equal degree of elevation. The sunk semicircle of the orchestra contained no spectators, and was destined for another purpose. It was otherwise, however, with the Romans, but we are not at present considering the distribution of their theatres.

The stage consisted of a strip which stretched from one end of the building to the other, and of which the depth bore little proportion to this breadth. This was called the logeum, in the Latin, *pulpitum*, and the usual place for persons who spoke was in the middle of it. Behind this middle part, the scene went inward in a quadrangular form, with less depth, however, than breadth. The space here comprehended was called the proscenium. The remaining part of the logeum, to the right and left of the scene, had, both before the brink which adjoined the orchestra, and behind, a wall possessing no scenical decorations, but entirely simple, or at most architecturally ornamented, which was elevated to an equal height with the uppermost steps for the audience.

The decoration was contrived in such a manner, that the principal object in front covered the background, and the prospects of distance were given at two sides, the very reverse of the mode adopted by us. This had also its rules: on the left appeared the town to which the palace, temple, or whatever occupied the middle, belonged; on the right the open country, landscape, mountains, seashore, etc. The lateral decorations were composed of triangles, which turned on an axis fastened underneath; and in this manner the change of scene was effected. In the hindmost decoration it is probable that many things were exhibited in a bodily form which are only painted with us. When a palace or temple was represented, there appeared in the proscenium an altar, which answered a number of purposes in the performance of the pieces.

The decoration was for the most part architectural, but it was also not unfrequently a painted landscape, as in Prometheus, where it represented Caucasus; or in Philoctetus, where the desert island of Lemnos, with its rocks and his cave, were exhibited. It is clear, from a passage of Plato, that the Greeks, in the deceptions of theatrical perspective, carried things much further than we might have inferred from some wretched landscapes discovered in Herculaneum.

In the back wall of this scene there was a large main entrance, and two side entrances. It has been maintained that from them it might be discovered whether an actor played a principal or under part, as in the first case he came in at the main entrance, and in the second, at the side doors. But this should be understood with the distinction, that it must have been regulated according to the nature of the piece. As the hindmost decoration was generally a palace, in which the principal characters of royal descent resided, they naturally came through the great door, while the servants resided in the wings. There were two other entrances; the one at the end of the logeum, from whence the inhabitants of the town came; the other underneath in the orchestra, which was the side for those who had to come from a distance: they ascended a staircase of the logeum opposite to the orchestra, which could be applied to all sorts of purposes, according to circumstances. The entrance, therefore, with respect to the lateral decorations, declared the place from whence the players were supposed to come; and it might naturally happen, that the principal characters were in a situation to avail themselves with propriety of the two last-mentioned entrances. The situation of these entrances serves to explain many passages in the ancient dramas, where the persons standing in the middle see some one advancing, long before he approaches them. Beneath the seats of the spectators a stair was somewhere constructed, which was called the Charonic, and through which the shadows of the departed, without being seen by the audience, ascended into the orchestra, and then, by the stair which we formerly mentioned, made their appearance on the stage. The nearest brink of the logeum sometimes represented the seashore. The Greeks were well skilled in availing themselves even of what lay beyond the decoration, and making it subservient to scenical effect. I doubt not, therefore, that in the "Eumenides" the spectators were twice addressed as an assembled people; first, by Pythia, when she calls upon the Greeks to consult the oracle; and a second time, when Pallas, by a herald, commands silence throughout the place of judgment. The frequent addresses to heaven were undoubtedly directed to a real heaven; and when Electra, on her first appearance, exclaims: "O holy light, and thou air which fillest the expanse between earth and heaven!" she probably turned towards the rising sun. The whole of this procedure is highly deserving of praise; and though modern critics have censured the mixture of reality and imitation, as destructive of theatrical illusion, this only proves that they have misunderstood the essence of the illusion which can be produced by an artificial representation. If we are to be truly deceived by a picture, that is, if we are to believe in the reality of the object which we see, we must not perceive its limits, but look at it through an opening; the frame at once declares it for a picture. In scenical decorations we are now unavoidably compelled to make use of architectural contrivances, productive of the same effect as the frames of pictures. It is consequently much better to avoid this, and to renounce the modern illusion, though it may have its advantages, for the sake of extending the view beyond the mere decoration. It was, generally speaking, a principle of the Greeks, that everything imi-

tated on the stage should, if possible, consist of actual representation; and only where this could not be done were they satisfied
with a symbolical exhibition.

The machinery for the descent of the gods through the air,
or the withdrawing of men from the earth, was placed aloft behind the walls of the two sides of the scene, and consequently
removed from the sight of the spectators. Even in the time of
Æschylus great use was made of it, as he not only brings
Oceanus through the air on a griffin, but also introduces the
whole choir of ocean nymphs, at least fifteen in number, in a
winged chariot. There were hollow places beneath the stage,
and contrivances for thunder and lightning, for the apparent fall
or burning of a house, etc.

An upper story could be added to the furthermost wall of the
scene, when they wished to represent a tower with a wide prospect, or anything similar. The encyclema could be thrust behind
the great middle entrance, a machine of a semicircular form
within, and covered above, which represented the objects contained in it as in a house. This was used for producing a great
theatrical effect, as we may see from many pieces. The side
door of the entrance would naturally be then open, or the curtain which covered it withdrawn.

A stage curtain, which, we clearly see from a description of
Ovid, was not dropped, but drawn upwards, is mentioned both
by Greek and Roman writers, and the Latin appellation, aulæum,
is even borrowed from the Greeks. I suspect, however, that the
curtain on the Attic stage was not in use at its commencement.
In the pieces of Æschylus and Sophocles the scene is evidently
empty at the opening as well as the conclusion, and therefore it
did not require any contrivance for preventing the view of the
spectators. However, in many of the pieces of Euripides, perhaps
also in the "Œdipus Tyrannus," the stage is at once filled, and
represents a standing group, who could not have been first assembled under the eyes of the spectators. It must be recollected,
that it was only the comparatively small proscenium, and not the
logeum, which was covered by the curtain; for, from its great
breadth, to have attempted to screen the logeum would have been
almost impracticable, without answering any good end.

The entrances of the chorus were beneath in the orchestra,
in which it generally remained, and in which also it performed
its solemn dance going backwards and forwards during the choral

songs.   In the front of the orchestra, opposite to the middle of
the scene, there was an elevation with steps, resembling an altar,
as high as the stage, which was called thymele.   This was the
station of the chorus when it did not sing, but merely took an
interest in the action.   The leader of the chorus then took his
station on the top of the thymele, to see what was passing on
the stage, and to communicate with the characters.   For though
the choral song was common to the whole, yet when it entered
into the dialogue one person spoke for the rest; and hence we
are to account for the shifting from "thou" to "ye" in addressing
them.   The thymele was situated in the very centre of the building; all the measurements were calculated from it, and the semicircle of the amphitheatre was described round that point.   It
was, therefore, an excellent contrivance to place the chorus, who
were the ideal representatives of the spectators, in the very situation where all the radii were concentrated.

From " Lectures on Dramatic Literature."
Black's translation.

ARTHUR SCHOPENHAUER

(1788–1860)

SCHOPENHAUER was born at Dantzic, Germany, February 22d, 1788. After a short novitiate in the office of a Hamburg merchant, where he had been placed by his father, he decided that he was unfit for business and determined to become great in literature. Studying at Göttingen and beginning his literary work with the deepest problems of philosophy, he published in 1813 his monograph "On the Fourfold Root of the Principle of Sufficient Reason," and in 1819 followed it with his most celebrated work, "The World as Will and Idea." After spending several years as a tutor at the University of Berlin, he went to Frankfort-on-the-Main, where he lived from 1831 until his death, September 21st, 1860. His shorter essays, which were published in 1851, are artistically the best which have come from any professional philosopher of Germany. Schopenhauer knows how to condense his thought to the utmost possible extent without making it obscure, and to expand as much as he pleases without making it so abstract that it ceases to be intelligible. His admirers are not generally inclined to admit that he is a humorist, but there is a latent suspicion of an undertone of humor in his deepest philosophy. His "pessimism" reduces itself to the proposition that the world as men make it "must be some kind of a mistake." At another time, he compares it to "a drop of water seen through a microscope, a single drop teeming with infusoria, or a speck of cheese full of mites invisible to the naked eye." This is pessimism, but, after all, it is much less bitter than that of Swift. Indeed, Schopenhauer's view of the world as it manifests itself through selfishness, is in no essential respect different from that presented in the opening chapters of the Book of Genesis, which account for human life and for the physical and moral conditions under which it is passed as the result of degeneracy or a "Fall" into conditions which destroy the wholly unfit and force those who are fit for survival to improve. When a world controlled by the impulses of selfish struggle is said to be either "a hell or a hospital," the pessimism of the definition depends on the conclusion from it. Those who argue from it to negation must become hopeless and useless. But while St. Paul and St. John agree with the most extreme modern pessimists in conceding the weariness and uselessness

of the life natural to the world, they made this conclusion merely
the premise for asserting the infinite possibility of increasing efficiency, to be achieved through Faith and Love, operating as governing motives of action. Schopenhauer's theory that the body is "the
Will objectified" is related on one side to the Pythagorean idea
that the Will or the soul it represents, must necessarily take such
shapes in animal life as represent its moral qualities; and on the
other side it seems to bear a not less distinct relation to the Darwinian hypothesis of the gradual modification of species as a result
of Will determining the habits of typical individuals of the class.

W. V. B.

BOOKS AND AUTHORSHIP

THERE are, first of all, two kinds of authors: those who write
for the subject's sake, and those who write for writing's
sake. While the one have had thoughts or experiences which
seem to them worth communicating, the others want money, and
so they write for money. Their thinking is part of the business
of writing. They may be recognized by the way in which they
spin out their thoughts to the greatest possible length; then, too,
by the very nature of their thoughts, which are only half-true,
perverse, forced, vacillating; again, by the aversion they generally show to saying anything straight out, so that they may seem
other than they are. Hence their writing is deficient in clearness and definiteness, and it is not long before they betray that
their only object in writing at all is to cover paper. This sometimes happens with the best authors: now and then, for example,
with Lessing in his "Dramaturgie," and even in many of Jean
Paul's romances. As soon as the reader perceives this, let him
throw the book away; for time is precious. The truth is that
when an author begins to write for the sake of covering paper
he is cheating the reader; because he writes under the pretext
that he has something to say.

Writing for money and reservation of copyright are, at bottom, the ruin of literature. No one writes anything that is worth
writing, unless he writes entirely for the sake of his subject.
What an inestimable boon it would be, if in every branch of literature there were only a few books, but those excellent! This
can never happen, as long as money is to be made by writing.
It seems as though the money lay under a curse; for every au-

thor degenerates as soon as he begins to put pen to paper in any way for the sake of gain. The best works of the greatest men all come from the time when they had to write for nothing or for very little. And here, too, that Spanish proverb holds good, which declares that honor and money are not to be found in the same purse —*"Honray provecho no caben en un saco."* The reason literature is in such a bad plight nowadays is simply and solely that people write books to make money. A man who is in want sits down and writes a book, and the public is stupid enough to buy it. The secondary effect of this is the ruin of language.

A great many bad writers make their whole living by that foolish mania of the public for reading nothing but what has just been printed — journalists, I mean. Truly, a most appropriate name. In plain language it is journeymen day-laborers!

Again, it may be said that there are three kinds of authors. First come those who write without thinking. They write from a full memory, from reminiscences; it may be, even straight out of other people's books. This class is the most numerous. Then come those who do their thinking whilst they are writing. They think in order to write,— and there is no lack of them. Last of all come those authors who think before they begin to write. They are rare.

Authors of the second class, who put off their thinking until they come to write, are like a sportsman who goes forth at random and is not likely to bring very much home. On the other hand, when an author of the third or rare class writes, it is like a *battue*. Here the game has been previously captured and shut up within a very small space, from which it is afterward let out, so many at a time, into another space, also confined. The game cannot possibly escape the sportsman; he has nothing to do but aim and fire,— in other words, write down his thoughts. This is a kind of sport from which a man has something to show.

But even though the number of those who really think seri ously before they begin to write is small, extremely few of them think about the subject itself: the remainder think only about the books that have been written on the subject, and what has been said by others. In order to think at all, such writers need the more direct and powerful stimulus of having other people's thoughts before them. These become their immediate theme, and the result is that they are always under their influence, and

so never, in any real sense of the word, original. But the former are roused to thought by the subject itself, to which their
thinking is thus immediately directed. This is the only class that
produces writers of abiding fame.

It must, of course, be understood that I am speaking here of
writers who treat of great subjects; not of writers on the art of
making brandy.

Unless an author takes the material on which he writes out
of his own head, that is to say, from his own observation, he is
not worth reading. Book manufacturers, compilers, the common
run of history writers, and many others of the same class, take
their material immediately out of books; and the material goes
straight to their finger tips without even paying freight or undergoing examination as it passes through their heads, to say nothing of elaboration or revision. How very learned many a man
would be if he knew everything that was in his own books!

.   .   .   .

A book can never be anything more than the impress of its
author's thoughts; and the value of these will lie either "in the
matter about which he has thought," or in the form which his
thoughts take; in other words, "what it is that he has thought
about it."

The matter of books is most various; and various also are
the several excellences attaching to books on the score of their
matter. By matter I mean everything that comes within the domain of actual experience; that is to say, the facts of history and
the facts of nature, taken in and by themselves and in their
widest sense. Here it is the thing treated of which gives its
peculiar character to the book; so that a book can be important,
whoever it was that wrote it.

But in regard to the form, the peculiar character of a book
depends upon the person who wrote it. It may treat of matters
which are accessible to every one and well known; but it is the
way in which they are treated, what it is that is thought about
them, that gives the book its value; and this comes from its author. If, then, from this point of view a book is excellent and
beyond comparison, so is its author. It follows that if a writer
is worth reading, his merit rises just in proportion as he owes little
to his matter; therefore, the better known and the more hackneyed
this is, the greater he will be. The three great tragedians
of Greece, for example, all worked at the same subject-matter.

So when a book is celebrated, care should be taken to note whether it is so on account of its matter or its form; and a distinction should be made accordingly.

Books of great importance on account of their matter may proceed from very ordinary and shallow people, by the fact that they alone have had access to this matter; books, for instance, which describe journeys in distant lands, rare natural phenomena, or experiments; or historical occurrences of which the writers were witnesses, or in connection with which they have spent much time and trouble in the research and special study of original documents.

On the other hand, where the matter is accessible to every one or very well known, everything will depend upon the form; and what it is that is thought about the matter will give the book all the value it possesses. Here only a really distinguished man will be able to produce anything worth reading; for the others will think nothing but what any one else can think. They will just produce an impress of their own minds; but this is a print of which every one possesses the original.

However, the public is very much more concerned to have matter than form; and for this very reason it is deficient in any high degree of culture. The public shows its preference in this respect in the most laughable way when it comes to deal with poetry; for there it devotes much trouble to the task of tracking out the actual events or personal circumstances in the life of the poet which served as the occasion of his various works; nay, these events and circumstances come in the end to be of greater importance than the works themselves; and rather than read Goethe himself, people prefer to read what has been written about him, and to study the legend of Faust more industriously than the drama of that name. And when Bürger declared that "people would write learned disquisitions on the question, who Leonora really was," we find this literally fulfilled in Goethe's case; for we now possess a great many learned disquisitions on Faust and the legend attaching to him. Study of this kind is, and remains, devoted to the material of the drama alone. To give such preference to the matter over the form is as though a man were to take a fine Etruscan vase, not to admire its shape or coloring, but to make a chemical analysis of the clay and paint of which it is composed.

The attempt to produce an effect by means of the material employed — an attempt which panders to this evil tendency of the public — is most to be condemned in branches of literature where any merit there may be lies expressly in the form; I mean, in poetical work. For all that, it is not rare to find bad dramatists trying to fill the house by means of the matter about which they write. For example, authors of this kind do not shrink from putting on the stage any man who is in any way celebrated, no matter whether his life may have been entirely devoid of dramatic incident; and sometimes, even, they do not wait until the persons immediately connected with him are dead.

The distinction between matter and form to which I am here alluding, also holds good of conversation. The chief qualities which enable a man to converse well are intelligence, discernment, wit, and vivacity; these supply the form of conversation. But it is not long before attention has to be paid to the matter of which he speaks; in other words, the subjects about which it is possible to converse with him — his knowledge. If this is very small, his conversation will not be worth anything, unless he possesses the above-named formal qualities in a very exceptional degree: for he will have nothing to talk about but those facts of life and nature which everybody knows. It will be just the opposite, however, if a man is deficient in these formal qualities, but has an amount of knowledge which lends value to what he says. This value will then depend entirely upon the matter of his conversation; for, as the Spanish proverb has it, *"Mas sabe el necio en su casa, que el sabio en la ageno"* — a fool knows more of his own business than a wise man of others'.

THE VANITY OF EXISTENCE

THIS vanity finds expression in the whole way in which things exist: in the infinite nature of Time and Space, as opposed to the finite nature of the individual in both; in the ever-passing present moment as the only mode of actual existence; in the interdependence and relativity of all things; in continual becoming without ever being; in constant wishing and never being satisfied; in the long battle which forms the history of life, where every effort is checked by difficulties, and stopped until they are overcome. Time is that in which all things pass away; it is merely the form under which the Will to Live — the Thing in

Itself and therefore imperishable — has revealed to it that its efforts are in vain; it is that agent by which at every moment all things in our hands become as nothing, and lose any real value they possess.

That which has been exists no more; it exists as little as that which has never been. But of everything that exists you must say, in the next moment, that it has been. Hence something of great importance now past is inferior to something of little importance now present, in that the latter is a reality, and related to the former as something to nothing.

A man finds himself, to his great astonishment, suddenly existing, after thousands and thousands of years of nonexistence: he lives for a little while; and then, again, comes an equally long period when he must exist no more. The heart rebels against this, and feels that it cannot be true. The crudest intellect cannot speculate on such a subject without having a presentiment that Time is something ideal in its nature. This ideality of Time and Space is the key to every true system of metaphysics; because it provides for quite another order of things than is to be met with in the domain of nature. This is why Kant is so great.

Of every event in our life we can say only for one moment that it is; forever after, that it was. Every evening we are poorer by a day. It might, perhaps, make us mad to see how rapidly our short span of time ebbs away, if it were not that in the furthest depths of our being we are secretly conscious of our share in the inexhaustible spring of eternity, so that we can always hope to find life in it again.

Considerations of the kind touched on above might, indeed, lead us to embrace the belief that the greatest wisdom is to make the enjoyment of the present the supreme object of life; because that is the only reality, all else being merely the play of thought. On the other hand, such a course might just as well be called the greatest folly; for that which in the next moment exists no more, and vanishes utterly, like a dream, can never be worth a serious effort.

The whole foundation on which our existence rests is the present — the ever-fleeting present. It lies, then, in the very nature of our existence to take the form of constant motion, and to offer no possibility of our ever attaining the rest for which we are always striving. We are like a man running downhill, who cannot keep on his legs unless he runs on, and will inevitably fall if he stops; or, again, like a pole balanced on the tip of one's finger; or like a planet, which would fall into its sun the moment it ceased to hurry forward on its way. Unrest is the mark of existence.

In a world where all is unstable, and naught can endure, but is swept onward at once in the hurrying whirlpool of change; where a man, if he is to keep erect at all, must always be advancing and moving, like an acrobat on a rope — in such a world, happiness is inconceivable. How can it dwell where, as Plato says, "continual Becoming and never Being" is the sole form of existence? In the first place, a man never is happy, but spends his whole life in striving after something which he thinks will make him so; he seldom attains his goal, and when he does, it is only to be disappointed; he is mostly shipwrecked in the end, and comes into harbor with masts and rigging gone. And then, it is all one whether he has been happy or miserable; for his life was never anything more than a present moment always vanishing; and now it is over.

At the same time it is a wonderful thing that, in the world of human beings as in that of animals in general, this manifold restless motion is produced and kept up by the agency of two simple impulses — hunger and the sexual instinct; aided a little, perhaps, by the influence of boredom, but by nothing else; and that, in the theatre of life, these suffice to form the *primum mobile* of how complicated a machinery, setting in motion how strange and varied a scene!

On looking a little closer, we find that inorganic matter presents a constant conflict between chemical forces, which eventually works dissolution; and on the other hand, that organic life is impossible without continual change of matter, and cannot exist if it does not receive perpetual help from without. This is the realm of finality; and its opposite would be an infinite existence, exposed to no attack from without, and needing nothing to support it; ἀεὶ ὡσαύτως ὄν, the realm of eternal peace; οὔτε γιγνόμενον οὔτε ἀπολλύμενον, some timeless, changeless state, one and undiversified; the negative knowledge of which forms the dominant note of the Platonic philosophy. It is to some such state as this that the denial of the Will to live opens up the way.

The scenes of our life are like pictures done in rough mosaic. Looked at close, they produce no effect. There is nothing beautiful to be found in them, unless you stand some distance off. So, to gain anything we have longed for is only to discover how vain and empty it is; and even though we are always living in expectation of better things, at the same time we often repent and long to have the past back again. We look upon the present as something to be put up with while it lasts, and serving only as the way toward our goal. Hence most people, if they glance back when they come to the end of life, will find that all along they have been living *ad interim;* they will be surprised to find the very thing they disregarded and let slip by unenjoyed was just the life in the expectation of which they passed all their time. Of how many a man may it not be said that hope made a fool of him until he danced into the arms of Death!

Then, again, how insatiable a creature is man. Every satisfaction he attains lays the seeds of some new desire, so that there is no end to the wishes of each individual Will. And why is this? The real reason is simply that, taken in itself, Will is the lord of all worlds; everything belongs to it, and therefore no one single thing can ever give it satisfaction, but only the whole, which is endless. For all that, it must rouse our sympathy to think how very little the Will, this lord of the world, really gets when it takes the form of an individual; usually only just enough to keep the body together. This is why man is so very miserable.

Life presents itself chiefly as a task — the task, I mean, of subsisting at all, *ganger sa vie.* If this is accomplished, life is a burden, and then there comes the second task of doing something with that which has been won — of warding off boredom, which, like a bird of prey, hovers over us, ready to fall wherever it sees a life secure from need. The first task is to win something; the second, to banish the feeling that it has been won; otherwise it is a burden.

Human life must be some kind of mistake. The truth of this will be sufficiently obvious if we only remember that man is a compound of needs and necessities hard to satisfy; and that even when they are satisfied, all he obtains is a state of painlessness, where nothing remains to him but abandonment to boredom. This is direct proof that existence has no real value in itself; for what is boredom but the feeling of the emptiness of life? If life — the craving for which is the very essence of our being — were possessed of any positive intrinsic value, there would be no such thing as boredom at all: mere existence would satisfy us in itself, and we should want for nothing. But as it is, we take no delight in existence except when we are struggling for something; and then distance and difficulties to be overcome make our goal look as though it would satisfy us — an illusion which vanishes when we reach it; or else when we are occupied with some purely intellectual interest — where in reality we have stepped forth from life to look upon it from the outside, much after the manner of spectators at a play. And even sensual pleasure itself means nothing but a struggle and aspiration, ceasing the moment its aim is attained. Whenever we are not occupied in one of these ways, but cast upon existence itself, its vain and worthless nature is brought home to us; and this is what we mean by boredom. The hankering after what is strange and uncommon — an innate and ineradicable tendency of human nature — shows how glad we are at any interruption of that natural course of affairs which is so very tedious.

That this most perfect manifestation of the Will to live, the human organism, with the cunning and complex working of its machinery, must fall to dust and yield up itself and all its strivings to extinction — this is the naïve way in which Nature, who is always so true and sincere in what she says, proclaims the whole struggle of this Will as in its very essence barren and unprofitable. Were it of any value in itself, anything unconditioned and absolute, it could not thus end in mere nothing.

If we turn from contemplating the world as a whole, and, in particular, the generations of men as they live their little hour of mock existence and then are swept away in rapid succession; if we turn from this, and look at life in its small details, as presented, say, in a comedy, how ridiculous it all seems! It is like a drop of water seen through a microscope, a single drop teeming with infusoria, or a speck of cheese full of mites invisible to the naked eye. How we laugh as they bustle about so eagerly, and struggle with one another in so tiny a space! And whether here, or in the little span of human life, this terrible activity produces a comic effect.

It is only in the microscope that our life looks so big. It is an indivisible point, drawn out and magnified by the powerful lenses of Time and Space.

Complete.

PARABLES

The Apple Tree and the Fir

A WIDESPREADING apple tree stood in full bloom, and behind it a straight fir raised its dark and tapering head. "Look at the thousands of gay blossoms which cover me everywhere," said the apple tree; "what have you to show in comparison? Dark green needles!" "That is true," replied the fir, "but when winter comes, you will be bared of your glory; and I shall be as I am now."

Complete.

The Young Oak

O NCE, as I was botanizing under an oak, I found among a number of other plants of similar height one that was dark in color, with tightly closed leaves and a stalk that was very straight and stiff. When I touched it, it said to me in firm tones: "Let me alone; I am not for your collection, like these plants to which nature has given only a single year of life. I am a little oak."

So it is with a man whose influence is to last for hundreds of years. As a child, as a youth, often even as a full-grown man, nay, his whole life long, he goes about among his fellows, looking like them and seemingly as unimportant. But let him alone; he will not die. Time will come and bring those who know how to value him.

Complete.

The Balloon Mystery

T HE man who goes up in a balloon does not feel as though he were ascending; he only sees the earth sinking deeper and deeper under him.

This is a mystery which only those will understand who feel the truth of it.

Complete.

The Varnish of Nature

NATURE covers all her works with a varnish of beauty, like the tender bloom that is breathed, as it were, on the surface of a peach or plum. Painters and poets lay themselves out to take off this varnish, to store it up, and give it us to be enjoyed at our leisure. We drink deep of this beauty long before we enter upon life itself; and when afterward we come to see the works of nature for ourselves, the varnish is gone: the artists have used it up and we have enjoyed it in advance. Thus it is that the world so often appears harsh and devoid of charm, nay, actually repulsive. It were better to leave us to discover the varnish for ourselves. This would mean that we should not enjoy it all at once and in large quantities; we should have no finished pictures, no perfect poems; but we should look at all things in the genial and pleasing light in which even now a child of nature sometimes sees them — some one who has not anticipated his æsthetic pleasures by the help of art, or taken the charms of life too early.

Complete.

The Cathedral in Mayence

THE cathedral in Mayence is so shut in by the houses that are built round about it, that there is no one spot from which you can see it as a whole. This is symbolic of everything great or beautiful in the world. It ought to exist for its own sake alone, but before very long it is misused to serve alien ends. People come from all directions wanting to find in it support and maintenance for themselves; they stand in the way and spoil its effect. To be sure, there is nothing surprising in this, for in a world of need and imperfection everything is seized upon which can be used to satisfy want. Nothing is exempt from this service, no, not even those very things which arise only when need and want are for a moment lost sight of — the beautiful and the true, sought for their own sakes.

This is especially illustrated and corroborated in the case of institutions — whether great or small, wealthy or poor, founded, no matter in what century or in what land, to maintain and advance human knowledge, and generally to afford help to those intellectual efforts which ennoble the race. Wherever these institutions may be, it is not long before people sneak up to them under the pretense of wishing to further those special ends, while they are really led on by the desire to secure the emoluments which have been left for their furtherance, and thus to satisfy certain coarse and brutal instincts of their own. Thus it is that we come to have so many charlatans in every branch of knowledge. The charlatan takes very different shapes, according to circumstances; but at bottom he is a man who cares nothing about knowledge for its own sake, and only strives to gain the semblance of it that he may use it for his own personal ends, which are always selfish and material.

Complete.

The Fate of Samson

EVERY hero is a Samson. The strong man succumbs to the intrigues of the weak and the many; and if in the end he loses all patience, he crushes both them and himself. Or he is like Gulliver at Lilliput, overwhelmed by an enormous number of little men.

Complete.

Enlightened Rationalists

A MOTHER gave her children Æsop's "Fables" to read, in the hope of educating and improving their minds; but they very soon brought the book back, and the eldest, wise beyond his years, delivered himself as follows: "This is no book for us; it's much too childish and stupid. You can't make us believe that foxes and wolves and ravens are able to talk; we've got beyond stories of that kind!"

In these young hopefuls you have the enlightened Rationalists of the future.

Complete.

Co-operation among Porcupines

A NUMBER of porcupines huddled together for warmth on a cold day in winter; but, as they began to prick one another with their quills, they were obliged to disperse. However, the cold drove them together again, when just the same thing happened.   At last, after many turns of huddling and dispersing, they discovered that they would be best off by remaining at a little distance from one another.   In the same way the need of society drives the human porcupines together, only to be mutually repelled by the many prickly and disagreeable qualities of their nature.   The moderate distance which they at last discover to be the only tolerable condition of intercourse, in the code of politeness and fine manners; and those who transgress it are roughly told — in the English phrase — "to keep their distance."   By this arrangement the mutual need of warmth is only very moderately satisfied; but then people do not get pricked.   A man who has some heat in himself prefers to remain outside, where he will neither prick other people nor get pricked himself.

> Complete.   All the foregoing were translated
> by T. B. Saunders.

THE GARDEN OF LOVE.

After the Painting, "Liebesgarten," by C. Schweininger.

OLIVE SCHREINER

(*c.* 1863–)

THE writings of Olive Schreiner are the firstfruits which modern Africa offers to world-literature. From the fall of the Greek civilization in Egypt and of the Roman in Numidia until our own times, the "Dark Continent" has produced nothing except a few Arab songs and stories to which not even the most strained courtesy can impute literary quality. Olive Schreiner's "Dreams," however, have in them the unmistakable signs of such genius as immortalizes whatever it inspires. They are strange and fanciful, but they will not easily be forgotten. She comes of the Boer stock of Cape Colony. Her father was a Lutheran minister at Cape Town, and all her work shows the impression of this heredity. "The Story of an African Farm," which she published in 1883, was an immediate success, but it was not until "Dreams" appeared in 1890 that the full strength of her genius was evident. She left Africa for Europe in 1883, and she has since spent most of her time in England. She married Mr. Cronwright in 1894. Her latest publication, "An English South African's View of the Situation" (1899), deals with the overthrow of the Boer republics by the English "Conservatives."

IN A RUINED CHAPEL

THERE are four bare walls; there is a Christ upon the walls, in red, carrying his cross; there is a Blessèd Bambino with the face rubbed out; there is a Madonna in blue and red; there are Roman soldiers and a Christ with tied hands. All the roof is gone; overhead is the blue, blue Italian sky; the rain has beaten holes in the walls, and the plaster is peeling from it. The Chapel stands here alone upon the promontory, and by day and by night the sea breaks at its feet. Some say that it was set here by the monks from the island down below, that they might bring their sick here in times of deadly plague. Some say that it was set here that the passing monk and friars, as they hurried by upon the roadway, might stop and say their prayers here. Now no one stops to pray here, and the sick come no more to be healed.

Behind it runs the old Roman road. If you climb it and come and sit there alone on a hot sunny day you may almost hear at last the clink of the Roman soldiers upon the pavement, and the sound of that older time, as you sit there in the sun, when Hannibal and his men broke through the brushwood, and no road was.

Now it is very quiet. Sometimes a peasant girl comes riding by between her panniers, and you hear the mule's feet beat upon the bricks of the pavement; sometimes an old woman goes past with a bundle of weeds upon her head, or a brigand-looking man hurries by with a bundle of sticks in his hand; but for the rest the Chapel lies here alone upon the promontory, between the two bays and hears the sea break at its feet.

I came here one winter's day when the midday sun shone hot on the bricks of the Roman road. I was weary, and the way seemed steep. I walked into the Chapel to the broken window, and looked out across the bay. Far off, across the blue, blue water, were towns and villages, hanging white and red dots, upon the mountain sides, and the blue mountains rose up into the sky, and now stood out from it and now melted back again.

The mountains seemed calling to me, but I knew there would never be a bridge built from them to me; never, never, never! I shaded my eyes with my hand and turned away. I could not bear to look at them.

I walked through the ruined Chapel, and looked at the Christ in red carrying his cross, and the Blessèd rubbed-out Bambino, and the Roman soldiers, and the folded hands, and the rod; and I went and sat down in the open porch upon a stone. At my feet was the small bay, with its white row of houses buried among the olive trees; the water broke in a long, thin, white line of foam along the shore; and I leaned my elbows on my knees. I was tired, very tired; tired with a tiredness that seemed older than the heat of the day and the shining of the sun on the bricks of the Roman road; and I lay my head upon my knees; I heard the breaking of the water on the rocks three hundred feet below, and the rustling of the wind among the olive trees and the ruined arches, and then I fell asleep there. I had a dream.

A man cried up to God, and God sent down an angel to help him; and the angel came back and said, " I cannot help that man."

God said, "How is it with him?"

And the angel said, "He cries out continually that one has injured him; and he would forgive him and he cannot."

God said, "What have you done for him?"

The angel said, "All——. I took him by the hand, and I said, 'See, when other men speak ill of that man do you speak well of him; secretly, in ways he shall not know, serve him; if you have anything you value share it with him; so, serving him, you will at last come to feel possession in him, and you will forgive.' And he said, 'I will do it.' Afterward, as I passed by in the dark of night, I heard one crying out, 'I have done all. It helps nothing! My speaking well of him helps me nothing! If I share my heart's blood with him, is the burning within me less? I cannot forgive; I cannot forgive! Oh, God, I cannot forgive!'

"I said to him, 'See here, look back on all your past. See from your childhood all smallness, all indirectness that has been yours; look well at it, and in its light do you not see every man your brother? Are you so sinless you have a right to hate?'

"He looked, and said, 'Yes, you are right; I, too, have failed, and I forgive my fellow. Go, I am satisfied; I have forgiven'; and he laid him down peacefully and folded his hands on his breast, and I thought it was well with him. But scarcely had my wings rustled and I turned to come up here, when I heard one crying out on earth again, 'I cannot forgive! I cannot forgive! Oh, God, God, I cannot forgive! It is better to die than to hate! I cannot forgive! I cannot forgive!' And I went and stood outside his door in the dark, and I heard him cry, 'I have not sinned so, not so! If I have torn my fellow's flesh ever so little, I have kneeled down and kissed the wound with my mouth till it was healed. I have not willed that any soul should be lost through hate of me. If they have but fancied that I wronged them I have lain down on the ground before them that they might tread on me, and so, seeing my humiliation, forgive and not be lost through hating me; they have not cared that my soul should be lost; they have not willed to save me; they have not tried that I should forgive them!'

"I said to him, 'See here, be thou content; do not forgive; forget this soul and its injury; go on your way. In the next world perhaps——'

OLIVE SCHREINER

" He cried, 'Go from me, you understand nothing! What is the next world to me! I am lost now, to-day. I cannot see the sunlight shine, the dust is in my throat, the sand is in my eyes! Go from me, you know nothing! Oh, once again before I die to see that the world is beautiful! Oh, God, God, I cannot live and not love. I cannot live and hate. Oh, God, God, God!' So I left him crying out and came back here."

God said, " This man's soul must be saved."

And the angel said, " How ? "

God said, " Go down you, and save it."

The angel said, " What more shall I do ? "

Then God bent down and whispered in the angel's ear, and the angel spread out its wings and went down to earth.

And partly I woke, sitting there upon the broken stone with my head on my knee; but I was too weary to rise. I heard the wind roam through the olive trees and among the ruined arches, and then I slept again.

The angel went down and found the man with the bitter heart and took him by the hand, and led him to a certain spot.

Now the man wist not where it was the angel would take him, nor what he would show him there. And when they came the angel shaded the man's eyes with his wing, and when he moved it, the man saw somewhat on the earth before them. For God had given it to that angel to unclothe a human soul; to take from it all those outward attributes of form and color, and age, and sex, whereby one man is known from among his fellows and is marked off from the rest, and the soul lay before them bare, as a man turning his eye inward beholds himself.

They saw its past, its childhood, the tiny life with the dew upon it; they saw its youth when the dew was melting, and the creature raised its Lilliputian mouth to drink from a cup too large for it, and they saw how the water spilt; they saw its hopes that were never realized; they saw its hours of intellectual blindness, men call sin; they saw its hours of all-radiating insight, which men call righteousness; they saw its hour of strength, when it leaped to its feet crying, " I am omnipotent "; its hour of weakness, when it fell to the earth and grasped dust only; they saw what it might have been, but never would be.

The man bent forward.

And the angel said, "What is it?"

He answered, "It is I! it is myself!" And he went forward as if he would have lain his heart against it; but the angel held him back and covered his eyes.

Now God had given power to the angel further to unclothe that soul, to take from it all those outward attributes of time and place and circumstance whereby the individual life is marked off from the life of the whole.

Again the angel uncovered the man's eyes, and he looked. He saw before him that which in its tiny drop reflects the whole universe; he saw that which marks within itself the step of the furthest star, and tells how the crystal grows under ground where no eye has seen it; that which is where the germ in the egg stirs; which moves the out-stretched fingers of the little newborn babe, and keeps the leaves of the trees pointing upward; which moves where the jellyfish sail alone on the sunny seas, and is where the lichens form on the mountain's rocks.

And the man looked.

And the angel touched him.

But the man bowed his head and shuddered. He whispered, "It is God!"

And the angel recovered the man's eyes. And when he uncovered them there was one walking from them a little way off — for the angel had reclothed the soul in its outward form and vesture — and the man knew who it was.

And the angel said, "Do you know him?"

And the man said, "I know him," and he looked after the figure.

And the angel said, "Have you forgiven him?"

But the man said, "How beautiful my brother is!"

And the angel looked into the man's eyes, and he shaded his own face with his wing from the light. He laughed softly and went up to God.

But the men were together on earth.

I awoke.

The blue, blue sky was over my head, and the waves were breaking below on the shore. I walked through the little Chapel, and I saw the Madonna in blue and red, and the Christ carrying his cross, and the Roman soldiers with the rod, and the Blessèd Rambino with its broken face; and then I walked down the sloping road to the brick pathway. The olive trees stood up on either side of the road, their black berries and pale-green leaves stood out against the sky; and the little ice plants hung from the crevices in the stone wall. It seemed to me as if it must have rained while I was asleep. I thought I had never seen the heavens and the earth look so beautiful before. I walked down the road. The old, old, old tiredness was gone.

Presently there came a peasant boy down the path leading his ass; she had two large panniers fastened to her sides; and they went down the road before me.

I had never seen him before; but I should have liked to walk by him and to have held his hand — only he would not have known why.

Complete. From «Dreams.» Written at Alassio, Italy.

THE GARDENS OF PLEASURE

SHE walked upon the beds, and the sweet, rich scent arose; and she gathered her hands full of flowers. Then Duty, with his white, clear features, came and looked at her. Then she ceased from gathering, but she walked away among the flowers, smiling, and with her hands full.

Then Duty, with his still, white face, came again, and looked at her; but she, — she turned her head away from him. At last she saw his face, and she dropped the fairest of the flowers she had held, and walked silently away.

Then again he came to her. And she moaned, and bent her head low, and turned to the gate. But as she went out she looked back at the sunlight on the faces of the flowers, and wept in anguish. Then she went out and it shut behind her forever; but still in her hand she held of the buds she had gathered, and the scent was very sweet in the lonely desert.

But he followed her. Once more he stood before her with his still, white, death-like face. And she knew what he had come for; she unbent the fingers, and let the flowers drop out, the flowers she had loved so, and walked on without them, with dry, aching eyes. Then for the last time he came. And she showed him her empty hands, the hands that held nothing now. But still he looked. Then at length she opened her bosom and took out of it one small flower she had hidden there, and laid it on the sand. She had nothing more to give now, and she wandered away, and the gray sand whirled about her.

Complete. From « Dreams. »

IN A FAR-OFF WORLD

THERE is a world in one of the far-off stars, and things do not happen here as they happen there. In that world were a man and a woman; they had one work, and they walked together side by side on many days, and were friends — and that is a thing that happens now and then in this world also.

But there was something in that star-world that there is not here. There was a thick wood; where the trees grew closest, and the stems were interlocked, and the summer sun never shone, there stood a shrine. In the day all was quiet, but at night, when the stars shone or the moon glinted on the tree-tops, and all was quiet below, if one crept here quite alone and knelt on the steps of the stone altar, and uncovering one's breast, so wounded it that the blood fell down on the altar steps, then whatever he who knelt there wished for was granted him. And all this happens, as I said, because it is a far-off world and things often happen there as they do not happen here.

Now the man and the woman walked together; and the woman wished well to the man. One night when the moon was shining so that the leaves of all the trees glinted, and the waves of the sea were silvery, the woman walked alone to the forest. It was dark there; the moonlight fell only in little flecks on the dead leaves under her feet, and the branches were knotted tight overhead. Further in it got darker, not even a fleck of moonlight shone. Then she came to the shrine; she knelt down before it and prayed; there came no answer. Then she uncovered her breast; with a sharp two-edged stone that lay there she wounded it. The drops dripped slowly down onto the stone, and a voice cried, « What do you seek ? »

She answered, « There is a man; I hold him nearer than anything. I would give him the best of all blessings. »

The voice said, « What is it ? »

The girl said, « I know not, but that which is most good for him I wish him to have. »

The voice said, " Your prayer is answered; he shall have it. "

Then she stood up.   She covered her breast and held the garment tight upon it with her hand, and ran out of the forest, and the dead leaves fluttered under her feet.   Out in the moon-light the soft air was blowing, and the sand glittered on the beach.   She ran along the smooth shore, then suddenly she stood still.   Out across the water there was something moving.   She shaded her eyes and looked.   It was a boat; it was sliding swiftly over the moonlight water out to sea.   One stood upright in it; the face the moonlight did not show, but the figure she knew. It was passing swiftly; it seemed as if no one propelled it; the moonlight's shimmer did not let her see clearly, and the boat was far from shore, but it seemed almost as if there was another figure sitting in the stern.   Faster and faster it glided over the water away, away.   She ran along the shore; she came no nearer it.   The garment she had held closed fluttered open; she stretched out her arms, and the moonlight shone on her long loose hair.

Then a voice beside her whispered, " What is it ? "

She cried, " With my blood I bought the best of all gifts for him.   I have come to bring it him!   He is going from me!"

The voice whispered softly, " Your prayer was answered.   It was given him."

She cried, " What is it ? "

The voice answered, " It is that he might leave you."

The girl stood still.

Far out at sea the boat was lost to sight beyond the moon-light sheen.

The voice spoke softly, " Art thou contented ? "

She said, " I am contented."

At her feet the waves broke in long ripples softly on the shore.

Complete.   From " Dreams."

THE ARTIST'S SECRET

THERE was an artist once, and he painted a picture.   Other art-ists had colors richer and rarer, and painted more notable pictures.   He painted his with one color; there was a wonderful red glow on it; and the people went up and down, saying, " We like the picture, we like the glow."

The other artists came and said, "Where does he get his color from?" They asked him; and he smiled and said, "I cannot tell you"; and worked on with his head bent low.

And one went to the far East and bought costly pigments, and made a rare color and painted, but after a time the picture faded. Another read in the old books, and made a color rich and rare, but when he had put it on the picture it was dead.

But the artist painted on. Always the work got redder and redder, and the artist grew whiter and whiter. At last one day they found him dead before his picture, and they took him up to bury him. The other men looked about in all the pots and crucibles, but they found nothing they had not.

And when they undressed him to put his graveclothes on him, they found above his left breast the mark of a wound — it was an old, old wound, that must have been there all his life, for the edges were old and hardened; but Death, who seals all things, had drawn the edges together, and closed it up.

And they buried him. And still the people went about saying, "Where did he find his color from?"

And it came to pass that after a while the artist was forgotten — but the work lived.

Complete. From "Dreams."

SIR WALTER SCOTT

(1771–1832)

IR WALTER SCOTT's literary biographies are not in the strict-est sense essays. They are narratives rather than essays, but they belong to the literature of the English essay cycle and deserve to be studied as part of it. His incomparable gifts as a novelist were developed through a method which is incompatible with high excellence in essay writing. He was the greatest romance writer of his century and he became so because his mind expressed itself through the construction of romantic plots as naturally as Addison and Lamb expressed theirs through monologue, characterized by that kaleidoscopic shifting of topics which is the charm of the essay and the despair of the novel. Even when he is at his best as an essayist, Sir Walter is still the great novelist, with the virtue of the novelist rather than of the essayist. But the narrative style he loves rather enhances than detracts from the interest of his essays. Whatever he lacks in attention to the art of construction, he more than makes good by crowding incident on incident and anecdote on anecdote, until we forget to regret the loss of the great essayist he might have become had he not been the incomparable story-teller he is.

THE CHARACTER AND HABITS OF SWIFT

SWIFT was in person tall, strong, and well made, of a dark complexion, but with blue eyes, black and bushy eyebrows, nose somewhat aquiline, features which remarkably ex-pressed the stern, haughty, and dauntless turn of his mind. He was never known to laugh, and his smiles are happily character-ized by the well-known lines of Shakespeare. Indeed, the whole description of Cassius might be applied to Swift:—

« —————————————— He reads much,
He is a great observer, and he looks
Quite through the deeds of men.—
Seldom he smiles, and smiles in such a sort,
As if he mock'd himself, and scorn'd his spirit
That could be mov'd to smile at any thing.»

The features of the Dean have been preserved in several paintings, busts, and medals In youth he was reckoned hand-some, Pope observed that though his face had an expression of dullness, his eyes were very particular. They were as azure, he said, as the heavens, and had an unusual expression of acuteness. In old age the Dean's countenance conveyed an expression which, though severe, was noble and impressive. He spoke in public with facility and impressive energy; and as his talents for ready reply were so well calculated for political debate, it must have increased the mortification of Queen Anne's ministers, that they found themselves unable to secure him a seat on the bench of Bishops. The government of Ireland dreaded his eloquence as much as his pen.

His manners in society were, in his better days, free, lively, and engaging, not devoid of peculiarities, but bending them so well to circumstances that his company was universally courted. When age and infirmity had impaired the elasticity of his spirits and the equality of his temper, his conversation was still valued, not only on account of the extended and various acquaintance with life and manners, of which it displayed an inexhaustible fund, but also for the shrewd and satirical humor which seasoned his observations and anecdotes. This, according to Orrery, was the last of his powers which decayed, but the Dean himself was sensible that, as his memory failed, his stories were too often repeated. His powers of conversation and of humorous repartee were in his time regarded unrivaled; but, like most who have assumed a despotic sway in conversation, he was sometimes silenced by unexpected resistance. He was very fond of puns. Perhaps the application of the line of Virgil to the lady who threw down with her mantua a Cremona fiddle is the best that ever was made: —

« Mantua, væ miseræ nimium vicina Cremonæ ! »

The comfort which he gave an elderly gentleman who had lost his spectacles was more grotesque: "If this rain continues all night, you will certainly recover them in the morning betimes:

« Nocte pluit tota — redeunt spectacula mane. »

His pre-eminence in more legitimate wit is asserted by many anecdotes. A man of distinction not remarkable for regularity in his private concerns, chose for his motto, *"Eques haud male notus.* " " Better known than trusted," was the Dean's translation, when someone related the circumstance.

Swift had an odd humor of making extempore proverbs. Observing that a gentleman, in whose garden he walked with some friends, seemed to have no intention to request them to eat any of the fruit, Swift observed, it was a saying of his dear grandmother,

> " Always pull a peach
> When it is within your reach,"

and helping himself accordingly, his example was followed by the whole company. At another time, he framed an " old saying and true " for the benefit of a person who had fallen from his horse into the mire: —

> " The more dirt,
> The less hurt."

The man rose much consoled; but as he was a collector of proverbs himself, he wondered he had never before heard that used by the Dean upon the occasion. He threw some useful rules into rhyming adages; and indeed, as his " Journal to Stella " proves, had a felicity in putting rhymes together on any trifling occasion, which must have added considerably to the flow and facility of his poetical compositions.

In his personal habits he was cleanly, even to scrupulousness. At one period of his life he was said to lie in bed till eleven o'clock, and think of wit for the day; but latterly he was an early riser. Swift was fond of exercise, and particularly of walking. And although modern pedestrians may smile at his proposing to journey to Chester, by walking ten miles a day, yet he is said to have taken this exercise too violently, and to a degree prejudicial to his health. He was also a tolerable horseman, fond of riding, and a judge of the noble animal, which he chose to celebrate, as the emblem of moral merit, under the name of Houyhnhnm. Exercise he pressed on his friends, particularly upon Stella and Vanessa, as a sort of duty; and scarce any of his letters conclude without allusion to it; especially as relating to the preservation of his own health, which his constitutional fits of deafness and giddiness rendered very precarious. His habit of body in other respects appears to have been indifferent, with a tendency to scrofula, which, perhaps, hastened his mental disorder. But the immediate cause was the pressure of water upon the head, as appeared upon dissection after death.

Of his learning we have already spoken; it seems to have both been extensive and useful, but not profoundly scholastic. Of modern languages he spoke and wrote French with facility, and understood Italian. His Latin verses indicate an imperfect knowledge of prosody, and no great command of the language in which they are written. The poem called "Rupes Carberiæ," has, in particular, been severely criticized. It is seldom that Swift alludes to English literature; yet it is evident he had perused with attention those classics to which his name is now added. How carefully he had read Milton appears from his annotations on the "Paradise Lost," for the benefit of Stella. Chaucer also appears to have been his favorite, for I observe among his papers a memorandum of the oaths used in the "Canterbury Tales," classed with the personages by whom they are used. It appears from a note upon Mr. Todd's edition of Milton, that Swift was a peruser of the ancient romances of chivalry. But he never mentions the romances and plays of the period in which he lived, without expressing the most emphatic contempt. To the drama, particularly, he was so indifferent, that he never once alludes to the writings of Shakespeare, nor, wonderful to be told, does he appear to have possessed a copy of his works. After noticing this, it will scarce be held remarkable that the catalogue of his library only contains the works of three dramatic authors, Ben Jonson, Wycherley, and Rowe, the last two being presentation copies from the authors, in 1700 and 1702. History and classical authors formed the Dean's favorite studies, and, during the decay of his faculties, his reading was almost entirely confined to Clarendon.

Swift loved the country, like most men of genius, but rather practiced rural occupations than rural sports. At Quilca, Gaulstown, and Markethill, he delighted in acting as a sort of overseer or bailiff to those employed in improving the property of his friends, and he dwells fondly in his "Journal" on his plantations and canal at Laracor.

It does not appear from any part of his works, unless, perhaps, the Latin verses on the rocks of Carbery, that he was an admirer of the beautiful or romantic in landscapes; but he was a curious, though not a scientific, observer of any singular natural phenomena which came under his attention.

The humor of stubborn independence which influenced the Dean's whole character stamps it, at first examination, with a whole chain of paradoxes. A devout believer in the truths of Christianity, a constant observer of the rules of religion, and zealous even to slaying in the cause of the Church of England, Swift assumed an occasional levity of writing, speaking, and acting, which caused his being branded an infidel, a contemner of public ordinances, and a scoffer of church discipline. Nor was this all. A zealous friend of liberty in temporal politics, he acted during his whole life with the Tory party. Disliking Ireland even to virulent prejudice, he was the first and most effectual vindicator of her rights and liberties; and, charitable and benevolent to the extreme limits of a moderate revenue, he lay under the reproach of avarice and parsimony. An admirer of paradoxes, like Dr. Fuller, might have found points in his history, as well as opinions, capable of being placed in strong contrast. The first writer of his age was disgraced at college; the principal supporter of Queen Anne's last administration, whose interest had made many a prelate, was himself unable to attain that dignity; and he who in his writings exhibited a tone of the most bitter misanthropy, was in active life a steady patriot, a warm friend, and a bountiful patron. He had also this remarkable fate as a political writer, that, although his publishers were in four instances subjected to arrest and examination,—although large rewards were twice offered for the discovery of the author of works generally and truly ascribed to him,— yet he never personally felt the grasp of power;

> « For not a Judas could be found,
> To sell him for three hundred pound.»

Many of these apparent paradoxes arose from Swift's stern and unbending pride of temper, which rather contemned and avoided public applause than studied to present his character under favorable colors to the general eye. Even his politeness assumed often a singular turn of cynicism, and much of his conduct in life reminds us of his favorite style of composition, that irony

> « Which he was born to introduce,
> Refined at first, and showed its use.»

From the same cause he often exhibited, in his first address, a sternness and a bluntness of demeanor, which, detached from the mode in which he well knew how to repair the pain he had given, was harsh to his inferiors, and uncivil to those of higher rank. An anecdote which, though told by Mrs. Pilkington, is well attested, bears, that the last time he was in London he went to dine with the Earl of Burlington, who was then but newly married. The Earl being willing, it is supposed, to have some diversion, did not introduce him to his lady, nor mention his name. After dinner, said the Dean, "Lady Burlington, I hear you can sing; sing me a song." The lady looked on this unceremonious manner of asking a favor with distaste, and positively refused. He said, "She should sing, or he would make her. Why, madam, I suppose you take me for one of your poor English hedge parsons; sing when I bid you." As the Earl did nothing but laugh at this freedom, the lady was so vexed, that she burst into tears, and retired. His first compliment to her when he saw her again, was, "Pray, madam, are you as proud and as ill natured now as when I saw you last?" To which she answered with great humor, "No, Mr. Dean; I'll sing for you, if you please." From which time he conceived great esteem for her. The Dean received with complaisance such praise as was delicately administered; but it belonged to his character to repel whatever was extravagant or coarse. When a man professed to love Swift better than all his friends and relations, he said, "The man is a fool." And when Pope talked to him of a lady who admired him above all things, he replied, "Then I despise her heartily." In fact, he seems rather to have expected his friends to gratify him by implicit compliance with his humor, however whimsical, than by any verbal flattery disguising perhaps from himself, that such servile compliance was the grossest sort of practical adulation.

From "The Life of Swift."

LORD BYRON

A MIDST the general calmness of the political atmosphere, we have been stunned, from another quarter, by one of those death notes, which are pealed at intervals, as from an archangel's trumpet, to awaken the soul of a whole people at once. Lord Byron, who has so long and so amply filled the highest place in the public eye, has shared the lot of humanity. He died at Missolonghi, on the nineteenth of April, 1824. That mighty genius, which walked among men as something superior to ordinary mortality, and whose powers were beheld with wonder, and something approaching to terror, as if we knew not whether they were of good or of evil, is laid as soundly to rest as the poor peasant whose ideas never went beyond his daily task. The voice of just blame, and that of malignant censure, are at once silenced; and we feel almost as if the great luminary of heaven had suddenly disappeared from the sky, at the moment when every telescope was leveled for the examination of the spots which dimmed its brightness. It is not now the question, what were Byron's faults, what his mistakes; but, How is the blank which he has left in British literature to be filled up, Not, we fear, in one generation, which, among many highly gifted persons, has produced none who approached Byron in originality, the first attribute of genius. Only thirty-seven years old — so much already done for immortality — so much time remaining, as it seemed to us shortsighted mortals, to maintain and to extend his fame, and to atone for errors in conduct and levities in composition, — who will not grieve that such a race has been shortened, though not always keeping the straight path, such a light extinguished, though sometimes flaming to dazzle and bewilder? One word on this ungrateful subject ere we quit it forever.

The errors of Lord Byron arose neither from depravity of heart, — for nature had not committed the anomaly of uniting to such extraordinary talents an imperfect moral sense, — nor from feelings dead to the admiration of virtue. No man had ever a kinder heart for sympathy, or a more open hand for the relief of distress; and no mind was ever more formed for the enthusiastic admiration of noble actions, providing he was convinced that the actors had proceeded on disinterested principles. Lord Byron was totally free from the curse and degradation of literature, — its jealousies, we mean, and its envy. But his wonderful genius was of a nature which disdained restraint, even when restraint was most wholesome. When at school, the tasks in which he excelled were those only which he undertook voluntarily; and his situation as a young man of rank, with strong passions, and in the uncontrolled enjoyment of a considerable fortune, added to that impatience of strictures or coercion which was natural to him. As an author he refused to plead at the bar of criticism; as a man he would not submit to be morally amenable to the tribunal of public opinion. Remonstrances from a friend, of whose intentions and kindness he was secure, had often great weight with him; but there were few who could or dared venture on a task so difficult. Reproof he endured with impatience, and reproach hardened him in his error; so that he often resembled the gallant war steed who rushes forward on the steel that wounds him. In the most painful crisis of his private life, he evinced this irritability and impatience of censure in such a degree as almost to resemble the noble victim of the bullfight, which is more maddened by the squibs, darts, and petty annoyances of the unworthy crowds beyond the lists, than by the lance of his nobler, and, so to speak, his more legitimate antagonist. In a word, much of that in which he erred, was in bravado and scorn of his censors, and was done with the motive of Dryden's despot, "to show his arbitrary power." It is needless to say that his was a false and prejudiced view of such a contest; and that if the noble bard gained a species of triumph, by compelling the world to read poetry, though mixed with baser matter, because it was his, he gave, in return, an unworthy triumph to the unworthy, besides deep sorrow to those whose applause, in his cooler moments, he most valued.

It was the same with his politics, which on several occasions assumed a tone menacing and contemptuous to the constitution of his country; while, in fact, Lord Byron was in his own heart sufficiently sensible, not only of his privileges as a Briton, but of the distinction attending his high birth and rank, and was peculiarly sensitive of those shades which constitute what is termed the manners of a gentleman. Indeed, notwithstanding his having employed epigrams, and all the petty war of wit, when such would have been much better abstained from, he would have been found, had a collision taken place between the aristocratic and democratic parties in the state, exerting all his energies in defense of that to which he naturally belonged. His own feeling on these subjects he has explained in the very last canto of "Don Juan"; and they are in entire harmony with the opinions which we have seen expressed in his correspondence, at a moment when matters appeared to approach a serious struggle in his native country. "If we are to fall," he expressed himself to this purpose, "let the independent aristocracy and gentry of England suffer by the sword of an arbitrary prince, who has been born and bred a gentleman, and will behead us after the manner of our ancestors; but do not let us suffer ourselves to be massacred by the ignoble swarms of ruffians, who are endeavoring to throttle

their way to power." Accordingly, he expresses in the strongest
terms his purpose of resisting to the last extremity the tendency
to anarchy, which commercial distress had generated, and disaffec-
tion was endeavoring to turn to its own purposes. His poetry
expresses similar sentiments:—

> « It is not that I adulate the people;
>   Without me there are demagogues enough,
> And infidels to pull down every steeple,
>   And set up in their stead some proper stuff,
> Whether they may sow Skepticism to reap Hell,
>   As is the Christian dogma rather rough,
> I do not know;—I wish men to be free
>   As much from mobs as kings—from you as me.
> The consequence is, being of no party,
>   I shall offend all parties.»

We are not, however, Byron's apologists,—for now alas! he
needs none. His excellences will now be universally acknowledged, and his faults (let us hope and believe) not remembered
in his epitaph. It will be recollected what a part he has sustained in British literature since the first appearance of " Childe
Harold," a space of nearly sixteen years. There has been no re-
posing under the shade of his laurels, no living upon the resource
of past reputation; none of that coddling and petty precaution,
which little authors call " taking care of their fame." Byron let
his fame take care of itself. His foot was always in the arena,
his shield hung always in the lists; and, although his own gigantic renown increased the difficulty of the struggle, since he could
produce nothing, however great, which exceeded the public estimate of his genius, yet he advanced to the honorable contest
again and again and again, and came always off with distinction,
almost always with complete triumph. As various in composition
as Shakespeare himself (this will be admitted by all who are acquainted with his " Don Juan ") he has embraced every topic of
human life, and sounded every string on the divine harp, and
from its slightest to its most powerful and heart-astounding tones.
There is scarce a passion or a situation which has escaped his
pen; and he might be drawn, like Garrick, between the weeping
and the laughing muse, although his most powerful efforts have
certainly been dedicated to Melpomene. His genius seemed as
prolific as various. The most prodigal use did not exhaust his

powers, nay, seemed rather to increase their vigor. Neither "Childe Harold," nor any of the most beautiful of Byron's earlier tales, contain more exquisite morsels of poetry than are to be found scattered through the cantos of "Don Juan," amidst verses which the author appears to have thrown off with an effort as spontaneous as that of a tree resigning its leaves to the wind. But that noble tree will never more bear fruit or blossom! It has been cut down in its strength, and the past is all that remains to us of Byron. We can scarce reconcile ourselves to the idea — scarce think that the voice is silent forever, which, bursting so often on our ear, was often heard with rapturous admiration, sometimes with regret, but always with the deepest interest,—

"All that's bright must fade,
The brightest still the fleetest!"

With a strong feeling of awful sorrow, we take leave of the subject. Death creeps upon our most serious, as well as upon our most idle, employments; and it is a reflection solemn and gratifying that he found our Byron in no moment of levity, but contributing his fortune, and hazarding his life in behalf of a people only endeared to him by their past glories, and as fellow-creatures suffering under the yoke of a heathen oppressor.

From "Biographies."

JOHN SELDEN

(1584–1654)

JOHN SELDEN, remembered now as the author of Selden's "Table-Talk," was in his generation a man of great and varied activities. He was born in Sussex, England, December 16th, 1584, and was thus contemporary with many of the greatest men of what still remains the most remarkable age of England. Lyttleton, Herbert, Drayton, and Ben Jonson were among his intimates. He was a lawyer and jurist of reputation, and among his forgotten works are "England's Epinomis," "Janus Anglorum," and a "History of Luther," published in 1618 and suppressed. He was committed to the Tower for sedition in 1621 and seven years later he helped to draw up the Petition of Right. In 1640 he was elected to the Long Parliament, and he was a member of the committee which impeached Archbishop Laud. He died at London, November 30th, 1654.

TABLE–TALK

CHANGING SIDES

'TIS the trial of a man to see if he will change his side; and if he be so weak as to change once, he will change again.

Your country fellows have a way to try if a man be weak in the hams, by coming behind him and giving him a blow unawares; if he bend once, he will bend again.

The lords that fall from the king after they have got estates by base flattery at court and now pretend conscience, do as a vintner, that when he first sets up, you may go to his house, and carouse there; but when he grows rich, he turns conscientious, and will sell no wine upon the Sabbath Day.

Col. Goring, serving first the one side and then the other, did like a good miller that knows how to grind which way soevei the wind sits.

After Luther had made a combustion in Germany about religion, he was sent to by the Pope, to be taken off, and offered any preferment in the Church that he would make choice of: Luther answered, if he had offered half as much at first, he would have accepted it; but now he had gone so far, he could not come back. In truth, he had made himself a greater thing than they could make him; the German princes courted him, he was become the author of a sect ever after to be called Lutherans. So have our preachers done that are against the bishops; they have made themselves greater with the people than they can be made the other way; and, therefore, there is the less probability of bringing them off.

Complete.

CONTRACTS

IF OUR fathers have lost their liberty, why may not we labor to regain it? Answer: We must look to the contract; if that be rightly made, we must stand to it; if we once grant we may recede from contracts upon any inconveniency that may afterwards happen, we shall have no bargain kept. If I sell you a horse and do not like my bargain, I will have my horse again.

Keep your contracts — so far a divine goes; but how to make our contracts is left to ourselves; and as we agree upon the conveying of this house or that land, so it must be. If you offer me a hundred pounds for my glove, I tell you what my glove is, a plain glove, pretend no virtue in it, the glove is my own, I profess not to sell gloves, and we agree for a hundred pounds, I do not know why I may not with a safe conscience take it. The want of that common obvious distinction of *jus præceptivum* and *jus permissivum* does much trouble men.

Lady Kent articled with Sir Edward Herbert that he should come to her when she sent for him, and stay with her as long as she would have him, to which he set his hand; then he articled with her that he should go away when he pleased, and stay away as long as he pleased, to which she set her hand. This is the epitome of all the contracts in the world betwixt man and man, betwixt prince and subject; they keep them as long as they like them, and no longer.

Complete.

EVIL SPEAKING

HE THAT speaks ill of another, commonly before he is aware, makes himself such a one as he speaks against: for if he had civility or breeding, he would forbear such kind of language.

A gallant man is above ill words; an example we have in the old Lord of Salisbury, who was a great wise man. Stone had called some lord about court, "Fool": the lord complains and has Stone whipped; Stone cries, "I might have called my Lord of Salisbury 'fool' often enough before he would have had me whipped."

Speak not ill of a great enemy, but rather give him good words, that he may use you the better if you chance to fall into his hands. The Spaniard did this when he was dying. His confessor told him (to work him to repentance) how the devil tormented the wicked that went to hell: the Spaniard, replying, called the devil "my lord": "I hope my lord the devil is not so cruel." His confessor reproved him. "Excuse me," said the Don, "for calling him so; I know not into what hands I may fall, and if I happen into his I hope he will use me the better for giving him good words."

Complete.

THE MEASURE OF THINGS

WE MEASURE from ourselves; and as things are for our use and purpose, so we approve them. Bring a pear to the table that is rotten, we cry it down, "'Tis naught"; but bring a medlar that is rotten, and "'Tis a fine thing": and yet I'll warrant you the pear thinks as well of itself as the medlar does.

We measure the excellency of other men by some excellency we conceive to be in ourselves. Nash, a poet, poor enough (as poets used to be), seeing an alderman with his gold chain, upon his great horse, by way of scorn said to one of his companions, "Do you see yon fellow, how goodly, how big he looks? Why, that fellow cannot make a blank verse!"

Nay, we measure the goodness of God from ourselves; we measure his goodness, his justice, his wisdom, by something we

call just, good, or wise in ourselves; and in so doing we judge
proportionably to the country fellow in the play, who said if he
were a king he would live like a lord, and have peas and bacon
every day, and a whip that cried, "Slash!"

Complete.

WISDOM

A WISE man should never resolve upon anything, at least never
let the world know his resolution, for if he cannot arrive
at that he is ashamed. How many things did the king
resolve in his declaration concerning Scotland never to do, and
yet did them all! A man must do according to accidents and
emergencies.

Never tell your resolution beforehand; but when the cast is
thrown play it as well as you can to win the game you are at.
'Tis but folly to study how to play size-ace when you know not
whether you shall throw it or no.

Wise men say nothing in dangerous times. The lion, you
know, called the sheep to ask her if his breath smelt: she said,
" Aye "; he bit off her head for a fool. He called the wolf and
asked him: he said " No "; he tore him in pieces for a flatterer.
At last he called the fox and asked him: truly he had got a cold
and could not smell.

Complete.

WIT

WIT and wisdom differ; wit is upon the sudden turn, wisdom
is in bringing about ends.

Nature must be the groundwork of wit and art; otherwise whatever is done will prove but jack-pudding's work.

Wit must grow like fingers. If it be taken from others 'tis
like plums stuck upon blackthorns; there they are for a while,
but they come to nothing.

He that will give himself to all manner of ways to get money
may be rich; so he that lets fly all he knows or thinks may by
chance be satirically witty. Honesty sometimes keeps a man
from growing rich, and civility from being witty.

Women ought not to know their own wit, because they will still be showing it, and so spoil it; like a child that will continually be showing its fine new coat, till at length it all bedaubs it with its pah hands.

Fine wits destroy themselves with their own plots, in meddling with great affairs of state. They commonly do as the ape that saw the gunner put bullets in the cannon, and was pleased with it, and he would be doing so too: at last he puts himself into the piece, and so both ape and bullet were shot away together.

Complete.

WOMEN

"LET the women have power of their heads, because of the angels." The reason of the words, "because of the angels," is this: The Greek Church held an opinion that the angels fell in love with women; an opinion grounded upon that, Genesis vi. "The sons of God saw the daughters of men that they were fair." This fancy St. Paul discreetly catches, and uses it as an argument to persuade them to modesty.

The grant of a place is not good, by the canon law, before a man be dead: upon this ground some mischief might be plotted against him in present possession, by poisoning, or some other way. Upon the same reason a contract made with a woman, during her husband's life, was not valid.

Men are not troubled to hear a man dispraised, because they know, though he be naught, there's worth in others; but women are mightily troubled to hear any of them spoken against, as if the sex itself were guilty of some unworthiness.

Women and princes must both trust somebody; and they are happy or unhappy according to the desert of those under whose hands they fall. If a man knows how to manage the favor of a lady, her honor is safe, and so is a prince's.

Complete.

LUCIUS ANNÆUS SENECA

(*c.* 4 B. C.–65 A. D.)

ENECA was born at Corduba, in Spain, about 4 B. C. His parents brought him to Rome and educated him thoroughly in rhetoric and philosophy. He soon became celebrated as a pleader in the courts, and his writings raised him to eminence among the Stoics at a time when the despotism of a series of the worst tyrants made the Stoic philosophy of repression the only recourse of the intellectual classes at Rome. Seneca was a man of much flexibility of intellect and he became a Senator under Caligula; but under Claudius, Messalina caused him to be banished to Corsica, where he remained until recalled to become the tutor of Nero. The promise of virtue which characterized the early years of Nero's reign was due to Seneca's teaching, but when in 65 A. D. the philosopher was compelled by his pupil to commit suicide, it is not unfair to inquire of the system whether the same flaw in it which made so great a writer and teacher as Seneca himself one of the most notorious usurers of Rome, might not have been instrumental in making Nero what he became in the later years of his reign. Seneca's chief works as a moralist and essayist are "On Anger," "On Clemency," "On Benefits," "On Providence," and "On Tranquillity." His tragedies show that he had talent as a poet and maker of maxims scarcely inferior to that of Pope among the Moderns. His tragedies are imitated from Greek originals, it is true, but this is equally true of all other Latin verse. Among writers of Latin prose, Seneca ranks with Cicero in power of synthesis, but his prose style has found few imitators, while that of Cicero has been a model for students in all succeeding generations.

W. V. B.

ON ANGER

ARISTOTLE says that "certain passions, if one makes a proper use of them, act as arms": which would be true if, like weapons of war, they could be taken up or laid aside at the pleasure of their wielder. These arms, which Aristotle assigns to virtue, fight of their own accord, do not wait to be seized by the hand, and possess a man instead of being possessed by him.

We have no need of external weapons, Nature has equipped us sufficiently by giving us reason. She has bestowed this weapon upon us, which is strong, imperishable, and obedient to our will, not uncertain or capable of being turned against its master. Reason suffices by itself not merely to take thought for the future, but to manage our affairs: what, then, can be more foolish than for reason to beg anger for protection, that is, for what is certain to beg of what is uncertain? what is trustworthy of what is faithless? what is whole of what is sick? What, indeed? since reason is far more powerful by itself even in performing those operations in which the help of anger seems especially needful: for when Reason has decided that a particular thing should be done, she perseveres in doing it; not being able to find anything better than herself to exchange with. She, therefore, abides by her purpose when it has once been formed; whereas anger is often overcome by pity: for it possesses no firm strength, but merely swells like an empty bladder, and makes a violent beginning, just like the winds which rise from the earth and are caused by rivers and marshes, which blow furiously without any continuance: anger begins with a mighty rush, and then falls away, becoming fatigued too soon: that which but lately thought of nothing but cruelty and novel forms of torture is become quite softened and gentle when the time comes for punishment to be inflicted. Passion soon cools, whereas reason is always consistent: yet even in cases where anger has continued to burn, it often happens that although there may be many who deserve to die, yet after the death of two or three it ceases to slay. Its first onset is fierce, just as the teeth of snakes when first roused from their lair are venomous, but become harmless after repeated bites have exhausted their poison. Consequently those who are equally guilty are not equally punished, and often he who has done less is punished more, because he fell in the way of anger when it was fresher. It is altogether irregular; at one time it runs into undue excess, at another it falls short of its duty: for it indulges its own feelings and gives sentence according to its caprices, will not listen to evidence, allows the defense no opportunity of being heard, clings to what it has wrongly assumed, and will not suffer its opinion to be wrested from it, even when it is a mistaken one.

Reason gives each side time to plead; moreover, she herself demands adjournment, that she may have sufficient scope for the discovery of the truth; whereas anger is in a hurry: reason wishes to give a just decision; anger wishes its decision to be thought just: reason looks no further than the matter in hand; anger is excited by empty matters hovering on the outskirts of the case: it is irritated by anything approaching to a confident demeanor, a loud voice, and unrestrained speech, dainty apparel, high-flown pleading, or popularity with the public. It often condemns a man because it dislikes his patron; it loves and maintains error even when truth is staring it in the face. It hates to be proved wrong, and thinks it more honorable to persevere in a mistaken line of conduct than to retract it. I remember Gnæus Piso, a man who was free from many vices, yet of a perverse disposition, and one who mistook harshness for consistency. In his anger he ordered a soldier to be led off to execution because he had returned from furlough without his comrade, as though he must have murdered him if he could not show him. When the man asked for time for search, he would not grant it: the condemned man was brought outside the rampart, and was just offering his neck to the ax, when suddenly there appeared his comrade who was thought to be slain. Hereupon the centurion in charge of the execution bade the guardsman sheathe his sword, and led the condemned man back to Piso, to restore to him the innocence which fortune had restored to the soldier. They were led into his presence by their fellow-soldiers amid the great joy of the whole camp, embracing one another and accompanied by a vast crowd. Piso mounted the tribunal in a fury and ordered them both to be executed, both him who had not murdered and him who had not been slain. What could be more unworthy than this? Because one was proved to be innocent, two perished. Piso even added a third: for he actually ordered the centurion, who had brought back the condemned man, to be put to death. Three men were set up to die in the same place because one was innocent. Oh, how clever is anger at inventing reasons for its frenzy! "You," it says, "I order to be executed, because you have been condemned to death; you, because you have been the cause of your comrade's condemnation; and you, because when ordered to put him to death you disobeyed your general." He discovered the means of charging them with three crimes, because he could find no crime in them.

Irascibility, I say, has this fault—it is loath to be ruled: it is angry with the truth itself, if it comes to light against its will:

it assails those whom it has marked for its victims with shouting and riotous noise and gesticulation of the entire body together with reproaches and curses. Not thus does reason act: but if it must be so, she silently and quietly wipes out whole households, destroys entire families of the enemies of the state, together with their wives and children, throws down their very dwellings, levels them with the ground, and roots out the names of those who are the foes of liberty. This she does without grinding her teeth or shaking her head, or doing anything unbecoming to a judge, whose countenance ought to be especially calm and composed at the time when he is pronouncing an important sentence. "What need is there," asks Hieronymus, "for you to bite your own lips when you want to strike some one?" What would he have said, had he seen a proconsul leap down from the tribunal, snatch the fasces from the lictor, and tear his own clothes because those of others were not torn as fast as he wished. Why need you upset the table, throw down the drinking cups, knock yourself against the columns, tear your hair, smite your thigh and your breast? How vehement do you suppose anger to be, if it thus turns back upon itself, because it cannot find vent on another as fast as it wishes? Such men, therefore, are held back by the bystanders and are begged to become reconciled with themselves. But he who while free from anger assigns to each man the penalty which he deserves does none of these things. He often lets a man go after detecting his crime, if his penitence for what he has done gives good hope for the future, if he perceives that the man's wickedness is not deeply rooted in his mind, but is only, as the saying is, skin-deep. He will grant impunity in cases where it will hurt neither the receiver nor the giver. In some cases he will punish great crimes more leniently than lesser ones, if the former were the result of momentary impulse, not of cruelty, while the latter were instinct with secret, underhand, long-practiced craftiness. The same fault, committed by two separate men, will not be visited by him with the same penalty, if the one was guilty of it through carelessness, the other with a premeditated intention of doing mischief. In all dealing with crime he will remember that the one form of punishment is meant to make bad men better, and the other to put them out of the way. In either case he will look to the future, not to the past: for, as Plato says, "no wise man punishes any one because he has sinned, but that he may sin no more: for what is past cannot be recalled, but what is to come may be checked." Those, too, whom he wishes to make examples of the ill success of wickedness, he executes publicly, not merely in order that they themselves may die, but that by dying they may deter others from doing likewise. You see how free from any mental disturbance a man ought to be who has to weigh and consider all this, when he deals with a matter which ought to be handled with the utmost care,— I mean, the power of life and death. The sword of justice is ill placed in the hands of an angry man.

Neither ought it to be believed that anger contributes anything to magnanimity: what it gives is not magnanimity but vainglory. The increase which disease produces in bodies swollen with morbid humors is not healthy growth, but bloated corpulence. All those whose madness raises them above human considerations believe themselves to be inspired with high and sublime ideas; but there is no solid ground beneath, and what is built without foundation is liable to collapse in ruin. Anger has no ground to stand upon, and does not rise from a firm and enduring foundation, but is a windy, empty quality, as far removed from true magnanimity as foolhardiness from courage, boastfulness from confidence, gloom from austerity, cruelty from strictness. There is, I say, a great difference between a lofty and a proud mind: anger brings about nothing grand or beautiful. On the other hand, to be constantly irritated seems to me to be the part of a languid and unhappy mind, conscious of its own feebleness, like folk with diseased bodies covered with sores, who cry out at the lightest touch. Anger, therefore, is a vice which for the most part affects women and children. "Yet it affects men also." Because many men, too, have womanish or childish intellects. "But what are we to say? do not some words fall from angry men which appear to flow from a great mind?" Yes, to those who know not what true greatness is: as, for example, that foul and hateful saying, "Let them hate me, provided they fear me," which you may be sure was written in Sulla's time. I know not which was the worse of the two things he wished for, that he might be hated or that he might be feared. It occurs to his mind that some day people will curse him, plot against him, crush him: what prayer does he add to this? May all the gods curse him — for discovering a cure for hate so worthy of it. "Let them hate." How? "Provided they obey me"? No! "Provided they approve of me"? No! How then? "Provided they fear me"! I would not even be loved upon such terms. Do you imagine that this was a very spirited saying? You are wrong: this is not greatness, but monstrosity. You should not believe the words of angry men, whose speech is very loud and menacing, while their mind within them is as timid as possible: nor need you suppose that the most eloquent of men, Titus Livius, was right in describing somebody as being "of a great rather than a good disposition." The things cannot be separated: he must either be good or else he cannot be great, because I take greatness of mind to mean that it is unshaken, sound throughout, firm and uniform to its very foundation; such as cannot exist in evil dispositions. Such dispositions may be terrible, frantic, and destructive, but cannot possess greatness; because greatness rests upon goodness, and owes its strength to it. "Yet by speech, action, and all outward show they will make one think them great." True, they will say something which you may think shows a great spirit, like Gaius Cæsar, who when angry with heaven because it interfered with his ballet dancers, whom he imitated more carefully than he attended to them when they acted, and because it frightened his revels by its thunders, surely ill directed, challenged Jove to fight, and that to the death, shouting the Homeric verse:—

"Carry me off, or I will carry thee!"

How great was his madness. He must have believed either that he could not be hurt even by Jupiter himself, or that he could hurt even Jupiter itself. I imagine that this saying of his had no small weight in nerving the minds of the conspirators for their task: for it seemed to be the height of endurance to bear one who could not bear Jupiter.

There is therefore nothing great or noble in anger, even when it seems to be powerful and to contemn both gods and men alike. Any one who thinks that anger produces greatness of mind would think that luxury produces it: such a man wishes to rest on ivory, to be clothed with purple, and roofed with gold; to remove lands, embank seas, hasten the course of rivers, suspend woods in the air. He would think that avarice shows greatness of mind: for the avaricious man broods over heaps of gold and silver, treats whole provinces as merely fields on his estate, and has larger tracts of country under the charge of sin-

gle bailiffs than those which consuls once drew lots to administer.
He would think that lust shows greatness of mind: for the lust-
ful man swims across straits, castrates troops of boys, and puts
himself within reach of the swords of injured husbands with
complete scorn of death.   Ambition, too, he would think shows
greatness of mind: for the ambitious man is not content with office once a year, but, if possible, would fill the calendar of dignities
with his name alone, and cover the whole world with his titles.
It matters nothing to what heights or lengths these passions may
proceed: they are narrow, pitiable, groveling.   Virtue alone is
lofty and sublime, nor is anything great which is not at the same
time tranquil.

«On Anger,» Chaps. xvii., xviii., xix., xx., and xxi.,
complete.   Bohn edition.

MADAME DE SÉVIGNÉ

(MARIE DE RABUTIN-CHANTAL, MARQUISE DE SÉVIGNÉ)

(1626–1696)

ADAME DE SÉVIGNÉ, perhaps the most celebrated letter writer of modern times, was born at Paris, February 6th, 1626. She was carefully educated by her family, and at eighteen was married in the usual French way to the Marquis de Sévigné, by whom she had a daughter and a son. Her husband, who did not make her happy, was killed in a duel, and his widow devoted herself to the care of her children with such success that the letters written by her to her daughter are now read all over the civilized world. She died April 18th, 1696.

A BIT OF PARISIAN GOSSIP

I AM going to tell you a thing, the most astonishing, the most surprising, the most marvelous, the most miraculous, the most magnificent, the most confounding, the most unheard-of, the most singular, the most extraordinary, the most incredible, the most unforeseen, the greatest, the least, the rarest, the most common, the most public, the most private till to-day, the most brilliant, the most enviable; — in short, a thing of which there is but one example in past ages, and that not an exact one either; a thing that we cannot believe at Paris; how, then, will it gain credence at Lyons? a thing which makes everybody cry, "Lord have mercy upon us!" a thing which causes the greatest joy to Madame de Rohan and Madame de Hauterive; a thing, in fine, which is to happen on Sunday next, when those who are present will doubt the evidence of their senses; a thing which, though it is to be done on Sunday, yet perhaps will not be finished on Monday. I cannot bring myself to tell you; guess what it is. I give you three times to do it in. What, not a word to throw at a dog? Well, then, I find I must tell you. Monsieur de Lauzun is to be married next Sunday at the Louvre, to —————— pray guess to whom! I give you four times to do it in, — I give you six, —

I give you a hundred. Says Madame de Coulanges: "It is really very hard to guess; perhaps it is Madame de la Vallière." Indeed, madame, it is not. It is "Mademoiselle de Retz, then." No, nor she either; you are extremely provincial. "Lord bless me," say you, "what stupid wretches we are! it is Mademoiselle de Colbert all the while." Nay, now you are still further from the mark. "Why, then, it must certainly be Mademoiselle de Crequy." You have it not yet. Well, I find I must tell you at last. He is to be married next Sunday at the Louvre, with the king's leave, to Mademoiselle—Mademoiselle de——Mademoiselle—guess, pray guess her name; he is to be married to Mademoiselle, the great Mademoiselle; Mademoiselle, daughter to the late Monsieur; Mademoiselle, granddaughter of Henry IV; Mademoiselle d'Eu, Mademoiselle de Dombes, Mademoiselle de Montpensier, Mademoiselle d'Orleans, Mademoiselle, the king's cousin-german,—Mademoiselle, destined to the throne,—Mademoiselle, the only match in France that was worthy of Monsieur. What glorious matter for talk! If you should burst forth like a bedlamite, say we have told you a lie, that it is false, that we are making a jest of you, and that a pretty jest it is, without wit or invention; in short, if you abuse us, we shall think you are quite in the right; for we have done just the same things ourselves. Farewell, you will find by the letters you receive this post, whether we tell you truth or not.

Monsieur de Coulanges. Paris,
December 15th, 1670.

AN ARTISTIC FUNERAL

My Dear Child:—

I MUST return to narration, it is a folly I can never resist. Prepare, therefore, for a description. I was yesterday at a service performed in honor of the Chancellor Segnier at the Oratory. Painting, sculpture, music, rhetoric,—in a word, the four liberal arts,—were at the expense of it. Nothing could exceed the beauty of the decorations; they were finely imagined, and designed by Le Brun. The mausoleum reached to the top of the dome, adorned with a thousand lamps, and a variety of figures characteristic of him in whose honor it was erected. Beneath were four figures of Death, bearing the marks of his several dignities, as having taken away his honors with his life. One of

them held his helmet, another his ducal coronet, another the ensigns of his order, another his chancellor's mace. The four sister arts, painting, music, eloquence, and sculpture, were represented
in deep distress, bewailing the loss of their protector. The first
representation was supported by the four virtues, fortitude, temperance, justice, and religion. Above these, four angels, or genii,
received the soul of the deceased, and seemed preening their purple wings to bear their precious charge to heaven. The mausoleum was adorned with a variety of little seraphs, who supported
an illuminated shrine, which was fixed to the top of the cupola.
Nothing so magnificent or so well imagined was ever seen; it is
Le Brun's masterpiece. The whole church was adorned with
pictures, devices, and emblems, which all bore some relation to
the life, or office, of the chancellor; and some of his noblest actions were represented in painting. Madame de Verneuil offered
to purchase all the decoration at a great price; but it was unanimously resolved by those who had contributed to it, to adorn a
gallery with it, and to consecrate it as an everlasting monument
of their gratitude and magnificence. The assembly was grand
and numerous, but without confusion. I sat next to Monsieur
de Tulle, Madame Colbert and the Duke of Monmouth, who is
as handsome as when we saw him at the *palais royal.* (Let me
tell you in a parenthesis, that he is going to the army to join
the king.) A young father of the Oratory came to speak the funeral oration. I desired Monsieur de Tulle to bid him come
down, and to mount the pulpit in his place; since nothing could
sustain the beauty of the spectacle, and the excellence of the
music, but the force of his eloquence. My child, this young man
trembled when he began, and we all trembled for him. Our ears
were at first struck with a provincial accent; he is of Marseilles,
and called Lené. But as he recovered from his confusion, he became so brilliant; established himself so well; gave so just a measure of praise to the deceased; touched with so much address and
delicacy all the passages in his life where delicacy was required;
placed in so true a light all that was most worthy of admiration;
employed all the charms of expression, all the masterly strokes
of eloquence, with so much propriety and so much grace, that
every one present, without exception, burst into applause, charmed
with so perfect, so finished a performance. He is twenty-eight
years of age, the intimate friend of M. de Tulle, who accompanied him when he left the assembly. We were for naming him

the Chevalier Mascaron, and I think he will even surpass his friend. As for the music, it was fine beyond all description. Baptiste exerted himself to the utmost, and was assisted by all the king's musicians. There was an addition made to that fine "Miserere," and there was a "Libera" which filled the eyes of the whole assembly with tears; I do not think the music in heaven could exceed it. There were several prelates present. I desired Guitaut to look for the good Bishop of Marseilles, but we could not see him. I whispered him, that if it had been the funeral oration of any person living, to whom he might have made his court by it, he would not have failed to have been there. This little pleasantry made us laugh, in spite of the solemnity of the ceremony. My dear child, what a strange letter is this! I fancy I have almost lost my senses! What is this long account to you? To tell the truth, I have satisfied my love of description.

Written from Paris, May 6th, 1672, to her daughter.

TO MADAME DE GRIGNAN

WHEN we reckon without Providence, we must frequently reckon twice. I was dressed from head to foot by eight o'clock; I had drunk my coffee, heard mass, taken leave of everybody, the mules were loaded, and the tinkling of their bells gave me notice that it was time to mount my litter; my room was full of people, entreating me not to think of setting out on account of the heavy rain which had fallen incessantly for several days, and was then pouring more violently than ever; but I resisted all their arguments, resolving to abide by the promise I made you in my letter of yesterday, of being with you by Thursday, at furthest: at that very instant, in came M. de Grignan in his nightgown and slippers, and talked to me very gravely of the rashness of such an undertaking, saying that the muleteer would not be able to follow the litter; that my mules would fall into some ditch on the road; that my people would be so wet and fatigued that they would not be able to lend me assistance; so that I changed my mind in a moment, and yielded to his sage remonstrances: and now, my dear child, the trunks are brought back, the mules are unharnessed, the footmen and maids are drying themselves by the fire, for they were wet

through in only crossing the courtyard; and I dispatch you this
messenger, knowing your goodness will make you uneasy, and
wishing to lessen my own uneasiness, being very anxious about
your health; for this man will either bring me word here, or
meet one on the road.   In short, my dear, he will be with you
at Grignan on Thursday instead of me; and I shall set out the
first moment it pleases God and M. de Grignan, who is become
absolute master of me, and well knows my reasons for wishing
so much to be at Grignan.   I should be glad if this affair could
be kept a secret from M. de la Garde, for he will take a most
unmerciful pleasure in finding everything turn out as he foretold; but let him take care, and not grow vain upon this pretended gift of prophecy.

                                                    Lambesc, 1672.

THE EARL OF SHAFTESBURY

(ANTHONY ASHLEY COOPER, THIRD EARL OF SHAFTESBURY)

(1671–1713)

NTHONY ASHLEY COOPER, third Earl of Shaftesbury, was born in London, February 26th, 1671. He had for a teacher no less a person than John Locke, by whom he was subjected to an experimental system of education which succeeded so well that at the age of eleven Shaftesbury had already acquired the mastery of the classical languages for which he was noted. His chief work, "Characteristics of Men, Manners, Opinions, and Times," appeared in 1711. His "Inquiry concerning Virtue" and other notable essays were included in it. He died at Naples, February 15th, 1713.

DEGENERACY AND THE PASSIONS

IT HAPPENS with mankind that whilst some are by necessity confined to labor, others are provided with abundance of all things by the pains and labor of inferiors. Now, if amongst the superior and easy sort there be not something of fit and proper employment raised in the room of what is wanting in common labor and toil; if instead of an application to any sort of work, such as has a good and honest end in society (as letters, sciences, arts, husbandry, public affairs, economy, or the like), there be a thorough neglect of all duty or employment, a settled idleness, supineness, and inactivity; this of necessity must occasion a most relaxed and dissolute state; it must produce a total disorder of the passions, and break out in the strangest irregularities imaginable.

We see the enormous growth of luxury in capital cities, such as have been long the seat of empire. We see what improvements are made in vice of every kind, where numbers of men are maintained in lazy opulence, and wanton plenty. It is otherwise with those who are taken up in honest and due employment and have been well inured to it from their youth. This we may observe in the hardy remote provincials, the inhabitants of smaller towns, and the industrious sort of common people; where it is rare to meet with any instances of those irregularities, which are known in courts and palaces, and in the rich foundations of easy and pampered priests.

Now if what we have advanced concerning an inward constitution be real and just; if it be true that Nature works by a just order and regulation as well in the passions and affections as in the limbs and organs which she forms; if it appears withal, that she has so constituted this inward part, that nothing is so essential to it as exercise; and no exercise is so essential as that of social or natural affection: it follows that where this is removed or weakened, the inward part must necessarily suffer and be impaired. Let indolence, indifference, and insensibility be studied as an art, or cultivated with the utmost care; the passions thus restrained will force their prison, and in one way or other procure their liberty, and find full employment. They will be sure to create to themselves unusual and unnatural exercise, where they are cut off from such as is natural and good. And thus in the room of orderly and natural affection, new and unnatural must be raised, and all inward order and economy destroyed.

One must have a very imperfect idea of the order of nature in the formation and structure of animals to imagine that so great a principle, so fundamental a part as that of natural affection should possibly be lost or impaired, without any inward ruin or subversion of the temper and frame of mind.

Whoever is the least versed in this moral kind of architecture will find the inward fabric so adjusted and the whole so nicely built, that the barely extending of a single passion a little too far, or the continuance of it too long, is able to bring irrecoverable ruin and misery. He will find this experienced in the ordinary case of frenzy and distraction; when the mind, dwelling too long upon one subject (whether prosperous or calamitous), sinks under the weight of it, and proves what the necessity is, of a due balance and counterpoise in the affections. He will find that in every different creature, and distinct sex, there is a different and distinct order, set, or suit of passions, proportionable to the different order of life, the different functions, and capacities assigned to each. As the operations and effects are different, so are the springs and causes in each system. The inside work is fitted to the outward action and performance. So that where habits or affections are dislodged, misplaced, or changed; where those belonging to one species are intermixed with those belonging to another, there must of necessity be confusion and disturbance within.

All this we may observe easily, by comparing the more perfect with the imperfect natures, such as are imperfect from their birth, by having suffered violence within, in their earliest form and inmost matrix. We know how it is with monsters, such as are compounded of different kinds, or different sexes. Nor are they less monsters, who are misshapen or distorted in an inward part. The ordinary animals appear unnatural and monstrous, when they lose their proper instincts, forsake their kind, neglect their offspring, and pervert those functions or capacities bestowed by nature. How wretched must it be, therefore, for Man, of all other creatures, to lose that sense and feeling, which is proper to him as a man, and suitable to his character and genius! How unfortunate must it be for a creature, whose dependence on society is greater than any other's, to lose that natural affection by which he is prompted to the good and interest of his species, and community! Such, indeed, is man's natural share of this affection, that he, of all other creatures, is plainly the least able to bear solitude. Nor is anything more apparent than that there is naturally in every man such a degree of social affection as inclines him to seek the familiarity and friendship of his fellows. It is here that he lets loose a passion, and gives reins to a desire, which can hardly by any struggle or inward violence be withheld; or if it be, is sure to create a sadness, dejection, and melancholy in the mind. For whoever is unsociable, and voluntarily shuns society, or commerce with the world, must of necessity be morose and ill-natured. He, on the other side, who is withheld by force or accident, finds in his temper the ill effects of this restraint. The inclination, when suppressed, breeds discontent; and, on the contrary, affords a healing and enlivening joy, when acting at its liberty, and with full scope: as we may see particularly, when, after a time of solitude and long absence, the heart is opened, the mind disburdened, and the secrets of the breast unfolded to a bosom friend.

This we see yet more remarkably instanced in persons of the most elevated stations; even in princes, monarchs, and those who seem by their condition to be above ordinary human commerce, and who affect a sort of distant strangeness from the rest of mankind. But their carriage is not the same towards all men. The wiser and better sort, it is true, are often held at a distance as unfit for their intimacy or secret trust. But, to compensate this, there are others substituted in their room who, though they have the least merit, and are perhaps the most vile and contemptible of men, are sufficient, however, to serve the purpose of an imaginary friendship, and can become favorites in form. These are the subjects of humanity in the Great. For these, we see them often in concern and pain; in these, they easily confide; to these, they can with pleasure communicate their power and greatness,— be open, free, generous, confiding, bountiful; as rejoicing in the action itself: having no intention or aim beyond it; and their interest, in respect of policy, often standing a quite contrary way. But where neither the love of mankind, nor the passion for favorites prevails, the tyrannical temper fails not to show itself in its proper colors, and to the life, with all the bitterness, cruelty, and mistrust, which belong to that solitary and gloomy state of uncommunicative and unfriendly greatness. Nor needs there any particular proof from history, or present time, to second this remark.

Thus it may appear, how much natural affection is predominant; how it is inwardly joined to us, and implanted in our natures; how interwoven with our other passions; and how essential to that regular motion and course of our affections, on which our happiness and self-enjoyment so immediately depend.

And thus we have demonstrated, that as, on one side, to have the natural and good affections is to have the chief means and power of self-enjoyment, so, on the other side, to want them is certain misery and ill.

From « Inquiry concerning Virtue. »

PERCY BYSSHE SHELLEY

(1792–1822)

SHELLEY wrote a considerable number of essays which were edited by Mrs. Shelley after his death. All of them show the effects of his inclination to metaphysics, which was even stronger than that of Coleridge. His prose is often remarkable, but it does not demonstrate the genius which makes his verse unmistakably the product of one of the greatest lyric poets of modern times. Born in Sussex, England, August 4th, 1792, Shelley was schooled for six years at Eton and then sent to the University of Oxford which expelled him for writing a pamphlet on «The Necessity of Atheism.» In the year of his expulsion, he married Harriet Westbrook, a girl of sixteen, the daughter of a tavern keeper. Three years later he deserted her for Mary Wollstonecraft, whom, after the suicide of his wife in 1816, he married. In 1818 he went with her to Italy and they were living together at Spezia when Shelley was drowned, July 8th, 1822, by the capsizing of the boat in which he and his friend, Edward Williams, were sailing on the bay of Spezia. Shelley's body was recovered and burned in the presence of Byron, Leigh Hunt, and Trelawney.

BENEVOLENCE

THERE is a class of emotions which we instinctively avoid. A human being, such as is man considered in his origin, a child a month old, has a very imperfect consciousness of the existence of other natures resembling itself. All the energies of its being are directed to the extinction of the pains with which it is perpetually assailed. At length it discovers that it is surrounded by natures susceptible of sensations similar to its own. It is very late before children attain to this knowledge. If a child observes, without emotion, its nurse or its mother suffering acute pain, it is attributable rather to ignorance than insensibility. So soon as the accents and gestures, significant of pain, are referred to the feelings which they express, they awaken in the mind of the beholder a desire that they should cease. Pain is thus apprehended to be evil for its own sake, without any other

necessary reference to the mind by which its existence is perceived than such as is indispensable to its perception. The tendencies of our original sensations, indeed, all have for their object
the preservation of our individual being. But these are passive
and unconscious. In proportion as the mind acquires an active
power, the empire of these tendencies becomes limited. Thus an
infant, a savage, and a solitary beast, is selfish, because its mind
is incapable of receiving an accurate intimation of the nature of
pain as existing in beings resembling itself. The inhabitant of
a highly civilized community will more acutely sympathize with
the sufferings and enjoyments of others than the inhabitant of a
society of a less degree of civilization. He who shall have cultivated his intellectual powers by familiarity with the highest
specimens of poetry and philosophy will usually sympathize more
than one engaged in the less refined functions of manual labor.
Every one has experience of the fact that to sympathize with
the sufferings of another is to enjoy a transitory oblivion of his
own.

The mind thus acquires, by exercise, a habit, as it were, of
perceiving and abhorring evil, however remote from the immediate sphere of sensations with which that individual mind is conversant. Imagination or mind employed in prophetically imaging
forth its objects is that faculty of human nature on which every
gradation of its progress, nay, every, the minutest, change depends. Pain or pleasure, if subtly analyzed, will be found to consist entirely in prospect. The only distinction between the selfish
man and the virtuous man is that the imagination of the former
is confined within a narrow limit, whilst that of the latter em-
braces a comprehensive circumference. In this sense, wisdom
and virtue may be said to be inseparable, and criteria of each
other. Selfishness is the offspring of ignorance and mistake; it
is the portion of unreflecting infancy, and savage solitude, or of
those whom toil or evil occupations have blunted or rendered
torpid; disinterested benevolence is the product of a cultivated
imagination, and has an intimate connection with all the arts
which add ornament, or dignity, or power, or stability to the social state of man. Virtue is thus entirely a refinement of civilized life; a creation of the human mind; or, rather, a combination
which it has made, according to elementary rules contained
within itself, of the feelings suggested by the relations established between man and man.

All the theories which have refined and exalted humanity, or those which have been devised as alleviations of its mistakes and evils, have been based upon the elementary emotions of disinterestedness, which we feel to constitute the majesty of our nature. Patriotism, as it existed in the ancient republics, was never, as has been supposed, a calculation of personal advantages. When Mutius Scævola thrust his hand into the burning coals, and Regulus returned to Carthage, and Epicharis sustained the rack silently, in the torments of which she knew that she would speedily perish, rather than betray the conspirators to the tyrant, these illustrious persons certainly made a small estimate of their private interest. If it be said that they sought posthumous fame, instances are not wanting in history which prove that men have even defied infamy for the sake of good. But there is a great error in the world with respect to the selfishness of fame. It is certainly possible that a person should seek distinction as a medium of personal gratification. But the love of fame is frequently no more than a desire that the feelings of others should confirm, illustrate, and sympathize with our own. In this respect it is allied with all that draws us out of ourselves. It is the "last infirmity of noble minds." Chivalry was likewise founded on the theory of self-sacrifice. Love possesses so extraordinary a power over the human heart, only because disinterestedness is united with the natural propensities. These propensities themselves are comparatively impotent in cases where the imagination of pleasure to be given, as well as to be received, does not enter into the account. Let it not be objected that patriotism, and chivalry, and sentimental love, have been the fountains of enormous mischief. They are cited only to establish the proposition that, according to the elementary principles of mind, man is capable of desiring and pursuing good for its own sake.

Complete. From «Speculations on Morals.»

ON GOOD AND BAD ACTIONS

THE internal influence, derived from the constitution of the mind from which they flow, produces that peculiar modification of actions which makes them intrinsically good or evil.

To attain an apprehension of the importance of this distinction, let us visit, in imagination, the proceedings of some metropolis. Consider the multitude of human beings who inhabit it, and survey, in thought, the actions of the several classes into which they are divided. Their obvious actions are apparently uniform: the stability of human society seems to be maintained sufficiently by the uniformity of the conduct of its members, both with regard to themselves, and with regard to others. The laborer arises at a certain hour, and applies himself to the task enjoined him. The functionaries of government and law are regularly employed in their offices and courts. The trader holds a train of conduct from which he never deviates. The ministers of religion employ an accustomed language, and maintain a decent and equable regard. The army is drawn forth, the motions of every soldier are such as they were expected to be; the general commands, and his words are echoed from troop to troop. The domestic actions of men are, for the most part, undistinguishable one from the other, at a superficial glance. The actions which are classed under the general appellation of marriage, education, friendship, etc., are perpetually going on, and, to a superficial glance, are similar one to the other.

But, if we would see the truth of things, they must be stripped of this fallacious appearance of uniformity. In truth, no one action has, when considered in its whole extent, any essential resemblance with any other. Each individual who composes the vast multitude which we have been contemplating has a peculiar frame of mind, which, whilst the features of the great mass of his actions remain uniform, impresses the minuter lineaments with its peculiar hues. Thus, whilst his life, as a whole, is like the lives of other men, in detail it is most unlike, and the more subdivided the actions become; that is, the more they enter into that class which have a vital influence on the happiness of others and his own, so much the more are they distinct from those of other men.

> ———" Those little, nameless unremembered acts
> Of kindness and of love,"

as well as those deadly outrages which are inflicted by a look, a word — or less — the very refraining from some faint and most evanescent expression of countenance; these flow from a profounder source than the series of our habitual conduct, which, it has been already said, derives its origin from without. These are the actions, and such as these, which make human life what it is, and are the fountains of all the good and evil with which

Its entire surface is so widely and impartially overspread; and though they are called minute, they are called so in compliance with the blindness of those who cannot estimate their importance. It is in the due appreciating the general effects of their peculiarities, and in cultivating the habit of acquiring decisive knowledge respecting the tendencies arising out of them in particular cases, that the most important part of moral science consists. The deepest abyss of these vast and multitudinous caverns it is necessary that we should visit.

This is the difference between social and individual man. Not that this distinction is to be considered definite, or characteristic of one human being as compared with another, it denotes rather two classes of agency, common in a degree to every human being. None is exempt, indeed, from that species of influence which affects, as it were, the surface of his being, and gives the specific outline to his conduct. Almost all that is ostensible submits to that legislature created by the general representation of the past feelings of mankind — imperfect as it is from a variety of causes, as it exists in the government, the religion, and domestic habits. Those who do not nominally, yet actually, submit to the same power. The external features of their conduct, indeed, can no more escape it than the clouds can escape from the stream of the wind; and his opinion, which he often hopes he has dispassionately secured from all contagion of prejudice and vulgarity, would be found, on examination, to be the inevitable excrescence of the very usages from which he vehemently dissents. Internally all is conducted otherwise; the efficiency, the essence, the vitality of actions, derives its color from what is no way contributed to from any external source. Like the plant, which, while it derives the accident of its size and shape from the soil in which it springs, and is cankered, or distorted, or inflated, yet retains those qualities which essentially divide it from all others; so that hemlock continues to be poison, and the violet does not cease to emit its odor in whatever soil it may grow.

We consider our own nature too superficially. We look on all that in ourselves with which we can discover a resemblance in others; and consider those resemblances as the materials of moral knowledge. It is in the differences that it actually consists.

Complete. From « Speculations on Morals. »

ANCIENT LITERATURE AND MODERN PROGRESS

THE modern nations of the civilized world owe the progress which they have made — as well in those physical sciences in which they have already excelled their masters, as in the moral and intellectual inquiries, in which, with all the advantage of the experience of the latter, it can scarcely be said that they have yet equaled them — to what is called the Revival of Learning; that is, the study of the writers of the age which preceded and immediately followed the government of Pericles, or of subsequent writers, who were, so to speak, the rivers flowing from those immortal fountains. And though there seems to be a principle in the modern world, which, should circumstances analogous to those which modeled the intellectual resources of the age to which we refer into so harmonious a proportion again arise, would arrest and perpetuate them, and consign their results to a more equal, extensive, and lasting improvement of the condition of man — though justice and the true meaning of human society are, if not more accurately, more generally understood; though perhaps men know more, and therefore are more, as a mass, yet this principle has never been called into action, and requires indeed a universal and almost appalling change in the system of existing things. The study of modern history is the study of kings, financiers, statesmen, and priests. The history of ancient Greece is the study of legislators, philosophers, and poets; it is the history of men, compared with the history of titles. What the Greeks were was a reality, not a promise. And what we are and hope to be is derived, as it were, from the influence and inspiration of these glorious generations.

Whatever tends to afford a further illustration of the manners and opinions of those to whom we owe so much, and who were, perhaps, on the whole, the most perfect specimens of humanity of whom we have authentic record, were infinitely valuable. Let us see their errors, their weaknesses, their daily actions, their familiar conversation, and catch the tone of their society. When we discover how far the most admirable community ever framed was removed from that perfection to which human society is impelled by some active power within each bosom to aspire, how great ought to be our hopes, how resolute our struggles. For the Greeks of the Periclean age were widely different from us. It is to be lamented that no modern writer has hitherto dared to show them precisely as they were. Barthélemi cannot be denied the praise of industry and system; but he never forgets that he is a Christian and a Frenchman. Wieland, in his delightful novels, makes, indeed, a very tolerable Pagan, but cherishes, too, many political prejudices, and refrains from diminishing the interest of his romances by painting sentiments in which no European of modern times can possibly sympathize. There is no book which shows the Greeks precisely as they were; they seem all written for children, with the caution that no practice or sentiment highly inconsistent with our present manners should be mentioned, lest those manners should receive outrage and violation. But there are many to whom the Greek language is inaccessible, who ought not to be excluded by this prudery from possessing an exact and comprehensive conception of the history of man; for there is no knowledge concerning what man has been and may be, from partaking of which a person can depart, without becoming in some degree more philosophical, tolerant, and just.

From an unfinished essay on
«Athenian Literature.»

IX—215

SIR PHILIP SIDNEY

(1554–1586)

IR PHILIP SIDNEY, author of "Arcadia," and the "Defense of Poesy" was born in Kent, England, November 29th, 1554. After leaving the University of Oxford, he traveled several years in various European countries "to complete his education." On his return he came into such high favor with Queen Elizabeth that she called him one of the "jewels of her crown." At the age of twenty-two he was pronounced "one of the ripest statemen in Europe," by no less a judge of statesmanship than William the Silent. This early ripeness of intellect is attested by his "Arcadia," his "Sonnets," his "Defense of Poesy," and other works he left behind when he died at the early age of thirty-two, as a result of a wound received at the battle of Zutphen, September 22d, 1586. It is said by the critical that the story of his generosity in passing to a dying soldier the cup of water he was about to drink when wounded at Zutphen is not sufficiently attested to be regarded as historical, but it is one of the things which it is well to believe on the general principle that it is much easier for the critical to assert a negative than to prove it.

THE USES OF POETRY

SINCE poetry is of all human learnings the most ancient, and of most fatherly antiquity, as from whence other learnings have taken their beginnings; since it is so universal that no learned nation doth despise it, nor barbarous nation is without it; since both Roman and Greek gave such divine names unto it, the one of prophesying, the other of making, and that indeed that name of making is fit for him, considering that where all other arts retain themselves within their subject, and receive, as it were, their being from it, the poet only, only bringeth his own stuff, and doth not learn a conceit out of a matter, but maketh matter for a conceit; since neither his description nor end containeth any evil, the thing described cannot be evil; since his effects be so good as to teach goodness, and delight the learners of it; since therein (namely, in moral doctrine, the chief of all knowl-

edges) he doth not only far pass the historian, but, for instruct-
ing, is well nigh comparable to the philosopher; for moving,
leaveth him behind him; since the Holy Scripture (wherein there
is no uncleanness) hath whole parts in it poetical, and that even
our Savior Christ vouchsafed to use the flowers of it; since all
his kinds are not only in their united forms, but in their severed
dissections fully commendable; I think, and think I think rightly,
the laurel crown appointed for triumphant captains, doth worthily,
of all other learnings, honor the poet's triumph.

But because we have ears as well as tongues, and that the
lightest reasons that may be will seem to weigh greatly if nothing be put in the counterbalance, let us hear, and, as well as we
can, ponder what objections be made against this art, which may
be worthy either of yielding or answering.

First, truly, I note, not only in these μισομούσοι, poet haters,
but in all that kind of people who seek a praise by dispraising
others, that they do prodigally spend a great many wandering
words in quips and scoffs, carping and taunting at each thing,
which, by stirring the spleen, may stay the brain from a thorough
beholding the worthiness of the subject. Those kind of objections, as they are full of a very idle uneasiness (since there is
nothing of so sacred a majesty but that an itching tongue may
rub itself upon it), so deserve they no other answer, but, instead
of laughing at the jest, to laugh at the jester. We know a playing wit can praise the discretion of an ass, the comfortableness
of being in debt, and the jolly commodities of being sick of the
plague; so of the contrary side, if we will turn Ovid's verse,—

« Ut lateat virtus proximitate mali.»

" That good lies hid in nearness of the evil," Agrippa will be as
merry in the showing the Vanity of Science as Erasmus was in
the commending of Folly; neither shall any man or matter escape some touch of these smiling railers. But for Erasmus and
Agrippa, they had another foundation than the superficial part
would promise. Marry, these other pleasant fault-finders, who
will correct the verb before they understand the noun, and con-
fute others' knowledge before they confirm their own; I would
have them only remember that scoffing cometh not of wisdom;
so as the best title in true English they got with their merri-
ments is to be called good fools; for so have our grave fore
fathers ever termed that humorous kind of jesters.

But that which giveth greatest scope to their scorning humor is rhyming and versing. It is already said, and, as I think, truly said, it is not rhyming and versing that maketh poesy; one may be a poet without versing, and a versifier without poetry. But yet, presuppose it were inseparable, as, indeed, it seemeth Scaliger judgeth truly, it were an inseparable commendation; for if "oratio" next to "ratio," speech next to reason, be the greatest gift bestowed upon mortality, that cannot be praiseless which doth most polish that blessing of speech; which considereth each word, not only as a man may say by his forcible quality, but by his best-measured quantity; carrying even in themselves a harmony; without, perchance, number, measure, order, proportion be in our time grown odious.

But lay aside the just praise it hath, by being the only fit speech for music — music, I say, the most divine striker of the senses; thus much is undoubtedly true, that if reading be foolish without remembering, memory being the only treasure of knowledge, those words which are fittest for memory are likewise most convenient for knowledge. Now, that verse far exceedeth prose in the knitting up of the memory, the reason is manifest: the words, besides their delight, which hath a great affinity to memory, being so set as one cannot be lost, but the whole work fails: which, accusing itself, calleth the remembrance back to itself, and so most strongly confirmeth it. Besides, one word so, as it were, begetting another, as, be it in rhyme or measured verse, by the former a man shall have a near guess to the follower. Lastly, even they that have taught the art of memory have showed nothing so apt for it as a certain room divided into many places, well and thoroughly known; now that hath the verse in effect perfectly, every word having his natural seat, which seat must needs make the word remembered. But what needs more in a thing so known to all men? Who is it that ever was a scholar that doth not carry away some verses of Virgil, Horace, or Cato, which in his youth he learned, and even to his old age serve him for hourly lessons? as, —

"Percontatorem fugito: nam garrulus idem est.
Dum sibi quisque placet credula turba sumus."

But the fitness it hath for memory is notably proved by all delivery of arts, wherein, for the most part, from grammar to logic, mathematics, physic, and the rest, the rules chiefly necessary to be borne away are compiled in verses. So that verse being in itself sweet and orderly, and being best for memory, the only handle of knowledge, it must be in jest that any man can speak against it.

From « Defense of Poesy. »

THE UNIVERSE NO CHANCE MEDLEY

You say, because we know not the causes of things, therefore Fear was the mother of Superstition; nay, because we know that each effect hath a cause, that hath engendered a true and lively devotion. For this goodly work of which we are, and in which we live, hath not his being by chance; on which opinion it is beyond marvel by what chance any brain could stumble. For if it be eternal, as you would seem to conceive of it, eternity and chance are things unsufferable together. For that is chanceable which happeneth; and if it happen, there was a time before it happened when it might have not happened; or else it did not happen, and so, if chanceable, not eternal. And as absurd it is to think that, if it had a beginning, his beginning was derived from chance; for chance could never make all things of nothing: and if there were substances before which by chance should meet to make up this work, thereon follows another bottomless pit of absurdities. For then those substances must needs have been from ever, and so eternal; and that eternal causes should bring forth chanceable effects is as sensible as that the sun should be the author of darkness. Again if it were chanceable, then was it not necessary; whereby you take away all consequents. But we see in all things, in some respect or other, necessity of consequence; therefore, in reason, we must needs know that the causes were necessary. Lastly, chance is variable, or else it is not to be called chance; but we see this work is steady and permanent. If nothing but chance had glued those pieces of this All, the heavy parts would have gone infinitely downward, the light infinitely upward, and so never have met to have made up this goodly body. For, before there was a heaven or earth, there was neither a heaven to stay the height of the ring, or an earth which, in respect of the round walls of heaven, should become a centre. Lastly, perfect order, perfect beauty, perfect constancy,— if these be the children of chance, let wisdom be counted the root of wickedness.

But, you will say, it is so by nature; as much as if you said it is so because it is so. If you mean of many natures conspiring together, as in a popular government, to establish this fair estate, as if the elementish and ethereal parts should in their town-house set down the bounds of each one's office, then consider what follows: that there must needs have been a wisdom which made them concur. For their natures, being absolutely contrary, in nature rather would have sought each other's ruin than have served as well-consorted parts to such an unexpressible harmony. For that contrary things should meet to make up a perfection without force and wisdom above their powers is absolutely impossible, unless you will fly to that hissed-out opinion of chance again. But you may perhaps affirm that one universal nature, which hath been forever, is the knitting-together of these many parts to such an excellent unity. If you mean a nature of wisdom, goodness, and providence, which knows what it doth, then say you that which I seek of you, and cannot conclude those blasphemies with which you defiled your mouth and mine ears. But if you mean a nature as we speak of the fire, which goeth upward it knows not why, and of the nature of the sea, which in ebbing and flowing seems to observe so just a dance and yet understands no music, it is but still the same absurdity superscribed with another title. For this word One being attributed to that which is All is but one mingling of many, and many ones; as in a less matter when we say one kingdom which contains many cities, or one city which contains many persons; wherein the under-ones, if there be not a superior power and wisdom, cannot by nature regard any preservation but of themselves; no more we see they do, since the water willingly quenches the fire, and drowns the earth, so far are they from a conspired unity; but that a right heavenly nature, indeed, as it were unnaturing them, doth so bridle them.

Again, it is as absurd in nature that from a unity many contraries should proceed, still kept in a unity, as that from the number of contrarieties a unity should arise. I say still, if you banish both a singularity and a plurality of judgment from among them, then, if so earthly a mind can lift itself up so high, do but conceive how a thing whereto you give the highest and most excellent kind of being, which is eternity, can be of a base and vilest degree of being, and next to a not-being, which is so to be as not to enjoy his own being. I will not here call all your senses to witness, which can hear nor see nothing which yields not most evident evidence of the unspeakableness of that wisdom, each thing being directed to an end of preservation; so proper effects of judgment as speaking and laughing are of mankind. But what mad fury can ever so inveigle any conceit as to see our mortal and corruptible selves to have a reason, and that this universality, whereof we are but the least pieces, should be utterly devoid thereof? As if one should say that one's foot might be wise, and himself foolish. This heard I once alleged against such a godless mind as yours, who, being driven to acknowledge this beastly absurdity, that our bodies should be better than the whole world if it had the knowledge whereof the other were void, he sought, not able to answer directly, to shift it off in this sort: that, if that reason were true, then must it follow also that the world must have in it a spirit that could write and read too, and be learned, since that was in us commendable. Wretched fool! not considering that books be but supplies of defects, and so are praised because they help our want, and therefore cannot be incident to the Eternal Intelligence, which needs no recording of opinions to confirm his knowledge, no more than the sun wants wax to be the fuel of his glorious lightfulness.

This world, therefore, cannot otherwise consist but by a mind of wisdom which governs it, which whether you will allow to be the Creator thereof, as undoubtedly he is, or the soul and governor thereof, most certain it is that, whether he govern all, or make all, his power is above either his creatures or his government. And if his power be above all things, then, consequently, it must needs be infinite, since there is nothing above it to limit it; for that beyond which there is nothing must needs be boundless and infinite. If his power be infinite, then likewise must his knowledge be infinite; for else there should be an infinite proportion of power which he should not know how to use, the unsensibleness whereof I think even you can conceive; and if infinite, then must nothing, no, not the estate of flies, which you with so unsavory scorn did jest at, be unknown to him; for if there were, then were his knowledge bounded, and so not infinite. If his knowledge and power be infinite, then must needs his goodness and justice march in the same rank; for infiniteness of power and knowledge, without like measure of goodness, must necessarily bring forth destruction and ruin, and not ornament and preservation.   Since, then, there is a God, and an all-knowing God, so as he seeth into the darkness of all natural secrets, which is the heart of man, and sees therein the deepest dissembled thoughts — nay, sees the thoughts before they be thought; since he is just to exercise his might, and mighty to perform his justice, assure thyself, most wicked woman, that hast so plaguily a corrupted mind as thou canst not keep thy sickness to thyself, but must most wickedly infect others — assure thyself, I say, for what I say depends of everlasting and unremovable causes, that the time will come when thou shalt know that power by feeling it, when thou shalt see his wisdom in the manifest-ing thy ugly shamefulness, and shalt only perceive him to have been a Creator in thy destruction.

From « Arcadia.» Book III.

LYDIA H. SIGOURNEY

(1791–1865)

YDIA HUNTLEY, who as Lydia H. Sigourney, became one of the most celebrated American authoresses of the first half of the nineteenth century, was born at Norwich, Connecticut, September 1st, 1791. Until her marriage in 1819 to Charles Sigourney she taught school, but when her husband's fortune became impaired she attempted professional writing in the hope of helping him, and succeeded probably much beyond her expectations. She wrote essays, poems, sketches, and stories in great numbers to supply the demand she had created. Her work was helpful to her generation and frequently has a decided literary quality. She died at Hartford, Connecticut, June 10th, 1865. Among her books are "Letters to Young Ladies," "Gleanings," "The Man of Uz and Other Poems," "Olive Leaves," and "Lucy Howard's Journal."

THE END OF ALL PERFECTION

I HAVE seen a man in the glory of his days, and in the pride of his strength. He was built like the strong oak, that strikes its root deep in the earth — like the tall cedar, that lifts its head above the trees of the forest. He feared no danger — he felt no sickness — he wondered why any should groan or sigh at pain. His mind was vigorous like his body; he was perplexed at no intricacy, he was daunted at no obstacle. Into hidden things he searched, and what was crooked he made plain. He went forth boldly upon the face of the mighty deep. He surveyed the nations of the earth. He measured the distances of the stars, and called them by their names. He gloried in the extent of his knowledge, in the vigor of his understanding, and strove to search even into what the Almighty had concealed. And when I looked upon him, I said with the poet, "What a piece of work is man! how noble in reason! how infinite in faculties! in form and moving, how express and admirable! in action how like an angel! in apprehension how like a god!"

I returned — but his look was no more lofty, nor his step proud. His broken frame was like some ruined tower. His hairs were white and scattered, and his eye gazed vacantly upon the passers-by. The vigor of his intellect was wasted, and of all that he had gained by study, nothing remained. He feared when there was no danger, and where was no sorrow he wept. His decaying memory had become treacherous. It showed him only broken images of the glory that had departed. His house was to him like a strange land, and his friends were counted as enemies. He thought himself strong and healthful, while his feet tottered on the verge of the grave. He said of his son, "He is my brother"; of his daughter, "I know her not." He even inquired what was his own name. And as I gazed mournfully upon him, one who supported his feeble frame, and ministered to his many wants, said to me, "Let thine heart receive instruction, for thou hast seen an end of all perfection!"

I have seen a beautiful female, treading the first stages of youth, and entering joyfully into the pleasures of life. The glance of her eye was variable and sweet, and on her cheek trembled something like the first blush of the morning. Her lips moved, and there was melody, and when she floated in the dance, her light form, like the aspen, seemed to move with every breeze.

I returned — she was not in the dance. I sought her among her gay companions, but I found her not. Her eye sparkled not there — the music of her voice was silent. She rejoiced on earth no more. I saw a train — sable and slow-paced. Sadly they bore towards an open grave what once was animated and beautiful. As they drew near, they paused, and a voice broke the solemn silence: "Man that is born of a woman is of few days and full of misery. He cometh up, and is cut down like a flower, he fleeth as it were a shadow, and never continueth in one stay." Then they let down into the deep, dark pit, that maiden whose lips but a few days since were like the half-blown rosebud. I shuddered at the sound of clods falling upon the hollow coffin. Then I heard a voice saying, "Earth to earth, ashes to ashes, dust to dust." They covered her with the damp soil, and the uprooted turf of the valley, and turned again to their own homes. But one mourner lingered to cast himself upon the tomb. And as he wept he said, "There is no beauty, nor grace, nor loveliness, but what vanisheth like the morning dew. I have seen an end of all perfection!"

I saw an infant, with a ruddy brow, and a form like polished ivory. Its motions were graceful, and its merry laughter made other hearts glad. Sometimes it wept,— and again it rejoiced,— when none knew why. But whether its cheek dimpled with smiles, or its blue eyes shone more brilliant through tears, it was beautiful. It was beautiful because it was innocent. And careworn and sinful men admired, when they beheld it. It was like the first blossom which some cherished plant has put forth, whose cup sparkles with a dewdrop, and whose head reclines upon the parent stem.

Again I looked. It had become a child. The lamp of reason had beamed into its mind. It was simple, and single-hearted, and a follower of the truth. It loved every little bird that sang in the trees, and every fresh blossom. Its heart danced with joy as it looked around on this good and pleasant world. It stood like a lamb before its teachers — it bowed its ear to instruction — it walked in the way of knowledge. It was not proud, nor stubborn, nor envious, and it had never heard of the vices and vanities of the world. And when I looked upon it, I remembered our Savior's words, "Except ye become as little children, ye cannot enter into the kingdom of heaven."

I saw a man, whom the world calls honorable. Many waited for his smile. They pointed to the fields that were his, and talked of the silver and gold which he had gathered. They praised the stateliness of his domes, and extolled the honor of his family. But the secret language of his heart was, "By my wisdom have I gotten all this." So he returned no thanks to God, neither did he fear or serve him. As I passed along, I heard the complaints of the laborers, who had reaped his fields — and the cries of the poor, whose covering he had taken away. The sound of feasting and revelry was in his mansion, and the unfed beggar came tottering from his door. But he considered not that the cries of the oppressed were continually entering into the ears of the Most High. And when I knew that this man was the docile child whom I had loved, the beautiful infant on whom I had gazed with delight, I said in my bitterness, "Now have I seen an end of all perfection!" And I laid my mouth in the dust.

Complete.

JEAN CHARLES LEONARD DE SISMONDI

(1773–1842)

ISMONDI, the celebrated historian of Italy and of Italian literature, was born at Geneva, Switzerland, May 9th, 1773. His father, a village pastor, was named "Simonde," a patronymic which the son for literary and other purposes altered to the more aristocratic one of "de Sismondi." The Simonde family emigrated from Geneva during the French Revolution, and after spending a short time in England, settled at Pescia, near Lucca, in Italy, where Sismondi received the bent which resulted in his most celebrated works. His "History of the Italian Republics" appeared between 1807 and 1818, and his "Literature of the South of Europe" between 1813 and 1829. He wrote, besides, a "History of France," a number of works on Political Economy and "Julia Severa," a historical novel, which appeared in 1829. He died at Geneva, June 25th, 1842.

ROMANTIC LOVE AND PETRARCH'S POETRY

NEVER did passion burn more purely than in the love of Petrarch for Laura. Of all the erotic poets, he alone never expresses a single hope offensive to the purity of a heart which had been pledged to another. When Petrarch first beheld her, on the sixth of April, 1327, Laura was in the church of Avignon. She was the daughter of Audibert de Noves, and wife of Hugues de Sade, both of Avignon. When she died of the plague, on the sixth of April, 1348, she had been the mother of eleven children. Petrarch has celebrated, in upwards of three hundred sonnets, all the little circumstances of this attachment; those precious favors which, after an acquaintance of fifteen or twenty years, consisted at most of a kind word, a glance not altogether severe, a momentary expression of regret or tenderness at his departure, or a deeper paleness at the idea of losing her beloved and constant friend. Yet even these marks of an attachment so pure and unobstrusive, and which he had so often struggled to subdue, were repressed by the coldness of Laura, who, to preserve her lover, cautiously abstained from giving the least encouragement to his love. She avoided his presence, except at church, in the brilliant levees of the papal court, or in the country, where, surrounded by her friends, she is described by Petrarch as exhibiting the semblance of a queen, pre-eminent amongst them all in the grace of her figure, and the brilliancy of her beauty.   It does not appear that, in the whole course of these twenty years, the poet ever addressed her, unless in the presence of witnesses.   An interview with her alone would surely have been celebrated in a thousand verses; and, as he has left us four sonnets on the good fortune he enjoyed in having an opportunity of picking up her glove, we may fairly presume that he would not have passed over in silence so happy a circumstance as a private interview.   There is no poet, in any language, so perfectly pure as Petrarch, so completely above all reproach of levity and immorality; and this merit, which is due equally to the poet and to his Laura, is still more remarkable, when we consider that the models which he followed were by no means entitled to the same praise.   The verses of the Troubadours and of the Trouveres were very licentious.   The court of Avignon, at which Laura lived, the Babylon of the West, as the poet himself often terms it, was filled with the most shameful corruption; and even the Popes, more especially Clement V. and Clement VI. had afforded examples of great depravity.   Indeed, Petrarch himself, in his intercourse with other ladies, was by no means so reserved.   For Laura he had conceived a sort of religious and enthusiastic passion; such as mystics imagine they feel towards the Deity, and such as Plato supposes to be the bond of union between elevated minds.   The poets who have succeeded Petrarch have amused themselves with giving representations of a similar passion, of which, in fact, they had little or no experience.

In order to appreciate the full beauty of Petrarch's sonnets, it would be necessary to write the history of his attachment, as M. Ginguené has so ably done; and thus to assign to every sonnet the place to which its particular sentiment destines it.   But it would be even more necessary that I should myself be sensible of the excellence of these poems, and that I should feel that charm which has enchanted every nation and every age.   To this I must acknowledge that I am a stranger.   I could have wished, in order to comprehend and to become interested in the passion of Petrarch, that there should have been a somewhat better understanding between the lovers; that they should have had a more intimate knowledge of each other; and that, by this means, we might ourselves have been better acquainted with both.

I could have wished to have seen some impression made upon the sensibility of this loving and long-loved lady; to have seen her heart, as well as her mind, enlarging itself and yielding to the constancy and the purity of true friendship, since virtue denied a more tender return. It is tiresome to find the same veil, always shading not only the figure, but the intellect and the heart of the woman who is celebrated in these monotonous verses. If the poet had allowed us a fairer view of her, he would have been less likely to fall into exaggerations, into which my imagination, at least, is unable to follow him. How desirable would it be that he should have recalled her to our minds by thought, by feeling, and by passion, rather than by a perpetual play upon the words Laura (the laurel), and l'aura (the air). The first of these conceits, more especially, is incessantly repeated, nor merely in the poems alone. Throughout Petrarch's whole life, we are in doubt whether it is of Laura or of the laurel that he is enamored; so great is the emotion which he expresses, whenever he beholds the latter; so passionately does he mention it; and so frequently has he celebrated it in his verses. Nor is that personified heart, to which Petrarch perpetually addresses himself, less fatiguing. It speaks, it answers, it argues, it is ever upon his lips, in his eyes, and yet ever at a distance. He is always absent, and we cannot avoid wishing that during his banishment, he would for once cease to speak of it. Judging from these conceits, and from the continual personification of beings which have no personal attributes, it has always appeared to me that Petrarch is by no means so great a poet as Dante, because he is less of a painter. There is scarcely one of his sonnets, in which the leading idea is not completely at variance with the principles of painting, and which does not, therefore, escape from the imagination. Poetry may be called a happy union of two of the fine arts. It has borrowed its harmonies from music, and its images from painting. But to confound the two objects which poetry has thus in view is to be equally in error; whether we attempt, by an image, to represent a coincidence in sound, as when the laurel is put for Laura; or whether we wish to call up an image by sounds, as when, neglecting the rules of harmony, we produce a discordance suited to the object we design to paint, and make the serpents of which we are speaking hiss in our verses.

From «Literature of the South of Europe.»

SAMUEL SMILES

(1812–)

AMUEL SMILES was born at Haddington, Scotland, in 1812. He began life as a physician, practicing at Haddington and in Leeds. Becoming editor of the Leeds Times, he gave up medicine for journalism and essay writing, and in such books as "Character," "Thrift," and "Self-Help," he has almost created a school of his own. His essays are characterized by a wealth of incident and anecdote which makes them interesting and entertaining even when they are most didactic. Besides his essays Smiles wrote a "History of Ireland," a "Life of George Stephenson," "Brief Biographies," and "The Huguenots in France." From 1845 to 1866 he was an officer of various English railway companies. The whole tendency of his writings is to establish a more efficient faith in honesty and persistent industry as the basis of success in life and business.

MEN WHO CANNOT BE BOUGHT

Thou must be brave thyself,
If thou the truth would teach;
Live truly and thy life shall be
A great and noble creed.

'Tis a very good world we live in,
To lend, or to spend, or to give in;
But to beg, or to borrow, or to get a man's own
'Tis the very worst world that ever was known.
— *Bulwer Lytton.*

Good name in man or woman, dear my lord,
Is the immediate jewel of their souls:
Who steals my purse, steals trash: 'tis something, nothing,
'Twas mine, 'tis his, and has been slave to thousand;
But he that filches from me my good name,
Robs me of that which not enriches him,
And makes me poor indeed.
— *Shakespeare.*

L'honneur vaut mieux que l'argent.
— **French Proverb.**

FIRST, there are men who can be bought. There are rogues innumerable, who are ready to sell their bodies and souls for money and for drink. Who has not heard of the elections which have been made void through bribery and corruption? This is not the way to enjoy liberty or to keep it. The men who sell themselves are slaves; their buyers are dishonest and unprincipled. Freedom has its humbugs. "I'm standing on the soil of liberty," said an orator. "You ain't," replied a bootmaker in the audience. "You're standing in a pair of boots you never paid me for."

The tendency of men is ever to go with the majority — to go with the huzzas. "Majority," said Schiller, "what does that mean? Sense has ever centred in the few. Votes should be weighed, not counted. That state must sooner or later go to ruin where numbers sway and ignorance decides."

When the secession from the Scotch Church took place, Norman Macleod said it was a great trial to the flesh to keep by the unpopular side, and to act out what conscience dictated as the line of duty. Scorn and hissing greeted him at every turn. "I saw a tomb to-day," he says, in one of his letters, "in the chapel of Holyrood, with this inscription, 'Here lies an honest man!' I only wish to live in such a way as to entitle me to the same éloge."

The ignorant and careless are at the mercy of the unprincipled; and the ignorant are as yet greatly in the majority. When a French quack was taken before the Correctional Tribunal at Paris for obstructing the Pont Neuf, the magistrate said to him, "Sirrah! how is it you draw such crowds about you, and extract so much money from them in selling your 'infallible' rubbish?" "My lord," replied the quack, "how many people do you think cross the Pont Neuf in the hour?" "I don't know," said the judge. "Then I can tell you — about ten thousand; and how many of these do you think are wise?" "Oh, perhaps a hundred!" "It is too many," said the quack; "but I leave the hundred persons to you, and take the nine thousand and nine hundred for my customers!"

Men are bribed in all directions. They have no spirit of probity, self-respect, or manly dignity. If they had, they would spurn bribes in every form. Government servants are bribed to pass goods, fit or unfit for use. Hence soldiers' half-tanned shoes give way on a march; their shoddy coats become ragged;

their tinned provisions are found rotten. Captain Nares had a sad account to give of the feeding of his sailors while in the Arctic regions. All this is accomplished by bribery and corruption in the lower quarters of the civil service.

Much is done in the way of illicit commissions. A check finds its way to a certain official, and he passes the account. Thus many a man becomes rich upon a moderate salary. After a great act of corruption had been practiced by the servant of a public company, a notice was placed over the office door to this effect: "The servants of the company are not allowed to take bribes." The cook gets a commission from the tradesman; the butler has a secret understanding with the wine merchant.

"These illicit commissions," says the Times, "do much to poison business relations. But if the vice were ever to mount from the servants' hall or the market and invade any public office, there would be an end to efficiency or confidence in public men. It is all-important that the public service should be pure, and that no suspicion should rest on the name of any official in a post of confidence. It would be an evil day if it were generally suspected that civil servants took backsheesh or *pots de vin.*"

An inventor suggested a method for registering the number of persons entering an omnibus, but the secretary was unable to entertain it. "It is of no use to us," he said; "the machine which we want is one that will make our men honest, and that, I am afraid, we are not likely to meet with." We want honest men! is the cry everywhere. The police courts too often reveal the stealing and swindling of men in whom confidence has been placed; and the result is that they are dragged down from confidence to ruin. It is trustworthy character that is most wanted. Character is reliableness; convincing other men by your acts that you can be trusted.

Abroad it is the same. Russia, Egypt, and Spain are the worst. In Russia the corruption of public servants, even of the highest grade, is most gross. You must buy your way by gold. Bribery in every conceivable form is practiced — from arrangements between furnishers and the officials who should control them, to the direct handling over of the goods — is undeniably prevalent. The excuse is that the public servants are so badly paid. The Moscow and Petersburg Railway was constructed at great expense. Vast sums were paid to engineers and workmen, and stolen by overseers and directors. Prince Mentchikoff accompanied his Imperial Master in a jaunt through the capital, undertaken for the benefit of the Persian embassador, who was making a visit to the country. The Persian surveyed golden domes, granite pillars, glittering miles of shops, with true Oriental indifference. The Emperor at last bent toward his favorite and whispered with an air of vexation, "Can't we find anything that will astonish this fellow?" "Yes, your Majesty," replied the Prince; "show him the accounts of the Moscow and Petersburg Railway!" At Alexandria, in Egypt, the "leakage," as it is called, is enormous, unless bought off by gold. In Spain, every ship has to work its way into port after bribing the customs officers. The excuse is the same as in Russia; the civil servants of Spain cannot live except by taking bribes.

Even in republics men are apt and willing to be bribed. Money gets over many difficulties; it solves many problems. In America, the cream of republics, bribery is conducted in a wholesale way. The simple salary of an official is not sufficient. Even the highest in office is bribed by presents of carriages and horses, and even by hard cash. The most far-seeing and honest of American statesmen see that jobbery and corruption are fast undermining the efficiency of the administration, and debasing the standard of public virtue.

It has been the same all over the world. It does not matter what the form of government is called — whether a monarchy, an aristocracy, or a republic. It is not the form of government, but the men who administer it. Selfishly used, political power is a curse; intelligently and impartially used, it may be one of the greatest blessings to a community. If selfishness begins with the governing classes, woe to the country that is governed. The evil spreads downward, and includes all classes, even the poorest. The race of life becomes one for mere pelf and self. Principle is abandoned. Honesty is a forgotten virtue. Faith dies out, and society becomes a scramble for place and money.

Yet there are men who have refused to be bought, in all times and ages. Even the poorest, inspired by duty, have refused to sell themselves for money. Among the North American Indians a wish for wealth is considered unworthy of a brave man — so that the chief is often the poorest of his tribe. The best benefactors of the race have been poor men, among the Israelites, among the Greeks, and among the Romans. Elisha was at the plow when called to be a prophet, and Cincinnatus was in his fields when called to lead the armies of Rome. Socrates and Epaminondas were among the poorest men in Greece. Such, too, were the Galilean fishermen, the inspired founders of our faith.

Aristides was called The Just from his unbending integrity. His sense of justice was spotless, and his self-denial unimpeachable. He fought at Marathon, at Salamis, and commanded at the battle of Platea. Though he had borne the highest offices in the state, he died poor. Nothing could buy him; nothing could induce him to swerve from his duty. It is said that the Athenians became more virtuous from contemplating his bright example. In the representation of one of the tragedies of Æschylus, a sentence was uttered in favor of moral goodness, on which the eyes of the audience turned involuntarily from the actor to Aristides.

Phocion, the Athenian general, a man of great bravery and foresight, was surnamed The Good. Alexander the Great, when overrunning Greece, endeavored to win him from his loyalty. He offered him riches, and the choice of four cities in Asia. The answer of Phocion bespoke the spotless character of the man. "If Alexander really esteems me," he said, "let him leave me my honesty."

Yet Demosthenes, the eloquent, could be bought. When Harpalus, one of Alexander's chiefs, came to Athens, the orators had an eye upon his gold. Demosthenes was one of them. What is eloquence without honesty? On his visit to Harpalus, the chief perceived that Demosthenes was much pleased with one of the king's beautifully engraved cups. He desired him to take it in his hand that he might feel its weight. "How much might it bring?" asked Demosthenes. "It will bring you twenty talents," replied Harpalus. That night the cup was sent to Demosthenes, with twenty talents in it. The present was not refused. The circumstance led to the disgrace of the orator, and he soon after poisoned himself.

Cicero, on the other hand, refused all presents from friends, as well as from the enemies of his country. Some time after his assassination Cæsar found one of his grandsons with a book of Cicero's in his hands. The boy endeavored to hide it, but Cæsar took it from him. After having run over it, he returned it to the boy, saying, "My dear child, this was an eloquent man, and a lover of his country."

Bias, when asked why he did not, like others of his country-men, load himself with part of his property when all were obliged to fly, said, "Your wonder is without reason; I am carrying all my treasures with me."

When Diocletian had quitted the imperial purple for some time, Maximilian invited him to reassume the reins of government. Diocletian replied, "If I could show you the cabbages that I have planted with my own hands at Salona, and the fine melons that I have been ripening, and the delightful plantations I have made about my villa, I should no longer be urged to relinquish the enjoyment of happiness for the pursuit of power."

What he had worked for was his own, the fruit of his own labor and pains. He had imbibed the spirit of industry, which gives perseverance to the worker, enterprise to the warrior, and firmness to the statesman. Labor shuts up the first avenues to dishonesty; it opens a broader field for the display of every talent; and inspires with a new vigor the performance of every social and religious duty. Hence the Romans desired to call Diocletian back to his political duties.

Contentment is also better than luxury or power; indeed, it is natural wealth. Mary, sister of Elizabeth, often wished that she had been born a milkmaid instead of a queen. She would have been saved the torture of unrequited love, and the degradation of power through the hands of her ministers. Many martyrs would have been saved from burning.

Brave and honest men do not work for gold. They work for love, for honor, for character. When Socrates suffered death rather than abandon his views of right morality; when Las Casas endeavored to mitigate the tortures of the poor Indians, they had no thought of money or country. They worked for the elevation of all that thought, and for the relief of all that suffered.

When Michael Angelo was commanded by the Pope to undertake the direction of the works of St. Peter's, he consented only upon condition that he should receive no salary, but that he should labor "for the love of God alone." "Keep your money," said Wiertz of Brussels to a gentleman who wished to buy one of his pictures; "gold gives the deathblow to art." At the same time it must be confessed that Wiertz was a man of outré character.

In political life, place and money are too much in request. The gift of office, when not fairly earned by public service, proves often the corruption of morals. It is the substitution of an inferior motive for a patriotic one; and wherever it prevails from considerations of personal favoritism, it degrades politics and debases character.

Andrew Marvell was a patriot of the old Roman build. He lived in troublous times. He was born at Hull at the beginning of the reign of Charles I. When a young man, he spent four years at Trinity College, Cambridge. He afterward traveled through Europe. In Italy he met Milton, and continued his friend through life. On his return to England the civil war was raging. It does not appear that he took any part in the struggle, though he was always a defender and promoter of liberty. In 1660 he was elected member of Parliament for his native town, and during his membership he wrote to the mayor and his constituents by almost every post, telling them of the course of affairs in Parliament.

Marvell did not sympathize with Milton's antimonarchical tendencies. His biographer styles him "the friend of England, Liberty, and Magna Charta." He had no objections to a properly restricted monarchy, and therefore favored the Restoration. The people longed for it, believing that the return of Charles II. would prove the restoration of peace and loyalty. They were much mistaken. Marvell was appointed to accompany Lord Carlisle on an embassy to Russia, showing that he was not reckoned an enemy to the court. During his absence much evil had been done. The restored king was constantly in want of money. He took every method, by selling places and instituting monopolies, to supply his perpetual need. In one of Marvell's letters to his constituents he said, "The court is at the highest pitch of want and luxury, and the people are full of discontent." In a trial of two Quakers, Pen and Mead, at the Old Bailey, the recorder, among the rest, commended the Spanish Inquisition, saying "it would never be well till we had something like it."

The king continued to raise money unscrupulously, by means of his courtiers and apostate patriots. He bought them up by bribes of thousands of pounds. But Marvell was not to be bought. His satires upon the court and its parasites were published. They were read by all classes, from the king to the tradesman. The king determined to win him over. He was

SAMUEL SMILES

threatened, he was flattered, he was thwarted, he was caressed, he was beset with spies, he was waylaid by ruffians, and courted by beauties. But no Delilah could discover the secret of his strength. His integrity was proof alike against danger and against corruption. Against threats and bribes, pride is the ally of principle. In a court which held no man to be honest, and no woman chaste, this soft sorcery was cultivated to perfection; but Marvell, revering and respecting himself, was proof against its charms.

It has been said that Lord Treasurer Danby, thinking to buy over his old schoolfellow, called upon Marvell in his garret. At parting, the lord treasurer slipped into his hand an order on the treasury for £1,000, and then went to his chariot. Marvell, looking at the paper, calls after the treasurer, "My lord, I request another moment." They went up again to the garret, and Jack, the servant boy, was called. "Jack, child, what had I for dinner yesterday?" "Don't you remember, sir? you had the little shoulder of mutton that you ordered me to bring from a woman in the market." "Very right, child. What have I for dinner to-day?" "Don't you know, sir, that you bid me lay by the blade bone to broil?" "'Tis so, very right, child, go away." "My lord," said Marvell, turning to the treasurer, "do you hear that? Andrew Marvell's dinner is provided; there's your piece of paper. I want it not. I knew the sort of kindness you intended. I live here to serve my constitutents: the ministry may seek men for their purpose; I am not one."

Marvell conducted himself nobly to the end. He remained unimpeachable in his character. He was the true representative of his constituents. Though not poor, his mode of living was simple and frugal. In July, 1678, he visited his constituents for the last time. Shortly after his return to London, without any previous illness or visible decay, he expired. Some say he died from poison. That may not be true. But certainly he died an honest man. He always preserved his purity. He ever defended the right. He was "beloved by good men; feared by bad; imitated by few; and scarce paralleled by any." These are the words on his tombstone at Hull.

Ben Jonson, like Marvell, was sturdy and plain spoken. When Charles I. sent that brave poet a tardy and slight gratuity during his poverty and sickness, Ben sent back the money, with the message, "I suppose he sends me this because I live in an alley; tell him his soul lives in an alley."

Goldsmith also was a man who would not be bought. He had known the depths of poverty. He had wandered over Europe, paying his way with his flute. He had slept in barns and under the open sky. He tried acting, ushering, doctoring. He starved amid them all. Then he tried authorship, and became a gentleman. But he never quite escaped from the clutches of poverty. He described himself as "in a garret writing for bread, and expecting to be dunned for a milk score." One day Johnson received a message from Goldsmith, stating that he was in great distress. The doctor went to see him, and found that his landlady had arrested him for his rent. The only thing he had to dispose of was a packet of manuscript. Johnson took it up, and found it to be the "Vicar of Wakefield." Having ascertained its merit, Johnson took it to a bookseller and sold it for sixty pounds.

Poor though he was then, and poor though he was at the end of his life,—for he died in debt,—Goldsmith could not be bought. He refused to do dirty political work. About £50,000 annually was then expended by Sir Robert Walpole in secret-service money. Daily scribblers were suborned to write up the acts of the administration, and to write down those of their opponents. In the time of Lord North "Junius" was in opposition. It was resolved to hire Goldsmith to baffle his terrible sarcasm. Dr. Scott, chaplain to Lord Sandwich, was deputed to negotiate with him. "I found him," says Dr. Scott, "in a miserable suite of chambers in the Temple. I told him my authority. I told how I was empowered to pay for his exertions; and, would you believe it?—he was so absurd as to say, 'I can earn as much as will supply my wants without writing for any party; the assistance you offer is therefore unnecessary to me'; and so I left him in his garret!"

Thus did poor and noble Goldsmith spurn the wages of unrighteousness! He preferred using his pen to write the famous tale of "Goody Two Shoes" for the amusement of children rather than become the hack pamphleteer of political prostitutes.

Pulteney, the leader of the Opposition in the House of Commons, having in one of his speeches made a Latin quotation, was corrected by Sir Robert Walpole, who offered to wager a guinea on the inaccuracy of the lines. The bet was accepted, the classic was referred to, and Pulteney was found to be right. The minister threw a guinea across the table, and Pulteney, on taking it

up, called the house to witness that this was the first guinea of
the public money he had ever put into his pocket! The very
coin thus lost and won is preserved in the British Museum, as
the "Pulteney Guinea."

                                        From "Duty."

ADAM SMITH

(1723–1790)

ADAM SMITH, author of the "Wealth of Nations," and one of the most celebrated economists of modern times, was born in Fifeshire, Scotland, June 5th, 1723. After completing his own scholastic education at Glasgow and Oxford, he taught Rhetoric and Belles-Lettres at Edinburgh, Logic at Glasgow, and finally Moral Philosophy in the latter university. In 1778 he was appointed Commissioner of Customs at Edinburgh; in 1787 was chosen Lord Rector of the University of Glasgow. His "Inquiry into the Nature and Causes of the Wealth of Nations" appeared in 1776, and his "Theory of Moral Sentiments" in 1759. He died at Edinburgh, July 17th, 1790. He wrote industriously on what seems to have been a wide range of topics, but just before his death he selected a few essays from the mass of his manuscripts and directed that all the rest should be burned. This was accordingly done, perhaps to the advantage of his reputation, but certainly to the disadvantage of posterity, as even the worst and most unpolished writing of a man of his intellectual rank may be more valuable than the masterpieces of mediocrity.

JUDGING OTHERS BY OURSELVES

WHEN the original passions of the person principally concerned are in perfect concord with the sympathetic emotions of the spectator, they necessarily appear to this last just and proper, and suitable to their objects; and, on the contrary, when, upon bringing the case home to himself, he finds that they do not coincide with what he feels, they necessarily appear to him unjust and improper, and unsuitable to the causes which excite them. To approve of the passions of another, therefore, as suitable to their objects, is the same thing as to observe that we entirely sympathize with them; and not to approve of them as such is the same thing as to observe that we do not entirely sympathize with them. The man who resents the injuries that have been done to me, and observes that I resent them precisely as he does, necessarily approves of my resentment. The man whose sympathy keeps time to my grief cannot but admit the reasonableness of my sorrow. He who admires the same poem, or the same picture, and admires them exactly as I do, must surely allow the justness of my admiration. He who laughs at the same joke, and laughs along with me, cannot well deny the propriety of my laughter. On the contrary, the person who, upon these different occasions, either feels no such emotion as that which I feel, or feels none that bears any proportion to mine, cannot avoid disapproving my sentiments on account of their dissonance with his own. If my animosity goes beyond what the indignation of my friend can correspond to; if my grief exceeds what his most tender compassion can go along with; if my admiration is either too high or too low to tally with his own; if I laugh loud and heartily when he only smiles, or, on the contrary, only smile when he laughs loud and heartily; in all these cases, as soon as he comes from considering the object, to observe how I am affected by it, according as there is more or less disproportion between his sentiments and mine, I must incur a greater or less degree of his disapprobation: and upon all occasions his own sentiments are the standards and measures by which he judges of mine.

To approve of another man's opinions is to adopt those opinions, and to adopt them is to approve of them. If the same arguments which convince you convince me likewise, I necessarily approve of your conviction; and if they do not, I necessarily disapprove of it: neither can I possibly conceive that I should do the one without the other. To approve or disapprove, therefore, of the opinions of others is acknowledged by everybody to mean no more than to observe their agreement or disagreement with our own. But this is equally the case with regard to our approbation or disapprobation of the sentiments or passions of others.

There are, indeed, some cases in which we seem to approve without any sympathy or correspondence of sentiments, and in which, consequently, the sentiment of approbation would seem to be different from the perception of this coincidence. A little attention, however, will convince us that even in these cases our approbation is ultimately founded upon a sympathy or correspondence of this kind. I shall give an instance in things of a very frivolous nature, because in them the judgments of mankind are less apt to be perverted by wrong systems. We may often approve of a jest, and think the laughter of the company quite just and proper, though we ourselves do not laugh, because, perhaps, we are in a grave humor, or happen to have our attention engaged with other objects. We have learned, however, from experience, what sort of pleasantry is upon most occasions capable of making us laugh, and we observe that this is one of that kind. We approve, therefore, of the laughter of the company, and feel that it is natural and suitable to its object; because, though in our present mode we cannot easily enter into it, we are sensible that upon most occasions we should very heartily join in it.

The same thing often happens with regard to all the other passions. A stranger passes by us in the street with all the marks of the deepest affliction; and we are immediately told that he has just received the news of the death of his father. It is impossible that, in this case, we should not approve of his grief. Yet it may often happen, without any defect of humanity on our part, that, so far from entering into the violence of his sorrow, we should scarce conceive the first movements of concern upon his account. Both he and his father, perhaps, are entirely unknown to us, or we happen to be employed about other things, and do not take time to picture out in our imagination the different circumstances of distress which must occur to him. We have learned, however, from experience, that such a misfortune naturally excites such a degree of sorrow, and we know that if we took time to consider his situation fully in all its parts, we should, without doubt, most sincerely sympathize with him. It is upon the consciousness of this conditional sympathy, that our approbation of his sorrow is founded, even in those cases in which that sympathy does not actually take place; and the general rules derived from our preceding experience of what our sentiments would commonly correspond with, correct upon this, as upon many other occasions, the impropriety of our present emotions.

The sentiment or affection of the heart from which any action proceeds, and upon which its whole virtue or vice must ultimately depend, may be considered under two different aspects, or in two different relations; first, in relation to the cause which excites it, or the motive which gives occasion to it; and second, in relation to the end which it proposes, or the effect which it tends to produce.

In the suitableness or unsuitableness, in the proportion or disproportion which the affection seems to bear to the cause or object which excites it, consists the propriety or impropriety, the decency or ungracefulness of the consequent action.

In the beneficial or hurtful nature of the effects which the affection aims at, or tends to produce, consists the merit or demerit of the action, the qualities by which it is entitled to reward, or is deserving of punishment.

Philosophers have, of late years, considered chiefly the tendency of affections, and have given little attention to the relation which they stand in to the cause which excites them. In common life, however, when we judge of any person's conduct, and of the sentiments which directed it, we constantly consider them under both these aspects. When we blame in another man the excesses of love, of grief, of resentment, we not only consider the ruinous effect which they tend to produce, but the little occasion which was given for them. The merit of his favorite, we say, is not so great, his misfortune is not so dreadful, his provocation is not so extraordinary, as to justify so violent a passion. We should have indulged, we say, perhaps have approved of the violence of his emotion, had the cause been in any respect proportioned to it.

When we judge in this manner of any affection as proportioned or disproportioned to the cause which excites it, it is scarce possible that we should make use of any other rule or canon but the correspondent affection in ourselves. If, upon bringing the case home to our own breast, we find that the sentiments which it gives occasion to, coincide and tally with our own, we necessarily approve of them as proportioned and suitable to their objects; if otherwise, we necessarily disapprove of them, as extravagant and out of proportion.

Every faculty in one man is the measure by which he judges of the like faculty in another. I judge of your sight by my sight, of your ear by my ear, of your reason by my reason, of your resentment by my resentment, of your love by my love. I neither have, nor can have, any other way of judging about them.

Chap. iii., « Of Sympathy,» complete. From
« Theory of Moral Sentiments.»

THE DIVISION OF LABOR

OBSERVE the accommodation of the most common artificer or day laborer in a civilized and thriving country, and you will perceive that the number of people, of whose industry a part, though but a small part, has been employed in procuring him this accommodation, exceeds all computation. The woolen coat, for example, which covers the day laborer, as coarse and rough as it may appear, is the produce of the joint labor of a great multitude of workmen. The shepherd, the sorter of the wool, the wool comber or carder, the dyer, the scribbler, the spinner, the weaver, the fuller, the dresser, with many others, must all join their different arts in order to complete even this homely production. How many merchants and carriers, besides, must have been employed in transporting the materials from some of those workmen to others, who often live in a very distant part of the country! How much commerce and navigation in particular, how many shipbuilders, sailors, sail makers, rope makers, must have been employed in order to bring together the different drugs made use of by the dyer, which often come from the remotest corners of the world! What a variety of labor, too, is necessary in order to produce the tools of the meanest of those workmen! To say nothing of such complicated machines as the ship of the sailor, the mill of the fuller, or even the loom of the weaver, let us consider only what a variety of labor is requisite in order to form that very simple machine, the shears with which the shepherd clips the wool. The miner, the builder of the furnace for smelting the ore, the feller of the timber, the burner of the charcoal to be made use of in the smelting house, the brickmaker, the bricklayer, the workmen who attend the furnace, the millwright, the forger, the smith, must all of them join their different arts in order to produce them. Were we to examine in the same manner all the different parts of his dress and household furniture, the coarse linen shirt which he wears next his skin, the shoes which cover his feet, the bed which he lies on, and all the different parts which compose it, the kitchen grate at which he prepares his victuals, the coals which he makes use of for that purpose, dug from the bowels of the earth, and brought to him, perhaps, by a long sea and a long land carriage, all the other utensils of his kitchen, all the furniture of his table,

the knives and forks, the earthen or pewter plates upon which
he serves up and divides his victuals, the different hands employed in preparing his bread and his beer, the glass window
which lets in the heat and the light, and keeps out the wind and
the rain, with all the knowledge and art requisite for preparing
that beautiful and happy invention, without which these northern
parts of the world could scarce have afforded a very comfortable
habitation, together with the tools of all the different workmen
employed in producing those different conveniences; if we examine, I say, all these things, and consider what a variety of
labor is employed about each of them, we shall be sensible that,
without the assistance and co-operation of many thousands, the
very meanest person in a civilized country could not be provided,
even according to what we very falsely imagine the easy and
simple manner in which he is commonly accommodated. Compared, indeed, with the more extravagant luxury of the great, his
accommodation must, no doubt, appear extremely simple and
easy; and yet it may be true, perhaps, that the accommodation
of a European prince does not always so much exceed that of
an industrious and frugal peasant, as the accommodation of the
latter exceeds that of many an African king, the absolute master
of the lives and liberties of ten thousand naked savages.

From «Wealth of Nations.»

HORACE SMITH

(1779–1849)

ORACE SMITH, joint author with his brother James of the famous "Rejected Addresses," was born at London, December 31st, 1779. The "Rejected Addresses" made the brothers so celebrated that Horace found a field for indulging his inclination towards humorous essay writing. His "Gayeties and Gravities," published in three volumes in 1826, deserve to be read much more frequently than they have been since his death in 1849. The occasion of the "Rejected Addresses" was the rebuilding of Drury Lane Theatre in 1812, and the offer of a prize of £50 for an address to be recited at the dedication in October of that year. On noticing the advertisement of the prize, the Smith brothers conceived the idea of writing and publishing as having been rejected by the managers a volume of addresses which they imputed to Wordsworth, Southey, Coleridge, Crabbe, Byron, Moore, Scott, and Bowles. The parodies were so clever and the idea which inspired them so attractively comic that the "Rejected Addresses" at once took the hold on English literature which the passage of time has shown to be a permanent one.

THE DIGNITY OF A TRUE JOKE

The gravest beast is an ass; the gravest bird is an owl; the gravest fish is an oyster; and the gravest man a fool.
—Joe Miller.

GRAVITY, says Lord Bolingbroke, is the very essence of imposture. A quack or a pretender is generally a very grave and reverend signior; and though I would not venture to assert that the converse of this proposition is invariably true, I must confess that as I am apt to doubt the virtue of an obtrusive Puritan and rigorist, so am I marvelously prone to suspect the wisdom of your serious and solemn Precisian. While the shallow pedant endeavors to impose upon the world by a serious and pompous deportment, minds of a superior order will be often found abandoning themselves to playfulness and puerility. Plato, after discoursing philosophy with his disciples upon the promon-

tory of Sunium, frequently indulged the gayety of his heart by
relaxing into a vein of the most trivial jocoseness; but once seeing a grave formalist approach in the midst of their trifling, he
exclaimed, "Silence, my friends! let us be wise now; here is a
fool coming." This man's race is not extinct. Reader! hast
thou not sometimes encountered a starched-looking quiz, who
seemed to have steeped his countenance in vinegar to preserve it
from the infection of laughter?—a personage of whom it might
be pronounced, as Butler said of the Duke of Buckingham, that
he endures pleasures with less patience than other men do their
pains?—a staid, important, dogged, square-rigged, mathematical-
minded sort of an animal? Question him, and I will lay my
head to yours (for I like to take the odds), that whatever tolerance he may be brought to admit for other deviations from the
right line of gravity, he will profess a truculent and implacable
hatred of that most kind-hearted, sociable, and urbane witticism,
termed—a Pun.

Oh, the Anti-risible rogue! Oh, the jesticide—the Hilarifuge!
the extinguisher of "quips and cranks and wanton wiles";—the
queller of quirks, quiddets, quibbles, equivocation, and quizzing!
the gagger of gigglers! the Herod of witlings, and Procrustes of
full-grown Punsters! Look at his atrabilarious complexion; it is
the same that Cæsar feared in Brutus and Cassius: such a fellow
is indeed fit for treasons, stratagems, and plots; he has no music
in his soul, for he will not let us even play upon words. Will
nothing but pure wit serve thy turn, most sapient Sir? Well,
then set us the example—

———"Lay on, Macduff,
And damn'd be he that first cries, Hold! enough!"

How,—dumbfounded? Not quite;—methinks I hear him quot-
ing Dr. Johnson's stale hyperbole, "Sir, the man that would
commit a pun would pick a pocket"; to which I would oppose
an equally valid dictum of an illustrious quibbler, "Sir, no man
ever condemned a good pun who was able to make one." I
know not a more aggrieved and unjustly proscribed character in
the present day than the poor painstaking punster. He is the
pariah of the dining table; it is the fashion to run him down: and
as every dull ass thinks that he may have a kick at the prostrate
witling, may I be condemned to pass a whole week without punning (a fearful adjuration!) if I do not show that the greatest

sages, poets, and philosophers of all ages have been enrolled upon this proscribed list!

Even in Holy Writ, whatever might have been the intention of the speaker, there is authority for a play upon words equivalent to a pun. When Simon Bar-Jona, for his superior faith, received the name of Peter (which in Greek signifies a stone or rock), the divine bestower of that appellation exclaimed, "I say unto thee, that thou art Peter, and upon this rock will I build my church," etc. Homer has made the wily Ulysses save his life by means of a pun. In the ninth book of the "Odyssey" that hero informs the Cyclops that his name is Noman; and when the monster, after having had his eye put out in his sleep, awakes in agony, he thus roars to his companions for assistance:—

> "Friends! No-man kills me. No-man in the hour
> Of sleep oppresses me with fraudful power.—
> If No-man hurt thee, but the hand divine
> Inflicts disease, it fits thee to resign.
> To Jove, or to thy father Neptune pray,
> The brethren cried, and instant strode away"—

a joke upon which Euripides dilates with huge delight in the drama of the "Cyclops." * It will be observed that Pope has preserved the equivoque in his translation, which attests his respect for this most ancient *jeu de mots;* while Ulysses is described as hurrying away in high glee, "pleased with the effect of conduct and of art," which is an evidence that Homer felicitated himself upon the happiness of the thought. This passage exhibits a very rude and primitive state of the art; for had any modern Cyclopses been invoked to aid their comrade, under similar circumstances, they would have seen through so flimsy a trick only with one eye.

Later Greek writers were by no means slow in following so notable an example. Plutarch has preserved several of these *Pterœnta*, or flying words, particularly King Philip's celebrated pun to the physician who attended him when his collar bone was broken; and Diogenes the Cynic made so happy an equivoque upon a damsel's eye, which the profligate Didymus undertook to cure, that Scaliger said he would rather have been author of it

* Cibber, in translating the Italian opera of "Polifemo," make Ulysses answer, "I take no name"; whereby all that followed became unintelligible, and the Greek pun was most ingeniously spoilt.   H. S.

than King of Navarre. From the comic authors a whole galaxy of similar jokes might be collected; but I reserve the specification for a new edition of Hierocles, the Joe Miller of Alexandria, which I am preparing for the press in ten volumes quarto.

The Romans, who imitated the Greeks in everything, were not likely to forget their puns, *verbaque apta joco.* Cicero informs us that Cæsar was a celebrated performer in this way. Horace in his seventh Satire, giving an account of the quarrel between Persius and Rupilius Rex, before Brutus the Pretor, makes the former exclaim, "*Per magnos, Brute, Deos te oro, qui reges consuêris tollere, cur non hunc Regem jugulas?*" thus playing upon the names of both parties. Martial was an accomplished punster; and Ovid not only quibbled upon words, but metamorphosed them into a thousand phantasies and vagaries.

The same valuable privilege formed the staple commodity of the ancient Oracles; for if the presiding deities had not been shrewd punsters, or able to inspire the Pythoness with ready equivoques, the whole establishment must speedily have been declared bankrupt. Sometimes, indeed, they only dabbled in accentuation, and accomplished their prophecies by the transposition of a stop, as in the well-known answer to a soldier inquiring his fate in the war for which he was about to embark. "*Ibis, redibis. Nunquam in bello, peribis.*" The warrior set off in high spirits upon the faith of this prediction, and fell in the first engagement, when his widow had the satisfaction of being informed that he should have put the full stop after the word "*nunquam,*" which would probably have put a full stop to his enterprise and saved his life. More commonly, however, they betook themselves to a positive pun, the double construction of which enabled them to be always right: sometimes playing upon a single word, and sometimes upon the whole clause of a sentence. When Crœsus, about to make war upon Cyrus, consulted the Delphian priestess, he was told that in crossing the river Halys he would overturn a great empire — which could hardly fail to be true; for, if he succeeded, he would subvert the Assyrian kingdom; if he failed, his own would be overwhelmed. Pyrrhus received a similar response as to the fate of his expedition against the Romans. "*Credo equidem Æacidas Romanos vincere posse*"; which might import either that the Æacides, from whom Pyrrhus was descended, would conquer the Romans, or precisely the reverse: such are the advantages of a double accusative.

Christianity, by superseding these Oracles, did not, most for-tunately, extinguish quibbling, for which we have the authority of one of the earliest Popes. Some Pagan English youths of extraordinary beauty being presented to him, he exclaimed, " *Non Angli, sed Angeli forent, si essent Christiani.*"

Heraldic bearings are supposed to have been invented to dis-tinguish the different nations, armies, and clans, that were con-gregated together in the Crusades; and the mottoes assumed upon this occasion, if we may judge by those of England, bore almost universally some punning allusion to the name or device of the chief. The similar epigraphs still retained by the Vernon, Fortescue, and Cavendish families, as well as by numerous others, may be viewed as so many venerable testimonies to the antiquity of punning in this our happy island.

There is not one of our sterling old English writers from whom we might not glean some specimen of this noble art; which seems to have attained its golden age in that Augustan era of our literature — the reign of our renowned Queen Elizabeth, when clergymen punned in the pulpit, judges upon the bench, and criminals in their last dying speeches. Then was it that the deer-stealing attorney's clerk fled from Stratford, and introducing whole scenes of punning into his immortal plays, eliciting quib-bles not less affluently from the mouths of fools and porters, than from the dread lips of the weird sisters, " who palter with us in a double sense," established upon an imperishable basis the glory of his favorite science of Paronomasia; — a glory irradiat-ing and reflected by the whole galaxy of dramatic talent with which he was surrounded.

Succeeding writers, though they have never equaled this splendor of quibble, have not failed to deposit occasional offer-ings upon the altar of Janus, the god of puns. Dryden pretended to be angry, when being in a coffeehouse with his back towards Rowe, one of his friends said to him, " You are like a waterman: you look one way and Rowe another"; but, though unwilling to be the object of a pun, he had no compunction in being the au-thor of many, for the support of which assertion the reader may consult his dramatic works. Addison's opinion of this laugh-provoking practice may be collected from the 440th Number of the Spectator, wherein he describes a society, who had established among themselves an infirmary for the cure of all defects of tem-per and infractions of good manners. " After dinner a very hon-

est fellow chancing to let a pun fall from him, his neighbor cried
out, 'to the infirmary!' at the same time pretending to be sick at
it, as having the same natural antipathy to a pun which some have
to a cat. This produced a long debate. Upon the whole, the
punster was acquitted and his neighbor sent off." Pope's authority we have already cited. Gay was probably the author of
the play upon his own name, when he observed that the great
success of his "Beggar's Opera," whilst Rich was proprietor of
the theatre, had made Gay rich and Rich gay. But what shall
we say of Swift, the punster's *vade mecum*, the Hierarch, the
Pontifex, Magnus Apollo of the tribe; the Alpha and Omega, the
first and last of the professors of equivocation; whose mind
was an ever-springing fountain of quiddets, and the thread of
whose life was an unbroken string of puns from his first to his
second childhood? Impossible as it is to do justice to the memory of so great a man, I feel the eulogomania swelling within
me; and that I may effectually check its yearnings, I leap athwart
a measureless hiatus, and revert to that lugubrious, somnolent,
single-sensed, and no-witted Antipunster, whom I apostrophized
in the outset.

And now, thou word measurer, thou line-and-rule mechanic,
thou reasoning but not ruminating animal, now that I have produced these authorities, limited to a narrow list from the want of
room, not of materials, wilt thou have the ridiculous arrogance
to affect contempt for a pun? That genuine wit which thou pre-
tendest to worship (as the Athenians built an altar to the unknown Deity), has been defined to be an assimilation of distant
ideas; and what is a pun but an eliciter of remote meanings,
which, though they may not always amount to a definite idea,
are at all events the materials of one, and therefore ingredients
in the composition of real wit? These Protean combinations are
the stimulants of fancy, the titillators of the imagination, the
awakeners of the risible faculties; and to condemn them because
the same happy results may be produced by a more rare and difficult process is either an exemplification of the fox and the sour
grapes, or the pride of mental luxury, which would quarrel with
all gratifications that are cheap and accessible. The sterling
commodity is scarce — let us prize it the more when we encounter
it; but in the meantime let us not reject a good substitute when
it is presented. Gooseberry wine is no very lofty succedaneum
for sparking Champagne, but it is better than fasting. Some

may not like the flavor of the beverage, but none would think of
abusing the caterer who puts upon the table the best liquor that
his cellar affords.   These sullen stupidities are reserved for an
Antipunster.

Complete.   From « Gayeties and
Gravities.»

UGLY WOMEN

Un homme rencontre une femme, et est choqué de sa laideur;
bientôt, si elle n'a pas de prétentions, sa physionomie lui fait oublier
les défauts de ses traits, il la trouve aimable, et conçoit qu'on puisse
l'aimer; huit jours après il a des espérances, huit jours après on les
lui retire, huit jours après il est fou.— " *De l'Amour.*"

THE ancient inhabitants of Amathus, in the island of Cyprus,
were the most celebrated statuaries in the world, which
they almost exclusively supplied with gods and goddesses.
Every one who had a mind to be in the vogue ordered his deity
from those fashionable artists: even Jupiter himself was hardly
considered orthodox and worship-worthy, unless emanating from
the established Pantheon of the Cypriots; and as to Juno, Venus,
Minerva, and Diana, it was admitted that they had a peculiar
knack in their manufacture, and it need hardly be added that
they drove a thriving trade in those popular goddesses.   But this
monopoly was more favorable to the fortunes than to the happiness
of the parties.   By constantly straining above humanity, and as-
piring to the representation of celestial beauty; by fostering the
enthusiasm of their imaginations in the pursuit of the beau
ideal,— they acquired a distaste, or at least an indifference, for
mortal attractions, and turned up their noses at their fair country-
women for not being Junos and Minervas.   Not one of them
equaled the model which had been conjured up in their minds,
and not one of them, consequently, would they deign to notice.
At the public games, the women were all huddled together,
whispering and looking glum, while the men congregated as far
from them as possible, discussing the beau ideal.   Had they been
prosing upon politics, you might have sworn it was an English
party.   Dancing was extinct, unless the ladies chose to lead out
one another; the priests waxed lank and woe-begone for want of
the marriage offerings; Hymen's altar was covered with as many
cobwebs as a poor's box; successive moons rose and set without

a single honeymoon, and the whole island threatened to become an antinuptial colony of bachelors and old maids.

In this emergency, Pygmalion, the most eminent statuary of the place, falling in love with one of his own works, a figure of Diana, which happened to possess the beau ideal in perfection, implored Venus to animate the marble; and she, as is well known to every person conversant with authentic history, immediately granted his request. So far as this couple were concerned, one would have imagined that the evil was remedied; but, alas! the remedy was worse than the disease. The model of excellence was now among them, alive and breathing; the men were perfectly mad, beleaguering the house from morn to night to get a peep at her; all other women were treated with positive insult, and, of course, the whole female population was possessed by all the Furies. Marmorea (such was the name of the animated statue) was no Diana in the flesh, whatever she might have been in the marble: if the scandalous chronicles of those days may be believed, she had more than one favored lover; certain is it that she was the cause of constant feuds and battles in which many lives were lost, and Pygmalion himself was at last found murdered in the neighborhood of his own house. The whole island was now on the point of a civil war on account of this philanthropical Helen, when one of her disappointed wooers, in a fit of jealousy, stabbed her to the heart, and immediately after threw himself from a high rock into the sea.

Such is the tragedy which would probably be enacting at the present moment in every country of the world, but for the fortunate circumstance that we have no longer any fixed standard of beauty, real or imaginary, and by a necessary and happy consequence no determinate rule of ugliness. In fact, there are no such animals as ugly women, though we still continue to talk of them as we do of harpies, gorgons, and chimeras. There is no deformity that does not find admirers, and no loveliness that is not deemed defective. Anamaboo, the African prince, received so many attentions from a celebrated belle of London, that in a moment of tenderness, he could not refrain from laying his hand on his heart and exclaiming, "Ah! madam, if heaven had only made you a negress, you would have been irresistible!" And the same beauty, when traveling among the Swiss Cretins, heard several of the men ejaculating, "How handsome she is! what a pity that she wants a goitre!" Plain women were formerly so

common, that they were termed "ordinary," to signify the frequency of their occurrence; in these happier days the phrase,
"extra-ordinary," would be more applicable. However parsimoni-
ous, or even cruel, nature may have been in other respects, they
all cling to admiration by some solitary tenure that redeems them
from the unqualified imputation of unattractiveness. One has an
eye that, like Charity, covers a multitude of sins; another is a
female Samson, whose strength consists in her hair; a third holds
your affections by her teeth; a fourth is a Cinderella who wins
hearts by her pretty little foot; a fifth makes an irresistible appeal from her face to her figure, and so on, to the end of the
catalogue. An expressive countenance may always be claimed in
the absence of any definite charm; if even this be questionable,
the party generally contrives to get a reputation for great clever-
ness; and if that, too, be inhumanly disputed, envy itself must
allow that she is "excessively amiable."

Still it must be acknowledged that however men may differ
as to the details, they agree as to results, and crowd about an
acknowledged beauty, influenced by some secret attraction, of
which they are themselves unconscious, and of which the source
has never been clearly explained. It would seem impossible that
it should originate in any sexual symptoms, since we feel the
impulsion without carrying ourselves, even in idea, beyond the
present pleasure of gazing, and are even sensibly affected by
the sight of beautiful children; yet it cannot be an abstract admiration, for it is incontestable that neither men nor women are
so vehemently impressed by the contemplation of beauty in their
own as in the opposite sex. This injustice towards our own half
of humanity might be assigned to a latent envy, but that the
same remark applies to the pleasure we derive from statues, of
the proportions of which we could hardly be jealous. Ugly
statues may be left to their fate without any compunctious visit-
ings of nature; but our conduct towards women whom we conceive to be in a similar predicament is by no means entitled to
the same indulgence. We shuffle away from them at parties,
and sneak to the other end of the dinner table, as if their features were catching; and as to their falling in love and possessing the common feelings of their sex, we laugh at the very
idea. And yet these pariahs of the drawing-room generally atone
by interior talent for what they want in exterior charms; as if
the Medusa's head were still destined to be carried by Minerva.

Nature seldom lavishes her gifts upon one subject: the peacock has no voice; the beautiful camellia japonica has no odor; and belles, generally speaking, have no great share of intellect. Some visionaries amuse themselves with imagining that the complacency occasioned by the possession of physical charms conduces to moral perfection.—

> « Why doth not beauty, then, refine the wit,
> And good complexion rectify the will ? »

This is a fond conceit, unwarranted by earthly test, though destined perhaps to be realized in a happier state of existence.

What a blessing for these unhandsome damsels whom we treat still more unhandsomely by our fastidious neglect, that some of us are less squeamish in our tastes, and more impartial in our attentions! Solomon proves the antiquity of the adage, " *De gustibus nil disputandum*," for he compares the hair of his beloved to a flock of goats appearing from Mount Gilead, and in a strain of enamored flattery exclaims, " Thy eyes are like the fish pools in Heshbon, by the gate of Bath-rabbim; thy nose like the tower of Lebanon looking towards Damascus." Now I deem it as becoming to see a woman standing behind a good roomy nose as to contemplate a fair temple with a majestic portico; but it may be questioned whether a nose like the tower of Lebanon be not somewhat too elephantine and bordering on the proboscis. The *nez retroussé* is smart and piquant; the button nose, like all other diminutives, is endearing; and even the snub absolute has its admirers. Cupid can get over it, though it have no bridge, and jumps through a wall-eye like a harlequin. As to the latter feature, my taste may be singular, perhaps bad, but I confess that I have a penchant for that captivating cast, sometimes invidiously termed a squint. Its advantages are neither few nor unimportant. Like a bowl, its very bias makes it sure of hitting the jack, while it seems to be running out of the course; and it has, moreover, the invaluable property of doing execution without exciting suspicion, like the Irish guns with crooked barrels, made for shooting round a corner. Common observers admire the sun in its common state, but philosophers find it a thousand times more interesting when suffering a partial eclipse; while the lovers of the picturesque are more smitten with its rising and setting than with its meridian splendor. Such men must be enchanted with a strabismus or squint, where they may behold the ball of sight emerging from the nasal East, or setting in its Occidental depths, presenting every variety of obscuration. With regard to teeth, also, a very erroneous taste prevails. Nothing can be more stiff and barrack-like than that uniformity of shape and hue which is so highly vaunted, for the merest tyro in landscape will tell us that castellated and jagged outlines, with a pleasing variety of tints, are infinitely more pictorial and pleasing. Patches of bile in the face are by no means to be deprecated; they impart to it a rich mellow tone of autumnal coloring, which we would in vain seek in less gifted complexions: and I am most happy to vindicate the claims of a moderate beard upon the upper lip, which is as necessary to the perfect beauty of the mouth as are the thorns and moss to a rose, or the leaves to a cherry. If there be any old maids still extant, while misogynists are so rare, the fault must be attributable to themselves, and they must incur all the responsibility of their single blessedness.

In the connubial lottery ugly women possess an advantage to which sufficient importance has not been attached. It is a common observation that husband and wife frequently resemble one another; and many ingenious theorists, attempting to solve the problem by attributing it to sympathy, contemplation of one another's features, congeniality of habits and modes of life, etc., have fallen into the very common error of substituting the cause for the effect. This mutual likeness is the occasion, not the result, of marriage. Every man, like Narcissus, becomes enamored of the reflection of himself, only choosing a substance instead of a shadow. His love for any particular woman is self-love at second hand, vanity reflected, compound egotism. When he sees himself in the mirror of a female face, he exclaims, "How intelligent, how amiable, how interesting! — how admirably adapted for a wife!" and forthwith makes his proposals to the personage so expressly and literally calculated to keep him in countenance. The uglier he is, the more need he has of this consolation; he forms a romantic attachment to the "fascinating creature with the snub nose," or the "bewitching girl with the roguish leer" (Anglicè — squint), without once suspecting that he is paying his addresses to himself, and playing the inamorato before a looking glass. Take self-love from love, and very little remains: it is taking the flame from Hymen's torch and leaving the smoke. The same feeling extends to his progeny: he would rather see

them resemble himself, particularly in his defects, than be modeled after the chubbiest cherubs or cupids that ever emanated
from the studio of Canova. One sometimes encounters a man of
a most unqualified hideousness, who obviously considers himself
an Adonis; and when such a one has to seek a congenial Venus,
it is evident that her value will be in the inverse ratio of her
charms. Upon this principle ugly women will be converted into
belles, perfect frights will become irresistible, and none need despair of conquests if they have but the happiness to be sufficiently
plain.

The best part of beauty, says Bacon, is that which a statue
or painting cannot express. As to symmetry of form and superficial grace, sculpture is exquisitely perfect, but the countenance
is of too subtle and intangible a character to be arrested by any
modification of marble. Busts, especially where the pupil of the
eye is unmarked, have the appearance of mere masks, and are
representations of little more than blindness and death. Painting
supplies by coloring and shade much that sculpture wants; but,
on the other hand, it is deficient in what its rival possesses —
fidelity of superficial form. Nothing can compensate for our in-
ability to walk round a picture, and choose various points of
view. Facility of production, meanness of material, and vulgarity
of association have induced us to look down with unmerited contempt upon those waxen busts in the perfumers' shops, which, as
simple representations of female nature, have attained a perfection that positively amounts to the kissable. That delicacy of
tint and material which so admirably adapts itself to female beauty
forms, however, but a milk-maidish representation of virility, and
the men have, consequently, as epicene and androgynous an aspect as if they had just been bathing in the Salmacian fountain.

Countenance, however, is not within the reach of any of these
substances or combinations. It is a species of moral beauty, as
superior to mere charm of surface as mind is to matter. It is,
in fact, visible spirit, legible intellect, diffusing itself over the
features, and enabling minds to commune with each other by
some secret sympathy unconnected with the senses. The heart
has a silent echo in the face, which frequently carries to us a
conviction diametrically opposite to the audible expressions of the
mouth; and we see, through the eyes, into the understanding of
the man, long before it can communicate with us by utterance.
This emanation of character is the light of a soul destined to the

skies, shining through its tegument of clay, and irradiating the countenance, as the sun illuminates the face of nature before it rises above the earth to commence its heavenly career. Of this indefinable charm all women are alike susceptible: it is to them what gunpowder is to warriors; it levels all distinctions, and gives to the plain and the pretty, to the timid and the brave, an equal chance of making conquests. It is, in fine, one among a thousand proofs of that system of compensation, both physical and moral, by which a superior power is perpetually evincing his benignity; affording to every human being a commensurate chance of happiness, and inculcating upon all, that when they turn their faces towards heaven, they should reflect the light from above, and be animated by one uniform expression of love, resignation, and gratitude.

Complete. From «Gayeties and
Gravities.»

SYDNEY SMITH

(1771–1845)

YDNEY SMITH was celebrated in his generation as an orator, wit, clergyman, essayist, and philosopher, with an incidental reputation as a book reviewer, at a time when, as he himself has suggested, book reviewers did not necessarily " prejudice " themselves by acquiring in advance a knowledge of the books they were writing about. His table-talk and his humor in conversation seem to have been almost, if not quite, unrivaled in the history of English " wits," but his essays, as a rule, are far from demonstrating the humor which would be expected from his reputation. They are often characterized, however, by brilliant flashes of wit which, when the reader is least expecting it, illuminate whole pages of logic. And again they develop from what had been apparently the deepest seriousness into the most striking and effective irony. Sydney Smith was born at Woodford, England, June 3d, 1771. After beginning life as a curate in a small village on Salisbury Plain, he spent several years in Edinburgh where he helped to found the Edinburgh Review, of which he became the first editor. He lectured on moral philosophy, at the Royal Institution of London, from 1804 to 1808. In 1809 he became rector of a Yorkshire parish, where it is said there had been no clergyman before him for a century. After remaining there for twenty years be became prebend of Bristol, and in 1831 canon of St. Paul's. He died in London, February 22d, 1845. His " Plymley Letters " advocating Catholic emancipation were published in 1807 and 1808, and in 1839 his contributions to the Edinburgh Review were collected and republished. These essays, which include his best works, are generally printed in the same volume with his speeches, which include what is perhaps the most celebrated political speech of the nineteenth century,— that in which he compared Tory opposition to reform to the attempt of Mrs. Partington of Sidmouth to mop the Atlantic out of her front door during the great flood at that place in 1824.

WIT AND HUMOR

I wish, after all I have said about wit and humor, I could satisfy myself of the good effects upon the character and disposition; but I am convinced the probable tendency of both is to corrupt the understanding and the heart. I am not speaking of wit where it is kept down by more serious qualities of mind, and thrown into the background of the picture; but where it stands out boldly and emphatically, and is evidently the master quality in any particular mind. Profound wits, though they are generally courted for the amusement they afford, are seldom respected for the qualities they possess. The habit of seeing things in a witty point of view, increases, and makes incursions from its own proper regions, upon principles and opinions which are ever held sacred by the wise and good. A witty man is a dramatic performer: in process of time, he can no more exist without applause than he can exist without air; if his audience be small, or if they are inattentive, or if a new wit defrauds him of any portion of his admiration, it is all over with him — he sickens and is extinguished. The applauses of the theatre on which he performs are so essential to him that he must obtain them at the expense of decency, friendship, and good feeling. It must always be probable, too, that a mere wit is a person of light and frivolous understanding. His business is not to discover relations of ideas that are useful, and have a real influence upon life, but to discover the more trifling relations which are only amusing; he never looks at things with the naked eye of common sense, but is always gazing at the world through a Claude Lorraine glass, — discovering a thousand appearances which are created only by the instrument of inspection, and covering every object with factitious and unnatural colors. In short, the character of a mere wit it is impossible to consider as very amiable, very respectable, or very safe. So far the world, in judging of wit where it has swallowed up all other qualities, judge aright; but I doubt if they are sufficiently indulgent to this faculty where it exists in a lesser degree, and as one out of many other ingredients of the understanding. There is an association in men's minds between dullness and wisdom, amusement and folly, which has a powerful influence in decision upon character, and is not overcome without considerable difficulty. The reason is, that the outward signs of a dull man and a wise man are the same, and so are the outward signs of a frivolous man and a witty man; and we are not to expect that the majority will be disposed to look to much more than the outward sign. I believe the fact to be, that wit is very seldom the only eminent quality which resides in the mind of any man; it is commonly accompanied by many other talents of every description, and ought to be considered as a strong evidence of a fertile and superior understanding. Almost all the great poets, orators, and statesmen of all times have been witty. Cæsar, Alexander, Aristotle, Descartes, and Lord Bacon were witty men; so were Cicero, Shakespeare, Demosthenes, Boileau, Pope, Dryden, Fontenelle, Jonson, Waller, Cowley, Solon, Socrates, Dr. Johnson, and almost every man who has made a distinguished figure in the House of Commons. I have talked of the danger of wit: I do not mean by that to enter into commonplace declamation against faculties because they are dangerous; — wit is dangerous, eloquence is dangerous, a talent for observation is dangerous, everything is dangerous that has efficacy and vigor for its characteristics; nothing is safe but mediocrity. The business is, in conducting the understanding well, to risk something; to aim at uniting things that are commonly incompatible. The meaning of an extraordinary man is, that he is eight men, not one man; that he has as much wit as if he had no sense, and as much sense as if he had no wit; that his conduct is as judicious as if he were the dullest of human beings, and his imagination as brilliant as if he were irretrievably ruined. But when wit is combined with sense and information; when it is softened by benevolence, and restrained by strong principle; when it is in the hands of a man who can use it and despise it, who can be witty and something much better than witty, who loves honor, justice, decency, good-nature, morality, and religion ten thousand times better than wit; — wit is then a beautiful and delightful part of our nature. There is no more interesting spectacle than to see the effects of wit upon the different characters of men; than to observe it expanding caution, relaxing dignity, unfreezing coldness,— teaching age, and care, and pain, to smile,— extorting reluctant gleams of pleasure from melancholy, and charming even the pangs of grief. It is pleasant to observe how it penetrates through the coldness and awkwardness of society, gradually bringing men nearer together, and, like the combined force of wine and oil, giving every man a glad heart and shining countenance.

Genuine and innocent wit, like this, is surely the flavor of the
mind! Man could direct his ways by plain reason, and support
his life by tasteless food; but God has given us wit, and flavor,
and brightness, and laughter, and perfumes, to enliven the days
of man's pilgrimage, and to "charm his pained steps over the
burning marle."

EDGEWORTH ON BULLS

WE HARDLY know what to say about this rambling, scram-
bling book;* but that we are quite sure the author, when he
began any sentence in it, had not the smallest suspicion
of what it was about to contain. We say the author, because,
in spite of the mixture of sexes in the title-page, we are strongly
inclined to suspect that the male contributions exceed the female
in a very great degree. The essay on "Bulls" is written much
with the same mind, and in the same manner, as a schoolboy
takes a walk: he moves on for ten yards on the straight road,
with surprising perseverance; then sets out after a butterfly, looks
for a bird's nest, or jumps backwards and forwards over a ditch.
In the same manner, this nimble and digressive gentleman is
away after every object which crosses his mind. If you leave
him at the end of a comma, in a steady pursuit of his subject, you
are sure to find him, before the next full stop, a hundred yards
to the right or left, frisking, capering, and grinning, in a high
paroxysm of merriment and agility. Mr. Edgeworth seems to
possess the sentiments of an accomplished gentleman, the information of a scholar, and the vivacity of a first-rate harlequin. He is
fuddled with animal spirits, giddy with constitutional joy; in such
a state he must have written on, or burst. A discharge of ink
was an evacuation absolutely necessary, to avoid fatal and ple-
thoric congestion.

The object of the book is to prove that the practice of making bulls is not more imputable to the Irish than to any other people; and the manner in which he sets about it is to quote examples
of bulls produced in other countries. But this is surely a singular
way of reasoning the question; for there are goitres out of Va-
lais, extortioners who do not worship Moses, oatcakes out of the

* "An Essay on Irish Bulls," 1802, written by Miss Edgeworth in col-
laboration with her father.

Tweed, and balm beyond the precincts of Gilead. If nothing can be said to exist pre-eminently and emphatically in one country, which exists at all in another, then Frenchmen are not gay, nor Spaniards grave, nor are gentlemen of the Milesian race remarkable for their disinterested contempt of wealth in their connubial relations. It is probable there is some foundation for a character so generally diffused; though it is also probable that such foundation is extremely enlarged by fame. If there were no foundation for the common opinion, we must suppose national characters formed by chance; and that the Irish might, by accident, have been laughed at as bashful and sheepish; which is impossible. The author puzzles himself a good deal about the nature of bulls, without coming to any decision about the matter. Though the question is not a very easy one, we shall venture to say that a bull is an apparent congruity, and real incongruity, of ideas, suddenly discovered. And if this account of bulls be just, they are (as might have been supposed) the very reverse of wit; for as wit discovers real relations, that are not apparent, bulls admit apparent relations that are not real. The pleasure arising from wit proceeds from our surprise at suddenly discovering two things to be similar, in which we suspected no similarity. The pleasure arising from bulls proceeds from our discovering two things to be dissimilar, in which a resemblance might have been suspected. The same doctrine will apply to wit, and to bulls in action. Practical wit discovers connection or relation between actions, in which duller understandings discover none; and practical bulls originate from an apparent relation between two actions, which more correct understandings immediately perceive to have no relation at all.

Louis XIV. being extremely harassed by the repeated solicitations of a veteran officer for promotion, said one day, loud enough to be heard, "That gentleman is the most troublesome officer I have in my service." "That is precisely the charge," said the old man, "which your Majesty's enemies bring against me."

"An English gentleman," says Mr. Edgeworth, in a story cited from Joe Miller, "was writing a letter in a coffeehouse; and perceiving that an Irishman stationed behind him was taking that liberty which Parmenio used with his friend Alexander, instead of putting his seal upon the lips of the curious impertinent, the English gentleman thought proper to reprove the Hibernian, if not with delicacy, at least with poetical justice.

He concluded writing his letter in these words: 'I would say more, but a damned tall Irishman is reading over my shoulder every word I write.'

"'You lie, you scoundrel,' said the self-convicted Hibernian."

The pleasure derived from the first of these stories proceeds from the discovery of the relation that subsists between the object he had in view, and the assent of the officer to an observation so unfriendly to that end. In the first rapid glance which the mind throws upon his words, he appears, by his acquiescence, to be pleading against himself. There seems to be no relation between what he says and what he wishes to effect by speaking.

In the second story, the pleasure is directly the reverse. The lie given was apparently the readiest means of proving his innocence, and really the most effectual way of establishing his guilt. There seems for a moment to be a strong relation between the means and the object; while, in fact, no irrelation can be so complete.

What connection is there between pelting stones at monkeys and gathering cocoanuts from lofty trees? Apparently none. But monkeys sit upon cocoanut trees; monkeys are imitative animals; and if you pelt a monkey with a stone, he pelts you with a cocoanut in return. This scheme of gathering cocoanuts is very witty, and would be more so, if it did not appear useful; for the idea of utility is always inimical to the idea of wit. There appears, on the contrary, to be some relation between the revenge of the Irish rebels against a banker, and the means which they took to gratify it, by burning all his notes wherever they found them; whereas they could not have rendered him a more essential service. In both these cases of bulls, the one verbal, the other practical, there is an apparent congruity and real incongruity of ideas. In both the cases of wit, there is an apparent incongruity and a real relation.

It is clear that a bull cannot depend upon mere incongruity alone; for if a man were to say that he would ride to London upon a cocked hat, or that he would cut his throat with a pound of pickled salmon, this, though completely incongruous, would not be to make bulls, but to talk nonsense. The stronger the apparent connection, and the more complete the real disconnection of the ideas, the greater the surprise and the better the bull. The less apparent, and the more complete the relations established by wit, the higher gratification does it, afford. A great deal of the

IX—218

pleasure experienced from bulls proceeds from the sense of superiority in ourselves. Bulls which we invented, or knew to be invented, might please, but in a less degree, for want of this additional zest.

As there must be apparent connection, and real incongruity, it is seldom that a man of sense and education finds any form of words by which he is conscious that he might have been deceived into a bull. To conceive how the person has been deceived, he must suppose a degree of information very different from, and a species of character very heterogeneous to, his own; a process which diminishes surprise, and consequently pleasure. In the above-mentioned story of the Irishman overlooking the man writing, no person of ordinary sagacity can suppose himself betrayed into such a mistake; but he can easily represent to himself a kind of character that might have been so betrayed. There are some bulls so extremely fallacious, that any man may imagine himself to have been betrayed into them; but these are rare: and, in general, it is a poor, contemptible species of amusement; a delight in which evinces a very bad taste in wit.

Whether the Irish make more bulls than their neighbors, is, as we have before remarked, not a point of much importance; but it is of considerable importance, that the character of a nation should not be degraded; and Mr. Edgeworth has great merit in his very benevolent intention of doing justice to the excellent qualities of the Irish. It is not possible to read his book, without feeling a strong and a new disposition in their favor. Whether the imitation of the Irish manner be accurate in his little stories we cannot determine; but we feel the same confidence in the accuracy of the imitation that is often felt in the resemblance of a portrait, of which we have never seen the original. It is no very high compliment to Mr. Edgeworth's creative powers to say he could not have formed anything which was not real, so like reality; but such a remark only robs Peter to pay Paul, and gives everything to his powers of observation, which it takes from those of his imagination. In truth, nothing can be better than his imitation of the Irish manner: It is first-rate painting.

Edgeworth and Co. have another faculty in great perfection. They are eminently masters of the pathos. The Firm drew tears from us in the stories of little Dominick, and of the Irish beggar, who killed his sweetheart: Never was any grief more natural or simple. The first, however, ends in a very foolish way;

> "——*formosa superne*
> *Desinit in piscem.*"

We are extremely glad that our avocations did not call us from Bath to London on the day that the Bath coach conversation took place. We except from this wish the story with which the conversation terminates; for as soon as Mr. Edgeworth enters upon a story he excels.

We must confess we have been much more pleased with Mr. Edgeworth in his laughing and in his pathetic, than in his grave and reasoning, moods. He meant, perhaps, that we should; and it certainly is not very necessary that a writer should be profound on the subject of bulls. Whatever be the deficiencies of the book, they are, in our estimation, amply atoned for by its merits; by none more than that lively feeling of compassion which pervades it for the distresses of the wild, kind-hearted, blundering poor of Ireland.

Complete. From the Edinburgh
Review 1803.

TABLE–TALK

On a Habitual Bore

LORD CHESTERTON we have often met with, and suffered a good deal from his lordship: a heavy, pompous, meddling peer, occupying a great share of the conversation — saying things in ten words which required only two, and evidently convinced that he is making a great impression; a large man with a large head, and a very candid manner. Knowing enough to torment his fellow-creatures, not to instruct them; the intimate of young ladies, and the natural butt and target of wit. It is easy to talk of carnivorous animals and beasts of prey; but does such a man, who lays waste a whole civilized party of beings by prosing, reflect upon the joy he spoils, and the misery he creates, in the course of his life? and that any one who listens to him through politeness, would prefer toothache or earache to his conversation? Does he consider the extreme uneasiness which ensues when the company have discovered a man to be an extremely absurd person, at the same time that it is absolutely impossible to convey, by words or manner, the most distant suspicion of the discovery? And, then, who punishes this bore? What sessions or what assizes for him? What bill is found against him? Who indicts him? When the judges have gone their vernal and autumnal rounds, the sheepstealer disappears — the swindler gets ready for the Bay — the solid parts of the murderer are preserved in anatomical collections. But after twenty years of crime, the bore is discovered in the same house, in the same attitude, eating the same soup — untried — unpunished — undissected.

Monk Lewis's Tragedy of "Alfonso"

THIS tragedy delights in explosions. Alfonso's empire is destroyed by a blast of gunpowder, and restored by a clap of thunder. After the death of Cæsario, and a short exhortation to that purpose by Orsino, all the conspirators fall down in a thunderclap, ask pardon of the king and are forgiven. This mixture of physical and moral power is beautiful! How interesting a waterspout would appear among Mr. Lewis's kings and queens. We anxiously look forward, in his next tragedy, to a fall of snow, three or four feet deep, or expect a plot shall gradually unfold itself by means of a general thaw.

A Dinner Party

AN EXCELLENT and well-arranged dinner is a most pleasing occurrence, and a great triumph of civilized life. It is not only the descending morsel and the enveloping sauce, but the rank, wealth, wit, and beauty which surround the meats; the learned management of light and heat; the silent and rapid services of the attendants; the smiling and sedulous host, proffering gusts and relishes; the exotic bottles; the embossed plate; the pleasant remarks; the handsome dresses; the cunning artifices in fruit and farina! The hour of dinner, in short, includes everything of sensual and intellectual gratification, which a great nation glories in producing.

CLASSICAL GLORY

DR. GENGE, the celebrated Grecian, upon hearing the praises of the great king of Prussia, entertained considerable doubts whether the king, with all his victories, knew how to conjugate a Greek verb in μ.

OFFICIAL DRESS

THE Americans, we believe, are the first persons who have discarded the tailor in the administration of justice, and his auxiliary the barber,— two persons of endless importance in codes and pandects of Europe. A judge administers justice, without a calorific wig and party-colored gown, in a coat and pantaloons. He is obeyed, however; and life and property are not badly protected in the United States. We shall be denounced by the laureate as atheists and jacobins; but we must say that we have doubts whether one atom of useful influence is added to men in important situations by any color, quantity, or configuration of cloth and hair. The true progress of refinement, we conceive, is to discard all the mountebank drapery of barbarous ages. One row of gold and fur falls off after another from the robe of power, and is picked up and worn by the parish beadle and the exhibitor of wild beasts. Meantime, the afflicted wiseacre mourns over equality of garment, and wotteth not of two men, whose doublets have cost alike, how one shall command and the other obey.

PULPIT ELOQUENCE

PULPIT discourses have insensibly dwindled from speaking to reading,— a practice, of itself, sufficient to stifle every germ of eloquence. It is only by the fresh feelings of the heart, that mankind can be very powerfully affected. What can be more ludicrous than an orator delivering stale indignation, and fervor of a week old; turning over whole pages of violent passions, written out in German text; reading the tropes and apostrophes into which he is hurried by the ardor of his mind; and so affected at a preconcerted line and page, that he is unable to proceed any further!

IMPERTINENCE OF OPINION

IT IS always considered as a piece of impertinence in England, if a man of less than two or three thousand a year has any opinions at all upon important subjects.

PARASITES

NATURE descends down to infinite smallness. A great man has his parasites; and if you take a large, buzzing bluebottle fly, and look at it in a microscope, you may see twenty or thirty little ugly insects crawling about it, which, doubtless, think their fly to be the bluest, grandest, merriest, most important animal in the universe; and are convinced the world would be at an end if it ceased to buzz.

THE THEATRE

THERE is something in the word Playhouse which seems so closely connected, in the minds of some people, with sin and Satan, that it stands in their vocabulary for every species of abomination. And yet why? Where is every feeling more roused in favor of virtue than at a good play? Where is goodness so feelingly, so enthusiastically learned? What so solemn as to see the excellent passions of the human heart called forth by a great actor, animated by a great poet? To hear Siddons repeat what Shakespeare wrote? To behold the child and his mother — the noble and the poor artisan — the monarch and his subjects — all ages and all ranks convulsed with one common passion — wrung with one common anguish, and, with loud sobs and cries, doing involuntary homage to the God that made their hearts! What wretched infatuation to interdict such amusements as these! What a blessing that mankind can be allured from sensual gratification, and find relaxation and pleasure in such pursuits!

MARY FAIRFAX SOMERVILLE

(1780–1872)

RS. SOMERVILLE, whose "Connection of the Physical Sciences" and similar works gave her high rank among the scientific essayists of the nineteenth century, was born at Jedburgh, Scotland, December 26th, 1780. Her father, Sir William George Fairfax, was an admiral in the British navy. She had, and improved to an extraordinary degree, the advantages of her education and position. After the death of her first husband, Capt. Samuel Greig, she married her cousin, Dr. William Somerville, who encouraged and assisted her in the study of the physical sciences. After translating Laplace's "Mécanique Céleste," in 1831, she published her "Connection of the Physical Sciences" four years later, and in 1848 her "Physical Geography." Her "Molecular and Microscopic Science" appeared in 1866 and her "Personal Recollections" after her death, which occurred at Naples November 28, 1872.

THE LAWS OF MUSIC

WHEN the particles of elastic bodies are suddenly disturbed by an impulse, they return to their natural position by a series of isochronous vibrations, whose rapidity, force, and permanency depend upon the elasticity, the form, and the mode of aggregation which unites the particles of the body. These oscillations are communicated to the air, and on account of its elasticity they excite alternate condensations and dilatations in the strata of the fluid nearest to the vibrating body: from thence they are propagated to a distance. A string or wire stretched between two pins, when drawn aside and suddenly let go, will vibrate till its own rigidity and the resistance of the air reduce it to rest. These oscillations may be rotatory in every plane, or confined to one plane, according as the motion is communicated. In the pianoforte, where the strings are struck by a hammer at one extremity, the vibrations probably consist of a bulge running to and fro from end to end. Different modes of vibration may be obtained from the same sonorous body. Suppose a vibrating string to give the lowest C of the pianoforte, which is the fundamental note of the string; if it be lightly touched exactly in the middle so as to retain that point at rest, each half will then vibrate twice as fast as the whole, but in opposite directions; the ventral or bulging segments will be alternately above and below the natural position of the string, and the resulting note will be the octave above C. When a point at a third of the length of the string is kept at rest, the vibrations will be three times as fast as those of the whole string, and will give the twelfth above C. When the point of rest is one-fourth of the whole, the oscillations will be four times as fast as those of the fundamental note, and will give the double octave; and so on. These acute sounds are called the harmonics of the fundamental note. It is clear from what has been stated, that the string thus vibrating could not give these harmonics spontaneously unless it divided itself at its aliquot parts into two, three, four, or more segments in opposite states of vibration separated by points actually at rest. In proof of this, pieces of paper placed on the string at the half, third, fourth, or other aliquot points, according to the corresponding harmonic sound, will remain on it during its vibration, but will instantly fly off from any of the intermediate points. The points of rest called the nodal points of the string are a mere consequence of the law of interferences. For if a rope fastened at one end be moved to and fro at the other extremity so as to transmit a succession of equal waves along it, they will be successively reflected when they arrive at the other end of the rope by the fixed point, and in returning they will occasionally interfere with the advancing waves; and as these opposite undulations will at certain points destroy one another, the point of the rope in which this happens will remain at rest. Thus a series of nodes and ventral segments will be produced, whose number will depend upon the tension and the frequency of the alternate motions communicated to the movable end. So when a string fixed at both ends is put in motion by a sudden blow at any point of it, the primitive impulse divides itself into two pulses running opposite ways, which are each totally reflected at the extremities, and, running back again along the whole length, are again reflected at the other ends. And thus they will continue to run backward and forward, crossing one another at each traverse, and occasionally interfering, so as to produce nodes; so that the motion of a string fastened at both ends consists of a wave or pulse, continually doubled back on itself by reflection at the fixed extremities.

Harmonics generally coexist with the fundamental sound in the same vibrating body. If one of the lowest strings of the pianoforte be struck, an attentive ear will not only hear the fundamental note, but will detect all the others sounding along with it, though with less and less intensity as their pitch becomes higher. According to the law of coexisting undulations, the whole string and each of its aliquot parts are in different and independent states of vibration at the same time; and as all the resulting notes are heard simultaneously, not only the air but the ear also vibrates in unison with each at the same instant.

Harmony consists in an agreeable combination of sounds. When two chords perform their vibrations in the same time, they are in unison. But when their vibrations are so related as to have a common period after a few oscillations, they produce concord. Thus when the vibrations of two strings bear a very simple relation to each other, as where one of them makes two, three, four, etc., vibrations in the time the other makes one; or if it accomplishes three, four, etc., vibrations while the other makes two, the result is a concord which is the more perfect the shorter the common period. In discords, on the contrary, the beats are distinctly audible, which produces a disagreeable and harsh effect, because the vibrations do not bear a simple relation to one another, as where one of two strings makes eight vibrations while the other accomplishes fifteen. The pleasure afforded by harmony is attributed by Dr. Young to the love of order, and to a predilection for a regular repetition of sensations natural to the human mind, which is gratified by the perfect regularity and rapid recurrence of the vibrations. The love of poetry and dancing he conceives to arise in some degree from the rhythm of the one and the regularity of the motions in the other.

A blast of air passing over the open end of a tube, as over the reeds in Pan's pipes; over a hole in one side, as in the flute; or through the aperture called a reed with a flexible tongue, as in the clarinet, puts the internal column of air into longitudinal vibrations by the alternate condensations and rarefactions of its particles. At the same time the column spontaneously divides itself into nodes between which the air also vibrates longitudinally, but with a rapidity inversely proportional to the length of the divisions, giving the fundamental note or one of its harmonics.

The nodes are produced on the principle of interferences by the reflection of the longitudinal undulations of the air at the ends of the pipe, as in the musical string, only that in one case the undulations are longitudinal, and in the other transverse.

A pipe either open or shut at both ends when sounded vibrates entire, or divides itself spontaneously into two, three, four, etc., segments separated by nodes. The whole column gives the fundamental note by waves or vibrations of the same length with the pipe. The first harmonic is produced by waves half as long as the tube, the second harmonic by waves a third as long, and so on. The harmonic segments in an open and shut pipe are the same in number, but differently placed. In a shut pipe the two ends are nodes, but in an open pipe there is half a segment at each extremity, because the air at these points is neither rarefied nor condensed, being in contact with that which is external. If one of the ends of the open pipe be closed, its fundamental note will be an octave lower, the air will now divide itself into three, five, seven, etc., segments,—and the wave producing its fundamental note will be twice as long as the pipe, so that it will be doubled back. All these notes may be produced separately, by varying the intensity of the blast. Blowing steadily and gently, the fundamental note will sound; when the force of the blast is increased, the note will all at once start up an octave; when the intensity of the wind is augmented, the twelfth will be heard, and by continuing to increase the force of the blast the other harmonics may be obtained, but no force of wind will produce a note intermediate between these. The harmonics of a flute may be obtained in this manner, from the lowest C or D upward, without altering the fingering, merely by increasing the intensity of the blast, and altering the form of the lips. Pipes of the same dimensions, whether of lead, glass, or wood, give the same tone as to pitch under the same circumstances, which shows that the air alone produces the sound.

Metal springs fastened at one end, when forcibly bent, endeavor to return to rest by a series of vibrations, which give very pleasing tones, as in musical boxes. Various musical instruments have recently been constructed, consisting of metallic springs thrown into vibration by a current of air. Among the most perfect of these are Mr. Wheatstone's symphonion, concertina, and æolian organ, instruments of different effects and capabilities, but all possessing considerable execution and expression.

The syren is an ingenious instrument, devised by M. Cagniard de la Tour, for ascertaining the number of pulsations in a second corresponding to each pitch; the notes are produced by jets of air passing through small apertures arranged at regular distances in a circle on the side of a box, before which a disk revolves pierced with the same number of holes. During a revolution of the disk the currents are alternately intercepted and allowed to pass as many times as there are apertures in it, and a sound is produced whose pitch depends on the velocity of rotation.

A glass or metallic rod, when struck at one end, or rubbed in the direction of its length with a wet finger, vibrates longitudinally like a column of air, by the alternate condensation and expansion of its constituent particles, producing a clear and beautiful musical note of a high pitch, on account of the rapidity with which these substances transmit sound. Rods, surfaces, and, in general, all undulating bodies, resolve themselves into nodes. But in surfaces, the parts which remain at rest during their vibrations are lines, which are curved or plane according to the substance, its form, and the mode of vibration. If a little fine dry sand be strewed over the surface of a plate of glass or metal, and if undulations be excited by drawing the bow of a violin across its edge, it will emit a musical sound, and the sand will immediately arrange itself in the nodal lines, where alone it will accumulate and remain at rest, because the segments of the surface on each side will be in different states of vibration, the one being elevated while the other is depressed; and as these two motions meet in the nodal lines, they neutralize one another. These lines vary in form and position with the part where the bow is drawn across, and the point by which the plate is held. The motion of the sand shows in what direction the vibrations take place. If they be perpendicular to the surface, the sand will be violently tossed up and down, till it finds the points of rest. If they be tangential, the sand will only creep along the surface to the nodal lines. Sometimes the undulations are oblique, or compounded of both the preceding. If a bow be drawn across one of the angles of a square plate of glass or metal held firmly by the centre, the sand will arrange itself in two straight lines parallel to the sides of the plate, and crossing in the centre so as to divide it into four equal squares, whose motions will be contrary to each other. Two of the diagonal squares will make their excursions on one side of the plate, while the other two make their vibrations on the other side of it. This mode of vibration produces the lowest tone of the plate. If the plate be still held by the centre, and the bow applied to the middle of one of the sides, the vibrations will be more rapid, and the tone will be a fifth higher than in the preceding case; now the sand will arrange itself from corner to corner, and will divide the plate into four equal triangles, each pair of which will make their excursions on opposite sides of the plate. The nodal lines and pitch vary not only with the point where the bow is applied, but with the point by which the plate is held, which, being at rest, necessarily determines the direction of one of the quiescent lines. The forms assumed by the sand in square plates are very numerous, corresponding to all the various modes of vibration. The lines in circular plates are even more remarkable for their symmetry, and upon them the forms assumed by the sand may be classed in three systems. The first is the diametrical system, in which the figures consist of diameters dividing the circumference of the plate into equal parts, each of which is in a different state of vibration from those adjacent. Two diameters, for example, crossing at right angles, divide the circumference into four equal parts; three diameters divide it into six equal parts; four divide it into eight, and so on. In a metallic plate, these divisions may amount to thirty-six or forty. The next is the concentric system, where the sand arranges itself in circles, having the same centre with the plate; and the third is the compound system, where the figures assumed by the sand are compounded of the other two, producing very complicated and beautiful forms. Galileo seems to have been the first to notice the points of rest and motion in the sounding-board of a musical instrument; but to Chladni is due the whole discovery of the symmetrical forms of the nodal lines in vibrating plates. Prof. Wheatstone has shown in a paper read before the Royal Society, in 1833, that all Chladni's figures, and indeed all the nodal figures of vibrating surfaces, result from very simple modes of vibration, oscillating isochronously, and superposed upon each other; the resulting figure varying with the component modes of vibration, the number of the superpositions, and the angles at which they are superposed. For example, if a square plate be vibrating so as to make the sand arrange itself in straight lines parallel to one side of the plate, and if, in addition to this, such vibrations be excited as would have caused the sand to form in lines perpendicular to the first had the plate been at rest, the combined vibrations will make the sand form in lines from corner to corner. . . .

A musical string gives a very feeble sound when vibrating alone, on account of the small quantity of air set in motion. But when attached to a sounding-board, as in the harp and pianoforte, it communicates its undulations to that surface, and from thence to every part of the instrument; so that the whole system vibrates isochronously, and by exposing an extensive undulating surface, which transmits its undulations to a great mass of air, the sound is much reinforced. The intensity is greatest when the vibrations of the string or sounding body are perpendicular to the sounding-board, and least when they are in the same plane with it. The sounding-board of the pianoforte is better disposed than that of any other stringed instrument, because the hammers strike the strings so as to make them vibrate at right angles to it. In the guitar, on the contrary, they are struck obliquely, which renders the tone feeble, unless when the sides, which also act as a sounding-board, are deep. It is evident that the sounding-board and the whole instrument are agitated at once by all the superposed vibrations excited by the simultaneous or consecutive notes that are sounded, each having its perfect effect independently of the rest. A sounding-board not only reciprocates the different degrees of pitch, but all the nameless qualities of tone. This has been beautifully illustrated by Prof. Wheatstone in a series of experiments on the transmission through solid conductors of musical performances, from the harp, piano, violin, clarinet, etc. He found that all the varieties of pitch, quality, and intensity, are perfectly transmitted with their relative gradations, and may be communicated through conducting wires or rods of very considerable length, to a properly disposed sounding-board in a distant apartment. The sounds of an entire orchestra may be transmitted and reciprocated by connecting one end of a metallic rod with a sounding-board near the orchestra, so placed as to resound to all the instruments, and the other end with the sounding-board of a harp, piano, or guitar, in a remote apartment. Prof. Wheatstone observes, " The effect of this experiment is very pleasing; the sounds, indeed, have so little intensity as scarcely to be heard at a distance from the reciprocating instrument; but on placing the ear close to it, a diminutive band is heard, in which all the instruments preserve their distinctive qualities, and the pianos and fortes, the crescendos and diminu-

endos, their relative contrasts. Compared with an ordinary band
heard at a distance through the air, the effect is as a landscape
seen in miniature beauty through a concave lens, compared with
the same scene viewed by ordinary vision through a murky
atmosphere.»

Every one is aware of the reinforcement of sound by the resonance of cavities. When singing or speaking near the aperture
of a wide-mouthed vessel, the intensity of some one note in unison with the air in the cavity is often augmented to a great degree. Any vessel will resound, if a body vibrating the natural
note of the cavity be placed opposite to its orifice, and be large
enough to cover it; or at least to set a large portion of the adjacent air in motion. For the sound will be alternately reflected
by the bottom of the cavity and the undulating body at its
mouth. The first impulse of the undulating substance will be reflected by the bottom of the cavity, and then by the undulating
body, in time to combine with the second new impulse. This
reinforced sound will also be twice reflected in time to conspire
with the third new impulse; and as the same process will be repeated on every new impulse, each will combine with all its
echoes to reinforce the sound prodigiously. Prof. Wheatstone, to
whose ingenuity we are indebted for so much new and valuable
information on the theory of sound, has given some very striking
instances of resonance. If one of the branches of a vibrating
tuning fork be brought near the embouchure of a flute, the lateral
apertures of which are stopped so as to render it capable of producing the same sound as the fork, the feeble and scarcely audible sound of the fork will be augmented by the rich resonance
of the column of air within the flute, and the tone will be full
and clear. The sound will be found greatly to decrease by closing or opening another aperture; for the alteration in the length
of the column of air renders it no longer fit perfectly to recipro-
cate the sound of the fork. This experiment may be made on a
concert flute with a C tuning fork. But Prof. Wheatstone observes that in this case it is generally necessary to finger the
flute for B, because when blown into with the mouth the upper
lip partly covers the embouchure, which renders the sound about
a semitone flatter than it would be were the embouchure entirely
uncovered. He has also shown, by the following experiment,
that any one among several simultaneous sounds may be rendered separately audible. If two bottles be selected, and tuned

by filling them with such a quantity of water as will render them unisonant with two tuning forks which differ in pitch, on bringing both of the vibrating tuning forks to the mouth of each bottle alternately, in each case that sound only will be heard which is reciprocated by the unisonant bottle.

Several attempts have been made to imitate the articulation of the letters of the alphabet. About the year 1779 MM. Kratzenstein of St. Petersburg, and Kempelen of Vienna, constructed instruments which articulated many letters, words, and even sentences. Mr. Willis of Cambridge has recently adapted cylindrical tubes to a reed, whose length can be varied at pleasure by sliding joints. Upon drawing out a tube while a column of air from the bellows of an organ is passing through it, the vowels are pronounced in the order, i, e, a, o, u. On extending the tube they are repeated after a certain interval, in the inverted order, u, o, a, e, i. After another interval they are again obtained in the direct order, and so on. When the pitch of the reed is very high, it is impossible to sound some of the vowels, which is in perfect correspondence with the human voice, female singers being unable to pronounce u and o in their high notes. From the singular discoveries of M. Savart on the nature of the human voice, and the investigations of Mr. Willis on the mechanism of the larynx, it may be presumed that ultimately the utterance or pronunciation of modern languages will be conveyed, not only to the eye, but also to the ear of posterity. Had the Ancients possessed the means of transmitting such definite sounds, the civilized world would still have responded in sympathetic notes at the distance of many ages.

From «Connection of the Physical Sciences.»

ROBERT SOUTHEY

(1774-1843)

ROBERT SOUTHEY was born at Bristol, England, August 12th, 1774. After having been expelled from Westminster School for writing an essay on "Flogging" for the school paper, he was admitted, after considerable difficulty, to Balliol College, Oxford, where he formed associations which were decisive of his future. One of his college friends was Coleridge, with whom he was interested in the famous scheme of "pantisocracy," through which the young poets hoped to establish the millennium in the United States. The association helped to make Southey one of the Lake School of English poets. After a year of travel, and a brief term in an official position, he took up his residence in 1804 at Greta Hall, near Keswick, where he devoted himself to study with painstaking industry. Few men of his century equaled him in the range and variety of his studies. His "Commonplace Book" is astonishing. It would be hard to find anywhere else so great an amount of curious, entertaining, and generally useless information as he collected in it. He was a man of books rather than of the world, and the distinction shows in all he wrote, both of prose and verse. He became Poet Laureate of England in 1813,— an honor he owed not only to his talent, but to his conversion to "Conservatism" and his complete abandonment of "pantisocracy" and all similar millennium ideals. He died at Greta Hall, March 21st, 1843. Among his best-known prose works are his "History of Brazil," "Life of Nelson," and "The Doctor," — the latter a collection of highly original essays which show him at his best.

FAME

GUESS, reader, where I once saw a full-sized figure of Fame, erect, tiptoe, in the act of springing to take flight, and soar aloft, her neck extended, her head raised, the trumpet at her lips, and her cheeks inflated, as if about to send forth a blast which the whole city of London was to hear? Perhaps thou mayst have seen this very figure thyself, and surely if thou hast, thou wilt not have forgotten it. It was in the Borough Road, placed above a shopboard which announced that Mr. Somebody fitted up water-closets upon a new and improved principle.

But it would be well for mankind if Fame were never employed in trumpeting anything worse. There is a certain stage of depravity in which men derive an unnatural satisfaction from the notoriety of their wickedness, and seek for celebrity " *ob magnitudinem infamiæ, cujus apud prodigos novissima voluptas est. Ils veulent faire parler d'eux,*" says Bayle, " *et leur vanité ne serait pas satisfaite s'il n'y avait quelque chose de superlatif et d'éminent dans leur mauvaise reputation. Le plus haut degré de l'infamie est le but de leurs souhaits, et il y a des choses qu'ils ne feraient pas si elles n'étaient extraordinairement odieuses.*"

Plutarch has preserved the name of Chœrephanes, who was notorious among the Ancients for having painted such subjects as Giulio Romano has the everlasting infamy of having designed for the flagitious Aretine. He has also transmitted to posterity the name of Parmeno, famous for grunting like a pig; and of Theodorus, not less famous for the more difficult accomplishment of mimicking the sound of a creaking cart-wheel. Who would wish to have his name preserved for his beggarliness, like Pauson, the painter, and Codrus, the poet? or for his rascality and wickedness, like Phrynondas? or like Callianax, the physician, for callous brutality? Our doctor used to instance these examples when he talked of "the bubble reputation," which is sometimes to be had so cheaply, and yet for which so dear a price has often been paid in vain. It amused him to think by what odd or pitiful accidents that bubble might be raised. " Whether the regular practitioner may sneer at Mr. Ching," says the historian of Cornwall, " I knew not; but the Patent Worm Lozenges have gained our Launceston apothecary a large fortune, and secured to him perpetual fame."

Would not John Dory's name have died with him, and so been long ago dead as a doornail, if a grotesque likeness to him had not been discovered in the fish, which, being called after him, has immortalized him and his ugliness? But if John Dory could have anticipated this sort of immortality when he saw his own face in the glass, he might very well have "blushed to find it fame." There would have been no other memorial of Richard Jacquett at this day than the letters of his name in an old dead and obsolete hand, now well-nigh rendered illegible by time, if he had not, in the reign of Edward VI., been lord of the manor of Tyburn, with its appurtenances, wherein the gallows was included, wherefore, from the said Jacquett, it is presumed by antiquaries that the hangman hath been ever since corruptly called Jack Ketch. A certain William Dowsing, who, during the great Rebellion, was one of the parliamentary visitors for demolishing superstitious pictures and ornaments of churches, is supposed by a learned critic to have given rise to an expression in common use among schoolboys and blackguards. For this worshipful commissioner broke so many "mighty great angels" in glass, knocked so many apostles and cherubims to pieces, demolished so many pictures and stone crosses, and boasted with so much puritanical rancor of what he had done, that it is conjectured the threat of giving any one a dowsing preserves his rascally name. So, too, while Bracton and Fleta rest on the shelves of some public library, Nokes and Stiles are living names in the courts of law; and for John Doe and Richard Roe, were there ever two litigious fellows so universally known as these eternal antagonists?

Johnson tells a story of a man who was standing in an inn kitchen with his back to the fire, and thus accosted a traveler, who stood next to him, "Do you know, sir, who I am?" "No, sir," replied the traveler, "I have not that advantage." "Sir," said the man, "I am the great Twalmley, who invented the new flood-gate iron." Who but for Johnson would have heard of the great Twalmley now? Reader, I will answer the question which thou hast already asked, and tell thee that his invention consisted in applying a sliding door, like a flood gate, to an ironing box, flat irons having till then been used, or box irons with a door and a bolt.

Who was Tom Long the carrier? when did he flourish? what road did he travel? did he drive carts or wagons, or was it in the age of pack horses? Who was Jack Robinson? not the once well-known Robinson of the treasury (for his celebrity is now like a tale that is told), but the one whose name is in everybody's mouth, because it is so easily and so soon said. Who was Magg? and what was his diversion? was it brutal, or merely boorish? the boisterous exuberance of rude and unruly mirth, or the gratification of a tyrannical temper and a cruel disposition? Who was Crop the conjuror, famous in trivial speech as Merlin in romantic lore, or Doctor Faustus in the school of German extravagance? What is remembered now of Bully Dawson? All I have read of him is that he lived three weeks on the credit of a brass shilling, because nobody would take it of him. "There goes a story of Queen Elizabeth," says Ray, "that being presented with a collection of English proverbs, and told by the author that it contained them all, 'Nay,' replied she, 'Bate me an ace, quoth Bolton!' which proverb being instantly looked for, happened to be wanting in his collection." "Who this Bolton was," Ray says, "I know not, neither is it worth inquiring." Nevertheless, I ask who was Bolton; and when echo answers, "who?" say in my heart, "*Vanitas vanitatum, omnia vanitas.*" And having said this, conscience smites me with the recollection of what Pascal has said, "*Ceux qui écrivent contre la gloire, veulent avoir la gloire d'avoir bien écrit; et ceux qui le lisent, voulent avoir la gloire de l'avoir lu; et moi qui écris ceci, j'ai peut-être cette envie, et peut-être que ceux qui le lirent l'auront aussi.*"

Who was old Ross of Potern, who lived till all the world was weary of him? All the world has forgotten him now. Who was Jack Raker, once so well known that he was named proverbially as a scapegrace by Skelton, and in the "Ralph Roister Doister" of Nicholas Udall, that Udall who, on poor Tom Tusser's account, ought always to be called the bloody schoolmaster? Who was William Dickins, whose wooden dishes were sold so badly, that when any one lost by the sale of his wares, the said Dickins and his dishes were brought up in scornful comparison? Outroaring Dick was a strolling singer of such repute that he got twenty shillings a day by singing at Braintree Fair; but who was that desperate Dick that was such a terrible cutter at a chine of beef, and devoured more meat at ordinaries in discoursing of his frays and deep acting, of his flashing and hewing, than would serve half a dozen brewer's draymen? It is at this day doubtful whether it was Jack Drum, or Tim Drum, whose mode of entertainment no one wishes to receive;—for it was to haul a man in by the head and thrust him out by the neck and shoulders. Who was that other Dick who wore so queer a hatband, that it has ever since served as a standing comparison for all queer things? By what name besides Richard was he known? Where did he live, and when? His birth, parentage, education, life, character, and behavior, who can tell? "Nothing," said the doctor, "is remembered of him, except that he was familiarly called Dick, and that his queer hatband went nine times round and would not tie."

> "O vain world's glory and unsteadfast state
> Of all that lives on face of sinful earth!"

Who was Betty Martin, and wherefore should she so often be mentioned in connection with my precious eye or yours? Who was Ludlam, whose dog was so lazy that he leaned his head against a wall to bark? And who was Old Cole, whose dog was so proud that he took the wall of a dung cart, and got squeezed to death by the wheel? Was he the same person of whom the song says:—

> "Old King Cole
> Was a merry old soul,
> And a merry old soul was he"?

And was his dog proud because his master was called king? Here are questions to be proposed in the examination papers of some Australian Cambridge, two thousand years hence, when the people of that part of the world shall be as reasonably inquisitive concerning our affairs as we are now concerning those of the Greeks. But the Burneys, the Parrs, and the Porsons, the Elmsleys, Monks, and Blomfields of that age will puzzle over them in vain, for we cannot answer them now.

"Who was the Vicar of Bray? I have had long chase after him," said Mr. Brome to Rawlins, in 1735. "Simon Aleyn, or Allen, was his name; he was Vicar of Bray about 1540, and died in 1588; so he held the living near fifty years. You now partake of the sport that has cost me some pains to take. And if the pursuit after such game seems mean, one Mr. Vernon followed a butterfly nine miles before he could catch him." Reader, do not refuse your belief of this fact, when I can state to you, on my own recollection, that the late Dr. Shaw, the celebrated naturalist, a librarian of the British Museum, and known by the name of the learned Shavius, from the facility and abundance of his Latin compositions, pointed out to my notice there, many years ago, two volumes written by a Dutchman, upon the wings of a butterfly. "The dissertation is rather voluminous, sir, perhaps you will think," said the doctor, with somewhat of that apologetic air, which modest science is wont occasionally to assume in her communications with ignorance, "but it is immensely important." Good-natured excellent enthusiast! fully didst thou appreciate the book, the Dutchman, and, above all, the butterfly.

"I have known a great man," says Taylor, the water poet, "very expert on the Jew's-harp; a rich heir excellent at noddy; a justice of the peace skillful at quoits; a merchant's wife a quick gamester at Irish, especially when she came to bearing of men, that she would seldom miss entering." Injurious John Taylor! thus to defraud thy friends of their fame, and leave in irremediable oblivion the proper name of that expert Jew's-harper, that person excellent at noddy, that great quoits man, and that mistress who played so masterly a game at Irish! But I thank thee for this, good John the water poet; thou hast told us that Monsieur La Ferr, a Frenchman, was the first inventor of that admirable game of double-hand, hotcockles, etc., and that Gregory Dawson, an Englishman, devised the unmatchable mystery of blindman's-buff. But who can tell me what the game of carps was, the *Ludus Carparum*, which Hearne says was used in Oxford much, and being joined with cards, and reckoned as a kind of *alea*, is prohibited in some statutes? When Thomas Hearne, who learned whatever time forgot, was uncertain what game or play it really was, and could only conjecture that perhaps it might be a kind of backgammon, what antiquary can hope to ascertain it?

"Elizabeth Canning, Mary Squires, the gipsy, and Miss Blandy," says one who remembered their days of celebrity, "were such universal topics in 1752, that you would have supposed it the business of mankind to talk only of them; yet now, in 1790, ask a young man of twenty-five or thirty a question relative to these extraordinary personages, and he will be puzzled to answer."

Who now knows the steps of that dance, or has heard the name of its author, of which in our fathers' days it was said in verse, that —

> "Isaac's rigadoon shall live as long
> As Raphael's paintings, or as Virgil's song"?

Nay, who reads the poem wherein those lines are found, though the author predicted for them, in self-applauding pleasantry, that —

> "Whilst birds in air or fish in streams we find,
> Or damsels fresh with aged partners joined,
> As long as nymphs shall with attentive ear
> A fiddle rather than a sermon hear,
> So long the brightest eye shall oft peruse
> These useful lines of my instructive muse"?

Even of the most useful of those lines the "uses are gone by." Ladies before they leave the ballroom are now no longer fortified against the sudden change of temperature by a cup of generous white wine, mulled with ginger; nor is it necessary now to caution them at such times against a draught of cold small beer, because, as the poet in his own experience assured them,—

«Destruction lurks within the poisonous dose,
A fatal fever, or a pimpled nose.»

From «The Doctor.»

THE DOCTOR'S WISE SAYINGS

SCHOOL LEARNING

I AM sometimes inclined to think that pigs are brought up upon a wiser system than boys at a grammar school. The pig is allowed to feed upon any kind of offal, however coarse, on which he can thrive, till the time approaches when pig is to commence pork, or take a degree as bacon.

LOVERS OF LITERATURE

YOUR true lover of literature is never fastidious. I do not mean the *helluo librorum*, the swinish feeder, who thinks that every name which is to be found in a title-page, or on a tombstone, ought to be rescued from oblivion; nor those first cousins of the moth, who labor under a passion for black letter, and believe everything to be excellent which was written in the reign of Elizabeth. I mean the man of robust and healthy intellect, who gathers the harvest of literature into his barns, thrashes the straw, winnows the grain, grinds it at his own mill, bakes it in his own oven, and then eats the true bread of knowledge. If he take his loaf upon a cabbage leaf, and eat onions with his bread and cheese, let who will find fault with him for his taste — not I!

VANITY OF HUMAN FAME

AN OLD woman in a village of the west of England was told one day that the king of Prussia was dead, such a report having arrived when the great Frederick was in the noonday of his glory. Old Mary lifted up her great slow eyes at the news, and, fixing them in the fullness of vacancy upon her informant, replied, "Is a! is a! the Lord ha' mercy! Well, well! the king of Prussia! and who's he?" The "who's he?" of this old woman might serve as a text for a notable sermon upon ambition. "Who's he?" may now be asked of men greater as soldiers in their day than Frederick and Wellington; greater as discoverers than Sir Isaac, or Sir Humphrey. Who built the pyramids? Who ate the first oyster? *Vanitas vanitatum, omnia vanitas!*

RETIREMENT

I⊤ IS neither so easy a thing, nor so agreeable a one, as men commonly expect, to dispose of leisure when they retire from the business of the world. Their old occupations cling to them even when they hope that they have emancipated themselves. Go to any seaport town, and you will see that the sea captain, who has retired upon his well-earned earnings, sets up a weather cock in full view from his window, and watches the variations of the wind as duly as when he was at sea, though no longer with the same anxiety. A tallow chandler, having amassed a fortune, disposed of his business, and took a house in the country, not far from London, that he might enjoy himself; and, after a few months' trial of a holiday life, requested permission of his successor to come into town and assist him on melting days. The keeper of a retail spirit-shop, having in like manner retired from trade, used to employ himself by having one puncheon filled with water, and measuring it off by pints into another. A butcher in a small town, for some time after he had left off business, informed his old customers that he meant to kill a lamb once a week just for amusement.

PREACHING TO THE POOR

A WOMAN in humble life was asked one day on her way back from church whether she had understood the sermon—a stranger having preached. "Wud I hae the presumption!" was her simple and contented answer.

"Well, Master Jackson," said his minister, walking homeward after service, with an industrious laborer, who was a constant attendant, "well, Master Jackson, Sunday must be a blessed day of rest for you, who work so hard all the week! And you make good use of the day, for you are always to be seen at church."

"Aye, sir," replied Jackson, "it is, indeed, a blessed day; I works hard enough all the week; and then I comes to church o' Sundays, and sets me down, and lays my legs up, and thinks o' nothing."

VOLUMINOUS TRIFLING

DR. SHAW, the naturalist, was one day showing to a friend two volumes written by a Dutchman, upon the wings of a butterfly, in the British Museum. "The dissertation is rather voluminous, perhaps you will think," said the doctor gravely, "but it is immensely important."

PARLIAMENTARY JOKES

OF WHAT use a story may be, even in the most serious debates, may be seen from the circulation of old Joes in parliament, which are as current there as their current namesakes used to be in the city some threescore years ago. A jest, though it shall be as stale as last year's newspapers, and as flat as Lord Flounder's face, is sure to be received with laughter by the collective wisdom of the nation; nay, it is sometimes thrown out like a tub to the whale, or like a trail of carrion to draw off hounds from the scent.

BOOK MADNESS

A COLLECTOR of scarce books was one day showing me his small but curious hoard. "Have you ever seen a copy of this book?" he asked, with every volume that he put into my hands; and when my reply was that I had not, he always rejoined, with a look and tone of triumphant delight, "I should have been exceedingly sorry if you had!"

ÉMILE SOUVESTRE

(1806–1854)

ÉMILE SOUVESTRE, novelist and essayist, was born in Morlaix, Brittany, April 15th, 1806. He began life with no other means of support than his daily labor, and it was only after years of struggle as bookseller's clerk, schoolmaster, and journalist, that he finally won the reputation as a writer for which he had industriously striven. He wrote novels and dramas which were more popular during his life than his essays; but while the novels are now seldom read, his "Attic Philosopher in Paris" (Un Philosophe sous les Toits) continues to go through one edition after another. It is a collection of essays in half narrative style, with just enough plot to give the characters in them vitality. Souvestre died July 5th, 1854.

MISANTHROPY AND REPENTANCE

AUGUST 3d, nine o'clock P. M.— There are days when everything appears gloomy to us; the world is, like the sky, covered by a dark fog. Nothing seems in its place; we only see misery, improvidence, and cruelty; the world seems without God, and given up to all the evils of chance.

Yesterday I was in this unhappy humor. After a long walk in the faubourgs, I returned home, sad and dispirited.

Everything I had seen seemed to accuse the civilization of which we are so proud! I had wandered into a little by-street, with which I was not acquainted, and I found myself suddenly in the middle of those dreadful abodes where the poor are born, languish, and die. I looked at those decaying walls, which time has covered with a foul leprosy; those windows, from which dirty rags hang out to dry; those fetid gutters, which coil along the fronts of the houses like venomous reptiles! I felt oppressed with grief, and hastened on.

A little further on I was stopped by the hearse of a hospital, —a dead man, nailed down in his deal coffin, was going to his last abode, without funeral pomp or ceremony, and without followers. There was not here even that last friend of the outcast, — the dog, which a painter has introduced as the sole attendant at the pauper's burial! He whom they were preparing to commit to the earth was going to the tomb as he had lived, alone; doubtless, no one would be aware of his end. In this great battle of society, what signifies a soldier the less?

But what, then, is this human society, if one of its members can thus disappear, like a leaf carried away by the wind?

The hospital was near a barrack, at the entrance of which old men, women, and children were quarreling for the remains of the coarse bread which the soldiers had given them in charity! Thus, beings like ourselves daily wait, in destitution, on our compassion, till we give them leave to live! Whole troops of outcasts, in addition to the trials imposed on all God's children, have to endure the pangs of cold, hunger, and humiliation. Unhappy human commonwealth! where man is in a worse condition than the bee in its hive, or the ant in its subterranean city!

Ah! what then avails our reason? What is the good of so many high faculties, if we are neither the wiser nor the happier for them? Which of us would not exchange his life of labor and trouble with that of the birds of the air, to whom the whole world is a life of joy.

How well I understand the complaint of Mao, in the popular tales of the "Le Foyer Breton," who, when dying of hunger and thirst, says, as he looks at the bullfinches rifling the fruit trees,—

"Alas! those birds are happier than Christians; they have no need of inns, or butchers, or bakers, or gardeners. God's heaven belongs to them and earth spreads a continual feast before them! The tiny flies are their game, ripe grass their cornfields, and hips and haws their store of fruit. They have the right of taking everywhere, without paying or asking leave; thus comes it that the little birds are happy, and sing all the livelong day."

But the life of man in a natural state is like that of the birds; he equally enjoys nature. "The earth spreads a continual feast before him." What, then, has he gained by that selfish and imperfect association which forms a nation? Would it not be better for every one to return again to the fertile bosom of Nature, and live there upon her bounty in peace and liberty?

August 10th, four o'clock A. M.— The dawn casts a red glow on my bed curtains; the breeze brings in the fragrance of the gardens below; here I am again leaning on my elbows by the window, inhaling the freshness and gladness of this first wakening of the day.

My eye always passes over the roofs filled with flowers, warbling and sunlight with the same pleasure; but to-day it stops at the end of a buttress which separates our house from the next. The storms have stripped the top of its plaster covering, and dust, carried by the wind, has collected in the crevices, and, being fixed there by the rain, has formed a sort of aërial terrace, where some green grass has sprung up. Amongst it rises a stalk of wheat, which to-day is surmounted by a sickly ear that droops its yellow head.

This poor stray crop on the roofs, the harvest of which will fall to the neighboring sparrows, has carried my thoughts to the rich crops which are now falling beneath the sickle; it has recalled to me the beautiful walks I took as a child through my native province, when the threshing floors at the farmhouses resounded from every part with the sound of the flail, and when the carts, loaded with golden sheaves, came in by all the roads. I still remember the songs of the maidens, the cheerfulness of the old men, the open-hearted merriment of the laborers. There was, at that time, something in their looks both of pride and feeling. The latter came from thankfulness to God; the former from the sight of the harvest, the reward of their labor. They felt indistinctly the grandeur and the holiness of their part in the general work of the world; they looked with pride upon their mountains of corn sheaves, and they seemed to say — next to God, it is we who feed the world!

What a wonderful order there is in all human labor! Whilst the husbandman furrows his land, and prepares for every one his daily bread, the town artisan, far away, weaves the stuff in which he is to be clothed; the miner seeks under ground the iron for his plow; the soldier defends him against the invader; the judge takes care that the law protects his fields; the tax comptroller adjusts his private interests with those of the public; the merchant occupies himself in exchanging his products with those of distant countries; the men of science and of art add every day a few horses to this ideal team, which draws along the material world, as steam impels the gigantic trains of our iron roads! Thus all unite together, all help one another; the toil of each one benefits himself and all the world; the work has

been apportioned among the different members of the whole of
society by a tacit agreement. If, in this apportionment, errors
are committed, if certain individuals have not been employed
according to their capacities, these defects of detail diminish in
the sublime conception of the whole. The poorest man included
in this association has his place, his work, his reason for being
there; each is something in the whole.

There is nothing like this for man in the state of nature; as
he depends only upon himself, it is necessary that he be sufficient
for everything. All creation is his property; but he finds in it
as many hindrances as helps. He must surmount these obstacles
with the single strength that God has given him; he cannot
reckon on any other aid than chance and opportunity. No one
reaps, manufactures, fights, or thinks for him; he is nothing to
any one. He is a unit multiplied by the cipher of his own single
powers; while the civilized man is a unit multiplied by the powers
of the whole of society.

Yet, notwithstanding this, the other day, disgusted by the
sight of some vices in detail, I cursed the latter, and almost
envied the life of the savage.

One of the infirmities of our nature is always to mistake feeling for evidence, and to judge of the season by a cloud or a ray
of sunshine.

Was the misery, the sight of which made me regret a savage
life, really the effect of civilization ? Must we accuse society of
having created these evils, or acknowledge, on the contrary, that
it has alleviated them ? Could the women and children who were
receiving the coarse bread from the soldier hope in the desert
for more help or pity ? That dead man, whose forsaken state I
deplored, had he not found, by the cares of a hospital, a coffin,
and the humble grave where he was about to rest ? Alone, and
far from men, he would have died like the wild beast in his den,
and would now be serving as food for vultures! These benefits
of human society are shared, then, by the most destitute. Whoever eats the bread that another has reaped and kneaded is
under an obligation to his brother, and cannot say he owes him
nothing in return. The poorest of us has received from society
much more than his own single strength would have permitted
him to wrest from nature.

But cannot society give us more? Who doubts it ? Errors
have been committed in this distribution of tasks and workers.

Time will diminish the number of them; with new lights a better division will arise; the elements of society go on towards perfection, like everything else; the difficulty is to know how to adapt ourselves to the slow step of time, whose progress can never be forced on without danger.

August 14th, six o'clock A. M.— My garret window rises upon the roof like a massive watchtower. The corners are covered by large sheets of lead, which run into the tiles; the successive action of cold and heat has made them rise, and so a crevice has been formed in an angle on the right side. There a sparrow has built her nest.

I have followed the progress of this aërial habitation from the first day. I have seen the bird successively bring the straw, moss, and wool designed for the construction of her abode; and I have admired the persevering skill she expended in this difficult work. At first, my new neighbor spent her days in fluttering over the poplar in the garden, and in chirping along the gutters. A fine lady's life seemed the only one to suit her; then, all of a sudden, the necessity of preparing a shelter for her brood transformed our idler into a worker: she no longer gave herself either rest or relaxation. I saw her always either flying, fetching, or carrying; neither rain nor sun stopped her. A striking example of the power of necessity! We are not only indebted to it for most of our talents, but for many of our virtues!

Is it not necessity which has given the people of less favored climates that constant activity which has placed them so quickly at the head of nations? As they are deprived of most of the gifts of nature, they have supplied them by their industry; necessity has sharpened their understanding; endurance awakened their foresight. Whilst elsewhere man, warmed by an ever brilliant sun, and loaded with the bounties of the earth, was remaining poor, ignorant and naked in the midst of gifts he did not attempt to explore, here he was forced by necessity to wrest his food from the ground, to build habitations to defend himself from the intemperance of the weather, and to warm his body by clothing himself with the wool of animals. Work makes him both more intelligent and more robust: disciplined by it, he seems to mount higher on the ladder of creation, while those more favored by nature remain on the step the nearest to the brutes.

I made these reflections while looking at the bird, whose instinct seemed to have become more acute since she had been occupied in work. At last the nest was finished; she set up her household there, and I followed her through all the phases of her new existence.

When she had sat on the eggs and the young ones were hatched, she fed them with the most attentive care. The corner of my window had become a stage of moral action which fathers and mothers might come to take lessons from. The little ones soon became great, and this morning I have seen them take their first flight. One of them, weaker than the others, was not able to clear the edge of the roof, and fell into the gutter. I caught him with some difficulty, and placed him again on the tile in front of his house, but the mother has not noticed him. Once freed from the cares of a family, she has resumed her wandering life among the trees and along the roofs. In vain I have kept away from my window, to take from her every excuse for fear; in vain the feeble little bird has called to her with plaintive cries; his bad mother has passed by, singing and fluttering with a thousand airs and graces. Once only the father came near; he looked at his offspring with contempt, and then disappeared, never to return!

I crumbled some bread before the little orphan, but he did not know how to peck it with his bill. I tried to catch him, but he escaped into the forsaken nest. What will become of him there, if his mother does not come back!

August 15th, six o'clock. — This morning, on opening my window, I found the little bird dying upon the tiles; his wounds showed me that he had been driven from the nest by his unworthy mother. I tried in vain to warm him again with my breath; I felt the last pulsations of life; his eyes were already closed, and his wings hung down! I placed him on the roof in a ray of sunshine, and I closed my window. The struggle of life against death has always something gloomy in it; it is a warning to us.

Happily I hear some one in the passage; without doubt, it is my old neighbor; his conversation will distract my thoughts.

It was my portress. Excellent woman! She wished me to read a letter from her son the sailor, and begged me to answer it for her.

I kept it to copy into my journal. Here it is: —

Dear Mother : —

This is to tell you that I have been very well ever since the last time, except that last week I was nearly drowned with the boat, which would have been a great loss, as there is not a better craft anywhere.

A gust of wind capsized us; and just as I came up above water, I saw the captain sinking. I went after him, as was my duty, and, after diving three times, I brought him to the surface, which pleased him much; for when we were hoisted on board, and he had recovered his senses, he threw his arms round my neck, as he would have done to an officer.

I do not hide from you, dear mother, that this has delighted me. But it isn't all; it seems that fishing up the captain has reminded them that I had a good character, and they have just told me that I am promoted to be a sailor of the first class. Directly I knew it, I cried out, "My mother shall have coffee twice a day!" And really, dear mother, there is nothing now to hinder you, as I shall now have a larger allowance to send you.

I conclude by begging you to take care of yourself if you wish to do me good; for nothing makes me feel so well as to think that you want for nothing.

Your son, from the bottom of my heart,
JACQUES.

This is the answer the portress dictated to me: —

My good Jacquot: —

It makes me very happy to see that your heart is still as true as ever, and that you will never shame those who have brought you up. I need not tell you to take care of your life, because you know it is the same as my own, and that without you, dear child, I should wish for nothing but the grave; but we are not bound to live, while we are bound to do our duty.

Do not fear for my health, good Jacques. I was never better! I do not grow old at all, for fear of making you unhappy. I want nothing, and I live like a lady. I even had some money over this year, and as my drawers shut very badly, I put it into the savings bank, where I have opened an account in your name. So, when you come back, you will find yourself with an income. I have also furnished your chest with new linen, and I have knitted you three new sea jackets.

All your friends are well. Your cousin is just dead, leaving his widow in difficulties. I gave her your thirty francs remittance, and said that you had sent it to her; and the poor woman remembers you day and night in her prayers. So, you see, I have put that money in another sort of **savings** bank; but there it is our hearts which get the interest.

Good-bye, dear Jacquot; write to me often, and always remember the good God and your old mother,

PHROSINE MILLOT.

Good son, and worthy mother! how such examples bring us back to a love for the human race! In a fit of fanciful misanthropy, we may envy the fate of the savage, and prefer that of the bird to such as he; but impartial observation soon does justice to such paradoxes. We find, on examination, that in the mixed good and evil of human nature, the good so far abounds that we are not in the habit of noticing it, while the evil strikes us precisely on account of its being the exception. If nothing is perfect, nothing is so bad as to be without its compensation or its remedy. What spiritual riches are there in the midst of the evils of society! How much does the moral world redeem the material!

That which will ever distinguish man from the rest of creation is his power of deliberate affection and of enduring self-sacrifice. The mother who took care of her brood in the corner of my window devoted to them the necessary time for accomplishing the laws which insure the preservation of her kind; but she obeyed an instinct and not a rational choice. When she had accomplished the mission appointed her by Providence, she cast off the duty, as we get rid of a burden, and she returned again to her selfish liberty. The other mother, on the contrary, will go on with her task as long as God shall leave her here below; the life of her son will still remain, so to speak, joined to her own, and when she disappears from the earth, she will leave there that part of herself.

Thus, the affections make for our species an existence separate from all the rest of creation. Thanks to them, we enjoy a sort of terrestrial immortality; and if other beings succeed one another, man alone perpetuates himself.

Complete. «An Attic Philosopher in Paris,» Chap. viii.

HERBERT SPENCER

(1820–)

ERBERT SPENCER was born at Derby, England, April 27th, 1820. To his father, a schoolmaster at Derby, and to his father's brother, Rev. Thomas Spencer, rector at Hinton, he owed his early education and the first impulse towards the profound studies which made him the founder of "Synthetic Philosophy." He began life as an assistant in the office of a civil engineer, but in 1845 turned from engineering to the career of a writer, to which he devoted himself with remarkable industry and astonishing fertility during the remainder of the century. He worked with Darwin in elucidating the theories of evolution, but as against those who call him "a pupil of Darwin," his admirers cite the fact that in his "Principles of Psychology," published in 1855, he stated the principles of evolution four years before the appearance of "The Origin of Species." There is scarcely room for controversy on such a point, however, as only the "terminology" of the evolutionists of the nineteenth century was new. Their philosophy was itself an evolution. Spencer was really more remarkable, however, as a political essayist than in the science of which he was so fond. His determined and aggressive individualism did much to hold in check the "Collectionism" of Fourier, Marx, and Lassalle. To Spencer, society and all its institutions exist for man, not man for society. He reasoned that the only right society has to legislate for and to coerce the individual is that individuality may be the more fully developed through the establishment of a more nearly perfect justice. The only vitiating flaw in his severe logic was its consistency carried to its extreme. It made "the law of the survival of the fittest" apply against state aid, even to the helpless; and charity to the undeserving is by his theories almost criminal. It was on such consistencies as these that his opponents seized as they might have seized on the inconsistencies of a weaker intellect. They did not break his influence, however, and he became an inspiration for all who endeavor to check the tendency to restrictive legislation. The list of his works is so long and all are in one sense or another so important that it is hard to select from among them, but he himself no doubt intended to make the various volumes of his "Synthetic Philosophy" the great masterpiece of his life. His essay on "Education," his "Social Statics," "Data of Ethics,"

" The Man versus the State," and the essay on " The Philosophy of Style " are works which have had extensive circulation among general readers.

EVOLUTION OF THE PROFESSIONS

THE saying that we cannot put old heads on young shoulders figuratively expresses, among other truths, the truth that the beliefs which in youth result from small information joined with undisciplined thought and feeling cannot, until after long years, be replaced by the beliefs which wider knowledge and better balanced mental powers produce. And while it is usually impracticable to antedate the results of mental development and culture, it is also usually impracticable to arouse, during early stages, any such distrust of convictions then formed, as should be caused by the perception that there is much more to be learned.

This general remark, trite in substance though it is, I am prompted to make à *propos* of the profound change which study of many peoples in many places and times causes in those ideas of social organization which are current — ideas entertained not only by the young, but also by the majority of the old, who, relatively to the subject-matter to be investigated, are also young. For patient inquiry and calm thought make it manifest that sundry institutions regarded with strong prejudices have been essential institutions; and that the development of society has everywhere been determined by agencies — especially political and ecclesiastical — of characters condemned by the higher sentiments and incongruous with an advanced social ideal.

One in whom aversion to autocratic rule is strong does not willingly recognize the truth that without autocratic rule the evolution of society could not have commenced; and one to whom the thought of priestly control is repugnant cannot, without difficulty, bring himself to see that during early stages priestly control was necessary. But contemplation of the evidence, while proving these general facts, also makes it manifest that in the nature of things groups of men out of which organized societies germinate must, in passing from the homogeneous to the heterogeneous, have first assumed the form in which one individual predominates,— a nucleus of the group serving as a centre of initiation for all subsequent steps in development. Though, as fast as society advances, and especially as fast as the militant type yields place to the industrial type, a centralized and coercive control, political and ecclesiastical, becomes less needful, and plays a continually decreasing part in social evolution; yet the evidence compels us to admit that at first it was indispensable.

This generalization, which we saw variously illustrated by political institutions and ecclesiastical institutions, we now see again illustrated by professional institutions. As the foregoing chapters have shown, all the professions originate by differentiation from the agency which, beginning as political, becomes, with the apotheosis of the dead ruler, politico-ecclesiastical, and thereafter develops the professions chiefly from its ecclesiastical element. Egypt which, by its records and remains, exhibits so well the early phases of social progress, shows us how at first various governmental functions, including the professional, were mingled in the king and in the cluster of those who surrounded the king. Says Tiele: —

"A conflict between the authority of priest and king was hardly possible in earlier times, for then the kings themselves, their sons, and their principal officers of state were the chief priests, and the priestly dignities were not dissevered from nor held to be inconsistent with other and civil functions."

And again: —

"The priestly offices were state functions . . . which did not differ at all in kind from that of commander of the troops, governor of a district, architect, and chamberlain. In fact, both kinds of office were, for the most part, filled by the same persons."

And since, as Brugsch tells us, "Pharaoh's architects (the Mur-ket) . . . were often of the number of the king's sons and grandsons," we see that in the governing group the political, ecclesiastical, and professional functions were united.

No group of institutions illustrates with greater clearness the process of social evolution; and none shows more undeniably how social evolution conforms to the law of evolution at large. The germs out of which the professional agencies arise, forming at first a part of the regulative agency, differentiate from it at the same time that they differentiate from one another; and while severally being rendered more multiform by the rise

of subdivisions, severally become more coherent within themselves and more definitely marked off. The process parallels
completely that by which the parts of an individual organism
pass from their initial state of simplicity to their ultimate state
of complexity.

Originally one who was believed by himself and others to
have power over demons — the mystery man or medicine man —
using coercive methods to expel disease-producing spirits, stood
in the place of doctor; and when his appliances, at first supposed
to act supernaturally, came to be understood as acting naturally,
his office eventually lost its priestly character altogether: the resulting physician class, originally uniform, eventually dividing into
distinguishable subclasses while acquiring a definite embodi-
ment.

Less early, because implying more developed groups, arose
those who as exhibitors of joy, now in the presence of the living
ruler and now in the supposed presence of the deceased ruler,
were at first simultaneously singers and dancers, and, becoming
specialized from the people at large, presently became distinct
from one another; whence, in course of time, two groups of
professionals, whose official laudations, political or religious, extended in their range and multiplied in their kinds. And then
by like steps were separated from one another vocal and instrumental musicians, and eventually composers; within which classes
also there arose subdivisions.

Ovations, now to the living king and now to the dead king,
while taking saltatory and musical forms, took also verbal forms,
originally spontaneous and irregular, but presently studied and
measured; whence, first, the unrhythmical speech of the orator,
which under higher emotional excitement grew into the rhythmi-
cal speech of the priest poet, chanting verses — verses that finally
became established hymns of praise. Meanwhile from accompanying rude imitations of the hero's acts, performed now by one
and now by several, grew dramatic representations, which, little
by little elaborated, fell under the regulation of a chief actor,
who prefigured the playwright. And out of these germs, all per-
taining to worship, came eventually the various professions of
poets, actors, dramatists, and the subdivisions of these.

The great deeds of the hero god, recited, chanted, or sung, and
mimetically rendered, naturally came to be supplemented by details, so growing into accounts of his life; and thus the priest

poet gave origin to the biographer, whose narratives, being extended to less sacred personages, became secularized. Stories of the apotheosized chief or king, joined with stories of his companions and amplified by narratives of accompanying transactions, formed the first histories. And from these accounts of the doings of particular men and groups of men, partly true but passing by exaggeration into the mythical, came the wholly mythical, or fiction; which then and always preserved the biographico-historical character. Add to which that out of the criticisms and reflections scattered through this personal literature an impersonal literature slowly emerged; the whole group of these products having as their deepest root the eulogies of the priest poet.

Prompted as were the medicine men of savages and the priests of early civilized peoples to increase their influence, they were ever stimulated to acquire knowledge of natural actions and the properties of things; and, being in alleged communication with supernatural beings, they were supposed to acquire such knowledge from them. Hence, by implication, the priest became the primitive man of science; and led by his special experiences to speculate about the causes of things, thus entered the sphere of philosophy: both his science and his philosophy being pursued in the service of his religion.

Not only his higher culture, but his alleged intercourse with the gods, whose mouthpiece he was, made him the authority in cases of dispute; and being also, as historian, the authority concerning past transactions and traditional usages, or laws, he acquired in both capacities the character of judge. Moreover, when the growth of legal administration brought the advocate, he, though usually of lay origin, was sometimes clerical.

Distinguished in early stages as the learned man of the tribe or society, and especially distinguished as the possessor of that knowledge which was thought of most value — knowledge of unseen things — the priest of necessity became the first teacher. Transmitting traditional statements concerning ghosts and gods, at first to neophytes of his class only, but afterward to the cultured classes, he presently, beyond instruction in supernatural things, gave instruction in natural things; and, having been the first secular teacher, has retained a large share in secular teaching even down to our own days.

As making a sacrifice was the original priestly act, and as the building of an altar for the sacrifice was by implication a priestly act, it results that the making of a shelter over the altar, which in its developed form became the temple, was also a priestly act. When the priest, ceasing to be himself the executant, directed the artificers, he continued to be the designer; and when he ceased to be the actual designer, the master builder or architect thereafter continued to fulfill his general directions. And then the temple and the palace in sundry early societies, being at once the residence of the apotheosized ruler and the living ruler (even now a palace usually contains a small temple), and being the first kinds of developed architecture, eventually gave origin to secular architecture.

A rudely carved or modeled image of a man placed on his grave gave origin to the sculptured representation of a god inclosed in his temple. A product of priestly skill at the outset, it continued in some cases to be such among early civilized peoples; and always thereafter, when executed by an artisan, conformed to priestly direction. Extending presently to the representation of other than divine and semidivine personages, it eventually thus passed into its secularized form.

So was it with painting. At first used to complete the carved representation of the revered or worshiped personage, and being otherwise in some tribes used by the priest and his aids for exhibiting the tribal hero's deeds, it long remained subservient to religion, either for the coloring of statues (as it does still in Roman Catholic images of saints, etc.), or for the decoration of temples, or for the portraiture of deceased persons on sarcophagi and stelæ; and when it gained independence it was long employed almost wholly for the rendering of sacred scenes,—its eventual secularization being accompanied by its subdivision into a variety of kinds and of the executant artists into correlative groups.

Thus the process of professional evolution betrays throughout the same traits. In stages like that described by Huc as still existing among the Tibetans, where "the Lama is not merely a priest, he is the painter, poet, sculptor, architect, physician," there are joined in the same individual, or group of individuals, the potentialities out of which gradually arise the specialized groups we know as professions. While out of the one primitive class there come by progressive divergences many classes, each of these classes itself undergoes a kindred change: there are formed in it subdivisions and even sub-subdivisions, which become gradually more marked; so that, throughout, the advance is from an indefinite homogeneity to a definite heterogeneity.

In presence of the fact that the immense majority of mankind adhere pertinaciously to the creeds, political and religious, in which they are brought up; and in presence of the further fact that on behalf of their creeds, however acquired, there are soon enlisted prejudices which practically shut out adverse evidence, it is not to be expected that the foregoing illustrations, even joined with kindred illustrations previously given, will make them see that society is a growth and not a manufacture, and has its laws of evolution.

From prime ministers down to plowboys there is either ignorance or disregard of the truth that nations acquire their vital structures by natural processes and not by artificial devices. If the belief is not that social arrangements have been divinely ordered thus or thus, then it is that they have been made thus or thus by kings, or if not by kings, then by parliaments. That they have come about by small accumulated changes not contemplated by rulers is an open secret which only of late has been recognized by a few, and is still unperceived by the many, — educated as well as uneducated. Though the turning of the land into a food-producing surface, cleared, fenced, drained, and covered with farming appliances, has been achieved by men working for individual profit, not by legislative direction — though villages, towns, cities, have insensibly grown up under the desires of men to satisfy their wants — though by spontaneous co-operation of citizens have been formed canals, railways, telegraphs, and other means of communication and distribution, the natural forces which have done all this are ignored as of no account in political thinking. Our immense manufacturing system with its multitudinous inventions, supplying both home and foreign consumers, and the immense mercantile marine by which its products are taken all over the globe and other products brought back, have been naturally and not artificially originated. That transformation by which, in thousands of years, men's occupations have been so specialized that each, aiding to satisfy some small division of his fellow-citizen's needs has his own needs satisfied by the work of hundreds of others, has taken place without design and unobserved. Knowledge developing into science, which has become so vast in mass that no one can grasp a tithe of it, and which now guides productive activities at large has resulted from the workings of individuals prompted not by the ruling agency, but by their own inclinations. So, too, has been created the still vaster mass distinguished as literature, yielding the gratifications filling so large a space in our lives. Nor is it otherwise with the literature of the hour. That ubiquitous journalism which provides satisfactions for men's more urgent mental wants has resulted from the activities of citizens severally pursuing private benefits. And supplementing these come the innumerable companies, associations, unions, societies, clubs, subserving enterprise, philanthropy, culture, art, amusement; as well as the multitudinous institutions annually receiving millions by endowments and subscriptions: all of them arising from the unforced co-operations of citizens. And yet so hypnotized are nearly all by fixedly contemplating the doings of ministers and parliaments, that they have no eyes for this marvelous organization which has been growing for thousands of years without governmental help — nay, indeed, in spite of governmental hindrances. For in agriculture, manufactures, commerce, banking, journalism, immense injuries have been done by laws, — injuries afterward healed by social forces which have thereupon set up afresh the normal courses of growth. So unconscious are men of the life of the social organism that though the spontaneous actions of its units, each seeking livelihood, generate streams of food which touch at their doors every hour — though the water for their morning bath, the lights for their rooms, the fires in their grates, the bus or tram which takes them to the city, the business they carry on (made possible by the distributing system they share in), the evening Special they glance at, the theatre or concert to which they presently go, and the cab home, all result from the unprompted workings of this organized humanity, they remain blind. Though by its vital activities capital is drafted to places where it is most wanted, supplies of commodities balanced in every locality and prices universally adjusted — all without official supervision; yet, being oblivious of the truth that these processes are socially originated without design of any one, they cannot believe that society will be bettered by natural agencies. And hence when they see an evil to be cured or a good to be achieved, they ask for legal coercion as the only possible means.

More than this is true. If, as every parliamentary debate and every political meeting show, the demands for legislation pay no attention to that beneficent social development which has done so much and may be expected to increase in efficiency, still more do they ignore the laws of that development — still less do they recognize a natural order in the changes by which society passes from its lower to its higher stages. Though, as we have seen, the process of evolution exemplified in the genesis of the professions is similar in character to the process exemplified in the genesis of political and ecclesiastical institutions and everywhere else; and though the first inquiry rationally to be made respecting any proposed measure should be whether or not it falls within the lines of this evolution, and what must be the effects of running counter to the normal course of things; yet not only is no such question ever entertained, but one who raised it would be laughed down in any popular assemblage and smiled at as a dreamer in the House of Commons: the only course thought wise in either the cultured or the uncultured gathering being that of trying to estimate immediate benefits and evils.

Nor will any argument or any accumulation of evidence suffice to change this attitude until there has arisen a different type of mind and a different quality of culture. The politician will still spend his energies in rectifying some evils and making more — in forming, reforming, and again reforming — in passing acts to amend acts that were before amended; while social schemers will continue to think that they have only to cut up society and re-arrange it after their ideal pattern and its parts will join together again and work as intended

Complete.

MEDDLESOME AND CODDLING PATERNALISM

THE enthusiastic philanthropist, urgent for some act of parliament to remedy this evil or secure the other good, thinks it a very trivial and far-fetched objection that the people will be morally injured by doing things for them instead of leaving them to do things themselves. He vividly realizes the benefit he hopes to get achieved, which is a positive and readily imaginable thing: he does not realize the diffused, invisible, and slowly accumulating effect wrought on the popular mind, and so does not believe in it; or, if he admits it, thinks it beneath consideration. Would he but remember, however, that all national

character is gradually produced by the daily action of circumstances, of which each day's result seems so insignificant as not
to be worth mentioning, he would see that what is trifling when
viewed in its increments, may be formidable when viewed in its
sum total.   Or if he would go into the nursery, and watch how
repeated actions — each of them apparently unimportant, create,
in the end, a habit which will affect the whole future life; he
would be reminded that every influence brought to bear on human nature tells, and if continued, tells seriously.   The thoughtless mother who hourly yields to the requests: " Mamma, tie my
pinafore," " Mamma, button my shoe," and the like, cannot be
persuaded that each of these concessions is detrimental; but the
wiser spectator sees that if this policy be long pursued, and be
extended to other things, it will end in hopeless dependence.
The teacher of the old school who showed his pupil the way out
of every difficulty did not perceive that he was generating an
attitude of mind greatly militating against success in life.   The
modern instructor, however, induces his pupil to solve his difficulties himself; believes that in so doing he is preparing him to meet
the difficulties which, when he goes into the world, there will be
no one to help him through; and finds confirmation for this belief in the fact that a great proportion of the most successful
men are self-made.

Well, is it not obvious that this relationship between discipline
and success holds good nationally?   Are not nations made of
men; and are not men subject to the same laws of modification
in their adult as in their early years?   Is it not true of the
drunkard, that each carouse adds a thread to his bonds? of the
trader, that each acquisition strengthens the wish for acquisitions?
of the pauper, that the more you assist him the more he wants?
of the busy man, that the more he has to do the more he can
do?   And does it not follow that if every individual is subject
to this process of adaptation to conditions, a whole nation must
be so — that just in proportion as its members are little helped
by extraneous power they will become self-helping, and in proportion as they are much helped they will become helpless?
What folly is it to ignore these results because they are not direct, and not immediately visible.   Though slowly wrought out,
they are inevitable.   We can no more elude the laws of human
development than we can elude the law of gravitation; and so
long as they hold true must these effects occur.

If we are asked in what special directions this alleged help-lessness, entailed by much state superintendence, shows itself, we reply that it is seen in a retardation of all social growths requiring self-confidence in the people — in a timidity that fears all difficulties not before encountered — in a thoughtless content-ment with things as they are. Let any one, after duly watching the rapid evolution going on in England, where men have been comparatively little helped by governments — or better still, after contemplating the unparalleled progress of the United States, which is peopled by self-made men, and the recent descendants of self-made men; — let such a one, we say, go on to the Con-tinent, and consider the relatively slow advance which things are there making; and the still slower advance they would make but for English enterprise. Let him go to Holland, and see that though the Dutch early showed themselves good mechanics, and have had abundant practice in hydraulics, Amsterdam has been without any due supply of water until now that works are being established by an English company. Let him go to Berlin, and there be told that, to give that city a water supply such as Lon-don has had for generations, the project of an English firm is about to be executed by English capital, under English superin-tendence. Let him go to Paris, where he will find a similar lack, and a like remedy now under consideration. Let him go to Vienna, and learn that it, in common with other continental cities, is lighted by an English gas company. Let him go on the Rhone, on the Loire, on the Danube, and discover that Englishmen established steam navigation on those rivers. Let him inquire concerning the railways in Italy, Spain, France, Sweden, Denmark, how many of them are English projects, how many have been largely helped by English capital, how many have been executed by English contractors, how many have had English engineers. Let him discover, too, as he will, that where railways have been government made, as in Russia, the energy, the perseverance, and the practical talent developed in England and the United States have been called in to aid.

And then if these illustrations of the progressiveness of a self-dependent race, and the torpidity of paternally governed ones, do not suffice him, he may read Mr. Laing's successive volumes of European travel, and there study the contrast in detail. What, now, is the cause of this contrast? In the order of nature, a capacity for self-help must in every case have been brought into

existence by the practice of self-help; and, other things equal, a
lack of this capacity must in every case have arisen from the
lack of demand for it.   Do not these two antecedents and their
two consequents agree with the facts as presented in England
and Europe ? Were not the inhabitants of the two, some centuries ago, much upon a par in point of enterprise ?   Were not
the English even behind, in their manufactures, in their coloniza-
tion, and in their commerce ? Has not the immense relative change
the English have undergone in this respect been coincident with
the great relative self-dependence they have been since habitu-
ated to ?   And is not this change proximately ascribable to this
habitual self-dependence ? Whoever doubts it is asked to assign
a more probable cause.   Whoever admits it must admit that the
enervation of a people by perpetual state aids is not a trifling
consideration, but the most weighty consideration.   A general arrest of national growth he will see to be an evil greater than
any special benefits can compensate for.   And, indeed, when, after
contemplating this great fact, the overspreading of the earth by
the Anglo-Saxons, he remarks the absence of any parallel phenomenon exhibited by a continental race — when he reflects how
this difference must depend chiefly on difference of character, and
how such difference of character has been mainly produced by
difference of discipline; he will perceive that the policy pursued
in this matter may have a large share in determining a nation's
ultimate fate.

We are not sanguine, however, that argument will change the
convictions of those who put their trust in legislation.   With men
of a certain order of thought the foregoing reasons will have
weight.   With men of another order of thought they will have
little or none; nor would any accumulation of such reasons affect
them.   The truth that experience teaches has its limits.   The
experiences that will teach must be experiences that can be appreciated; and experiences exceeding a certain degree of complexity become inappreciable to the majority.   It is thus with
most social phenomena.   If we remember that for these two
thousand years and more, mankind have been making regulations for commerce, which have all along been strangling some
trades, and killing others with kindness; and that though the
proofs of this have been constantly before their eyes, they have
only just discovered that they have been uniformly doing mis-

chief;—if we remember that even now only a small portion of
them see this, we are taught that perpetually-repeated and ever-
accumulating experiences will fail to teach, until there exist the
mental conditions required for the assimilation of them. Nay, when
they are assimilated, it is very imperfectly. The truth they teach
is only half understood, even by those supposed to understand it
best. For example, Sir Robert Peel, in one of his last speeches,
after describing the immensely increased consumption consequent
on free trade, goes on to say:—

« If, then, you can only continue that consumption — if, by your
legislation, under the favor of Providence, you can maintain the demand for labor, and make your trade and manufactures prosperous,
you are not only increasing the sum of human happiness, but are
giving the agriculturists of this country the best chance of that increased demand which must contribute to their welfare.»— Times,
February 22d, 1850.

Thus the prosperity really due to the abandonment of all legislation, is ascribed to a particular kind of legislation. " You can
maintain the demand," he says; "you can make trade and manufactures prosperous"; whereas, the facts he quotes prove that
they can do this only by doing nothing. The essential truth of
the matter — that law had been doing immense harm, and that
this prosperity resulted not from law, but from the absence of
law — is missed; and his faith in legislation in general, which
should, by this experience, have been greatly shaken seemingly
remains as strong as ever. Here, again, is the House of Lords,
apparently not yet believing in the relationship of supply and
demand, adopting within these few weeks, the standing order—

« That before the first reading of any bill for making any work in
the construction of which compulsory power is sought to take thirty
houses or more inhabited by the laboring classes in any one parish
or place, the promoters be required to deposit in the office of the
clerk of the parliaments a statement of the number, description, and
situation of the said houses, the number (so far as they can be esti-
mated) of persons to be displaced, and whether any and what provision is made in the bill for remedying the inconvenience likely to
arise from such displacements. »

If, then, in the comparatively simple relationships of trade,
the teachings of experience remain for so many ages unperceived,
and are so imperfectly apprehended when they are perceived, it

is scarcely to be hoped that where all social phenomena — moral, intellectual, and physical — are involved, any due appreciation of the truths displayed will presently take place. The facts cannot yet get recognized as facts. As the alchemist attributed his successive disappointments to some disproportion in the ingredients, some impurity, or some too great temperature, and never to the futility of his process, or the impossibility of his aim, so every failure cited to prove the impotence of state regulations the law-worshiper explains away as being caused by this trifling oversight, or that little mistake, — all which oversights and mistakes, he assures you, will in future be avoided. Eluding the facts as he does after this fashion, volley after volley of them produce no effect.

Indeed, this faith in governments is in a certain sense organic, and can diminish only by being outgrown. A subtle form of fetichism, it is as natural to the present phase of human evolution as its grosser prototype was to an earlier phase. From the time when rulers were thought demigods, there has been a gradual decline in men's estimates of their power. This decline is still in progress, and has still far to go. Doubtless, every increment of evidence furthers it in some degree, though not to the degree that at first appears. Only in so far as it modifies character does it produce a permanent effect. For while the mental type remains the same, the removal of a special error is inevitably followed by the growth of other errors of the same genus. All superstitions die hard; and we fear that this belief in government omnipotence will form no exception.

From his « Essays.»

EDUCATION — WHAT KNOWLEDGE IS OF MOST WORTH?

IT HAS been truly remarked that, in order of time, decoration precedes dress. Among people who submit to great physical suffering that they may have themselves handsomely tattooed, extremes of temperature are borne with but little attempt at mitigation. Humboldt tells us that an Orinoco Indian, though quite regardless of bodily comfort, will yet labor for a fortnight to purchase pigment wherewith to make himself admired; and that the same woman who would not hesitate to leave her hut without a fragment of clothing on, would not dare to commit such a breach of decorum as to go out unpainted. Voyagers uniformly find that colored beads and trinkets are much more prized by wild tribes than are calicoes or broadcloths. And the anecdotes we have of the ways in which, when shirts and coats are given, they turn them to some ludicrous display, show how completely the idea of ornament predominates over that of use. Nay, there are still more extreme illustrations: witness the fact narrated by Captain Speke of his African attendants, who strutted about in their goatskin mantles when the weather was fine, but when it was wet, took them off, folded them up, and went about naked, shivering in the rain! Indeed, the facts of aboriginal life seem to indicate that dress is developed out of decorations. And when we remember that even among ourselves most think more about the fineness of the fabric than its warmth, and more about the cut than the convenience — when we see that the function is still in great measure subordinated to the appearance, we have further reason for inferring such an origin.

It is not a little curious that the like relations hold with the mind. Among mental as among bodily acquisitions, the ornamental comes before the useful. Not only in times past, but almost as much in our own era, that knowledge which conduces to personal well-being has been postponed to that which brings applause. In the Greek schools, music, poetry, rhetoric, and a philosophy which, until Socrates taught, had but little bearing upon action, were the dominant subjects; while knowledge, aiding the arts of life, had a very subordinate place. And in our own universities and schools at the present moment the like antithesis holds. We are guilty of something like a platitude when we say that throughout his after career a boy, in nine cases out of ten, applies his Latin and Greek to no practical purposes. The remark is trite that in his shop, or his office, in managing his estate or his family, in playing his part as director of a bank or a railway, he is very little aided by this knowledge he took so many years to acquire,— so little, that generally the greater part of it drops out of his memory; and if he occasionally vents a Latin quotation or alludes to some Greek myth, it is less to throw light on the topic in hand than for the sake of effect. If we inquire what is the real motive for giving boys a classical education, we find it to be simply conformity to public opinion. Men dress their children's minds as they do their bodies, in the prevailing fashion. As the Orinoco Indian puts on his paint before leaving his hut, not with a view to any direct benefit, but because he would be ashamed to be seen without it, so a boy's drilling in Latin and Greek is insisted on, not because of their intrinsic value, but that he may not be disgraced by being found ignorant of them — that he may have "the education of a gentleman " — the badge marking a certain social position, and bringing a consequent respect.

This parallel is still more clearly displayed in the case of the other sex. In the treatment of both mind and body, the decorative element has continued to predominate in a greater degree among women than among men. Originally personal adornment occupied the attention of both sexes equally. In these latter days of civilization, however, we see that in the dress of men the regard for appearance has, in a considerable degree, yielded to the regard for comfort; while in their education the useful has of late been trenching on the ornamental. In neither direction has this change gone so far with women. The wearing of ear rings, finger rings, bracelets; the elaborate dressings of the hair; the still occasional use of paint; the immense labor bestowed in making habiliments sufficiently attractive; and the great discomfort that will be submitted to for the sake of conformity; show how greatly, in the attiring of women, the desire of approbation overrides the desire for warmth and convenience. And similarly in their education, the immense preponderance of "accomplishments " proves how here, too, use is subordinated to display. Dancing, deportment, the piano, singing, drawing — what a large space do these occupy! If you ask why Italian and German are learned, you will find that, under all the sham reasons given, the real reason is, that a knowledge of those tongues is thought ladylike. It is not that the books written in them may be utilized, which they scarcely ever are, but that Italian and German songs may be sung, and that the extent of attainment may bring whispered admiration. The births, deaths, and marriages of kings, and other like historic trivialities, are committed to memory, not because of any direct benefits that can possibly result from knowing them, but because society considers them parts of a good education — because the absence of such knowledge may bring the contempt of others. When we have named reading, writing, spelling, grammar, arithmetic, and sewing, we have named about all the things a girl is taught with a view to their direct uses in life; and even some of these have more reference to the good opinion of others than to immediate personal welfare.

Thoroughly to realize the truth that with the mind as with the body the ornamental precedes the useful, it is needful to glance at its rationale. This lies in the fact that, from the far past down even to the present, social needs have subordinated individual needs, and that the chief social need has been the control of individuals. It is not, as we commonly suppose, that there are no governments but those of monarchs, and parliaments, and constituted authorities. These acknowledged governments are supplemented by other unacknowledged ones, that grow up in all circles, in which every man or woman strives to be king or queen or lesser dignitary. To get above some and be reverenced by them, and to propitiate those who are above us, is the universal struggle in which the chief energies of life are expended. By the accumulation of wealth, by style of living, by beauty of dress, by display of knowledge or intellect, each tries to subjugate others, and so aids in weaving that ramified network of restraints by which society is kept in order. It is not the savage chief only who, in formidable war paint, with scalps at his belt, aims to strike awe into his inferiors; it is not only the belle who, by elaborate toilet, polished manners, and numerous accomplishments, strives to "make conquests"; but the scholar, the historian, the philosopher, use their acquirements to the same end. We are none of us content with quietly unfolding our own individualities to the full in all directions, but have a restless craving to impress our individualities upon others, and in some way subordinate them. And this it is which determines the character of our education. Not what knowledge is of most real worth is the consideration, but what will bring most applause, honor, respect — what will most conduce to social position and influence — what will be most imposing. As throughout life not what we are, but what we shall be thought, is the question; so in education, the question is, not the intrinsic value of knowledge, so much as its extrinsic effects on others. And this being our dominant idea, direct utility is scarcely more regarded than by the barbarian when filing his teeth and staining his nails.

If there needs any further evidence of the rude, undeveloped character of our education, we have it in the fact that the comparative worths of different kinds of knowledge have been as yet scarcely even discussed — much less discussed in a methodic way with definite results. Not only is it that no standard of relative values has yet been agreed upon, but the existence of any such standard has not been conceived in any clear manner. And not only is it that the existence of any such standard has not been clearly conceived, but the need for it seems to have been scarcely even felt. Men read books on this topic, and attend lectures on that; decide that their children shall be instructed in these branches of knowledge, and shall not be instructed in those; and all under the guidance of mere custom, or liking, or prejudice, without ever considering the enormous importance of determining in some rational way what things are really most worth learning. It is true that in all circles we have occasional remarks on the importance of this or the other order of information. But whether the degree of its importance justifies the expenditure of the time needed to acquire it, and whether there are not things of more importance to which the time might be better devoted, are queries which, if raised at all, are disposed of quite summarily, according to personal predilections. It is true, also, that from time to time we hear revived the standing controversy respecting the comparative merits of classics and mathematics. Not only, however, is this controversy carried on in an empirical manner, with no reference to an ascertained criterion, but the question at issue is totally insignificant when compared with the general question of which it is part. To suppose that deciding whether a mathematical or a classical education is the best, in deciding what is the proper curriculum, is much the same thing as to suppose that the whole of dietetics lies in determining whether or not bread is more nutritive than potatoes!

The question, which we contend is of such transcendent moment, is not whether such or such knowledge is of worth, but what is its relative worth. When they have named certain advantages which a given course of study has secured them, persons are apt to assume that they have justified themselves, quite forgetting that the adequateness of the advantages is the point to be judged. There is, perhaps, not a subject to which men devote attention that has not some value. A year diligently spent in getting up heraldry would very possibly give a little further insight into ancient manners and morals, and into the origin of names. Any one who should learn the distances between all the towns in England might, in the course of his life, find one or two of the thousand facts he has acquired of some slight service when arranging a journey. Gathering together all the small gossip of a county, profitless occupation as it would be, might yet occasionally help to establish some useful fact,— say, a good example of hereditary transmission. But in these cases every one would admit that there was no proportion between the required labor and the probable benefit. No one would tolerate the proposal to devote some years of a boy's time to getting such information, at the cost of much more valuable information which he might else have got. And if here the test of relative value is appealed to and held conclusive, then should it be appealed to and held conclusive throughout. Had we time to master all subjects we need not be particular. To quote the old song: —

> « Could a man be secure
> That his days would endure
> As of old, for a thousand long years,
> What things might he know!
> What deeds might he do!
> And all without hurry or cares. »

« But we that have but span-long lives » must ever bear in mind our limited time for acquisition. And remembering how narrowly this time is limited, not only by the shortness of life, but also still more by the business of life, we ought to be especially solicitous to employ what time we have to the greatest advantage. Before devoting years to some subject which fashion or fancy suggests, it is surely wise to weigh with great care the worth of the results, as compared with the worth of various alternative results which the same years might bring if otherwise applied.

In education, then, this is the question of questions, which it is high time we discussed in some methodic way. The first in importance, though the last to be considered, is the problem, how to decide among the conflicting claims of various subjects on our attention. Before there can be a rational curriculum, we must settle which things it most concerns us to know; or, to use a word of Bacon, now unfortunately obsolete, we must determine the relative values of knowledges. . . .

How to live ? — that is the essential question for us. Not how to live in the mere material sense only, but in the widest sense. The general problem which comprehends every special problem is the right ruling of conduct in all directions under all circum-

stances.   In what way to treat the body; in what way to treat
the mind; in what way to manage our affairs; in what way to
bring up a family; in what way to behave as a citizen; in what
way to utilize all those sources of happiness which nature supplies—how to use all our faculties to the greatest advantage of
ourselves and others—how to live completely.   And this being
the great thing needful for us to learn, is, by consequence, the
great thing which education has to teach.   To prepare us for
complete living is the function which education has to discharge;
and the only rational mode of judging of any educational course
is to judge in what degree it discharges such function.

From «Education.»

BARUCH SPINOZA

(1632–1677)

BARUCH (or BENEDICT) SPINOZA was born in Amsterdam, November 24th, 1632,—John Locke, his coadjutor in the cause of free speech, being at that time an infant in arms in Somersetshire, England. Spinoza's parents were Jews, but his active mind, as it developed under the inspiration of Descartes, so exceeded the limits set by what was then considered orthodoxy, that in 1656 he was excommunicated by the synagogue at Amsterdam. His "Tractatus Theologico-Politicus," which appeared in 1670, may be due to this incident, and, if so, the modern world is fortunate because of the opposition to his theories which led him to make this notable plea for freedom of intellectual development. His "Ethics," the most celebrated modern exposition of Pantheism, was completed in 1674, but was not published until after his death, which occurred at The Hague, February 21st, 1677.

THAT IN A FREE STATE EVERY MAN MAY THINK WHAT HE LIKES AND SAY WHAT HE THINKS

IF MEN'S minds were as easily controlled as their tongues, every king would sit safely on his throne, and government by compulsion would cease; for every subject would shape his life according to the intentions of his rulers, and would esteem a thing true or false, good or evil, just or unjust, in obedience to their dictates. No man's mind, however, can possibly lie wholly at the disposition of another, for no one can willingly transfer his natural right of free reason and judgment, or be compelled so to do. For this reason government which attempts to control minds is accounted tyrannical, and it is considered an abuse of sovereignty and a usurpation of the rights of subjects, to seek to prescribe what shall be accepted as true, or rejected as false, or what opinions should actuate men in their worship of God. All these questions fall within a man's natural right, which he cannot abdicate even with his own consent.

I admit that the judgment can be biased in many ways, and to an almost incredible degree, so that while exempt from the direct external control it may be so dependent on another man's words, that it may fitly be said to be ruled by him; but although this influence is carried to great lengths, it has never gone so far as to invalidate the statement, that every man's understanding is his own, and that brains are as diverse as palates.

Moses, not by fraud, but by divine virtue, gained such a hold over the popular judgment that he was accounted superhuman, and believed to speak and act through the inspiration of the Deity; nevertheless, even he could not escape murmurs and evil interpretations. How much less, then, can other monarchs avoid them! Yet such unlimited power, if it exists at all, must belong to a monarch, and least of all to a democracy, where the whole or a great part of the people wield authority collectively. This is a fact which I think every one can explain for himself.

However unlimited, therefore, the power of a sovereign may be, however implicitly it is trusted as the exponent of law and religion, it can never prevent men from forming judgments according to their intellect, or being influenced by any given emotion. It is true that it has the power to treat as enemies all men whose opinions do not, on all subjects, entirely coincide with its own; but we are not discussing its strict powers, but its proper course of action. I grant that it has the power to rule in the most violent manner, and to put citizens to death for very trivial causes, but no one supposes it can do this with the approval of sound judgment. Nay, inasmuch as such things cannot be done without extreme peril to itself, we may even deny that it has the absolute power to do them, consequently the absolute right; for the rights of the sovereign are limited by his power.

Since, therefore, no one can abdicate his freedom of judgment and feeling; since every man is by indefeasible natural right the master of his own thoughts, it follows that men thinking in diverse and contradictory fashions, cannot, without disastrous results, be compelled to speak only according to the dictates of the supreme power. Not even the most experienced, to say nothing of the multitude, know how to keep silence. Men's common failing is to confide their plans to others, though there be need for secrecy, so that a government would be most harsh which deprived the individual of his freedom of saying and teaching what he thought; and would be moderate if such freedom were granted. Still we cannot deny that authority may be as much injured by words as by actions; hence, although the freedom we are discussing cannot be entirely denied to subjects, its unlimited concession would be most baneful; we must, therefore, now inquire how far such freedom can and ought to be conceded without danger to the peace of the state, or the power of the rulers; and this is my principal object.

It follows, plainly, from the explanation given above, of the foundations of a state, that the ultimate aim of government is not to rule, or restrain, by fear, nor to exact obedience, but, contrariwise, to free every man from fear, that he may live in all possible security; in other words, to strengthen his natural right to exist and work without injury to himself or others.

No, the object of government is not to change men from rational beings into beasts or puppets, but to enable them to develop their minds and bodies in security, and to employ their reason unshackled; neither showing hatred, anger, or deceit, nor watched with the eyes of jealousy and injustice. In fact, the true aim of government is liberty.

Now we have seen that in forming a state the power of making laws must either be vested in the body of the citizens, or in a portion of them, or in one man. For, although men's free judgments are very diverse, each one thinking that he alone knows everything, and although complete unanimity of feeling and speech is out of the question, it is impossible to preserve peace, unless individuals abdicate their right of acting entirely on their own judgment. Therefore, the individual justly cedes the right of free action, though not of free reason and judgment; no one can act against the authorities without danger to the state, though his feelings and judgment may be at variance therewith; he may even speak against them, provided that he does so from rational conviction, not from fraud, anger, or hatred, and provided that he does not attempt to introduce any change on his private authority.

For instance, supposing a man shows that a law is repugnant to sound reason, and should therefore be repealed; if he submits his opinion to the judgment of the authorities (who alone have the right of making and repealing laws), and meanwhile acts in nowise contrary to that law, he has deserved well of the state, and has behaved as a good citizen should; but if he accuses the authorities of injustice, and stirs up the people against them, of if he seditiously strives to abrogate the law without their consent, he is a mere agitator and rebel.

Thus we see how an individual may declare and teach what he believes, without injury to the authority of his rulers, or to the public peace; namely, by leaving in their hands the entire power of legislation as it affects action, and by doing nothing against their laws, though he be compelled often to act in contradiction to what he believes, and openly feels, to be best.

Such a course can be taken without detriment to justice and dutifulness; nay, it is the one which a just and dutiful man would adopt. We have shown that justice is dependent on the laws of the authorities, so that no one who contravenes their accepted decrees can be just, while the highest regard for duty is exercised in maintaining public peace and tranquillity; these could not be preserved if every man were to live as he pleased; therefore it is no less than undutiful for a man to act contrary to his country's laws, for if the practice become universal the ruin of states would necessarily follow.

Hence, so long as a man acts in obedience to the laws of his rulers, he in nowise contravenes his reason, for in obedience to reason he transferred the right of controlling his actions from his own hands to theirs. This doctrine we can confirm from actual custom, for in a conference of great and small powers, schemes are seldom carried unanimously, yet all unite in carrying out what is decided on, whether they voted for or against. But I return to my proposition.

From the fundamental notions of a state, we have discovered how a man may exercise free judgment without detriment to the supreme power; from the same premises we can no less easily determine what opinions would be seditious. Evidently those which by their very nature nullify the compact by which the right of free action was ceded. For instance, a man who holds that the Supreme Power has no rights over him, or that promises ought not to be kept, or that every one should live as he pleases, or other doctrines of this nature in direct opposition to the above-mentioned contract, is seditious, not so much from his actual opinions and judgment, as from the deeds which they involve; for he who maintains such theories abrogates the contract which tacitly, or openly, he made with his rulers. Other opinions which do not involve acts violating the contract, such as revenge, anger, and the like, are not seditious, unless it be in some corrupt state, where superstitious and ambitious persons, unable to endure men of learning, are so popular with the multitude that their word is more valued than the law.

However, I do not deny that there are some doctrines which, while they are apparently only concerned with abstract truths and falsehoods, are yet propounded and published with unworthy motives. This question we have discussed and shown that reason should nevertheless remain unshackled. If we hold to the principle that a man's loyalty to the state should be judged, like his loyalty to God, from his actions only, namely, from his charity towards his neighbors, we cannot doubt that the best government will allow freedom of philosophical speculation no less than of religious belief. I confess that from such freedom inconveniences may sometimes arise, but what question was ever settled so wisely that no abuses could possibly spring therefrom? He who seeks to regulate everything by law is more likely to arouse vices than to reform them. It is best to grant what cannot be abolished, even though it be in itself harmful. How many evils spring from luxury, envy, avarice, drunkenness, and the like, yet these are tolerated — vices as they are — because they cannot be prevented by legal enactments. How much more, then, should free thought be granted, seeing that it is in itself a virtue and that it cannot be crushed! Besides, the evil results can easily be checked, as I will show, by the secular authorities, not to mention that such freedom is absolutely necessary for progress in science and the liberal arts; for no man follows such pursuits to advantage unless his judgment be entirely free and unhampered.

But let it be granted that freedom may be crushed, and men be so bound down, that they do not dare to utter a whisper, save at the bidding of their rulers; nevertheless this can never be carried to the pitch of making them think according to authority, so that the necessary consequences would be that men would daily be thinking one thing and saying another, to the corruption of good faith, that mainstay of government, and to the fostering of hateful flattery and perfidy, whence spring stratagems, and the corruption of every good art.

It is far from possible to impose uniformity of speech, for the more rulers strive to curtail freedom of speech the more obstinately are they resisted; not indeed by the avaricious, the flatterers, and other numskulls, who think supreme salvation consists in filling their stomachs and gloating over their money bags, but by those whom good education, sound morality, and virtue have ren-

dered more free. Men, as generally constituted, are most prone
to resent the branding as criminal of opinions which they believe
to be true, and the proscription as wicked of that which inspires
them with piety towards God and man; hence they are ready to
forswear the laws and conspire against the authorities, thinking
it not shameful but honorable to stir up seditions and perpetrate
any sort of crime with this end in view. Such being the constitution of human nature, we see that laws directed against opinions affect the generous-minded rather than the wicked, and are
adapted less for coercing criminals than for irritating the upright;
so that they cannot be maintained without great peril to the
state.

Moreover, such laws are almost always useless, for those who
hold that the opinions proscribed are sound cannot possibly obey
the law; whereas those who already reject them as false, accept
the law as a kind of privilege, and make such boast of it, that
authority is powerless to repeal it, even if such a course be sub-
sequently desired.

To these considerations may be added what we said in treating of the history of the Hebrews. And, lastly, how many
schisms have arisen in the Church from the attempt of the authorities to decide by law the intricacies of theological controversy! If men were not allured by the hope of getting the law
and the authorities on their side; of triumphing over their adversaries in the sight of an applauding multitude, and of acquiring
honorable distinctions, they would not strive so maliciously, nor
would such fury sway their minds. This is taught not only by
reason, but by daily examples; for laws of this kind, prescribing
what every man shall believe and forbidding any one to speak or
write to the contrary, have often been passed, as sops or concessions to the anger of those who cannot tolerate men of enlight-
enment, and who, by such harsh and crooked enactments, can
easily turn the devotion of the masses into fury and direct it
against whom they will.

How much better would it be to restrain popular anger and
fury, instead of passing useless laws, which can only be broken
by those who love virtue and the liberal arts, thus paring down
the state till it is too small to harbor men of talent. What
greater misfortune for a state can be conceived than that honorable men should be sent like criminals into exile, because they
hold diverse opinions which they cannot disguise? What, I say,

can be more hurtful than that men who have committed no crime or wickedness should, simply because they are enlightened, be treated as enemies and put to death, and that the scaffold, the terror of evil doers, should become the arena where the high- est examples of tolerance and virtue are displayed to the people with all the marks of ignominy that authority can devise?

He that knows himself to be upright does not fear the death of a criminal, and shrinks from no punishment; his mind is not wrung with remorse for any disgraceful deed; he holds that death in a good cause is no punishment, but an honor, and that death for freedom is glory.

What purpose then is served by the death of such men; what example is proclaimed? The cause for which they die is un- known to the idle and the foolish, hateful to the turbulent, loved by the upright. The only lesson we can draw from such scenes is to flatter the persecutor, or else to imitate the victim.

If formal assent is not to be esteemed above conviction, and if governments are to retain a firm hold of authority and not be compelled to yield to agitators, it is imperative that freedom of judgment should be granted, so that men may live together in harmony, however diverse, or even openly contradictory their opinions may be. We cannot doubt that such is the best system of government and open to the fewest objections, since it is the one most in harmony with human nature. In a democracy, the most natural form of government, every one submits to the control of authority over his actions, but not over his judgment and reason; that is, seeing that all cannot think alike, the voice of the majority has the force of law, subject to repeal if circum- stances bring about a change of opinion. In proportion as the power of free judgment is withheld, we depart from the natural condition of mankind, and consequently the government becomes more tyrannical.

In order to prove that from such freedom no inconvenience arises, which cannot easily be checked by the exercise of the sovereign power, and that men's actions can easily be kept in bounds, though their opinions be at open variance, it will be well to cite an example. Such a one is not very far to seek. The city of Amsterdam reaps the fruit of this freedom in its own great prosperity and in the admiration of all other people. For in this most flourishing state, and most splendid city, men of every nation and religion live together in the greatest harmony, and ask no questions before trusting their goods to a fellow-citizen, save whether he be rich or poor, and whether he generally acts honestly, or the reverse. His religion and sect is considered of no importance; for it has no effect before the judges in gaining or losing a cause, and there is no sect so despised that its followers, provided that they harm no one, pay every man his due, and live uprightly, are deprived of the protection of the magisterial authority.

On the other hand, when the religious controversy between Remonstrants and Counter-Remonstrants began to be taken up by politicians and the states, it grew into a schism, and abundantly showed that laws dealing with religion and seeking to settle its controversies are much more calculated to irritate than to reform, and that they give rise to extreme license; further, it was seen that schisms do not originate in a love of truth, which is a source of courtesy and gentleness, but rather in an inordinate desire for supremacy. From all these considerations it is clearer than the sun at noonday, that the true schismatics are those who condemn other men's writings, and seditiously stir up the quarrelsome masses against their authors, rather than those authors themselves, who generally write only for the learned, and appeal solely to reason. In fact, the real disturbers of the peace are those who, in a free state, seek to curtail the liberty of judgment which they are unable to tyrannize over.

I have thus shown: I. That it is impossible to deprive men of the liberty of saying what they think. II. That such liberty can be conceded to every man without injury to the rights and authority of the sovereign power, and that every man may retain it without injury to such rights, provided that he does not presume upon it to the extent of introducing any new rights into the state, or acting in any way contrary to the existing laws. III. That every man may enjoy this liberty without detriment to the public peace, and that no inconveniences arise therefrom which cannot easily be checked. IV. That every man may enjoy it without injury to his allegiance. V. That laws dealing with speculative problems are entirely useless. VI. Lastly, that not only may such liberty be granted without prejudice to the public peace, to loyalty, and to the rights of rulers, but that it is even necessary for their preservation. For when people try to take it away, and bring to trial, not only the acts which alone are capable of offending, but also the opinions of mankind, they only succeed in surrounding their victims with an appearance of martyrdom, and raise their feelings of pity and revenge rather than of terror. Uprightness and good faith are thus corrupted, flatterers and traitors are encouraged, and sectarians triumph, inasmuch as concessions have been made to their animosity, and they have gained the state sanction for the doctrines of which they are the interpreters. Hence they arrogate to themselves the state authority and rights, and do not scruple to assert that they have been directly chosen by God, and that their laws are Divine, whereas the laws of the state are human, and should therefore yield obedience to the laws of God — in other words, to their own laws. Every one must see that this is not a state of affairs conducive to public welfare. Wherefore, the safest way for a state is to lay down the rule that religion is comprised solely in the exercise of charity and justice, and that the rights of rulers in sacred, no less than in secular matters, should merely have to do with actions, but that every man should think what he likes and say what he thinks.

I have thus fulfilled the task I set myself in this treatise. It remains only to call attention to the fact that I have written nothing which I do not most willingly submit to the examinations and approval of my country's rulers; and that I am willing to retract anything which they shall decide to be repugnant to the laws, or prejudicial to the public good. I know that I am a man, and as a man liable to error, but against error I have taken scrupulous care, and have striven to keep in entire accordance with the laws of my country, with loyalty and with morality.

Complete. Concluding chapter of the
« Tractatus Theologico-Politicus.»

MADAME DE STAËL,

(ANNE LOUISE GERMAINE NECKER, BARONNE DE STAËL-HOLSTEIN)

(1766–1817)

HE celebrated Necker, Minister of Finance under Louis XVI., did his best and most enduring work in the education of the daughter, who as "Madame de Staël" surpassed him in celebrity and in brilliancy. Born in Paris, April 22d, 1766, she passed her girlhood in her father's house at a time when it was frequented by some of the greatest men of the age. Buffon, Grimm, and Gibbon were among the early acquaintances who stimulated her intellect and encouraged her to effort. In 1788, two years after her marriage to the Swedish embassador, Baron de Staël-Holstein, she published her first notable essays under the title of "Letters on the Character and Writings of J. J. Rousseau." Her husband died in 1802, and for several years after his death she resided in Germany and Italy. Her celebrated novel, "Corinne," appeared in 1807 and established for her the high place in French literature she is never likely to lose. The philosophical purpose of the book is too plainly apparent to allow it to become popular with lovers of the romantic in fiction. It illustrates the fact that Madame de Staël is in all her literary instincts the essayist rather than the novelist. She has as much difficulty in expressing herself through direct narration as such writers as Irving and Hawthorne have in refraining from constructing a plot for their essays. The tendency to philosophical reflection and speculation which shows in her novels showed in her conversation also. It was one of the causes no doubt which made Napoleon detest her. He lost no opportunity of making her uncomfortable, and in 1812 his enmity drove her from France. She visited Austria, Russia, Sweden, and England, during her exile, returning to France after the fall of Napoleon, and dying at Paris, July 14th, 1817. Among her best-known works are "Germany," "Literature Considered in Its Relation to Social Institutions," "Considerations on the French Revolution," "Dramatic Essays," and "Ten Years of Exile."

OF THE GENERAL SPIRIT OF MODERN LITERATURE

I T MAY be to thought, and not to imagination, that we are indebted for the new acquisitions made to literature in the Middle
Ages. Imitation, the principle of the fine arts, as I have before remarked, does not admit of unlimited perfection; the Moderns, in this respect, can never proceed further than by following
the path traced out by the Ancients. But if the images of poetry
and description always remain nearly the same, more eloquence
is added to the passions by a new development of sensibility and
a profound knowledge of character, which gives a charm to our
superior specimens of literature, which cannot be attributed solely
to poetical imagination.

The Ancients esteemed men as their friends, while they
considered women in no other light than as slaves designed by
nature for that unhappy state; and, indeed, the greater part of
them were deserving of that appellation,—their minds were not
furnished with a single idea that could distinguish them from
the brute creation, nor were they enlightened by one generous
sentiment. This circumstance, without doubt, was the cause why
the Ancients represented in their tender scenes merely sensations.

The preference of the Ancients towards the softer sex was
solely influenced by their beauty; but the Moderns acknowledge
that superior talents and ties can alone insure their happiness or
misery, in that predilection to which they owe the destiny of
their lives.

Novels, those varied productions of modern genius, were almost entirely unknown to the Ancients; it is true, they composed
a few pastorals in that style, at a period when the Greeks endeavored to discover some employment as a relaxation during servitude. But before women had created an interest in domestic
life, there was nothing sufficiently desirable to excite the curiosity of men, whose time was almost entirely occupied by political
pursuits.

A greater number of shades were perceptible in the characters of women, which their wish to obtain power, and their fear
of subjection, presented to general view; but they were singularly useful in furnishing new secrets of emotion for the exercise of dramatic talents; their fear of death, their desire of life,
the devotion of themselves, their resentments, and, in short, every

sentiment which they were suffered to deliver, embellished literature with new expressions. The women, it may be said, not
being strictly answerable for their conduct, did not scruple to
relate what their different sentiments naturally suggested. A
solid understanding, with a scrutinizing discernment, may clearly
perceive these developments of the human heart when it appears
in a state of nature; it is for this reason that the modern moralists have, in general, so much the advantage over the Ancients
in regard to their subtlety in the knowledge of mankind.

With the Ancients, those who could not acquire fame had no
motive for development: but after the period when connections
were formed in domestic life, the communications of the mind
and the exercise of morals always existed, at least in a limited
circle; the children became dearer to the parents from reciprocal
tenderness, which more closely united the conjugal tie; and the
different affections assumed the appearance of that divine alliance
of friendship in love, of attraction and esteem, of a merited confidence and an involuntary seduction.

Advanced age that was crowned with glory and virtue, although it ceased to hope, might continue to be animated by the
emotions of the heart, and was consoled with a pensive melancholy which allowed individuals to remember, to regret, and still
to regard what had formerly claimed their affection. When
moral reflections have been united to the violent passions of
youth, they may be extended by an exalted remembrance to the
termination of existence, and present the same pleasing picture
through the awful variations of time.

A profound and melancholy sensibility is one of the greatest
beauties perceptible in some of our modern writings; this, without doubt, is owing to the fair sex, who, being ignorant of most
other things in life, except the art of pleasing, transmitted the
softness of their impressions to the style of certain authors. In
perusing those works which were composed since the renewal of
letters, we may in every separate page remark those ideas which
were wanting before they accorded to women a kind of civil
equality.

Generosity, courage, and humanity have in some respects a
different meaning. The Ancients founded the chief of their virtues on the love of their country; the qualities of women were
exercised in a different and an independent manner: — a sympathy for misfortune, a pity for weakness, an elevation of soul,

without any other aim than the enjoyment of that elevation, is much more in their nature than political virtues. The Moderns, influenced by women, easily gave way to philanthropy, and the mind acquired a more philosophical liberty when they were less under the empire of exclusive associations.

The only advantage which the writers of the last centuries have over the Ancients in their works of imagination is the talent of expressing a more delicate sensibility; and that of giving greater variety to situations and characters, from a more intimate knowledge of the human heart. But how much superior are the philosophers of the present era in the sciences, in method, in analysis, in the arrangement of ideas, and the chain of events.

Mathematical arguments resemble the two great ideas of metaphysics, space and eternity; millions of leagues may be added and centuries multiplied; each calculation is true, yet the term remains indefinite. The wisest step ever taken by the human understanding was, to renounce all doubtful systems and adopt methods capable of demonstration.

Although modern eloquence may be deficient in the emulation of a free people, nevertheless it acquires from philosophy and a melancholy imagination a new character, which has a very powerful effect. I do not think that among the Ancients there was one composition, or a single orator, that could equal Bossuet, Rousseau, or the English, in some of their poetry, or the German in some of their phrases, in the sublime art of affecting the heart. It is to the spirituality of the Christian ideas, and to the sombre truths of philosophy, that we must attribute the art of introducing, even into private discussions, general and affecting reflections which touched the heart, awakened recollection, and induced man to consider the interest of his fellow-creatures.

The Ancients knew how to add vigor to the arguments necessary to be used on every occasion; but, at the present period, the mind, through a succession of ages, has become so indifferent to the interest of individuals and also to that of nations, that the eloquent writer finds it necessary to adopt a more pathetic style, in order to awaken the feelings which are common to all men. Without doubt, it is requisite to strike the imagination with a lively and forcible impression of the object intended to create an interest; but the appeal to pity is never irresistible, except when melancholy represents what the imagination has portrayed.

The Moderns possess a readiness of expression, the sole aim of which is to engage the eloquence of thought; antiquity presents no model of this kind but Tacitus. Montesquieu, Pascal, and Machiavelli are eloquent by a single expression, by a striking epithet, or in a rapidity of imagery, the purpose of which is the elucidation of an idea, and the endeavor to enlarge and embellish what is intended to be explained. The impression given by this peculiar style may be compared to the effect produced by the disclosure of an important secret: it seems likewise as if a number of thoughts had preceded that which had just been expressed, and each separate idea appears connected with the most profound meditations; and that suddenly, and by a single word, we are permitted to extend our ideas to those immense regions which have been accurately traced by the efforts of genius.

The ancient philosophers exercised, so to speak, a magistracy of instruction among men; having always in view the general benefit, they enforced certain rules, and left nothing undone that was likely to enlighten mankind. The knowledge of morals must have advanced with the progress of human reason; but philosophical demonstrations are considered more applicable to that moral which is of the intellectual order. We must not compare modern virtues with those of the Ancients, as citizens; it is only in a free country where there can exist that constant duty and that generous relation between the citizens and their country. It is true that, in a despotic government, custom or prejudice may still inspire some brilliant acts of military courage; but the continued and painful attention given to civil employments and legislative virtues, added to the disinterested sacrifice of the greater part of their lives to the public, can only exist where there is a real passion for liberty: it is therefore in private qualities, sentiments of philanthropy, and in a few writings of a superior order, that we are to examine the progress of morals.

The principles of modern philosophy are much more conducive to happiness than those of the Ancients; the duties imposed by our moralists are courtesy, docility, pity, and affection. Filial reverence was holden in the highest estimation by the Ancients, and parental attachment is viewed in the same light by the Moderns; but without doubt, in the connection between father and son, it is more advantageous that the benefactor should be the individual whose tenderness is the strongest.

The Ancients could not be exceeded in their love of justice, but they did not consider benevolence as a duty; justice may be enforced by the laws, notwithstanding general opinion is the criterion of beneficence, and is sufficient to exclude from esteem the being who is insensible to the miseries of his fellow-creatures.

The Ancients only required of others to refrain from injuring them; and simply desired them not to stand in their sunshine, but that they might be left to nature and themselves. But the Moderns, endowed with softer sentiments, solicit assistance, support, and that interest which their situation inspires. They have constituted into a virtue everything that can be useful to mutual happiness; domestic ties are cemented by a rational liberty; and no one has an arbitrary power over his fellow-creature.

With the ancient people of the North, lessons of prudence, dexterity, and maxims which commanded a supernatural empire over their own afflictions, were placed among the first precepts of virtue: but the importance of duties is much better classed by the Moderns; the reciprocal obligation from man to man holds the first rank; what regards ourselves ought to be considered relatively to the influence which we may possess over the destiny of others. What each individual is to procure, to promote his own happiness, is a counsel and not an order; the strictest moral does not impute to man as a crime that grief which is natural, and which his feelings will not allow him to conceal, but that grief which he occasions to others.

In a word, that which both the Gospel and philosophy alike inculcate is the doctrine of humanity. We are taught to respect the gift of life; and the existence of man is now considered as sacred to man, and is not viewed with that political indifference which some of the Ancients believed compatible with the true principles of virtue. We now feel a sensation of horror at the sight of blood; and the warrior who is entirely indifferent to his own personal danger acquires a degree of honor when he shudders at being the necessary cause of destruction to another. If any circumstance at this period gives reason to apprehend that a condemnation has been unjust, that an innocent person has fallen a victim to a supposed justice, nations will listen with terror to the lamentations which arise from an irreparable misfortune; the sensation caused by an unmerited death is recorded from one generation to another; and even children will listen with horror to the recital of so great a grievance. When the eloquent Lally, twenty years after the death of his father, demanded in France the re-establishment of his manes, those young men who could not have seen or known the victim whom he wished to reclaim, felt themselves violently agitated, and shed tears in abundance, as if that fatal day, when innocence was sacrificed, could never be effaced from their remembrance.

Thus ages rolled on towards the conquest of liberty, for virtue is always its herald. Alas! by what means shall we banish the painful contrast which so forcibly strikes the imagination? One crime was recollected during a long succession of years; but we have since witnessed cruelties without number committed and forgotten at the same moment! And it was under the shadow of the republic, the noblest, the most glorious, and the proudest institution of the human mind, that those execrable crimes have been committed! Ah! how difficult do we find it to repel those melancholy ideas, every time we reflect upon the destiny of man: the horrid phantom of the revolution appears before us; in vain we wish to look back on times that are past; in vain we desire to recognize in late events the constant connection of abstract combinations; if in the regions of metaphysics one word awakens recollection, the emotions of the heart resume all their empire, and, no longer supported by reflection, we are suddenly plunged into the abyss of despair.

Nevertheless, let us not yield to this despondency, but return to general observations and literary ideas,—to anything and everything, in short, that can divert our attention from personal sentiments; they are of too painful a nature to be developed. Talents may be animated by a certain degree of emotion; but long and heavy affliction stifles the genius of expression; and when sorrow is become habitual to the mind, the imagination loses even the wish to express what it feels.

Complete. « The Influence of Literature
upon Society, » Chap. ix.

OF SPANISH AND ITALIAN LITERATURE

THE greatest part of the ancient manuscripts, the monuments of art, and, in short, all the remains of Roman splendor and knowledge, existed in Italy; and considerable expenses and the authority of public power were necessary in order to make the researches requisite to bring them to light. It was consequently in this country, where the sources of all scientific pursuits were to be found, that literature first made its reappearance, and commenced its career under the auspices of princes; for the different means which are indispensably necessary to the first progress, are immediately dependent upon the power and will of government.

The protection of the Italian princes greatly contributed to the revival of letters; but it must have been an obstacle to the light of philosophy, and those obstacles would have existed even if religious superstition had not, in many instances, been detrimental to the investigation of truth.

I must once more explain the meaning which I have constantly attached to the word Philosophy in the course of this work; what I mean by the use of that term is a more minute inquiry into the principles of political and religious institutions; the analysis of characters, and the events of history,— in a word, the study of the human heart and the natural rights of man. Such a philosophy imagines a state of liberty, or must necessarily lead towards it.

The men of letters in Italy were further from that independence requisite to this philosophy than any other nation; as they required pecuniary means and the approbation of princes, in order to discover those manuscripts of antiquity that were to serve them as guides.

There were in all the great cities of Italy numberless academies and universities; .these associations were particularly proper for the learned researches that were to rescue from oblivion so many superior compositions of antiquity. But these public establishments, even from the nature of their institutions, were entirely under the subjection of government; and the corporations, like all other orders, classes, and sects, were extremely useful to one particular aim, but much less favorable than the efforts of individual genius to the advancement of philosophy. We must add to these general reflections, that the long and patient researches requisite for the examination of the ancient manuscripts was peculiarly adapted to a monastic life; and the monks, in fact, were the most active in the study of literature. Thus the same cause which produced the revival of letters opposed the development of natural reason. The Italians took the first steps, and pointed out the way in which the human understanding has since made such immense progress; but they were destined never to make any advance in the path which they themselves had laid open.

In Italy the imagination was intoxicated by the inimitable charms of poetry and the fine arts; but the writers in prose were, in general, neither moralists nor philosophers, and their efforts to appear eloquent produced nothing but bombast. Nevertheless, as it is in the nature of the human understanding always to improve, the Italians, to whom philosophy was interdicted, and who could not, in poetry, exceed the limit prescribed to all arts,—that of perfection,—the Italians, I say, rendered themselves illustrious by the astonishing progress which, by their perseverance, they affected in the sciences. After the century of Leo X., after Ariosto and Tasso, their poetry visibly assumed a retrograde course; but, in Galileo, Cassini, and in others still more recently, they acquired a number of useful discoveries in nature which associated them for the intellectual perfection of the human species.

Superstition made many attempts to persecute Galileo, but a number of the Italian princes came to his relief. Religious fanaticism is very inimical to the arts and sciences, as well as to philosophy; but absolute regal power, or federal aristocracy, have often protected them, and are only averse to a philosophical independence.

In a country where priesthood is predominant, every evil and every prejudice have been often found united; but the diversity of governments in Italy lightened the yoke of priesthood by creating a rivalry between those states or princes, who secured the very limited independence necessary to the arts and sciences.

After having affirmed that it was in the sciences only that the Italians advanced progressively, and furnished their tribute towards the general knowledge of the human species, let us proceed to examine into each branch of intellectual learning, into philosophy, eloquence, and poetry, with the causes of the successes and failures of the Italian literature.

The subdivision of states in the same country is, in general, very favorable to philosophy; this is what I have occasion to show in speaking of the German literature. But in Italy this subdivision did not produce its natural effect; the despotism of the priests destroyed, in a great measure, the happy results which might have arisen from a federal government; it would perhaps have been better if the whole nation had been united under one government; their recollection would have been more active, and the sentiments it inspired would have produced a retrospect favorable to virtue.

Principalities, whether under a federal or a theocratical government, have each of them been a prey to civil wars, parties, and factions altogether unfavorable to liberty. The minds of men were depraved by mutual hatred, instead of being enlarged by the love of their country. Even while they submitted to tyranny, they were familiar with assassination; incredulity was occasionally found the companion of fanaticism, but sound reason was never to be met with.

The Italians, notwithstanding their general incredulity and their universal professions, were much more addicted to pleasantry than reasoning,— which led them to make a jest of their own existence. When they wished to lay aside their natural talent, the comic, and attempted eloquent orations, they were always mixed with the most absurd affectation. Their recollection of past grandeur, without one idea of present greatness, must necessarily produce the stupendous. The Italians might possess dignity, if there were any mixture of the gloomy or melancholy in their characters; but when the successors of the Romans, deprived of all national splendor, and all political liberty, are yet the gayest people on earth, it shows that there is a natural want of elevation of soul.

It was perhaps from antipathy to the Italian bombast, that Machiavelli used such extreme simplicity when he analyzed tyranny. It is very probable that he wished that the horror of crimes should arise from the development of their principles; and carrying his contempt rather too far even for the appearance of declamation, he left everything to the imagination of his readers. The reflections of Machiavelli upon Titus Livy are far superior to his " Prince." These reflections may be considered as one of the works in which the human understanding has showed itself to the greatest advantage; such a production belongs entirely to the genius of the author, and has no connection with the general character of the Italian literature.

The literature of the Spaniards ought to have been more remarkable than that of the Italians; it should have united the imagination of the North with that of the East, the Oriental grandeur with the splendor of chivalry, the martial spirit which repeated wars had exalted, and the poetry which was inspired by the beauty of their climate: but regal power, which served as a prop for superstition, stifled in their birth those puerile dispositions to glory.

The subdivision of states, although it precluded Italy from becoming one nation, gave sufficient liberty for the study of the sciences; but the united despotism of Spain, in encouraging the active power of the Inquisition, left no pursuit for thought, no resource nor means of escaping the yoke. We may, however, judge what the Spanish literature might have been, by some essays which may yet be collected.

The romances of the Moors established in Spain borrowed their respect for the fair sex from chivalry. This respect was not to be found in the national manners of the East. The Arabs who remained in Africa did not in this instance resemble the Arabs established in Spain; the Moors inspired the Spaniards with their spirit of magnificence; and the Spaniards reciprocally taught their love and their chivalric honor to the Moors. No mixture could be more favorable to works of imagination, if literature had been encouraged in Spain. Amongst their romances, the "Cid" gives us some idea of the grandeur which would have characterized the efforts of their genius. In the poem of Camoens, which is written in the same spirit as many of the Spanish productions, we find a most beautiful fiction in the phantom which defends the entrance of the Indian seas. In the comedies of Calderoni, and of Lopez de Vega, an elevation of sentiment always shines through the cloud of faults by which their beauties are veiled. The love and jealousy of the Spaniards have quite a different character from the sentiments represented in the Italian pieces; their expressions are very subtile, though not entirely insipid; they never portray perfidy of character nor depravity of manners: it is true, they have too much pompousness of style; but while we condemn their bombast, we are convinced of the truth of their sentiments. It is not the same in Italy: if the affectation of certain works were taken away, there would remain nothing at all; while, if we could remove that of the Spaniards, they would shortly attain to the perfection of dignity, courage, and the most affecting sensibility.

It was not possible that the elements of philosophy could be improved in Spain; the invasion of the North introduced nothing but the military spirit; and the Arabians were altogether enemies to philosophy: their absolute government, and the fatality of their religion, led them to detest the light of philosophy: this hatred caused them to burn the library of Alexandria. They, however, cultivated the sciences and poetry: but they studied the former like astrologers, and the latter like warriors. They cultivated their vocal talents, merely to sing their exploits; and they studied nature only with the hopes of attaining the magic art. They had no idea of strengthening their reason: and in reality, to what use could they have applied a faculty which would have overthrown what they most respected, despotism and superstition?

The Spaniards, strangers like the Italians to the labors of philosophy, were entirely diverted from all literary emulation by the gloomy and oppressive tyranny of the Inquisition. They drew no profit from the inexhaustible sources of poetic invention which the Arabians brought with them. Italy was in possession of the ancient monuments; was also immediately connected with the Greeks of Constantinople; and drew from Spain the Oriental style, which the Moors had introduced, but which the Spaniards neglected. . . .

In Italy everything conspired to fill the life of man with the agreeable sensations which naturally arise from their fine arts and their unclouded sun; but since this country has lost the empire of the world, it seems as if its inhabitants disdained a political existence; and, according to the maxims of Cæsar, they aspired to the first rank in pleasure, rather than the second place in the annals of fame.

Dante having, as well as Machiavelli, supported a character in the civil commotions of his country, in some of his poems we observe an energy in no degree analogous to the literature of his time; but the numberless faults with which we may reproach him, belonged without doubt to the century he lived in. It is only in the time of Leo X. that we remark a decided purity in the Italian literature; the ascendency of this prince was to the Italian government what unity might have been; the rays of knowledge were collected into one focus, in which taste also might have been concentrated, and literary judgments have proceeded from the same tribunal.

After the age of the Medici, the Italian literature made no progress of any kind, either because some central point was necessary to rally all the forces of the intellect, or, principally, because philosophy was not at all cultivated in Italy. When the literature of imagination has attained to the highest possible degree of perfection, the subsequent age belongs to philosophy, in order that the human understanding may not cease in its advancement towards perfection in some way or other. After

Racine, we have seen Voltaire; because, in the eighteenth century, men were more profound thinkers than in the seventeenth. But what could have been added to the excellence of poetry after Racine?

The Italians have no romances like those of the French and English, because the love which inspired them, not being a passion of the mind capable of any long continuation, their customs and manners were too licentious to preserve any interest in this style. Their comedies were filled with that kind of buffoonery which arises from the absurdities and vices; but we do not find, if we except a few pieces of Goldoni, one striking and variegated picture of the vices of the human heart, such as are found in the French comedies. The Italians simply wished to create laughter; no serious aim can be discovered through the veil of flippancy, and their comedies are not the picture of human life, but its caricature.

The Italians, even in their theatres, have often turned their priests into ridicule, although in other respects they were entirely subjected to them; but it was not with a philosophical view that they attacked the abuses of religion; they had not, like some of our writers a wish to reform the faults they complained of; it was easy to perceive that their real opinions were totally opposite to that kind of authority to which they were compelled to submit; but this spirit of opposition incited them to nothing more than a contempt for those who commanded esteem; it was like the cunning of children to their teachers; they were willing to obey them on condition they might be permitted to make sport of them.

It follows from this that all the works of the Italians, except those which treat on physical sciences, have nothing useful in view; which is absolutely necessary in order to give a real strength and solidity to their reflections. The works of Beccaria, Filangieri, and a few others, make the only exception to what I have now advanced.

One question more remains to be decided before I close,—which is, whether the Italians have carried the dramatic art to any length in tragedy.

For myself, in spite of the charms of Metastasio, and the energy of Alfieri, I do not think they have. The Italians have a lively invention in subjects, and a brilliancy in expression; but the personages which they represent are not characterized in a manner to leave any lasting traces on the mind; and the affliction which they portray excites but little sympathy. This may be occasioned by their moral and political situation, not allowing the mind its full display: their sensibility is not serious, their sadness is without melancholy, and their grandeur commands no respect. The Italian author was therefore obliged to have recourse entirely to himself; and, to compose a tragedy, he must not only forget all he sees, but renounce all his habitual ideas and impressions: and it is very difficult to find out the true basis of a tragedy which is so widely different from the general manners and customs of the time in which it was composed.

Vengeance is the passion which is the best described in the Italian tragedies: it is natural to their character to be suddenly roused by this sentiment in the midst of that habitual indolence in which they spent their lives; and their resentments were naturally expressed, because they really felt them.

The operas alone were followed, because at the opera was heard that enchanting music which was the glory and pleasure of Italy. The performers did not exert themselves in tragedy; fine acting would have been thrown away; they were not even heard; and it must ever be thus, when the art of touching the passions is not carried to a sufficient length to predominate over every other pleasure. The Italians did not require to be softened, and the authors for want of spectators, and the spectators for want of authors, did not give themselves up to the profound impressions of the dramatic art.

Metastasio, however, found out the secret of turning his operas almost into tragedies; and though compelled to struggle with all the difficulties imposed by the obligation of submitting to music, he still preserved many beauties of style and situation truly dramatic. It may be that there exist yet some other exceptions little known to strangers; but to draw the principal characters of any national literature, it is absolutely necessary to lay aside many details; there are no general ideas that are not contradicted by certain exemptions; but the mind would be incapable of ever forming any determination, if it were to stop at each particular instead of drawing a consequence from a collective whole.

Melancholy, that sentiment which is so fertile in works of genius, appears to have belonged almost exclusively to the people of the North. The Oriental style, which the Italians have often imitated, had a sort of melancholy of which we find some traces in the Arabian poetry, and likewise in the Hebrew psalms; but it has a character entirely distinct from that we shall find when we analyze the literature of the North.

The people of the East, whether Jews or Mahometans, were sustained and directed by their positive reliance on their religion. It was not that uncertain and undetermined apprehension which afforded the mind a more philosophical impression; the melancholy of the Orientals was that of men who were happy from every enjoyment of nature; they simply reflected with regret upon the brevity of human life, and the rapid decay of prosperity; while the melancholy of the people of the North was that which is inspired by the sufferings of the mind, the void which the absence of sensibility makes in the existence, and that continual musing upon the calamities of this life, and the uncertainty of their destiny in a life to come.

From « The Influence of Literature upon Society.»

SIR RICHARD STEELE

(1672–1729)

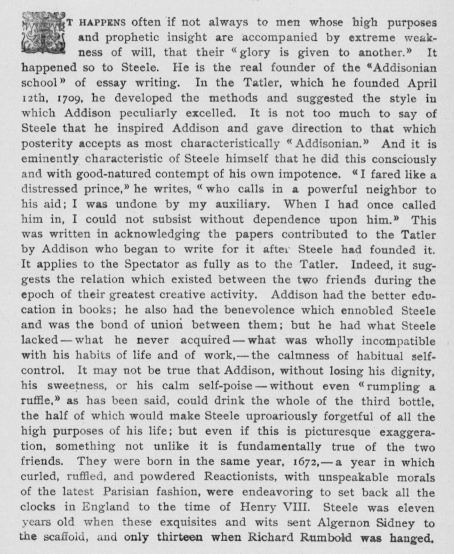T HAPPENS often if not always to men whose high purposes and prophetic insight are accompanied by extreme weakness of will, that their "glory is given to another." It happened so to Steele. He is the real founder of the "Addisonian school" of essay writing. In the Tatler, which he founded April 12th, 1709, he developed the methods and suggested the style in which Addison peculiarly excelled. It is not too much to say of Steele that he inspired Addison and gave direction to that which posterity accepts as most characteristically "Addisonian." And it is eminently characteristic of Steele himself that he did this consciously and with good-natured contempt of his own impotence. "I fared like a distressed prince," he writes, "who calls in a powerful neighbor to his aid; I was undone by my auxiliary. When I had once called him in, I could not subsist without dependence upon him." This was written in acknowledging the papers contributed to the Tatler by Addison who began to write for it after Steele had founded it. It applies to the Spectator as fully as to the Tatler. Indeed, it suggests the relation which existed between the two friends during the epoch of their greatest creative activity. Addison had the better education in books; he also had the benevolence which ennobled Steele and was the bond of union between them; but he had what Steele lacked — what he never acquired — what was wholly incompatible with his habits of life and of work, — the calmness of habitual self-control. It may not be true that Addison, without losing his dignity, his sweetness, or his calm self-poise — without even "rumpling a ruffle," as has been said, could drink the whole of the third bottle, the half of which would make Steele uproariously forgetful of all the high purposes of his life; but even if this is picturesque exaggeration, something not unlike it is fundamentally true of the two friends. They were born in the same year, 1672, — a year in which curled, ruffled, and powdered Reactionists, with unspeakable morals of the latest Parisian fashion, were endeavoring to set back all the clocks in England to the time of Henry VIII. Steele was eleven years old when these exquisites and wits sent Algernon Sidney to the scaffold, and only thirteen when Richard Rumbold was hanged.

eviscerated, and cut into quarters for holding the belief that God is not sufficiently a respecter of persons to give one man a title from heaven to master another. It was in 1660, only twelve years before Steele's birth, that Thomas Harrison had been actually eviscerated alive in accordance with the sentence of a court controlled by the "Merry Monarch." It is not pleasant to remember such things; but if they are forgotten, it will be impossible to understand Steele or his mission. In 1701, when he began what he always considered his apostolate by writing "The Christian Hero," the morals of England were indescribably corrupt. He was at the time a captain in Lord Lucas's Fusiliers, having left Oxford without a degree to join the army as a private soldier. Debauchery and cruelty characterized the modes through which the pride of the ruling class manifested its impulses of domination. Captain Steele who wrote "The Christian Hero" in the hope that the standard of morals he thus set for others would incidentally elevate his own, was so far defeated in his purpose of shaming himself into sobriety and dignity, that in defending the ethics of "The Christian Hero," he felt obliged to fight a duel and wound dangerously one of the Wildrakes who had insulted him for advocating meekness, temperance, and soberness. In an eminently characteristic way, Steele followed this up by writing "The Funeral," "The Conscious Lover," and other comedies, with the well-defined purpose of redeeming himself from the suspicion of too much sanctity, or, as he says, "to enliven" his character. He had a deep, underlying, and governing purpose, however, which he never abandoned — drunk or sober! It was to use his pen to reform the manners of his time. The frequency of his own lapses under temptation served to make him more steadfast in this governing purpose by convincing him the more deeply of the need for his work as a means of helping to redeem others from sufferings of which his own infirmities made him aware. Thus we have illustrated in his life the remarkable contradiction of a feeble will joined to extraordinary tenacity of life purpose. In such feebleness, controlled by the inspiration of hopes of usefulness, he was one of the very "babes and sucklings" out of whose mouths is perfected the praise which belongs in fullness only to the perfect expression of the Divinely Human. Steele is often absurd, and sometimes irresistibly ludicrous in his career as a reformer and prophet. But whether he was writing essays on virtue for the Tatler and Spectator, or drunk under the table over which Addison presided with still unruffled dignity; whether he was accepting Addison's charity as the only means of escaping imprisonment for debt, or founding the Plebeian to oppose the Toryism into which he feared even Addison had lapsed, — at all times, in all the follies and mischances of his life, he had always in him the strength of the same idea which gave greatness to Chatham and Burke, to Brougham and Macaulay. He believed in the divine right of every man to grow better, larger, and stronger; he believed also in the divine duty of attempting it, no matter how feebly; he feared and fought against that " merriness " of morals which he saw destroying the people as he felt it destroying himself. His ideal was of larger liberty and higher living for England and all the world. No man was ever weaker against temptation, but this high purpose saved and glorified him. If it did not make him an Addison, it fitted him to become at some later stage of the continuous existence throughout the eternity in which he believed the " Christian hero " he had longed to be in this life — the hero we may say with certainty that Addison never even attempted to be. For certainly though the " wit," who scarcely rumpled his ruffles when in the extremest stages of dissolute living, may reform and become a saint, — as Addison did, — there is nothing specially characteristic of the hero in him.

Steele was born in Dublin in March, 1672. He first met Addison when they were boys together at the Charterhouse School, and they were afterwards college mates at Oxford. After leaving the army with the rank of Captain, Steele, through his favor of influential Whigs, was elected to Parliament, from which he was not very long afterwards expelled for " seditious language " published in the Crisis. George I. knighted him and appointed him to various offices, because of his ability as a Whig pamphleteer. Between 1709 and 1711 he founded and edited the Tatler, and followed it up with the Spectator, in which he was associated with Addison (1711–12). He founded successively the Guardian, Town Talk, the Tea Table, Chit Chat, the Plebeian, and the Theatre, none of which were notable successes financially. Steele was usually more concerned, however, with some moral, literary, or political purpose than with money-making or with " establishing a property." When he could find no other way of exerting his influence at what seemed to him a crisis, he would found a paper (as he did the Plebeian, in which he opposed Addison) and run it, either until money failed or he had accomplished his purpose. It is hard to tell which of the two events was more apt to be fatal to his newspaper enterprises, as without a definite, moral purpose to inspire him, he seems to have been incapable of long-sustained effort. He died September 1st, 1729, leaving his memory for a jest to his lovers and his influence on English literature for a blessing to the remotest posterity.   W. V. B.

THE CHARACTER OF ISAAC BICKERSTAFF

Rura mihi placeant, riguique in vallibus amnes,
Flumina amem sylvasque inglorius —
                    —Virg. Georg. II. 485.

My next desire is, void of care and strife,
To lead a soft, secure, inglorious life:
A country cottage near a crystal flood,
A winding valley and a lofty wood.
                    —Dryden.

GRECIAN COFFEEHOUSE, November 2d.

I HAVE received this short epistle from an unknown hand.

Sir: —

I have no more to trouble you with than to desire you would in your next help me to some answer to the inclosed concerning yourself. In the meantime I congratulate you upon the increase of your fame, which you see has extended itself beyond the bills of mortality.

Sir: —

That the country is barren of news has been the excuse, time out of mind, for dropping a correspondence with our friends in London,— as if it were impossible, out of a coffeehouse, to write an agreeable letter. I am too ingenuous to endeavor at the covering of my negligence with so common an excuse. Doubtless, amongst friends, bred, as we have been, to the knowledge of books as well as men, a letter dated from a garden, a grotto, a fountain, a wood, a meadow, or the banks of a river, may be more entertaining than one from Tom's, Will's, White's, or St. James's. I promise, therefore, to be frequent for the future in my rural dates to you. But, for fear you should, from what I have said, be induced to believe I shun the commerce of men, I must inform you that there is a fresh topic of discourse lately arisen amongst the ingenious in our part of the world, and is become the more fashionable for the ladies giving into it. This we owe to Isaac Bickerstaff, who is very much censured by some, and as much justified by others. Some criticize his style, his humor, and his matter; others admire the whole man. Some pretend, from the informations of their friends in town, to decipher the author; and others confess they are lost in their guesses. For my part, I must own myself a professed admirer of the paper, and desire you to send me a complete set, together with your thoughts of the squire and his lucubrations.

There is no pleasure like that of receiving praise from the praiseworthy; and I own it a very solid happiness, that these my lucubrations are approved by a person of so fine a taste as the author of this letter, who is capable of enjoying the world in the simplicity of its natural beauties. This pastoral letter, if I may so call it, must be written by a man who carries his entertainment wherever he goes, and is, undoubtedly, one of those happy men who appear far otherwise to the vulgar. I dare say he is not envied by the vicious, the vain, the frolic, and the loud; but is continually blessed with that strong and serious delight, which flows from a well-taught and liberal mind. With great respect to country sports, I may say, this gentleman could pass his time agreeably, if there were not a hare or a fox in his county. That calm and elegant satisfaction which the vulgar call melancholy is the true and proper delight of men of knowledge and virtue. What we take for diversion, which is a kind of forgetting ourselves, is but a mean way of entertainment, in comparison of that which is considering, knowing, and enjoying ourselves. The pleasures of ordinary people are in their passions; but the seat of this delight is in the reason and understanding. Such a frame of mind raises that sweet enthusiasm, which warms the imagination at the sight of every work of nature, and turns all round you into picture and landscape. I shall be ever proud of advices from this gentleman; for I profess writing news from the learned, as well as the busy world.

As for my labors, which he is pleased to inquire after, if they can but wear one impertinence out of human life, destroy a single vice, or give a morning's cheerfulness to an honest mind; in short, if the world can be but one virtue the better, or in any degree less vicious, or receive from them the smallest addition to their innocent diversions, I shall not think my pains, or indeed my life, to have been spent in vain.

Thus far as to my studies. It will be expected I should, in the next place, give some account of my life. I shall, therefore, for the satisfaction of the present age, and the benefit of posterity, present the world with the following abridgment of it.

It is remarkable that I was bred by hand, and ate nothing but milk until I was a twelve-month old; from which time, to the eighth year of my age, I was observed to delight in pudding and potatoes; and, indeed, I retain a benevolence for that sort of food to this day. I do not remember that I distinguished myself in anything at those years, but by my great skill at taw, for which I was so barbarously used, that it has ever since given me an aversion to gaming. In my twelfth year I suffered very much for two or three false concords.* At fifteen I was sent to the university, and stayed there for some time; but a drum passing by, being a lover of music, I enlisted myself for a soldier. As years came on, I began to examine things, and grew discontented at the times. This made me quit the sword, and take to the study of the occult sciences, in which I was so wrapped up, that Oliver Cromwell had been buried and taken up again five years before I heard he was dead. This gave me first the reputation of a conjurer, which has been of great disadvantage to me ever since, and kept me out of all public employments. The greater part of my later years has been divided between Dick's coffeehouse, the Trumpet in Sheer-lane, and my own lodgings.

FROM MY OWN APARTMENT, November 2d.

The evil of unseasonable visits has been complained of to me with much vehemence by persons of both sexes; and I am desired to consider this very important circumstance, that men may know how to regulate their conduct in an affair which concerns no less than life itself. For to a rational creature, it is almost the same cruelty to attack his life, by robbing him of so many moments of his time, or so many drops of his blood. The author of the following letter has a just delicacy in this point, and hath put it into a very good light: —

Mr. Bickerstaff: —   October 29th.

I am very much afflicted with the gravel, which makes me sick and peevish. I desire to know of you, if it be reasonable that any of my acquaintance should take advantage over me at this time, and afflict me with long visits, because they are idle, and I am confined. Pray, sir, reform the town in this matter. Men never consider whether the sick person be disposed for company, but make their visits to

* Isaac Bickerstaff, Esq., declares that he was sixty-three in 1709; he was born, therefore, in 1646; he could only be fifteen in 1661, when the body of Cromwell was exposed. Yet he was sent to the university at fifteen;—then he was a soldier, a cadet at the battle of Coldstream; afterward he took to the study of the occult sciences, and did not hear of Cromwell's fate till five years after it happened. Kept out of all public employments, the greater part of his later years was divided between Dick's coffeehouse, a tavern, or alehouse, and his own obscure lodgings in Sheer-lane. How was such a man qualified to decide on all subjects private and public? (Steele's note.)

humor themselves. You may talk upon this topic, so as to oblige all persons afflicted with chronical distempers, among which I reckon visits. Do not think me a sour man, for I love conversation and my friends; but I think one's most intimate friend may be too familiar, and that there are such things as unseasonable wit and painful mirth.

It is with some so hard a thing to employ their time, that it is a great good fortune when they have a friend indisposed, that they may be punctual in perplexing him, when he is recovered enough to be in that state which cannot be called sickness or health; when he is too well to deny company and too ill to receive them. It is no uncommon case, if a man is of any figure or power in the world, to be congratulated into a relapse.

WILL'S COFFEEHOUSE, November 2d.

I was very well pleased this evening, to hear a gentleman express a very becoming indignation against a practice which I myself have been very much offended at. "There is nothing," said he, "more ridiculous, than for an actor to insert words of his own in the part he is to act, so that it is impossible to see the poet for the player. You will have Penkethman and Bullock helping out Beaumont and Fletcher. It puts me in mind," continued he, "of a collection of antique statues which I once saw in a gentleman's possession, who employed a neighboring stonecutter to add noses, ears, arms, or legs, to the maimed works of Phidias or Praxiteles. You may be sure this addition disfigured the statue much more than time had. I remember Venus, that, by the nose he had given her, looked like mother Shipton; and a Mercury, with a pair of legs that seemed very much swelled with the dropsy."

I thought the gentleman's observations very proper, and he told me I had improved his thought in mentioning on this occasion those wise commentators who had filled up the hemistichs of Virgil; particularly that notable poet, who, to make the "Æneid" more perfect, carried on the story to Lavinia's wedding. If the proper officer will not condescend to take notice of these absurdities, I shall myself, as a censor of the people, animadvert upon such proceedings.

Complete. From the Tatler.

BICKERSTAFF AND MARIA

FROM MY OWN APARTMENT, October 19th.

IT IS my frequent practice to visit places of resort in this town where I am least known, to observe what reception my works meet with in the world, and what good effects I may promise myself from my labors, and it being a privilege asserted by Monsieur Montaigne, and others, of vainglorious memory, that we writers of essays may talk of ourselves, I take the liberty to give an account of the remarks which I find are made by some of my gentle readers upon these my dissertations.

I happened this evening to fall into a coffeehouse near the 'Change, where two persons were reading my account of the "Table of Fame."

The one of these was commenting as he read, and explaining who was meant by this and the other worthy, as he passed on. I observed the person over against him wonderfully intent and satisfied with his explanation. When he came to Julius Cæsar, who is said to have refused any conductor to the table: "No, no," said he, "he is in the right of it, he has money enough to be welcome wherever he comes"; and then whispered, "He means a certain colonel of the Trainbands." Upon reading that Aristotle made his claim with some rudeness, but great strength of reason; "Who can that be, so rough and so reasonable? It must be some Whig, I warrant you. There is nothing but party in these public papers." Where Pythagoras is said to have a golden thigh, "Aye, aye," said he, "he has money enough in his breeches; that is the alderman of our ward." You must know, whatever he read, I found he interpreted from his own way of life and acquaintance. I am glad my readers can construe for themselves these difficult points; but, for the benefit of posterity, I design, when I come to write my last paper of this kind, to make it an explanation of all my former. In that piece you shall have all I have commended with their proper names. The faulty characters must be left as they are, because we live in an age wherein vice is very general, and virtue very particular; for which reason the latter only wants explanation.

But I must turn my present discourse to what is of yet greater regard to me than the care of my writings; that is to say, the preservation of a lady's heart. Little did I think I should ever

have business of this kind on my hands more; but, as little as
any one who knows me would believe it, there is a lady at this
time who professes love to me. Her passion and good humor
you shall have in her own words: —

Mr. Bickerstaff: —
     I had formerly a very good opinion of myself; but it is now with-
drawn, and I have placed it upon you, Mr. Bickerstaff, for whom I
am not ashamed to declare I have a very great passion and tenderness. It is not for your face, for that I never saw; your shape and
height I am equally a stranger to; but your understanding charms
me, and I am lost if you do not dissemble a little love for me. I
am not without hopes; because I am not like the tawdry gay
things that are fit only to make bone-lace. I am neither childish young, nor beldam old, but, the world says, a good, agreeable
woman.
     Speak peace to a troubled heart, troubled only for you; and in
your next paper let me find your thoughts of me.
     Do not think of finding out who I am, for, notwithstanding your
interest in demons, they cannot help you either to my name, or a
sight of my face; therefore, do not let them deceive you.
     I can bear no discourse, if you are not the subject; and believe
me, I know more of love than you do of astronomy.
     Pray, say some civil things in return to my generosity, and you
shall have my very best pen employed to thank you, and I will confirm it.
                                        I am your admirer,
                                             MARIA.

     There is something wonderfully pleasing in the favor of
women; and this letter has put me in so good a humor, that
nothing could displease me since I received it. My boy breaks
glasses and pipes, and instead of giving him a knock on the
pate, as my way is, for I hate scolding at servants, I only say,
" Ah, Jack! thou hast a head, and so has a pin," or some such
merry expression. But, alas! how am I mortified when he is
putting on my fourth pair of stockings on these poor spindles of
mine! "The fair one understands love better than I astronomy!"
I am sure, without the help of that art, this poor meagre trunk
of mine is a very ill habitation for love. She is pleased to speak
civilly of my sense, but *Ingenium malè habitat* is an invincible
difficulty in cases of this nature. I had always, indeed, from a
passion to please the eyes of the fair, a great pleasure in dress.

Add to this, that I have writ songs since I was sixty, and have
lived with all the circumspection of an old beau, as I am. But
my friend Horace has very well said, "Every year takes something from us"; and instructed me to form my pursuits and desires according to the stage of my life; therefore, I have no
more to value myself upon than that I can converse with young
people without peevishness, or wishing myself a moment younger.
For which reason, when I am amongst them, I rather moderate
than interrupt their diversions. But though I have this complacency, I must not pretend to write to a lady civil things, as
Maria desires. Time was, when I could have told her, "I had
received a letter from her fair hands; and that, if this paper
trembled, as she read it, it then best expressed its author," or
some other gay conceit. Though I never saw her, I could have
told her, "that good sense and good humor smiled in her eyes;
that constancy and good nature dwelt in her heart; that beauty
and good breeding appeared in all her actions." When I was
five-and-twenty, upon sight of one syllable, even wrong spelt, by
a lady I never saw, I could tell her, "that her height was that
which was fit for inviting our approach, and commanding our
respect; that a smile sat on her lips, which prefaced her expressions before she uttered them, and her aspect prevented her
speech. All she could say, though she had an infinite deal of
wit, was but a repetition of what was expressed by her form;
her form! which struck her beholders with ideas more moving and forcible than ever were inspired by music, painting, or eloquence." At this rate I panted in those days; but
ah! sixty-three! I am very sorry I can only return the agreeable Maria a passion expressed rather from the head than the
heart.

Dear Madam: —
    You have already seen the best of me, and I so passionately love
you that I desire we may never meet. If you will examine your
heart, you will find that you join the man with the philosopher; and
if you have that kind opinion of my sense as you pretend, I question
not but you add to it complexion, air, and shape; but, dear Molly, a man
in his grand climacteric is of no sex. Be a good girl, and conduct
yourself with honor and virtue, when you love one younger than
myself. I am, with the greatest tenderness, your innocent lover,

                                                      I. B

                              Complete. From the Tatler.

SIR ROGER AND THE WIDOW

————*Hærent infixi pectore vultus.*
          —*Virg*. Æn. IV. 4.

« Her looks were deep imprinted in his heart. »

IN MY first description of the company in which I pass most of
    my time, it may be remembered that I mentioned a great
    affliction which my friend Sir Roger had met with in his
youth; which was no less than a disappointment in love. It
happened this evening that we fell into a very pleasing walk at
a distance from his house. As soon as we came into it, " It is, "
quoth the good old man, looking round him with a smile, " very
hard that any part of my land should be settled upon one who
has used me so ill as the perverse widow did; and yet I am sure
I could not see a sprig of any bough of this whole walk of trees,
but I should reflect upon her and her severity. She has certainly
the finest hand of any woman in the world. You are to know,
this was the place wherein I used to muse upon her; and by that
custom I can never come into it, but the same tender sentiments
revive in my mind, as if I had actually walked with that beautiful creature under these shades. I have been fool enough to
carve her name on the bark of several of these trees; so unhappy
is the condition of men in love, to attempt the removing of their
passion by the methods which serve only to imprint it deeper.
She has certainly the finest hand of any woman in the world. »

Here followed a profound silence; and I was not displeased to
observe my friend falling so naturally into a discourse, which I
had ever before taken notice he industriously avoided. After a
very long pause, he entered upon an account of this great circumstance in his life, with an air which I thought raised my
idea of him above what I had ever had before; and gave me the
picture of that cheerful mind of his before it received that
stroke which has ever since affected his words and actions. But
he went on as follows:—

" I came to my estate in my twenty-second year, and resolved
to follow the steps of the most worthy of my ancestors who have
inhabited this spot of earth before me, in all the methods of
hospitality and good neighborhood, for the sake of my fame; and
in country sports and recreations, for the sake of my health. In

my twenty-third year I was obliged to serve as sheriff of the
county; and in my servants, officers, and whole equipage, indulged the pleasure of a young man (who did not think ill of
his own person) in taking that public occasion of showing my
figure and behavior to advantage. You may easily imagine to
yourself what appearance I made, who am pretty tall, rid well,
and was very well dressed, at the head of a whole county, with
music before me, a feather in my hat, and my horse well bitted.
I can assure you, I was not a little pleased with the kind looks
and glances I had from all the balconies and windows as I rode
to the hall where the assizes were held. But when I came there,
a beautiful creature, in a widow's habit, sat in court to hear
the event of a cause concerning her dower. This commanding
creature (who was born for the destruction of all who behold
her) put on such a resignation in her countenance, and bore the
whispers of all around the court with such a pretty uneasiness, I
warrant you, and then recovered herself from one eye to another,
until she was perfectly confused by meeting something so wistful
in all she encountered, that at last, with a murrain to her, she
cast her bewitching eye upon me. I no sooner met it but I bowed
like a great surprised booby; and knowing her cause was to be
the first which came on, I cried, like a great captivated calf as I
was, 'Make way for the defendant's witnesses.' This sudden
partiality made all the county immediately see the sheriff also
was become a slave to the fine widow. During the time her
cause was upon trial, she behaved herself, I warrant you, with
such a deep attention to her business, took opportunities to have
little billets handed to her counsel, then would be in such a pretty
confusion, occasioned, you must know, by acting before so
much company, that not only I, but the whole court, was prejudiced in her favor; and all that the next heir to her husband had
to urge was thought so groundless and frivolous, that when it
came to her counsel to reply, there was not half so much said as
every one besides in the court thought he could have urged to
her advantage. You must understand, sir, this perverse woman
is one of those unaccountable creatures that secretly rejoice in
the admiration of men, but indulge themselves in no further consequences. Hence it is that she has ever had a train of admirers,
and she removes from her slaves in town to those in the country,
according to the seasons of the year. She is a reading lady, and
far gone in the pleasures of friendship. She is always accom-

panied by a confidant, who is witness to her daily protesta-
tions against our sex, and consequently a bar to her first steps
towards love, upon the strength of her own maxims and declara-
tions.

"However, I must needs say this accomplished mistress of
mine has distinguished me above the rest, and has been known
to declare Sir Roger de Coverley was the tamest and most hu-
mane of all the brutes in the country. I was told she said so
by one who thought he rallied me; but upon the strength of this
slender encouragement of being thought least detestable, I made
new liveries, new paired my coach horses, sent them all to town
to be bitted, and taught to throw their legs well, and move altogether, before I pretended to cross the country, and wait upon
her. As soon as I thought my retinue suitable to the character
of my fortune and youth, I set out from hence to make my addresses. The particular skill of this lady has ever been to in-
flame your wishes, and yet command respect. To make her
mistress of this art, she has a greater share of knowledge, wit,
and good sense, than is usual even among men of merit. Then
she is beautiful beyond the race of women. If you will not let
her go on with a certain artifice with her eyes, and the skill of
beauty, she will arm herself with her real charms, and strike you
with admiration instead of desire. It is certain that if you were
to behold the whole woman, there is that dignity in her aspect,
that composure in her motion, that complacency in her manner,
that if her form makes you hope, her merit makes you fear. But
then again, she is such a desperate scholar, that no country gentleman can approach her without being a jest. As I was going to
tell you, when I came to her house, I was admitted to her
presence with great civility; at the same time she placed herself
to be first seen by me in such an attitude as I think you call
the posture of a picture, that she discovered new charms, and
I at last came towards her with such an awe as made me
speechless. This she no sooner observed but she made her advantage of it, and began a discourse to me concerning love and
honor, as they both are followed by pretenders, and the real
votaries to them. When she discussed these points in a discourse,
which I verily believe was as learned as the best philosopher in
Europe could possibly make, she asked me whether she was so
happy as to fall in with my sentiments on these important particulars. Her confidant sat by her, and upon my being in the

last confusion and silence, this malicious aid of hers, turning to her, says, 'I am very glad to observe Sir Roger pauses upon this subject, and seems resolved to deliver all his sentiments upon the matter when he pleases to speak.' They both kept their countenances, and after I had sat half an hour meditating how to behave before such profound casuists, I rose up and took my leave. Chance has since that time thrown me very often in her way, and she as often directed a discourse to me which I do not understand. This barbarity has kept me ever at a distance from the most beautiful object my eyes ever beheld. It is thus also she deals with all mankind, and you must make love to her, as you would conquer the sphinx, by posing her. But were she like other women, and that there were any talking to her, how constant must the pleasure of that man be, who could converse with a creature — but, after all, you may be sure her heart is fixed on some one or other; and yet I have been credibly informed; but who can believe half that is said! After she had done speaking to me, she put her hand to her bosom, and adjusted her tucker. Then she cast her eyes a little down, upon my beholding her too earnestly. They say she sings excellently; her voice in her ordinary speech has something in it inexpressibly sweet. You must know I dined with her at a public table the day after I first saw her, and she helped me to some tansy in the eye of all the gentlemen in the country. She has certainly the finest hand of any woman in the world. I can assure you, sir, were you to behold her, you would be in the same condition; for as her speech is music, her form is angelic. But I find I grow irregular while I am talking of her; but, indeed, it would be stupidity to be unconcerned at such perfection. Oh, the excellent creature! she is as inimitable to all women as she is inaccessible to all men."

I found my friend begin to rave, and insensibly led him towards the house, that we might be joined by some other company; and am convinced that the widow is the secret cause of all that inconsistency which appears in some parts of my friend's discourse; though he has so much command of himself as not directly to mention her, yet according to that of Martial, which one knows not how to render into English, *Dum tacet hanc loquitur*. I shall end this paper with that whole epigram, which represents with much humor my honest friend's condition: —

Quicquid agit Rufus, nihil est, nisi Nævia Rufo,
Si gaudet, si flet, si tacet, hanc loquitur:
Cœnat, propinat, poscit, negat, annuit, una est
Nævia; si non sit Nævia, mutus erit,
Scriberit hesternâ patri cum luce salutem,
Nævia lux, inquit, Nævia numen, ave.
                              —Mart. Epig. LXIX., 1. i.

«Let Rufus weep, rejoice, stand, sit, or walk,
  Still he can nothing but of Nævia talk;
  Let him eat, drink, ask questions, or dispute,
  Still he must speak of Nævia, or be mute.
  He writ to his father, ending with this line,
  I am, my lovely Nævia, ever thine.»
                              Complete.   From the Spectator.

THE COVERLEY FAMILY PORTRAITS

Abnormis sapiens —
            — Hor. Lib. II., Sat. II. 3.

« Of plain good sense, untutor'd in the schools. »

I was this morning walking in the gallery, when Sir Roger entered at the end opposite to me, and, advancing towards me,
    said he was glad to meet me among his relations the De
Coverleys, and hoped I liked the conversation of so much good
company who were as silent as myself. I knew he alluded to
the pictures, and as he is a gentleman who does not a little
value himself upon his ancient descent, I expected he would
give me some account of them. We were now arrived at the
upper end of the gallery, when the knight faced towards one
of the pictures, and as we stood before it, he entered into the
matter, after his blunt way of saying things, as they occur to his
imagination, without regular introduction, or care to preserve the
appearance of chain of thought.

    " It is," said he, " worth while to consider the force of dress;
and how the persons of one age differ from those of another,
merely by that only. One may observe also, that the general
fashion of one age has been followed by one particular set of
people in another, and by them preserved from one generation
to another. Thus the vast jutting coat and small bonnet, which
was the habit in Henry the Seventh's time, is kept on in the yeo-
men of the guard; not without a good and politic view, because

they look a foot taller, and a foot and a half broader; besides, that the cap leaves the face expanded, and consequently more terrible, and fitter to stand at the entrance of palaces.

This predecessor of ours you see is dressed after this manner, and his cheeks would be no larger than mine, were he in a hat as I am. He was the last man that won a prize in the Tilt-yard (which is now a common street before Whitehall). You see the broken lance that lies there by his right foot. He shivered that lance of his adversary all to pieces; and bearing himself, look you, sir, in this manner, at the same time he came within the target of the gentleman who rode against him, and taking him with incredible force before him on the pommel of his saddle, he in that manner rid the tournament over, with an air that showed he did it rather to perform the .rule of the lists than expose his enemy; however, it appeared he knew how to make use of a victory, and with a gentle trot he marched up to a gallery, where their mistress sat (for they were rivals), and let him down with laudable courtesy and pardonable insolence. I do not know but it might be exactly where the coffeehouse is now.

" You are to know this my ancestor was not only of a military genius, but fit also for the arts of peace, for he played on the bass viol as well as any gentleman at court; you see where his viol hangs by his basket-hilt sword. The action at the Tilt-yard you may be sure won the fair lady, who was a maid of honor, and the greatest beauty of her time; here she stands the next picture. Your see, sir, my great great great grandmother has on the new-fashioned petticoat, except that the modern is gathered at the waist. My grandmother appears as if she stood in a large drum, whereas the ladies now walk as if they were in a gocart. For all this lady was bred at court, she became an excellent country wife, she brought ten children, and when I show you the library, you shall see in her own hand (allowing for the difference of the language) the best receipt now in England both for a hasty pudding and a white-pot.

" If you please to fall back a little, because it is necessary to look at the three next pictures at one view; these are three sisters. She on the right hand, who is so very beautiful, died a maid; the next to her, still handsomer, had the same fate, against her will; this homely thing in the middle had both their portions added to her own, and was stolen by a neighboring gentleman, a man of stratagem and resolution, for he poisoned three mastiffs to come at her, and knocked down two deer stealers in carrying her off. Misfortunes happen in all families. The theft of this romp, and so much money, was no great matter to our estate. But the next heir that possessed it was this soft gentleman whom you see there. Observe the small buttons, the little boots, the laces, the slashes about his clothes, and, above all, the posture he is drawn in (which, to be sure, was his own choosing), you see he sits with one hand on a desk writing and looking, as it were, another way, like an easy writer, or a sonneteer. He was one of those that had too much wit to know how to live in the world; he was a man of no justice, but great good manners; he ruined everybody that had anything to do with him, but never said a rude thing in his life; the most indolent person in the world; he would sign a deed that passed away half his estate, with his gloves on, but would not put on his hat before a lady if it were to save his country. He is said to be the first that made love by squeezing the hand. He left the estate with ten thousand pounds debt upon it; but, however, by all hands I have been informed that he was every way the finest gentleman in the world. That debt lay heavy on our house for one generation, but it was retrieved by a gift from that honest man you see there, a citizen of our name, but nothing at all akin to us. I know Sir Andrew Freeport has said behind my back that this man was descended from one of the ten children of the maid of honor I showed you above; but it was never made out. We winked at the thing, indeed, because money was wanting at that time.»

Here I saw my friend a little embarrassed, and turned my face to the next portraiture.

Sir Roger went on with his account of the gallery in the following manner: "This man [pointing to him I looked at] I take to be the honor of our house. Sir Humphrey de Coverley; he was in his dealings as punctual as a tradesman, and as generous as a gentleman. He would have thought himself as much undone by breaking his word, as if it were to be followed by bankruptcy. He served his country as a knight of the shire to his dying day. He found it no easy matter to maintain an integrity in his words and actions, even in things that regarded the offices which were incumbent upon him, in the care of his own affairs and relations of life, and therefore dreaded (though he had great talents) to go into employments of state, where he must be exposed to the snares of ambition. Innocence of life and great ability were the distinguishing parts of his character; the latter, he had often observed, had led to the destruction of the former, and he used frequently to lament that great and good had not the same signification. He was an excellent husbandman, but had resolved not to exceed such a degree of wealth; all above it he bestowed in secret bounties many years after the sum he aimed at for his own use was attained. Yet he did not slacken his industry, but to a decent old age spent the life and fortune which was superfluous to himself, in the service of his friends and neighbors."

Here we were called to dinner, and Sir Roger ended the discourse of this gentleman, by telling me, as we followed the servant, that this his ancestor was a brave man, and narrowly escaped being killed in the civil wars. "For," said he, "he was sent out of the field upon a private message the day before the battle of Worcester." The whim of narrowly escaping by having been within a day of danger, with other matters above mentioned, mixed with good sense, left me at a loss whether I was more delighted with my friend's wisdom or simplicity.

Complete. From the Spectator.

ON CERTAIN SYMPTOMS OF GREATNESS

Nimirum insanus paucis videatur, eò quòd
Maxima pars hominum morbo jactatur eodem.
— *Hor.* Lib. II., Sat. III. 120.

By few, forsooth, a madman he is thought,
For half mankind the same disease have caught.
— *Francis.*

FROM MY OWN APARTMENT, January 30th.

THERE is no affection of the mind so much blended in human nature, and wrought into our very constitution, as pride.

It appears under a multitude of disguises, and breaks out in ten thousand different symptoms. Every one feels it in himself, and yet wonders to see it in his neighbor. I must confess, I met with an instance of it the other day where I should very little have expected it. Who would believe the proud person I am going to speak of is a cobbler upon Ludgate-hill? This artist being naturally a lover of respect, and considering that his circumstances are such that no man living will give it him, has contrived the figure of a beau, in wood; who stands before him in a bending posture, with his hat under his left arm, and his right hand extended in such a manner as to hold a thread, a piece of wax, or an awl, according to the particular service in which his master thinks fit to employ him. When I saw him, he held a candle in this obsequious posture. I was very well pleased with the cobbler's invention, that had so ingeniously contrived an inferior, and stood a little while contemplating this inverted idolatry, wherein the image did homage to the man. When we meet with such a fantastic vanity in one of this order, it is no wonder if we may trace it through all degrees above it, and particularly through all the steps of greatness. We easily see the absurdity of pride when it enters into the heart of a cobbler; though in reality it is altogether as ridiculous and unreasonable, wherever it takes possession of a human creature. There is no temptation to it from the reflection upon our being in general, or upon any comparative perfection, whereby one man may excel another. The greater a man's knowledge is, the greater motive he may seem to have for pride; but in the same proportion as the one rises, the other sinks, it being the chief office of wisdom to discover to us our weaknesses and imperfections.

As folly is the foundation of pride, the natural superstructure of it is madness. If there was an occasion for the experiment, I would not question to make a proud man a lunatic in three weeks' time, provided I had it in my power to ripen his frenzy with proper applications. It is an admirable reflection in Terence, where it is said of a parasite, "*Hic homines ex stultis facit insanos*" "This fellow," says he, "has an art of converting fools into madmen." When I was in France, the region of complaisance and vanity, I have often observed that a great man who has entered a levee of flatterers humble and temperate has grown so insensibly heated by the court which was paid him on all sides, that he has been quite distracted before he could get into his coach.

If we consult the collegiates of Moor-fields, we shall find most of them are beholden to their pride for their introduction into that magnificent palace. I had, some years ago, the curiosity to inquire into the particular circumstances of these whimsical freeholders; and learned from their own mouths the condition and character of each of them. Indeed, I found that all I spoke to were persons of quality. There were at that time five duchesses, three earls, two heathen gods, an emperor, and a prophet. There were also a great number of such as were locked up from their estates, and others who concealed their titles. A leather seller of Taunton whispered me in the ear that he was the "Duke of Monmouth," but begged me not to betray him. At a little distance from him sat a tailor's wife, who asked me, as I went, if I had seen the sword bearer, upon which I presumed to ask her who she was, and was answered, "My lady mayoress."

I was very sensibly touched with compassion towards these miserable people; and, indeed, extremely mortified to see human nature capable of being thus disfigured. However, I reaped this benefit from it, that I was resolved to guard myself against a passion which makes such havoc in the brain, and produces so much disorder in the imagination. For this reason I have endeavored to keep down the secret swellings of resentment, and stifle the very first suggestions of self-esteem; to establish my mind in tranquillity, and over-value nothing in my own or in another's possession.

For the benefit of such whose heads are a little turned, though not to so great a degree as to qualify them for the place of which I have been now speaking, I shall assign one of the sides of the college which I am erecting, for the cure of this dangerous distemper.

The most remarkable of the persons, whose disturbance arises from pride, and whom I shall use all possible diligence to cure, are such as are hidden in the appearance of quite contrary habits and dispositions. Among such, I shall, in the first place, take care of one who is under the most subtle species of pride that I have observed in my whole experience.

The patient is a person for whom I have a great respect, as being an old courtier, and a friend of mine in my youth. The man has but a bare subsistence, just enough to pay his reckoning with us at the Trumpet: but, by having spent the beginning of his life in the hearing of great men and persons of power, he is always promising to do good offices to introduce every man he converses with into the world; will desire one of ten times his substance to let him see him sometimes, and hints to him that he does not forget him. He answers to matters of no consequence with great circumspection; but, however, maintains a general civility in his words and actions, and an insolent benevolence to all whom he has to do with. This he practices with a grave tone and air; and though I am his senior by twelve years, and richer by forty pounds per annum, he had yesterday the impudence to commend me to my face, and tell me, "he should be always ready to encourage me." In a word, he is a very insignificant fellow, but exceeding gracious. The best return I can make him for his favors is to carry him myself to Bedlam and see him well taken care of.

The next person I shall provide for is of a quite contrary character, that has in him all the stiffness and insolence of quality, without a grain of sense or good-nature, to make it either respected or beloved. His pride has infected every muscle of his face; and yet, after all his endeavors to show mankind that he contemns them, he is only neglected by all that see him, as not of consequence enough to be hated.

For the cure of this particular sort of madness, it will be necessary to break through all forms with him, and familiarize his carriage by the use of a good cudgel. It may likewise be of great benefit to make him jump over a stick half a dozen times every morning.

A third, whom I have in my eye, is a young fellow, whose lunacy is such that he boasts of nothing but what he ought to be ashamed of. He is vain of being rotten, and talks publicly of having committed crimes which he ought to be hanged for by the laws of his country.

There are several others whose brains are hurt with pride, and whom I may hereafter attempt to recover; but shall conclude my present list with an old woman, who is just dropping into her grave, that talks of nothing but her birth. Though she has not a tooth in her head, she expects to be valued for the blood in her veins, which she fancies is much better than that which glows in the cheeks of Belinda, and sets half the town on fire.

Complete. From the Tatler.

HOW TO BE HAPPY THOUGH MARRIED

—— Garrit aniles
Ex re fabellas ——
—Hor. Lib. II., Sat. VI. 78.

"He tells an old wife's tale very pertinently."

IX—224

FROM MY OWN APARTMENT, December 5th.

MY BROTHER Tranquillus being gone out of town for some days, my sister Jenny sent me word she would come and dine with me, and therefore desired me to have no other company. I took care accordingly, and was not a little pleased to see her enter the room with a decent and matron-like behavior, which I thought very much became her. I saw she had a great deal to say to me, and easily discovered in her eyes, and the air of her countenance, that she had abundance of satisfaction in her heart, which she longed to communicate. However, I was resolved to let her break into her discourse her own way, and reduced her to a thousand little devices and intimations to bring me to the mention of her husband. But finding I was resolved not to name him, she began of her own accord. " My husband," said she, " gives his humble service to you," to which I only answered, " I hope he is well"; and, without waiting for a reply, fell into other subjects. She at last was out of all patience, and said, with a smile and manner that I thought had more beauty and spirit than I had ever observed before in her, " I did not think, brother, you had been so ill natured. You have seen, ever since I came in, that I had a mind to talk of my husband, and you will not be so kind as to give me an occasion." " I did not know," said I, " but it might be a disagreeable subject to you. You do not take me for so old fashioned a fellow as to think of entertaining a young lady with the discourse of her husband. I know nothing is more acceptable than to speak of one who is to be so, but to speak of one who is so! indeed, Jenny, I am a better-bred man than you think me." She showed a little dislike at my raillery; and, by her bridling up, I perceived she expected to be treated hereafter not as Jenny Distaff, but Mrs. Tranquillus. I was very well pleased with this change in her humor; and, upon talking with her on several subjects, I could not but fancy I saw a great deal of her husband's way and manner in her remarks, her phrases, the tone of her voice, and the very air of her countenance. This gave me an unspeakable satisfaction, not only because I had found her a husband, from whom she could learn many things that were laudable, but also because I looked upon her imitation of him as an infallible sign that she entirely loved him. This is an observation that I never knew fail, though I do not remember that any other has made it. The natural shyness of her sex hindered her from telling me the greatness of her own passion; but I easily collected it from the representation she gave me of his. "I have everything," says she, "in Tranquillus, that I can wish for; and enjoy in him, what, indeed, you have told me were to be met with in a good husband, the fondness of a lover, the tenderness of a parent, and the intimacy of a friend." It transported me to see her eyes swimming in tears of affection when she spoke. "And is there not, dear sister," said I, "more pleasure in the possession of such a man than in all the little impertinencies of balls, assemblies, and equipage, which it cost me so much pains to make you contemn?" She answered, smiling, "Tranquillus has made me a sincere convert in a few weeks, though I am afraid you could not have done it in your whole life. To tell you truly, I have only one fear hanging upon me, which is apt to give me trouble in the midst of all my satisfactions: I am afraid, you must know, that I shall not always make the same amiable appearance in his eye that I do at present. You know, brother Bickerstaff, that you have the reputation of a conjurer; and, if you have any one secret in your art to make your sister always beautiful, I should be happier than if I were mistress of all the worlds you have shown me in a starry night." "Jenny," said I, "without having recourse to magic, I shall give you one plain rule that will not fail of making you always amiable to a man who has so great a passion for you, and is of so equal and reasonable a temper as Tranquillus. Endeavor to please, and you must please; be always in the same disposition as you are when you ask for this secret, and you may take my word, you will never want it. An inviolable fidelity, good humor, and complacency of temper outlive all the charms of a fine face, and make the decays of it invisible."

We discoursed very long upon this head, which was equally agreeable to us both; for, I must confess, as I tenderly love her, I take as much pleasure in giving her instructions for her welfare, as she herself does in receiving them. I proceeded, therefore, to inculcate these sentiments by relating a very particular passage that happened within my own knowledge.

There were several of us making merry at a friend's house in a country village, when the sexton of the parish church entered the room in a sort of surprise, and told us, "that as he was digging a grave in the chancel, a little blow of his pickax opened a decayed coffin, in which there were several written papers."

Our curiosity was immediately raised, so that we went to the
place where the sexton had been at work, and found a great concourse of people about the grave. Among the rest there was an
old woman, who told us the person buried there was a lady
whose name I do not think fit to mention, though there is nothing in the story but what tends very much to her honor. This
lady lived several years an exemplary pattern of conjugal love,
and, dying soon after her husband, who every way answered her
character in virtue and affection, made it her deathbed request,
" that all the letters which she had received from him, both before and after her marriage, should be buried in the coffin
with her." These, I found upon examination, were the papers
before us. Several of them had suffered so much by time that
I could only pick out a few words; as my soul! lilies! roses!
dearest angel! and the like. One of them, which was legible
throughout, ran thus:—

Madam:—

If you would know the greatness of my love, consider that of your
own beauty. That blooming countenance, that snowy bosom, that
graceful person, return every moment to my imagination; the brightness of your eyes hath hindered me from closing mine since I last
saw you. You may still add to your beauties by a smile. A frown
will make me the most wretched of men, as I am the most passionate of lovers.

It filled the whole company with a deep melancholy, to compare the description of the letter with the person that occasioned
it, who was now reduced to a few crumbling bones, and a little
moldering heap of earth. With much ado I deciphered another
letter which began with, " My dear, dear wife." This gave me a
curiosity to see how the style of one written in marriage differed
from one written in courtship. To my surprise, I found the
fondness rather augmented than lessened, though the panegyric
turned upon a different accomplishment. The words were as follows:—

Before this short absence from you, I did not know that I loved
you so much as I really do; though, at the same time, I thought I
loved you as much as possible. I am under great apprehension lest
you should have any uneasiness whilst I am defrauded of my share
in it, and cannot think of tasting any pleasures that you do not partake with me. Pray, my dear, be careful of your health, if for no

other reason but because you know I could not outlive you. It is natural in absence to make professions of an inviolable constancy; but towards so much merit it is scarce a virtue, especially when it is but a bare return to that of which you have given me such continued proofs ever since our first acquaintance. I am, etc.

It happened that the daughter of these two excellent persons was by when I was reading this letter. At the sight of the coffin, in which was the body of her mother, near that of her father, she melted into a flood of tears. As I had heard a great character of her virtue, and observed in her this instance of filial piety, I could not resist my natural inclination of giving advice to young people, and therefore addressed myself to her. "Young lady," said I, "you see how short is the possession of that beauty, in which nature has been so liberal to you. You find the melancholy sight before you is a contradiction to the first letter that you heard on that subject; whereas, you may observe the second letter, which celebrates your mother's constancy, is itself, being found in this place, an argument of it. But, madam, I ought to caution you not to think the bodies that lie before you your father and your mother. Know their constancy is rewarded by a nobler union than by this mingling of their ashes, in a state where there is no danger or possibility of a second separation."

Complete. From the Tatler.

PÆTUS AND ARRIA

Quicquid agunt homines ——
—— nostri est farrago libelli.
—*Juv.* Sat. I. 85, 86.

" Whate'er men do, or say, or think, or dream,
Our motley paper seizes for its theme."

WHITE'S CHOCOLATEHOUSE, September 23d.

I HAVE taken upon me no very easy task in turning all my thoughts on panegyric, when most of the advices I receive tend to the quite contrary purpose; and I have few notices but such as regard follies and vices. But the properest way for me to treat is to keep in general upon the passions and affections of men, with as little regard to particulars as the nature of the thing will admit. However, I think there is something so passionate in the circumstances of the lovers mentioned in the following letter, that I am willing to go out of my way to obey what is commanded in it:—

Sir:—   LONDON, September 17th.

Your design of entertaining the town with the characters of the ancient heroes, as persons shall send an account to Mr. Morphew, encourages me and others to beg of you that, in the meantime, if it is not contrary to the method you have proposed, you would give us one paper upon the subject of the death of Pætus and his wife, when Nero sent him an order to kill himself; his wife, setting him the example, died with these words: " Pætus, it is not painful." You must know the story, and your observations upon it will oblige, sir,

Your most humble servant.

When the worst man that ever lived in the world had the highest station in it, human life was the object of his diversion; and he sent orders frequently, out of mere wantonness, to take off such and such, without so much as being angry with them. Nay frequently, his tyranny was so humorous, that he put men to death because he could not but approve of them. It came one day to his ear that a certain married couple, Pætus and Arria, lived in a more happy tranquillity and mutual love than any other persons who were then in being. He listened with great attention to the account of their manner of spending their time together, of the constant pleasure they were to each other in all their words and actions; and found, by exact information, that they were so treasonable as to be much more happy than his imperial Majesty himself. Upon which he writ Pætus the following billet:—

Pætus, you are hereby desired to despatch yourself. I have heard a very good character of you; and therefore leave it to yourself whether you will die by dagger, sword, or poison. If you outlive this order above an hour, I have given directions to put you to death by torture.

NERO.

This familiar epistle was delivered to his wife Arria, who opened it.

One must have a soul very well turned for love, pity, and indignation, to comprehend the tumult this unhappy lady was thrown into upon this occasion. The passion of love is no more to be understood by some tempers than a problem in a science

by an ignorant man; but he that knows what affection is will
have, upon considering the condition of Arria, ten thousand
thoughts flowing upon him, which the tongue was not formed to
express; but the charming statue is now before my eyes, and
Arria, in her unutterable sorrow, has more beauty than ever
appeared in youth, in mirth, or in triumph. These are the great
and noble incidents which speak the dignity of our nature, in
our sufferings and distresses. Behold, her tender affection for
her husband sinks her features into a countenance which appears
more helpless than that of an infant; but again, her indignation
shows in her visage and her bosom a resentment as strong as
that of the bravest man. Long she stood in this agony of alternate rage and love; but at last composed herself for her dissolution, rather than survive her beloved Pætus. When he came
into her presence, he found her with the tyrant's letter in one
hand and a dagger in the other. Upon his approach to her,
she gave him the order: and at the same time stabbing herself,
"Pætus," says she, "it is not painful," and expired. Pætus immediately followed her example. The passion of these memorable
lovers was such, that it illuded the rigor of their fortune, and
baffled the force of a blow, which neither felt, because each
received it for the sake of the other. The woman's part in this
story is by much the more heroic, and has occasioned one of the
best epigrams transmitted to us from antiquity.*

> *Casta suo gladium cum traderet Arria Pæto*
> *Quem de visceribus traxerat ipsa suis;*
> *Si qua fides, vulnus quod feci, non dolet, inquit*
> *Sed quod tu facies hoc mihi, Pæte, dolet.*
> —*Mart*. Epig. I. 14.

«When the chaste Arria reached the reeking sword,
Drawn from her bosom, to her honor'd lord,
Trust me, she said, for this I do not grieve,
I die by that which Pætus must receive.»

Complete. From the Tatler—No. 72

THE RING OF GYGES

Secretosque pios, his dantem jura Catonem.
—*Virg*. Æn. VIII. 670.

Apart from these, the happy souls he draws,
And Cato's pious ghost dispensing laws.
—*Dryden.*

SHEER-LANE, February 24th.

IT IS an argument of a clear and worthy spirit in a man to be able to disengage himself from the opinions of others, so far as not to let the deference due to the sense of mankind ensnare him to act against the dictates of his own reason. But the generality of the world are so far from walking by any such maxim, that it is almost a standing rule to do as others do, or be ridiculous. I have heard my old friend, Mr. Hart, speak it as an observation among the players, "that it is impossible to act with grace, except the actor has forgot that he is before an audience." Until he is arrived at that, his motion, his air, his every step and gesture, has something in them which discovers he is under a restraint, for fear of being ill received; or if he considers himself as in the presence of those who approve his behavior, you see an affectation of that pleasure run through his whole carriage. It is as common in life, as upon the stage, to behold a man in the most indifferent action betray a sense he has of doing what he is about gracefully. Some have such an immoderate relish for applause that they expect it for things which in themselves are so frivolous that it is impossible, without this affectation, to make them appear worthy either of blame or praise. There is Will Glare, so passionately intent upon being admired, that when you see him in public places, every muscle of his face discovers his thoughts are fixed upon the consideration of what figure he makes. He will often fall into a musing posture, to attract observation; and is then obtruding himself upon the company, when he pretends to be withdrawn from it. Such little arts are the certain and infallible tokens of a superficial mind, as the avoiding observation is the sign of a great and sublime one. It is therefore extremely difficult for a man to judge even of his own actions, without forming to himself an idea of what he should act, were it in his power to execute all his desires without the observation of the rest of the world. There is an allegorical fable in Plato, which seems to admonish us that we are very little acquainted with ourselves, while we know our actions are to pass the censures of others; but, had we the power to accomplish all our wishes unobserved, we should then easily inform ourselves how far we are possessed of real and intrinsic virtue. The fable I was going to mention is that of Gyges, who is said to have had an enchanted ring, which had in it a miraculous quality, making him who wore it visible or invisible, as he turned it to or from his body. The use Gyges made of his occasional invisibility was, by the advantage of it, to violate a queen, and murder a king. Tully takes notice of this allegory, and says very handsomely, "that a man of honor who had such a ring would act just in the same manner as he would without it." It is indeed no small pitch of virtue, under the temptation of impunity, and the hopes of accomplishing all a man desires, not to transgress the rules of justice and virtue; but this is rather not being an ill man, than being positively a good one; and it seems wonderful that so great a soul as that of Tully should not form to himself a thousand worthy actions, which a virtuous mind would be prompted to by the possession of such a secret. There are certainly some parts of mankind who are guardian beings to the other. Sallust could say of Cato, "That he had rather be than appear good," but, indeed, this eulogium rose no higher than, as I just now hinted, to an inoffensiveness, rather than an active virtue. Had it occurred to the noble orator to represent, in his language, the glorious pleasures of a man secretly employed in beneficence and generosity, it would certainly have made a more charming page than any he has left behind him. How might a man, furnished with Gyges's secret, employ it in bringing together distant friends; laying snares for creating good-will in the room of groundless hatred; in removing the pangs of an unjust jealousy, the shyness of an imperfect reconciliation, and the tremor of an lawful love! Such a one could give confidence to bashful merit, and confusion to overbearing impudence.

Certain it is, that secret kindnesses done to mankind are as beautiful as secret injuries are detestable. To be invisibly good is as godlike as to be invisibly ill, diabolical. As degenerate as we are apt to say the age we live in is, there are still amongst us men of illustrious minds, who enjoy all the pleasures of good actions, except that of being commended for them. There happens, among other very worthy instances of a public spirit, one which I am obliged to discover, because I know not otherwise how to obey the commands of the benefactor. A citizen of London has given directions to Mr. Rayner, the writing master of St. Paul's school, to educate at his charge ten boys, who shall be nominated by me, in writing and accounts, until they shall be fit for any trade; I desire, therefore, such as know any proper objects for receiving this bounty, to give notice thereof to

Mr. Morphew, or Mr. Lillie; and they shall, if properly qualified, have instructions accordingly.

Actions of this kind have in them something so transcendent, that it is an injury to applaud them, and a diminution of that merit which consists in shunning our approbation. We shall therefore leave them to enjoy that glorious obscurity; and silently admire their virtue who can contemn the most delicious of human pleasures, that of receiving due praise. Such celestial dispositions very justly suspend the discovery of their benefactions, until they come where their actions cannot be misinterpreted, and receive their first congratulations in the company of angels.

ADVERTISEMENT

Whereas, Mr. Bickerstaff, by a letter bearing date this twenty-fourth of February, has received information that there are in and about the Royal Exchange a sort of people commonly known by the name of Whetters, who drink themselves into an intermediate state of being neither drunk nor sober before the hours of Exchange, or business; and in that condition buy and sell stocks, discount notes, and do many other acts of well-disposed citizens; this is to give notice that from this day forward no Whetter shall be able to give or indorse any note, or execute any other point of commerce, after the third half-pint, before the hour of one: and whoever shall transact any matter or matters with a Whetter, not being himself of that order, shall be conducted to Moor-fields upon the first application of his next of kin.

N. B. No tavern near the Exchange shall deliver wine to such as drink at the bar standing, except the same shall be three-parts of the best cider; and the master of the house shall produce a certificate of the same from Mr. Tintoret, or some other credible wine-painter.

Whereas the model of the intended Bedlam is now finished, and the edifice itself will be very suddenly begun, it is desired that all such as have relations whom they would recommend to our care would bring in their proofs with all speed, none being to be admitted, of course, but lovers, who are put into an immediate regimen. Young politicians also are received without fees or examination.

Complete. From the Tatler.

THE ART OF PLEASING

Principibus placuisse viris non ultima laus est.
—*Hor*. Epist. I. 17, 35.

To please the great is not the smallest praise.
—*Creech*.

THE desire of pleasing makes a man agreeable or unwelcome to those with whom he converses, according to the motive from which that inclination appears to flow. If your concern for pleasing others arises from an innate benevolence, it never fails of success; if from a vanity to excel, its disappointment is no less certain. What we call an agreeable man is he who is endowed with that natural bent to do acceptable things from a delight he takes in them merely as such; and the affectation of that character is what constitutes a fop. Under these leaders one may draw up all those who make any manner of figure, except in dumb show. A rational and select conversation is composed of persons who have the talent of pleasing with delicacy of sentiments flowing from habitual chastity of thought; but mixed company is frequently made up of pretenders to mirth, and is usually pestered with constrained, obscene, and painful witticisms. Now and then you meet with a man so exactly formed for pleasing that it is no matter what he is doing or saying — that is to say, that there need be no manner of importance in it to make him gain upon everybody who hears or beholds him. This felicity is not the gift of nature only, but must be attended with happy circumstances, which add a dignity to the familiar behavior which distinguishes him whom we call an agreeable man. It is from this that everybody loves and esteems Polycarpus. He is in the vigor of his age and the gayety of life, but has passed through very conspicuous scenes in it; though no soldier, he has shared the danger, and acted with great gallantry and generosity, on a decisive day of battle. To have those qualities which only make other men conspicuous in the world as it were supernumerary to him, is a circumstance which gives weight to his most indifferent actions; for as a known credit is ready cash to a trader, so is acknowledged merit immediate distinction, and serves in the place of equipage, to a gentleman. This renders Polycarpus graceful in mirth, important in business, and regarded with love in every ordinary occurrence. But not to dwell upon characters which have such particular recommendations to our hearts, let us turn our thoughts rather to the methods of pleasing which must carry men through the world who cannot pretend to such advantages. Falling in with the particular humor or manner of one above you, abstracted from the general rules of good behavior, is the life of a slave. A parasite differs in nothing from the meanest servant but that the footman hires himself for bodily labor, subjected to go and come at the will of his master, but the other gives up his very soul: he is prostituted to speak, and professes to think, after the mode of him whom he courts. This servitude to a patron, in an honest nature would be more grievous than that of wearing his livery; therefore we shall speak of those methods only which are worthy and ingenuous.

The happy talent of pleasing either those above you or below you seems to be wholly owing to the opinion they have of your sincerity. This quality is to attend the agreeable man in all the actions of his life; and I think there need be no more said in honor of it than that it is what forces the approbation even of your opponents. The guilty man has an honor for the judge who, with justice, pronounces against him the sentence of death itself. The author of the sentence at the head of this paper was an excellent judge of human life, and passed his own in company the most agreeable that ever was in the world. Augustus lived amongst his friends as if he had his fortune to make in his own court. Candor and affability, accompanied with as much power as ever mortal was vested with, were what made him in the utmost manner agreeable among a set of admirable men, who had thoughts too high for ambition, and views too large to be gratified by what he could give them in the disposal of an empire, without the pleasures of their mutual conversation. A certain unanimity of taste and judgment, which is natural to all of the same order in the species, was the band of this society; and the emperor assumed no figure in it but what he thought was his due, from his private talents and qualifications, as they contributed to advance the pleasures and sentiments of the company.

Cunning people, hypocrites, all who are but half virtuous or half wise, are incapable of tasting the refined pleasure of such an equal company as could wholly exclude the regard of fortune in their conversations. Horace, in the discourse from whence I take the hint of the present speculation, lays down excellent rules for conduct in conversation with men of power; but he speaks it with an air of one who had no need of such an application for anything which related to himself. It shows he understood what it was to be a skillful courtier, by just admonitions against importunity, and showing how forcible it was to speak modestly of your own wants. There is indeed something so shameless in taking all opportunities to speak of your own affairs that he who is guilty of it towards him on whom he depends, fares like the beggar who exposes his sores, which, instead of moving compassion, makes the man he begs of turn away from the object.

I cannot tell what is become of him, but I remember about sixteen years ago an honest fellow who so justly understood how disagreeable the mention or appearance of his wants would make him that I have often reflected upon him as a counterpart of Irus, whom I have formerly mentioned. This man, whom I have missed for some years in my walks, and have heard was some way employed about the army, made it a maxim that good wigs, delicate linen, and a cheerful air, were to a poor dependent the same that working tools are to a poor artificer. It was no small entertainment to me, who knew his circumstances, to see him who had fasted two days, attribute the thinness they told him of to the violence of some gallantries he had lately been guilty of. The skillful dissembler carried this on with the utmost address; and if any suspected his affairs were narrow, it was attributed to indulging himself in some fashionable vice rather than an irreproachable poverty, which saved his credit with those on whom he depended.

The main art is to be as little troublesome as you can, and make all you hope for come rather as a favor from your patron than claim from you. But I am here prating of what is the method of pleasing so as to succeed in the world, when there are crowds who have — in city, town, court, and country — arrived to considerable acquisitions, and yet seem incapable of acting in any constant tenor of life, but have gone on from one successful error to another: therefore I think I may shorten this inquiry after the method of pleasing, and as the old beau said to his son, once for all, " Pray, Jack, be a fine gentleman," so may I to my reader abridge my instructions and finish the art of pleasing in a word, "Be rich."

Complete.

BENIGNITY

Consuetudinem benignitatis largitioni munerum longè antepono. Hæc est gravium hominum atque magnorum; illa quasi assentatorum populi, multitudinis levitatem voluptate quasi titillantium. — Cicero.

«I esteem a habit of benignity greatly preferable to munificence The former is peculiar to great and distinguished persons; the latter belongs to flatterers of the people, who tickle the levity of the multitude with a kind of pleasure.»

W HEN we consider the offices of human life, there is, methinks, something in what we ordinarily call generosity; which, when carefully examined, seems to flow rather from a loose and unguarded temper than an honest and liberal mind. For this reason it is absolutely necessary that all liberality should have for its basis and support, frugality. By this means the beneficent spirit works in a man from the convictions of reason, not from the impulses of passion. The generous man in the ordinary acceptation, without respect to the demands of his own family, will soon find upon the foot of his account that he has sacrificed to fools, knaves, flatterers, or the deservedly unhappy, all the opportunities of affording any future assistance where it ought to be. Let him therefore reflect that, if to bestow be in itself laudable, should not a man take care to secure an ability to do things praiseworthy as long as he lives? Or could there be a more cruel piece of raillery upon a man who should have reduced his fortune below the capacity of acting according to his natural temper than to say of him, «That gentleman was generous»? My beloved author therefore has, in the sentence on the top of my paper, turned his eye with a certain satiety from beholding the addresses to the people by largesses and public entertainments, which he asserts to be in general vicious, and are always to be regulated according to the circumstances of time and a man's own fortune. A constant benignity in commerce with the rest of the world, which ought to run through all a man's actions, has effects more useful to those whom you oblige, and is less ostentatious in yourself. He turns his recommendation of this virtue on commercial life; and, according to him, a citizen who is frank in his kindnesses, and abhors severity in his demands; he who, in buying, selling, lending, doing acts of good neighborhood, is just and easy; he who appears naturally averse to disputes, and above the sense of little sufferings — bears a nobler character, and does much more good to mankind than any other man's fortune, without commerce, can possibly support. For the citizen, above all other men, has opportunities of arriving at "that highest fruit of wealth," to be liberal without the least expense of a man's own fortune. It is not to be denied but such a practice is liable to hazard; but this therefore adds to the obligation that, among traders, he who obliges is as much concerned to keep the favor a secret as he who receives it. The unhappy distinctions among us in England are so great that to celebrate the intercourse of commercial friendship, with which I am daily made acquainted, would be to raise the virtuous man so many enemies of the contrary party. I am obliged to conceal all I know of "Tom the Bounteous," who lends at the ordinary interest, to give men of less fortune opportunities of making greater advantages. He conceals, under a rough air and distant behavior, a bleeding compassion and womanish tenderness. This is governed by the most exact circumspection, that there is no industry wanting in the person whom he is to serve, and that he is guilty of no improper expenses. This I know of Tom; but who dare say it of so known a Tory? The same care I was forced to use some time ago in the report of another's virtue, and said fifty instead of a hundred, because the man I pointed at was a Whig. Actions of this kind are popular, without being invidious; for every man of ordinary circumstances looks upon a man who has this known benignity in his nature as a person ready to be his friend upon such terms as he ought to expect it; and the wealthy who may envy such a character can do no injury to its interests but by the imitation of it, in which the good citizens will rejoice to be rivaled. I know not how to form to myself a greater idea of human life than in what is the practice of some wealthy men whom I could name, that make no step to the improvement of their own fortunes wherein they do not also advance those of other men who would languish in poverty without that munificence. In a nation where there are so many public funds to be supported, I know not whether he can be called a good subject who does not embark some part of his fortune with the state, to whose vigilance he owes the security of the whole. This certainly is an immediate way of laying an obligation upon many, and extending your benignity the furthest a man can possibly who is not engaged in commerce. But he who trades, besides giving the state some part of this sort of credit he gives his banker, may, in all the occurrences of his life, have his eye upon removing want from the door of the industrious, and defending the unhappy upright man from bankruptcy. Without this benignity, pride or vengeance will precipitate a man to choose the receipt of half his demands from one whom he has undone, rather than the whole from one to whom he has shown mercy. This benignity is essential to the character of a fair trader, and any man who designs to enjoy his wealth with honor and self-satisfaction; nay, it would not be hard to maintain that the practice of supporting good and industrious men would carry a man further even to his profit than indulging the propensity of serving and obliging the fortunate. My author argues on this subject in order to incline men's minds to those who want them most, after this manner: "We must always consider the nature of things, and govern ourselves accordingly. The wealthy man, when he has repaid you, is upon a balance with you; but the person whom you favored with a loan, if he be a good man, will think himself in your debt after he has paid you. The wealthy and the conspicuous are not obliged by the benefits you do them; they think they conferred a benefit when they received one. Your good offices are always suspected, and it is with them the same thing to expect their favor as to receive it. But the man below you, who knows, in the good you have done him, you respected himself more than his circumstances, does not act like an obliged man only to him from whom he has received a benefit, but also to all who are capable of doing him one. And whatever little offices he can do for you, he is so far from magnifying it that he will labor to extenuate it in all his actions and expressions. Moreover, the regard to what you do to a great man at best is taken notice of no further than by himself or his family; but what you do to a man of a humble fortune, provided always that he is a good and a modest man, raises the affections towards you of all men of that character, of which there are many, in the whole city."

There is nothing gains a reputation to a preacher so much as his own practice; I am therefore casting about what act of benignity is in the power of a spectator. Alas! that lies but in a very narrow compass; and I think the most immediately under my patronage are either players, or such whose circumstances bear an affinity with theirs. All, therefore, I am able to do at this time of this kind is to tell the town that on Friday, the eleventh of this instant, April, there will be performed, in York Buildings, a concert of vocal and instrumental music, for the benefit of Mr. Edward Keen, the father of twenty children; and that this day the haughty George Powell hopes all the good-natured part of the town will favor him, whom they applauded in "Alexander," "Timon," "Lear," and "Orestes," with their company this night, when he hazards all his heroic glory for their approbation in the humbler condition of honest Jack Falstaff.

Complete.

THE DREAM OF FAME

Hic manus ob patriam pugnando vulnera passi, —
Quique pii vates, et Phœbo digna locuti;
Inventas aut qui vitam excoluere per artes,
Quique sui memores alios fecere merendo.
                    —Virg. Æn. VI. 660.

Here patriots live, who, for their country's good,
In fighting fields were prodigal of blood;
Here poets worthy their inspiring god,
And of unblemish'd life, make their abode:
And searching wits, of more mechanic parts,
Who grac'd their age with new-invented arts:
Those who to worth their bounty did extend;
And those who knew that bounty to commend.
                    —Dryden.

FROM MY OWN APARTMENT, October 14th.

THERE are two kinds of immortality; that which the soul really enjoys after this life, and that imaginary existence by which men live in their fame and reputation. The best and greatest actions have proceeded from the prospect of the one or the other of these; but my design is to treat only of those who have chiefly proposed to themselves the latter, as the principal reward of their labors. It was for this reason that I excluded from my Tables of Fame all the great founders and votaries of religion; and it is for this reason also, that I am more than ordinary* anxious to do justice to the persons of whom I am now going to speak; for, since fame was the only end of all their

* Steele is above modern rules of syntax.

IX—22½

enterprises and studies, a man cannot be too scrupulous in allotting them their due proportion of it. It was this consideration which made me call the whole body of the learned to my assistance; to many of whom I must own my obligations for the catalogues of illustrious persons, which they have sent me in upon this occasion. I yesterday employed the whole afternoon in comparing them with each other; which made so strong an impression upon my imagination, that they broke my sleep for the first part of the following night, and at length threw me into a very agreeable vision, which I shall beg leave to describe in all its particulars.

I dreamed that I was conveyed into a wide and boundless plain that was covered with prodigious multitudes of people, which no man could number. In the midst of it there stood a mountain, with its head above the clouds. The sides were extremely steep, and of such a particular structure that no creature which was not made in a human figure could possibly ascend it. On a sudden there was heard from the top of it a sound like that of a trumpet, but so exceeding sweet and harmonious, that it filled the hearts of those who heard it with raptures, and gave such high and delightful sensations, as seemed to animate and raise human nature above itself. This made me very much amazed to find so very few in that innumerable multitude who had ears fine enough to hear or relish this music with pleasure; but my wonder abated when, upon looking round me, I saw most of them attentive to three sirens, clothed like goddesses, and distinguished by the names of Sloth, Ignorance, and Pleasure. They were seated on three rocks, amidst a beautiful variety of groves, meadows, and rivulets, that lay on the borders of the mountain. While the base and groveling multitude of different nations, ranks, and ages were listening to these delusive deities, those of a more erect aspect and exalted spirit separated themselves from the rest, and marched in great bodies towards the mountain from whence they heard the sound, which still grew sweeter the more they listened to it.

On a sudden methought this select band sprang forward, with a resolution to climb the ascent, and follow the call of that heavenly music. Every one took something with him that he thought might be of assistance to him in his march. Several had their swords drawn, some carried rolls of paper in their hands, some had compasses, others quadrants others telescopes, and others pencils. Some had laurels on their heads, and others buskins on their legs; in short, there was scarce any instrument of a mechanic art, or liberal science, which was not made use of on this occasion. My good demon, who stood at my right hand during the course of this whole vision, observing in me a burning desire to join that glorious company, told me, "he highly approved that generous ardor with which I seemed transported; but, at the same time, advised me to cover my face with a mask all the while I was to labor on the ascent." I took his counsel without inquiring into his reasons. The whole body now broke into different parties, and began to climb the precipice by ten thousand different paths. Several got into little alleys, which did not reach far up the hill, before they ended, and led no further; and I observed that most of the artisans, which considerably diminished our number, fell into these paths.

We left another considerable body of adventurers behind us, who thought they had discovered byways up the hill, which proved so very intricate and perplexed that, after having advanced in them a little, they were quite lost among the several turns and windings; and though they were as active as any in their motions, they made but little progress in the ascent. These, as my guide informed me, were men of subtle tempers, and puzzled politics, who would supply the place of real wisdom with cunning and artifice. Among those who were far advanced in their way, there were some that by one false step fell backward and lost more ground in a moment than they had gained for many hours, or could be ever able to recover. We were now advanced very high, and observed that all the different paths which ran about the sides of the mountain began to meet in two great roads; which insensibly gathered the whole multitude of travelers into two great bodies. At a little distance from the entrance of each road there stood a hideous phantom that opposed our further passage. One of these apparitions had his right hand filled with darts, which he brandished in the face of all who came up that way. Crowds ran back at the appearance of it, and cried out, Death. The spectre that guarded the other road was Envy. She was not armed with weapons of destruction like the former; but by dreadful hissings, noises of reproach, and a horrid distracted laughter, she appeared more frightful than Death itself, insomuch that abundance of our company were discouraged from passing any further, and some appeared ashamed of having come so far. As for myself, I must confess, my heart shrunk within me at the sight of these ghastly appearances; but, on a sudden, the voice of the trumpet came more full upon us, so that we felt a new resolution reviving in us; and in proportion as this resolution grew, the terrors before us seemed to vanish. Most of the company, who had swords in their hands, marched on with great spirit, and an air of defiance, up the road that was commanded by Death; while others, who had thought and contemplation in their looks, went forward in a more composed manner up the road possessed by Envy. The way above these apparitions grew smooth and uniform, and was so delightful, that the travelers went on with pleasure, and in a little time arrived at the top of the mountain. They here began to breathe a delicious kind of ether, and saw all the fields about them covered with a kind of purple light, that made them reflect with satisfaction on their past toils; and diffused a secret joy through the whole assembly, which showed itself in every look and feature. In the midst of these happy fields there stood a palace of very glorious structure. It had four great folding doors, that faced the four several quarters of the world. On the top of it was enthroned the goddess of the mountain, who smiled upon her votaries, and sounded the silver trumpet which had called them up, and cheered them in their passage to her palace. They had now formed themselves into several divisions,— a band of historians taking their stations at each door, according to the persons whom they were to introduce.

On a sudden, the trumpet, which had hitherto sounded only a march, or a point of war, now swelled all its notes into triumph and exultation. The whole fabric shook, and the doors flew open. The first who stepped forward was a beautiful and blooming hero, and as I heard by the murmurs round me, Alexander the Great. He was conducted by a crowd of historians. The person who immediately walked before him was remarkable for an embroidered garment, who, not being well acquainted with the place, was conducting him to an apartment appointed for the reception of fabulous heroes. The name of this false guide was Quintus Curtius. But Arrian and Plutarch, who knew better the avenues of this palace, conducted him into the great hall, and placed him at the upper end of the first table. My good demon, that I might see the whole ceremony, conveyed me to a corner of this room, where I might perceive all that passed, without being seen myself. The next who entered was a charming virgin, leading in a venerable old man that was blind. Under her left arm she bore a harp, and on her head a garland. Alexander, who was very well acquainted with Homer, stood up at his entrance, and placed him on his right hand. The virgin, who it seems was one of the nine sisters that attended on the goddess of Fame, smiled with an ineffable grace at their meeting, and retired.

Julius Cæsar was now coming forward; and, though most of the historians offered their service to introduce him, he left them at the door, and would have no conductor but himself.

The next who advanced was a man of a homely but cheerful aspect, and attended by persons of greater figure than any that appeared on this occasion. Plato was on his right hand, and Xenophon on his left. He bowed to Homer, and sat down by him. It was expected that Plato would himself have taken a place next to his master, Socrates; but on a sudden there was heard a great clamor of disputants at the door, who appeared with Aristotle at the head of them. That philosopher, with some rudeness, but great strength of reason, convinced the whole table that a title to the fifth place was his due, and took it accordingly.

He had scarce sat down, when the same beautiful virgin that had introduced Homer, brought in another, who hung back at the entrance, and would have excused himself, had not his modesty been overcome by the invitation of all who sat at the table. His guide and behavior made me easily conclude it was Virgil. Cicero next appeared and took his place. He had inquired at the door for one Lucceius to introduce him; but, not finding him there, he contented himself with the attendance of many other writers, who all, except Sallust, appeared highly pleased with the office.

We waited some time in expectation of the next worthy, who came in with a great retinue of historians whose names I could not learn, most of them being natives of Carthage. The person thus conducted, who was Hannibal, seemed much disturbed, and could not forbear complaining to the board of the affronts he had met with among the Roman historians, "who attempted," says he, "to carry me into the subterraneous apartment; and perhaps would have done it, had it not been for the impartiality of this gentleman," pointing to Polybius, "who was the only person, except my own countrymen, that was willing to conduct me hither.»

The Carthaginian took his seat, and Pompey entered with great dignity in his own person, and preceded by several historians. Lucan the poet was at the head of them, who, observing Homer and Virgil at the table, was going to sit down himself, had not the latter whispered him that whatever pretense he might otherwise have had, he forfeited his claim to it, by coming in as one of the historians. Lucan was so exasperated with the repulse, that he muttered something to himself; and was heard to say, «that since he could not have a seat among them himself, he would bring in one who alone had more merit than their whole assembly,» upon which he went to the door, and brought in Cato of Utica. That great man approached the company with such an air that showed he contemned the honor which he laid a claim to. Observing the seat opposite to Cæsar was vacant, he took possession of it, and spoke two or three smart sentences upon the nature of precedency, which, according to him, consisted not in place, but in intrinsic merit; to which he added, «that the most virtuous man, wherever he was seated, was always at the upper end of the table.» Socrates, who had a great spirit of raillery with his wisdom, could not forbear smiling at a virtue which took so little pains to make itself agreeable. Cicero took the occasion to make a long discourse in praise of Cato, which he uttered with much vehemence. Cæsar answered him with a great deal of seeming temper; but, as I stood at a great distance from them, I was not able to hear one word of what they said. But I could not forbear taking notice, that, in all the discourse which passed at the table, a word or nod from Homer decided the controversy.

After a short pause, Augustus appeared, looking round him with a serene and affable countenance upon all the writers of his age, who strove among themselves which of them should show him the greatest marks of gratitude and respect. Virgil rose from the table to meet him; and though he was an acceptable guest to all, he appeared more such to the learned than the military worthies.

The next man astonished the whole table with his appearance. He was slow, solemn, and silent in his behavior, and wore a raiment curiously wrought with hieroglyphics. As he came into the middle of the room, he threw back the skirt of it, and discovered a golden thigh. Socrates, at the sight of it, declared against keeping company with any who were not made of flesh and blood; and, therefore, desired Diogenes the Laertian to lead him to the apartment allotted for fabulous heroes, and worthies of dubious existence. At his going out, he told them, "that they did not know whom they dismissed; that he was now Pythagoras, the first of philosophers, and that formerly he had been a very brave man at the siege of Troy." "That may be very true," said Socrates; "but you forget that you have likewise been a very great harlot in your time." This exclusion made way for Archimedes, who came forward with a scheme of mathematical figures in his hand, among which I observed a cone and a cylinder.

Seeing this table full, I desired my guide, for variety, to lead me to the fabulous apartment, the roof of which was painted with gorgons, chimeras, and centaurs, with many other emblematical figures, which I wanted both time and skill to unriddle. The first table was almost full: at the upper end sat Hercules, leaning an arm upon his club; on his right hand were Achilles and Ulysses, and between them Æneas; on his left were Hector, Theseus, and Jason; the lower end had Orpheus, Æsop, Phalaris, and Musæus. The ushers seemed at a loss for a twelfth man, when, methought, to my great joy and surprise, I heard some at the lower end of the table mention Isaac Bickerstaff; but those of the upper end received it with disdain, and said, "if they must have a British worthy, they would have Robin Hood." While I was transported with the honor that was done me, and burning with envy against my competitor, I was awakened by the noise of the cannon which were then fired for the taking of Mons. I should have been very much troubled at being thrown out of so pleasing a vision on any other occasion; but thought it an agreeable change to have my thoughts diverted from the greatest among the dead and fabulous heroes to the most famous among the real and the living.

Complete. From the Tatler.

OF PATRIOTISM AND PUBLIC SPIRIT

———*Fuit hæc sapientia quondam*
Publica privatis secernere.
—*Hor*. Ars Poet. 396.

"Our sage forefathers wisely understood
To sep'rate public from the private good."

FROM MY OWN APARTMENT, June 9th.

WHEN men look into their own bosoms, and consider the generous seeds which are there planted, that might, if rightly
cultivated, ennoble their lives, and make their virtue venerable to futurity; how can they, without tears, reflect on the
universal degeneracy from that public spirit, which ought to be
the first and principal motive of all their actions? In the Grecian and Roman nations, they were wise enough to keep up
this great incentive, and it was impossible to be in the fashion
without being a patriot. All gallantry had its first source from
hence; and to want a warmth for the public welfare was a
defect so scandalous that he who was guilty of it had no pretense to honor or manhood. What makes the depravity among
us in this behalf the more vexatious and irksome to reflect upon
is that the contempt of life is carried as far amongst us as it
could be in those memorable people; and we want only a proper
application of the qualities which are frequent among us, to be
as worthy as they. There is hardly a man to be found who will
not fight upon any occasion which he thinks may taint his own
honor. Were this motive as strong in everything that regards
the public as it is in this our private case, no man would pass his
life away without having distinguished himself by some gallant
instance of his zeal towards it in the respective incidents of his
life and profession. But it is so far otherwise, that there cannot
at present be a more ridiculous animal than one who seems to
regard the good of others. He, in civil life, whose thoughts turn
upon schemes which may be of general benefit, without further
reflection, is called a projector; and the man whose mind seems
intent upon glorious achievements, a knight-errant. The ridicule among us runs strong against laudable actions; nay, in
the ordinary course of things, and the common regards of life,
negligence of the public is an epidemic vice. The brewer in his
excise, the merchant in his customs, and, for aught we know,
the soldier in his muster rolls, think never the worse of themselves for being guilty of their respective frauds towards the
public. This evil is come to such a fantastical height that he
is a man of a public spirit, and heroically affected to his country, who can go so far as even to turn usurer with all he has in
her funds. There is not a citizen in whose imagination such a
one does not appear in the same light of glory as Codrus,
Scævola, or any other great name in old Rome. Were it not

for the heroes of so much per cent. as have regard enough for
themselves and their nation to trade with her with their wealth,
the very notion of public love would long before now have van-
ished from among us.   But however general custom may hurry
us away in the stream of a common error, there is no evil, no
crime, so great as that of being cold in matters which relate to
the common good.   This is in nothing more conspicuous than in
a certain willingness to receive anything that tends to the diminution of such as have been conspicuous instruments in our
service.   Such inclinations proceed from the most low and vile
corruption, of which the soul of man is capable.   This effaces
not only the practice, but the very approbation of honor and
virtue; and has had such an effect that, to speak freely, the
very sense of public good has no longer a part even of our
conversations.   Can then the most generous motive of life, the
good of others, be so easily banished the breast of man?   Is it
possible to draw all our passions inward?   Shall the boiling heat
of youth be sunk in pleasures, the ambition of manhood in selfish intrigues?   Shall all that is glorious, all that is worth the
pursuit of great minds, be so easily rooted out?   When the universal bent of a people seems diverted from the sense of their
common good and common glory, it looks like a fatality, and
crisis of impending misfortune.

The generous nations we just now mentioned understood this
so very well that there was hardly an oration ever made which
did not turn upon this general sense, "That the love of their
country was the first and most essential quality in an honest
mind."   Demosthenes, in a cause wherein his fame, reputation,
and fortune, were embarked, puts his all upon this issue; "Let
the Athenians," says he, "be benevolent to me, as they think I
have been zealous for them."   This great and discerning orator
knew there was nothing else in nature could bear him up
against his adversaries, but this one quality of having shown
himself willing or able to serve his country.   This certainly is
the test of merit; and the first foundation for deserving good-
will is having it yourself.   The adversary of this orator at that
time was Æschines, a man of wily arts and skill in the world,
who could, as occasion served, fall in with a national start of
passion, or sullenness of humor; which a whole nation is sometimes taken with as well as a private man, and by that means
divert them from their common sense, into an aversion for

receiving anything in its true light. But when Demosthenes had awakened his audience with that one hint of judging by the general tenor of his life towards them, his services bore down his opponent before him, who fled to the covert of his mean arts, until some more favorable occasion should offer against the superior merit of Demosthenes.

It were to be wished that love of their country were the first principle of action in men of business, even for their own sakes; for, when the world begins to examine into their conduct, the generality, who have no share in, or hopes of any part in power or riches, but what is the effect of their own labor or property, will judge of them by no other method than that of how profitable their administration has been to the whole. They who are out of the influence of men's fortune or favor will let them stand or fall by this one only rule; and men who can bear being tried by it are always popular in their fall. Those who cannot suffer such a scrutiny are contemptible in their advancement.

But I am here running into shreds of maxims from reading Tacitus this morning, that has driven me from my recommendation of public spirit, which was the intended purpose of this lucubration. There is not a more glorious instance of it than in the character of Regulus. This same Regulus was taken prisoner by the Carthaginians, and was sent by them to Rome, in order to demand some Punic noblemen, who were prisoners, in exchange for himself; and was bound by an oath, that he would return to Carthage if he failed in his commission. He proposes this to the senate, who were in suspense upon it, which Regulus observing, without having the least notion of putting the care of his own life in competition with the public good, desired them to consider that he was old and almost useless; that those demanded in exchange were men of daring tempers, and great merit in military affairs; and wondered they would make any doubt of permitting him to go back to the short tortures prepared for him at Carthage, where he should have the advantage of ending a long life both gloriously and usefully. This generous advice was consented to; and he took his leave of his country and his weeping friends, to go to certain death, with that cheerful composure, as a man, after the fatigue of business in a court or a city, retires to the next village for the air.

Complete.   From the Tatler.

OF MEN WHO ARE NOT THEIR OWN MASTERS

Stultitia patiuntur opes.
— *Hor.* Lib. I., Epist. XVIII. 29.

« Their folly pleads the privilege of wealth.»

FROM MY OWN APARTMENT, June 2d.

I HAVE received a letter which accuses me of partiality in the administration of the censorship; and says that I have been very free with the lower part of mankind, but extremely cautious in representations of matters which concern men of condition. This correspondent takes upon him also to say, the upholsterer was not undone by turning politician, but became bankrupt by trusting his goods to persons of quality; and demands of me that I should do justice upon such as brought poverty and distress upon the world below them, while they themselves were sunk in pleasures and luxury, supported at the expense of those very persons whom they treated with negligence, as if they did not know whether they dealt with them or not. This is a very heavy accusation, both of me, and such as the man aggrieved accuses me of tolerating. For this reason I resolved to take this matter into consideration; and upon very little meditation could call to my memory many instances which made this complaint far from being groundless. The root of this evil does not always proceed from injustice in the men of figure, but often from a false grandeur which they take upon them in being unacquainted with their own business; not considering how mean a part they act, when their names and characters are subjected to the little arts of their servants and dependants. The overseers of the poor are a people who have no great reputation for the discharge of their trust; but are much less scandalous than the overseers of the rich. Ask a young fellow of a great estate who was that odd fellow that spoke to him in a public place, he answers, « one that does my business. » It is, with many, a natural consequence of being a man of fortune that they are not to understand the disposal of it; and they long to come to their estates, only to put themselves under new guardianship. Nay, I have known a young fellow, who was regularly bred an attorney, and was a very expert one until he had an estate fallen to him. The moment that happened, he, who could

before prove the next land he cast his eye upon his own, and
was so sharp that a man at first sight would give him a small
sum for a general receipt, whether he owed him anything or not;
such a one, I say, have I seen, upon coming to an estate, forget
all his diffidence of mankind, and become the most manageable
thing breathing. He immediately wanted a stirring man to take
upon him his affairs, to receive and pay, and do everything
which he himself was now too fine a gentleman to understand.
It is pleasant to consider that he who would have got an estate,
had he not come to one, will certainly starve because one fell to
him; but such contradictions are we to ourselves, and any change
of life is insupportable to some natures.

It is a mistaken sense of superiority to believe a figure or
equipage gives men precedence to their neighbors. Nothing can
create respect from mankind, but laying obligations upon them;
and it may very reasonably be concluded that if it were put into
a due balance, according to the true state of the account, many
who believe themselves in possession of a large share of dignity
in the world must give place to their inferiors. The greatest of
all distinctions in civil life is that of debtor and creditor; and
there needs no great progress in logic to know which, in that
case, is the advantageous side. He who can say to another,
" Pray, master," or, " Pray, my lord, give me my own," can as
justly tell him, " It is a fantastical distinction you take upon you
to pretend to pass upon the world for my master or lord, when,
at the same time that I wear your livery, you owe me wages;
or, while I wait at your door, you are ashamed to see me until
you have paid my bill."

The good old way among the gentry of England, to maintain
their pre-eminence over the lower rank, was by their bounty,
munificence, and hospitality; and it is a very unhappy change, if
at present, by themselves or their agents, the luxury of the gentry is supported by the credit of the trader. This is what my
correspondent pretends to prove out of his own books, and those
of his whole neighborhood. He has the confidence to say that
there is a mughouse near Longacre, where you may every evening hear an exact account of distresses of this kind. One complains that such a lady's finery is the occasion that his own wife
and daughter appear so long in the same gown. Another, that
all the furniture of her visiting apartment are no more hers than
the scenery of a play are the proper goods of the actress. Nay,

at the lower end of the same table, you may hear a butcher and poulterer say that, at their proper charge, all that family has been maintained since they last came to town.

The free manner in which people of fashion are discoursed on at such meetings is but a just reproach of their failures in this kind; but the melancholy relations of the great necessities tradesmen are driven to, who support their credit in spite of the faithless promises which are made them, and the abatement which they suffer when paid by the extortion of upper servants, is what would stop the most thoughtless man in the career of his pleasures, if rightly represented to him.

If this matter be not very speedily amended, I shall think fit to print exact lists of all persons who are not at their own disposal, though above the age of twenty-one; and as the trader is made bankrupt for absence from his abode, so shall the gentleman for being at home, if, when Mr. Morphew calls, he cannot give an exact account of what passes in his own family. After this fair warning, no one ought to think himself hardly dealt with, if I take upon me to pronounce him no longer master of his estate, wife, or family, than he continues to improve, cherish, and maintain them upon the basis of his own property, without incursions upon his neighbor in any of these particulars.

According to that excellent philosopher, Epictetus, we are all but acting parts in a play; and it is not a distinction in itself to be high or low, but to become the parts we are to perform. I am by my office prompter on this occasion; and shall give those who are a little out in their parts such soft hints as may help them to proceed, without letting it be known to the audience they were out; but if they run quite out of character, they must be called off the stage, and receive parts more suitable to their genius. Servile complaisance shall degrade a man from his honor and quality, and haughtiness be yet more debased. Fortune shall no longer appropriate distinctions, but nature direct us in the disposition both of respect and discountenance. As there are tempers made for command, and others for obedience, so there are men born for acquiring possessions, and others incapable of being other than mere lodgers in the houses of their ancestors, and have it not in their very composition to be proprietors of anything. These men are moved only by the mere effects of impulse: then good-will and disesteem are to be regarded equally; for neither is the effect of their judgment. This loose temper is that which makes a man, what Sallust so well remarks to happen frequently in the same person, to be covetous of what is another's, and profuse of what is his own. This sort of men is usually amiable to ordinary eyes; but, in the sight of reason, nothing is laudable but what is guided by reason. The covetous prodigal is of all others the worst man in society. If he would but take time to look into himself, he would find his soul all over gashed with broken vows and promises; and his retrospect on his actions would not consist of reflections upon those good resolutions after mature thought, which are the true life of a reasonable creature, but the nauseous memory of imperfect pleasures, idle dreams, and occasioned amusements. To follow such dissatisfying pursuits, is it possible to suffer the ignominy of being unjust? I remember in Tully's "Epistle," in the recommendation of a man to an affair which had no manner of relation to money, it is said, "You may trust him, for he is a frugal man." It is certain he who has not regard to strict justice in the commerce of life can be capable of no good action in any other kind; but he who lives below his income lays up, every moment of life, armor against a base world, that will cover all his frailties while he is so fortified, and exaggerate them when he is naked and defenseless.

ADVERTISEMENT

A stagecoach sets out exactly at six from Nando's coffee-house to Mr. Tiptoe's dancing school, and returns at eleven every evening, for one shilling and fourpence.

N. B. Dancing shoes, not exceeding four inches height in the heels, and periwigs, not exceeding three feet in length, are carried in the coach box gratis.

Complete. From the Tatler.

SIR JAMES STEPHEN

(1789–1859)

IR JAMES STEPHEN, one of the noted essayists of the Edinburgh Review, was born in London, January 3d, 1789. He was a graduate of Cambridge University, and a successful lawyer, author of a volume of "Essays," a "History of France," and "Desultory and Systematic Reading," a lecture published in 1853. He served for some time as Undersecretary for the Colonies, and on his retirement was made Knight Commander of the Bath. In 1849 he became Regius Professor of Modern History at Cambridge. The appointment is credited to the influence of his essays in the Edinburgh Review, which were collected and republished under the title of "Essays on Ecclesiastical Biography and Other Subjects." He died at Coblenz September 15th, 1859.

CHRISTIANITY AND PROGRESS

IF SCIPIO had his dream of colloquies after death with the wise and good of all ages, the Eskimo has his heaven where sealskins may be procured in placid seas, and undying lamps are fed with inexhaustible supplies of the odorous grease of bears. Mahomet promised his Arabian converts "rivers of incorruptible water and rivers of milk, the taste whereof changeth not; gardens planted with shady trees, in each of which shall be two flowing fountains; couches, the linings whereof shall be of thick silk interwoven with gold, and beautous damsels, refraining their eyes from beholding any but their spouses, having complexions like rubies and pearls, and fine black eyes." The stream can rise no higher than the fountain. Our ideas of immortal good are but amplifications of our mortal enjoyments. To sublimate our conceptions of felicity, by associating together all innocent and not incompatible delights, and by subtracting from them every alloy of pain, satiety, and languor, is to create for ourselves the only heaven with the contemplation of which hope can be sustained and activity invigorated. He who carefully surveys the Elysium which reason or imagination has laid out and

planted for him in the next world will acquire far better acquaintance with the "happy gardens" to which choice or fortune
has directed him in this. Judged by this standard, and giving
him credit for having made his public confessions with entire
candor, the author of the "Theory of a Future Life" may be esteemed a wise and happy man — wise, because he has no fear
of acknowledging to himself or to others the dependence of his
spiritual on his animal economy, and affects no superhuman disdain of mere bodily gratifications; and happy, because his felicity
consists in bringing the body into that unresisting servitude to
the mind, without which freedom and serenity are but empty
words. Such as is his paradise in the highest conceivable degree,
such in the highest attainable degree must be his earthly Eden.
Dismiss it if you will as a midsummer night's dream; yet must
it be confessed that it is such a dream as could visit no slumbers
but those of one whose fancy was pure from sensual defilement,
and whose intellect had been trained to active exercise and to
close self-observation. Or, give the theorist credit for nothing
more than having skillfully selected the most alluring possibilities
of future good from the many celestial schemes with which the
poetry and the poetical prose of all ages abounds, and still it
will be true that the choice has been guided by opinions such as
every one would wish to adopt, and by tastes which in our better moments we should all desire to gratify. The time subtracted,
for such visions, from the scarcely more substantial delights
among which we are living, will send us back to the cares of
life, not less fitted resolutely to endure them; and to the pleasures of life, not less prepared wisely to enjoy them. . . .

There is in Christianity an expansive power, sometimes
repressed, but never destroyed; and that latent energy the Christian
strives to draw forth into life and action. Those mysteries which
shroud the condition and the prospects of our race, however inscru-
table to the slaves of appetite, are not absolutely impervious to a
soul purified by devout contemplation; and to these empyreal heights
he aspires at once to point and to lead the way. To him whose
foot is firmly planted on the eternal verities of heaven, there
belong motives of such force, and a courage so undaunted, as
should burst through all resistance; and he calls on those who
enjoy this high privilege to assert their native supremacy above
the sordid ambition, the frivolities, and the virulence of the lower
world. The voice thus raised in expostulation will die away, not

unheeded by the interior circle he addresses, nor unblessed by a meet recompense; but unrewarded, we fear, by the accomplishment of these exalted purposes. Eloquent as is the indignation with which our anonymous monitor regards the low level to which divine and human literature has fallen amongst us, and mean as is his estimate of the pursuits with which the men of his own days are engaged, a hope may perhaps, without presumption, be indulged, that less fastidious and not less capable judges will pronounce a more lenient sentence on us and on our doings.

In the great cycle of human affairs there are many stages, each essential to the consummation of the designs of Providence, and each separated by broad distinctions from the rest. They whose province it is to censure, and they whose desire it is to improve their age, will never find their sacred fires extinct from the mere want of fuel. History and theory are always at hand with humiliating contrasts to the times we live in. That men have been better or might be better than they are has been true since the first fathers of our race returned to their native dust, and will still be true as long as our planet shall be inhabited by their descendants. But below the agitated surface of the ocean, under currents are silently urging forward, on their destined path, the waters of the mighty deep, themselves impelled by that Power which none may question or resist. Human society obeys a similar influence. Laws as anomalous in appearance, as uniform in reality, as those which direct the planetary movements determine the present state, and regulate the progress of commonwealths, whether political, literary, or religious. Christianity demands the belief, and experience justifies the hope, that their ultimate tendency is towards the universal dominion of piety and virtue. But it is neither pious nor rational to suppose that this consummation can be attained by any sequence of identical causes constantly working out similar effects. The best generations, like the best men, are those which possess an individual and distinctive character. A chain of splendid biographies constitutes the history of past centuries. Whoever shall weave the chronicles of our own must take for his staple statistics illuminated by a skillful generalization. Once every eye was directed to the leaders of the world; now all are turned to the masses of which it is composed. Instead of Newtons presiding over royal societies, we have Dr. Birkbecks lecturing at mechanics' institutes. If no Wolseys arise to found colleges like that of Christ Church, Joseph

Lancaster and William Bell have emulated each other in works not less momentous at the Borough Road and Baldwin's Gardens. We people continents, though we have ceased to discover them. We abridge folios for the many, though we no longer write them for the few. . . .

We know not how to regret that Genius has from the moment abdicated her austere supremacy, and stooped to be popular and plain. Mackintosh surrendered his philosophy to the compilation of a familiar history of England. Faithless to his Peris and Glendowers, Mr. Moore is teaching the commonalty of the realm the sad tale of the woes inflicted on the land of his birth. No longer emulous of Porson, the Bishop of London devotes his learned desire to preparing cheap and easy lessons for the householders of his diocese. Lord Brougham arrests the current of his eloquence to instruct mechanics in the principles of the sciences which they are reducing to daily practice. Tracts for the times are extorted from the depositories of ecclesiastical tradition, obedient to the general impulse which they condemn, and constrained to render the Church argumentative, that they may render her oracular. Nay, the author of the "Natural History of Enthusiasm" himself, despite his own protests, yields at length to the current, and has become the periodical writer of monthly tracts, where, in good round controversial terms, the superficial multitude are called to sit in judgment on the claims of the early fathers to sound doctrine, good morals, and common sense. Let who will repine at what has passed, and at what is passing, if they will allow us to rejoice in what is to come. If we witness the growth of no immortal reputations, we see the expansion of universal intelligence. The disparities of human understanding are much the same in all times; but it is when the general level is the highest that the mighty of the earth rise to the most commanding eloquence.

From a review of "Physical Theory
of Another Life."

LAURENCE STERNE

(1713–1768)

THE author of "Tristram Shandy" and the "Sentimental Journey" was as incapable of writing an essay according to rule as he was of telling a story with a plot or a purpose. The "Chapter on Sleep" in "Tristram Shandy" is an essay, to be sure, complete in itself, and in every way admirable. It is one of the best in the English language, but it is accidental as far as Sterne is concerned. It was his deliberate and lifelong habit to begin nowhere in particular and never to end at all. This with his extensive and curious learning (which he is unkindly charged with borrowing in a great measure from Burton's "Anatomy of Melancholy") constitutes his peculiar excellence and his greatest charm. Time was when the "Sentimental Journey" and "Tristram Shandy" were considered improper books for family reading, but they have come to be "classics," and it is well known that all classics are not only safe but necessary *virginibus puerisque*. It must be noted also that whoever sets out to get his morals corrupted by Sterne will have much labor for his pains,— for it is a "Shandean" habit to tantalize the reader with fifty pages of curious philosophy as the price of getting at the suspicion of a doubtful jest. And moreover, though nothing is more delightful than five minutes of "Tristram Shandy," nothing could be more calculated to break the spirit than five hours of it. This, however, is not to Sterne's discredit. He is deliberately disconnected, writing in defiance of all the known laws of the mind's operation and still succeeding in impressing himself on the English literature of all time. He is not "purely original," for he followed Rabelais; but while Rabelais has found many imitators, Sterne himself has defied all. He was the first and last representative of a school of English humor of which the world needs nothing more than he has given it,— though of that it could spare nothing. He was born at Clonmel, Ireland, November 24th, 1713. His father was an English officer whose regiment was stationed at Clonmel, and Sterne, after remaining with the regiment until his tenth year, was then sent to school in England. He graduated at Cambridge in 1736, and took orders in the English Established Church, in the ministry of which he remained until his death, March 18th, 1768. His "Sermons" and several volumes of his letters are included with "Tristram Shandy" and the "Sentimental Journey" to make up the total of his works. The "Sermons" are described as

"Shandean" in their style, and when first published they were very popular. His best sermon, however, is the story of Le Fevre, in consideration of which he may fairly have asked the recording angel to shed tears enough over the unclerical parts of "Tristram Shandy" to allow its author to pass into heaven in full canonicals without the formality of a trial.

W. V. B.

A CHAPTER ON SLEEP

I WISH I could write a chapter upon sleep.

A fitter occasion could never have presented itself than what this moment offers, when all the curtains of the family are drawn, the candles put out, and no creature's eyes are open but a single one — for the other has been shut these twenty years — of my mother's nurse.

It is a fine subject.

And yet, as fine as it is, I would undertake to write a dozen chapters upon buttonholes, both quicker and with more fame, than a single chapter upon this.

Buttonholes! there is something lively in the very idea of 'em; and trust me, when I get amongst 'em, you gentry with great beards, look as grave as you will, I'll make merry work with my buttonholes — I shall have 'em all to myself, — 'tis a maiden subject — I shall run foul of no man's wisdom or fine saying in it.

But for sleep, I know I shall make nothing of it before I begin; I am no dab at your fine sayings, in the first place; and in the next, I cannot for my soul set a grave face upon a bad matter, and tell the world 'tis the refuge of the unfortunate, the enfranchisement of the prisoner, the downy lap of the hopeless, the weary, and the broken-hearted; nor could I set out with a lie in my mouth, by affirming that of all the soft and delicious functions of our nature, by which the great Author of it, in his bounty, has been pleased to recompense the sufferings wherewith his justice and his good pleasure has wearied us, that this is the chiefest (I know pleasures worth ten of it); or what a happiness it is to man, after the anxieties and passions of the day are over, and he lies down upon his back, that his soul shall be so seated within him, that whichever way she turns her eyes, the heavens shall look calm and sweet above her; no desire, or fear, or doubt, that troubles the air; nor any difficulty, past, present, or to come, that the imagination may not pass over without offense, in that sweet secession.

"God's blessing," said Sancho Panza, "be upon the man who first invented this self-same thing called Sleep; it covers a man all over like a cloak." Now there is more to me in this, and it speaks warmer to my heart and affections than all the dissertations squeezed out of the heads of the learned together upon the subject.

Not that I altogether disapprove of what Montaigne advances upon it; 'tis admirable in its way. I quote by memory.

The world enjoys other pleasures, says he, as they do that of sleep, without tasting or feeling it as it slips and passes by. We should study and ruminate upon it, in order to render proper thanks to him who grants it to us. For this end, I cause myself to be disturbed in my sleep, that I may the better and more sensibly relish it; and yet I see few, says he again, who live with less sleep, when need requires. My body is capable of a firm, but not of a violent and sudden agitation; I evade of late all violent exercises, I am never weary with walking, but from my youth I never liked to ride upon pavements. I love to lie hard and alone, and even without my wife. This last word may stagger the faith of the world; but remember, *"La Vraisemblance"* (as Bayle says in the affair of Liceti) *" n'est pas toujours du Cote de la Verite."* And so much for sleep.

Complete. "Life and Opinions of Tristram Shandy," Book IV., Chap. xv.

A PEASANT'S PHILOSOPHY

A SHOE coming loose from the forefoot of the thill horse, at the beginning of the ascent of Mount Taurira, the postilion dismounted, twisted the shoe off, and put it in his pocket. As the ascent was of five or six miles, and that horse our main dependence, I made a point of having the shoe fastened on again as well as we could; but the postilion had thrown away the nails, and the hammer in the chaise box being of no great use without them, I submitted to go on. He had not mounted half a mile higher, when, coming to a flinty piece of road, the poor devil lost a second shoe, and from off his other forefoot. I then got out of the chaise in good earnest; and seeing a house about a quarter of a mile to the left hand, with a great deal to do I prevailed upon the postilion to turn up to it. The look of the house, and of everything about it, as we drew nearer, soon reconciled me to the disaster. It was a little farmhouse, surrounded with about twenty acres of vineyard, and about as much corn; and close to the house on one side was a *potagerie* of an acre and a half, full of everything which could make plenty in a French peasant's house; and on the other side was a little wood, which furnished where-withal to dress it. It was about eight in the evening when I got to the house; so I left the postilion to manage his point as he could,—and for mine, I walked directly into the house.

The family consisted of an old gray-headed man and his wife, with five or six sons and sons in law and their several wives, and a joyous genealogy out of them. They were all sitting down to-gether to their lentil soup; a large wheaten loaf was in the middle of the table; and a flagon of wine at each end of it promised joy through the stages of the repast; 'twas a feast of love. The old man rose up to meet me, and with a respectful cordiality would have me sit down at the table; my heart was set down the moment I entered the room, so I sat down at once like a son of the family; and to invest myself in the character as speedily as I could, I instantly borrowed the old man's knife, and, taking up the loaf, cut myself a hearty luncheon; and as I did it, I saw a testimony in every eye, not only of an honest welcome, but of a welcome mixed with thanks that I had not seemed to doubt it. Was it this,—or tell me, Nature, what else it was,—that made this morsel so sweet; and to what magic I owe it, that the draught I took of their flagon was so delicious with it, that they remain upon my palate to this hour? If the supper was to my taste, the grace which followed it was much more so.

When supper was over, the old man gave a knock upon the table with the haft of his knife, to bid them prepare for the dance. The moment the signal was given, the women and girls ran all together into a back apartment to tie up their hair, and the young men to the door to wash their faces and change their sabots; and in three minutes every soul was ready, upon a little esplanade before the house, to begin. The old man and his wife came out last, and, placing me betwixt them, sat down upon a sofa of turf by the door. The old man had some fifty years ago been no mean performer upon the vielle; and at the age he was then of, touched it well enough for the purpose. His wife sung

now and then a little to the tune, then intermitted, and joined
her old man again as their children and grandchildren danced
before them.

It was not till the middle of the second dance, when, for
some pauses in the movement, wherein they all seemed to look
up, I fancied I could distinguish an elevation of spirit different
from that which is the cause or the effect of simple jollity. In a
word, I thought I beheld Religion mixing in the dance; but as I
had never seen her so engaged, I should have looked upon it now
as one of the illusions of an imagination which is eternally mis
leading me, had not the old man, as soon as the dance ended,
said that this was their constant way; and that all his life long
he had made it a rule, after supper was over, to call out his
family to dance and rejoice; believing, he said, that a cheerful and
contented mind was the best sort of thanks to Heaven that an
illiterate peasant could pay.   Or a learned prelate either, said I.

From the «Sentimental Journey.»

ROBERT LOUIS STEVENSON

(1850–1894)

FTER the death of Thackeray and Dickens, English prose fiction tended more and more towards "the novel with a purpose," and in the last quarter of the century, when Stevenson first made himself felt, the reading public was wholly under the power of fiction, which was properly classed as "degenerate." Much of it was radically unhealthy. It is no exaggeration to say that tons of fair, white paper were desecrated by "studies" of problems of physiology and psychology on which no healthy mind will wish to dwell — if for no other reason than that their existence as "problems" does not become evident except through abnormality in its most diseased and generally its most contagious form. Stevenson brought about a strong reaction. His "Doctor Jekyll and Mr. Hyde," the prose masterpiece of the nineteenth century, was in some sense a "problem book," but it deals with the whole problem of human life as a struggle between good and evil. Stevenson, who saw things, as he expresses it, "bare to the buff," felt this struggle in himself, and saw it everywhere in the world outside of himself. The expression he gives it in "Doctor Jekyll and Mr. Hyde" verges on the supernatural. In this book at least, Scott's greatest pupil is greater than his master. The romantic novel and the prose allegory found their perfect union and their climax in this book, which stands quite unique in English literature, since Stevenson himself never approached it afterwards. His other stories and novels show, however, a great and compelling genius for narration. In some of them it is almost too great to be endurable. "Treasure Island," for instance, is professedly a book for boys, but any one of any age who surrenders himself to it is apt to feel an effect from it comparable to nothing less violent than that of brandy. This intensity appears in all Stevenson's work. He had an extraordinary power of focusing all his energies,— a power as dangerous as it is unusual. It belongs only to genius and it cannot be exercised except at the expense of vitality. What Landor knew of "the pangs of approaching the gods," Stevenson felt as he gradually burned his life away in the brilliant flame of his own powers. He welcomed death with joy, as the reward of one who had done his best without sparing himself. There is nothing more pathetic in literature than the stanza he wrote for his own epitaph:—

ROBERT LOUIS STEVENSON.

After a Portrait Etched by Hollyer.

« Under the wide and starry sky,
  Dig me a grave and let me lie;
  Glad did I live and gladly I die
  And I laid me down with a will.

« This be the verse that they grave for me:
  ‹ Here he lies where he longed to be;
  Home is the sailor, home from the sea,
  And the hunter home from the hill.› »

No one who reads this will need to be told that its author was a poet capable of attaining the highest reaches of poetical expression. But Stevenson sang only in snatches. In some of these, he is more musical than Burns at his best. In such verses as:—

« It is ill to break the bonds which God decreed to bind;
  Still will we be the children of the heather and the wind, »

we hear echoes of such melody as the world had not known for eighteen hundred years. It appears from them, unmistakably, that Stevenson as a poet might have surpassed his highest successes in prose. Why he did not do so it is idle to inquire, but the cause is probably closely involved with the painful reactions which brought him his untimely death (Apia, Samoa, December 3d, 1894).

He was born at Edinburgh, November 13th, 1850. His father was a lighthouse engineer, a son of Robert Stevenson, and the family represented a Scottish ancestral tradition which inspired Stevenson's best work. He had all possible advantages of early training, including education at Edinburgh University and for the bar. After his first literary successes, he went to live in London, but, except in his deep love for Scotland, he was a cosmopolitan. He found his wife in America, and from 1889 he lived, or rather slowly died, in Samoa, where he had gone, that in spite of increasing weakness due to consumption, he might gain strength to complete his work. When he had completed it, the objection that remains against it, is that he did himself too little justice as a poet while putting into his novels the full intensity of a genius which in prose narrative is frequently too close to the intoxicating to be entirely healthy for those who indulge it without reserve. As an essayist, however, no such objection lies against him. Had he attempted his greatest success in essay writing instead of in fiction, he might have become easily first among the essayists of the nineteenth century. In delicacy, he is equaled only by Lamb, while he has the strength of Thackeray. But even when he is gayest or most commonplace, he never ceases to be unearthly. In his essays as in his poems and his fiction, he is the dying man who, having already awakened to realities beyond the earthly, is waiting for death as a deliverance and working for it as a reward.   W. V. B.

EL DORADO

IT SEEMS as if a great deal were attainable in a world where there are so many marriages and decisive battles, and where we all, at certain hours of the day, and with great gusto and dispatch, stow a portion of victuals finally and irretrievably into the bag which contains us. And it would seem also, on a hasty view, that the attainment of as much as possible was the one goal of man's contentious life. And yet, as regards the spirit, this is but a semblance. We live in an ascending scale when we live happily, one thing leading to another in an endless series. There is always a new horizon for onward-looking men, and although we dwell on a small planet, immersed in petty business and not enduring beyond a brief period of years, we are so constituted that our hopes are inaccessible, like stars, and the term of hoping is prolonged until the term of life. To be truly happy is a question of how we begin and not of how we end, of what we want and not of what we have. An aspiration is a joy forever, a possession as solid as a landed estate, a fortune which we can never exhaust and which gives us year by year a revenue of pleasurable activity. To have many of these is to be spiritually rich. Life is only a very dull and ill-directed theatre unless we have some interests in the piece; and to those who have neither art nor science, the world is a mere arrangement of colors, or a rough footway where they may very well break their shins. It is in virtue of his own desires and curiosities that any man continues to exist with even patience, that he is charmed by the look of things and people, and that he wakens every morning with a renewed appetite for work and pleasure. Desire and curiosity are the two eyes through which he sees the world in the most enchanted colors: it is they that make women beautiful or fossils interesting; and the man may squander his estate and come to beggary, but if he keeps these two amulets he is still rich in the possibilities of pleasure. Suppose he could take one meal so compact and comprehensive that he should never hunger any more; suppose him, at a glance, to take in all the features of the world and allay the desire for knowledge; suppose him to do the like in any province of experience — would not that man be in a poor way for amusement ever after?

One who goes touring on foot with a single volume in his knapsack reads with circumspection, pausing often to reflect, and often laying the book down to contemplate the landscape or the prints in the inn parlor; for he fears to come to an end of his entertainment, and be left companionless on the last stages of his journey. A young fellow recently finished the works of Thomas Carlyle, winding up, if we remember aright, with the ten notebooks upon Frederick the Great. "What!" cried the young fellow, in consternation, "is there no more Carlyle? Am I left to the daily papers?" A more celebrated instance is that of Alexander, who wept bitterly because he had no more worlds to subdue. And when Gibbon had finished the "Decline and Fall," he had only a few moments of joy; and it was with a "sober melancholy" that he parted from his labors.

Happily we all shoot at the moon with ineffectual arrows; our hopes are set on an inaccessible El Dorado; we come to an end of nothing here below. Interests are only plucked up to sow themselves again, like mustard. You would think, when the child was born, there would be an end to trouble; and yet it is only the beginning of fresh anxieties; and when you have seen it through its teething and its education, and at last its marriage, alas! it is only to have new fears, new quivering sensibilities, with every day; and the health of your children's children grows as touching a concern as that of your own. Again, when you have married your wife, you would think you were got upon a hilltop, and might begin to go downward by an easy slope. But you have only ended courting to begin marriage. Falling in love and winning love are often difficult tasks to overbearing and rebellious spirits; but to keep in love is also a business of some importance, to which both man and wife must bring kindness and good-will. The true love story commences at the altar, when there lies before the married pair a most beautiful contest of wisdom and generosity, and a life-long struggle towards an unattainable ideal. Unattainable? Aye, surely unattainable, from the very fact that there are two instead of one.

"Of making books there is no end," complained the preacher; and did not perceive how highly he was praising letters as an occupation. There is no end, indeed, to making books or experiments, or to travel, or to gathering wealth. Problem gives rise to problem. We may study forever, and we are never as learned as we would be. We have never made a statue worthy of our dreams. And when we have discovered a continent, or crossed a chain of mountains, it is only to find another ocean or

another plain upon the further side. In the infinite universe there is room for our swiftest diligence and to spare. It is not like the works of Carlyle, which can be read to an end. Even in a corner of it, in a private park, or in the neighborhood of a single hamlet, the weather and the seasons keep so deftly changing that although we walk there for a lifetime there will be always something new to startle and delight us.

There is only one wish realizable on the earth; only one thing that can be perfectly attained: Death. And from a variety of circumstances we have no one to tell whether it be worth attaining. A strange picture we make on our way to our chimeras, ceaselessly marching, grudging ourselves the time for rest; indefatigable, adventurous pioneers. It is true that we shall never reach the goal; it is even more than probable that there is no such place; and if we lived for centuries and were endowed with the powers of a god, we should find ourselves not much nearer what we wanted at the end. O toiling hands of mortals! O unwearied feet, traveling ye know not whither! Soon, soon, it seems to you, you must come forth on some conspicuous hilltop, and but a little way further, against the setting sun, descry the spires of El Dorado. Little do ye know your own blessedness; for to travel hopefully is a better thing than to arrive, and the true success is to labor.

Complete. From « Virginibus Puerisque.»

OLD MORTALITY

BOOKS AND TOMBSTONES

THERE is a certain graveyard, looked upon on the one side by a prison, on the other by the windows of a quiet hotel; below, under a steep cliff, it beholds the traffic of many lines of rail, and the scream of the engine and the shock of meeting buffers mount to it all day long. The aisles are lined with the inclosed sepulchres of families, door beyond door, like houses in a street; and in the morning the shadow of the prison turrets, and of many tall memorials, fall upon the graves. There, in the hot fits of youth, I came to be unhappy. Pleasant incidents are woven with my memory of the place. I here made friends with a certain plain old gentleman, a visitor on sunny mornings, gravely cheerful, who, with one eye upon the place that awaited him, chirped about his youth like winter sparrows; a beautiful housemaid of the hotel once, for some days together, humbly flirted with me from a window and kept my wild heart flying; and once — she possibly remembers — the wise Eugenia followed me to that austere inclosure. Her hair came down, and in the shelter of the tomb my trembling fingers helped her to repair the braid. But for the most part I went there solitary and, with irrevocable emotion, pored on the names of the forgotten. Name after name, and to each the conventional attributions and the idle dates; a regiment of the unknown that had been the joy of mothers, and had thrilled with the illusions of youth, and at last, in the dim sick room, wrestled with the pangs of old mortality. In that whole crew of the silenced there was but one of whom my fancy had received a picture; and he, with his comely, florid countenance, bewigged and habited in scarlet, and in his day combining fame and popularity, stood forth, like a taunt, among that company of phantom appellations. It was then possible to leave behind us something more explicit than these severe, monotonous, and lying epitaphs; and the thing left, the memory of a painted picture and what we call the immortality of a name, was hardly more desirable than mere oblivion. Even David Hume, as he lay composed beneath that « circular idea,» was fainter than a dream; and when the housemaid, broom in hand, smiled and beckoned from the open window, the fame of that bewigged philosopher melted like a raindrop in the sea.

And yet in soberness I cared as little for the housemaid as for David Hume. The interests of youth are rarely frank; his passions, like Noah's dove, come home to roost. The fire, sensibility, and volume of his own nature, that is all that he has learned to recognize. The tumultuary and gray tide of life, the empire of routine, the unrejoicing faces of his elders, fill him with contemptuous surprise; there also he seems to walk among the tombs of spirits; and it is only in the course of years, and after much rubbing with his fellowmen, that he begins by glimpses to see himself from without and his fellows from within; to know his own for one among the thousand undenoted countenances of the city street, and to divine in others the throb of human agony and hope. In the meantime he will avoid the hospital doors, the pale faces, the cripple, the sweet whiff of chloroform — for there, on the most thoughtless, the pains of others are burned home; but he will continue to walk, in a divine self-pity, the aisles of the forgotten graveyard. The length of man's life, which is endless to the brave and busy, is scorned by his ambitious thought. He cannot bear to have come for so little, and to go again so wholly. He cannot bear, above all, in that brief scene, to be still idle, and, by way of cure, neglects the little that he has to do. The parable of the talent is the brief epitome of youth. To believe in immortality is one thing, but it is first needful to believe in life. Denunciatory preachers seem not to suspect that they may be taken gravely and in evil part; that young men may come to think of time as of a moment, and with the pride of Satan wave back the inadequate gift. Yet here is a true peril; this it is that sets them to pace the graveyard alleys, and to read, with strange extremes of pity and derision, the memorials of the dead.

Books were the proper remedy: books of vivid human import, forcing upon their minds the issues, pleasures, business, importance, and immediacy of that life in which they stand; books of smiling or heroic temper, to excite or to console; books of a large design, shadowing the complexity of that game of consequences to which we all sit down, the hanger-back not least. But the average sermon flees the point, disporting itself in that eternity of which we know, and need to know, so little; avoiding the bright, crowded, and momentous fields of life where destiny awaits us. Upon the average book a writer may be silent; he may set it down to his ill-hap that when his own youth was in the acrid fermentation, he should have fallen and fed upon the cheerless fields of Obermann. Yet to Mr. Arnold, who led him to these pastures, he still bears a grudge. The day is perhaps not far off when people will begin to count " Moll Flanders," aye, or " The Country Wife," more wholesome and more pious diet than these guide books to consistent egoism.

But the most inhuman of boys soon wearies of the inhumanity of Obermann. And even while I still continued to be a haunter of the graveyard, I began insensibly to turn my attention to the gravediggers, and was weaned out of myself to observe the conduct of visitors. This was dayspring, indeed, to a lad in such great darkness. Not that I began to see men, or to try to see them, from within, nor to learn charity and modesty and justice from the sight; but still stared at them externally from the prison windows of my affectation. Once I remember to have observed two workingwomen with a baby halting by a grave;

there was something monumental in the grouping, one upright carrying the child, the other with bowed face crouching by her side. A wreath of immortelles under a glass dome had thus attracted them; and, drawing near, I overheard their judgment on that wonder. "Eh! what extravagance!" To a youth afflicted with the callosity of sentiment, this quaint and pregnant saying appeared merely base.

My acquaintance with gravediggers, considering its length, was unremarkable. One, indeed, whom I found plying his spade in the red evening, high above Allan Water and in the shadow of Dunblane Cathedral, told me of his acquaintance with the birds that still attended on his labors; how some would even perch about him, waiting for their prey; and in a true Sexton's Calendar, how the species varied with the season of the year. But this was the very poetry of the profession. The others whom I knew were somewhat dry. A faint flavor of the gardner hung about them, but sophisticated and disbloomed. They had engagements to keep, not alone with the deliberate series of the seasons, but with mankind's clocks and hour-long measurement of time. And thus there was no leisure for the relishing pinch, or the hour-long gossip, foot on spade. They were men wrapped up in their grim business; they liked well to open long-closed family vaults, blowing in the key and throwing wide the grating; and they carried in their minds a calendar of names and dates. It would be "in fifty-twa" that such a tomb was last opened for "Miss Jemimy." It was thus they spoke of their past patients — familiarly, but not without respect, like old family servants. Here is indeed a servant, whom we forget that we possess; who does not wait at the bright table, or run at the bell's summons, but patiently smokes his pipe beside the mortuary fire, and in his faithful memory notches the burials of our race. To suspect Shakespeare in his maturity of a superficial touch savors of paradox; yet he was surely in error when he attributed insensibility to the digger of the grave. But perhaps it is on Hamlet that the charge should lie; or perhaps the English sexton differs from the Scotch. The "goodman delver," reckoning up his years of office, might have at least suggested other thoughts. It is a pride common among sextons. A cabinetmaker does not count his cabinets, nor even an author his volumes, save when they stare upon him from the shelves; but the gravedigger numbers his graves. He would indeed be something different from human if his solitary open-air and tragic labors left **not a broad** mark upon his mind. There, in his tranquil aisle, apart from city clamor, among the cats and robins and the ancient effigies and legends of the tomb, he waits the continual passage of his contemporaries, falling like minute drops into eternity. As they fall, he counts them; and this enumeration, which was at first perhaps appalling to his soul, in the process of years, and by the kindly influence of habit, grows to be his pride and pleasure. There are many common stories telling how he piques himself on crowded cemeteries. But I will rather tell of the old grave-digger of Monkton, to whose unsuffering bedside the minister was summoned. He dwelt in a cottage built into the wall of the churchyard; and through a bull's-eye pane above his bed he could see, as he lay dying, the rank grasses and the upright and recumbent stones. Dr. Laurie was, I think, a Moderate: 'tis certain, at least, that he took a very Roman view of deathbed dispositions, for he told the old man that he had lived beyond man's natural years, that his life had been easy and reputable, that his family had all grown up and been a credit to his care, and that it now behooved him unregretfully to gird his loins and follow the majority. The gravedigger heard him out; then he raised himself upon one elbow, and with the other hand pointed through the window to the scene of his lifelong labors. "Doctor," he said, "I ha'e laid three hunner and fower-score in that kirkyaird; an' it had been his wull," indicating Heaven, "I would ha'e likit weel to ha'e made out the fower hunner." But it was not to be; this tragedian of the fifth act had now another part to play, and the time had come when others were to gird and carry him.

THE HAUNTER OF GRAVES

I WOULD fain strike a note that should be more heroical; but the ground of all youth's suffering, solitude, hysteria, and haunting of the grave, is nothing else than naked, ignorant selfishness. It is himself that he sees dead; those are his virtues that are forgotten; his is the vague epitaph. Pity him but the more, if pity be your cue; for where a man is all pride, vanity, and personal aspiration, he goes through fire unshielded. In every part and corner of our life, to lose oneself is to be

gainer; to forget oneself is to be happy; and this poor, laughable and tragic fool has not yet learned the rudiments; himself,
giant Prometheus, is still ironed on the peaks of Caucasus. But
by and by his truant interests will leave that tortured body, slip
abroad and gather flowers. Then shall death appear before him
in an altered guise; no longer as a doom peculiar to himself,
whether fate's crowning injustice or his own last vengeance upon
those who fail to value him; but now as a power that wounds
him far more tenderly, not without solemn compensations, taking and giving, bereaving and yet storing up.

The first step for all is to learn to the dregs our own ignoble
fallibility. When we have fallen through story after story of
our vanity and aspiration, and sit rueful among the ruins, then
it is that we begin to measure the stature of our friends: how
they stand between us and our own contempt, believing in our
best; how, linking us with others, and still spreading wide the
influential circle, they weave us in and in with the fabric of contemporary life; and to what petty size they dwarf the virtues
and the vices that appeared gigantic in our youth. So that at
the last, when such a pin falls out — when there vanishes in the
least breath of time one of those rich magazines of life on
which we drew for our supply — when he who had first dawned
upon us as a face among the faces of the city, and, still growing, came to bulk on our regard with those clear features of the
loved and living man, falls in a breath to memory and shadow,
there falls along with him a whole wing of the palace of our
life.

THE HEAVEN OF NOBLE FAILURE

ONE such face I now remember; one such blank some half a
dozen of us labor to dissemble. In his youth he was most
beautiful in person; most serene and genial by disposition;
full of racy words and quaint thoughts. Laughter attended on
his coming. He had the air of a great gentleman, jovial and
royal with his equals, and to the poorest student gentle and attentive. Power seemed to reside in him exhaustless; we saw him
stoop to play with us, but held him marked for higher destinies;
we loved his notice; and I have rarely had my pride more gratified than when he sat at my father's table, my acknowledged

IX—227

friend.   So he walked among us, both hands full of gifts, carrying with nonchalance the seeds of a most influential life.

The powers and the ground of friendship are a mystery; but, looking back, I can discern that, in part, we love the thing he was, for some shadow of what he was to be. For with all his beauty, power, breeding, urbanity, and mirth, there was in those days something soulless in our friend. He would astonish us by sallies, witty, innocent, and inhumane; and by a misapplied Johnsonian pleasantry, demolish honest sentiment. I can still see and hear him, as he went his way along the lamplit streets, " *Là ci darem la mano* " on his lips, a noble figure of a youth, but following vanity and incredulous of good; and sure enough, somewhere on the high seas of life, with his health, his hopes, his patrimony, and his self-respect, miserably went down.

From this disaster, like a spent swimmer, he came desperately ashore, bankrupt of money and consideration; creeping to the family he had deserted; with broken wing, never more to rise. But in his face there was a light of knowledge that was new to it. Of the wounds of his body he was never healed; died of them gradually, with clear-eyed resignation; of his wounded pride, we knew only from his silence. He returned to that city where he had lorded it in his ambitious youth; lived there alone, seeing few; striving to retrieve the irretrievable; at times still grappling with that mortal frailty that had brought him down; still joying in his friend's successes; his laugh still ready but with kindlier music; and over all his thoughts the shadow of that unalterable law which he had disavowed and which had brought him low. Lastly, when his bodily evils had quite disabled him, he lay a great while dying, still without complaint, still finding interests; to his last step gentle, urbane, and with the will to smile.

The tale of this great failure is, to those who remain true to him, the tale of a success. In his youth he took thought for no one but himself; when he came ashore again, his whole armada lost, he seemed to think of none but others. Such was his tenderness for others, such his instinct of fine courtesy and pride, that of that impure passion of remorse he never breathed a syllable; even regret was rare with him, and pointed with a jest. You would not have dreamed, if you had known him then, that this was that great failure, that beacon to young men, over whose fall a whole society had hissed and pointed fingers. Often have we gone to him, red-hot with our own hopeful sorrows, railing on the rose leaves in our princely bed of life, and he would patiently give ear and wisely counsel; and it was only upon some return of our own thoughts that we were reminded what manner of man this was to whom we disembosomed: a man, by his own fault, ruined; shut out of the garden of his gifts; his whole city of hope both ploughed and salted; silently awaiting the deliverer. Then something took us by the throat; and to see him there, so gentle, patient, brave, and pious, oppressed but not cast down, sorrow was so swallowed up in admiration that we could not dare to pity him. Even if the old fault flashed out again, it but awoke our wonder that, in that lost battle, he should have still the energy to fight. He had gone to ruin with a kind of kingly abandon, like one who condescended; but once ruined, with the lights all out, he fought as for a kingdom. Most men, finding themselves the authors of their own disgrace, rail the louder against God or destiny. Most men, when they repent, oblige their friends to share the bitterness of that repentance. But he had held an inquest and passed sentence: *mene, mene;* and condemned himself to smiling silence. He had given trouble enough; had earned misfortune amply, and foregone the right to murmur.

Thus was our old comrade, like Samson, careless in his days of strength; but on the coming of adversity, and when that strength was gone that had betrayed him,—"for our strength is weakness,"— he began to blossom and bring forth. Well, now, he is out of the fight: the burden that he bore thrown down before the great deliverer. We —

> "in the vast cathedral leave him;
> God accept him,
> Christ receive him!"

THE DOOR OF IMMORTALITY

IF WE go now and look on these innumerable epitaphs, the pathos and the irony are strangely fled. They do not stand merely to the dead, these foolish monuments; they are pillars and legends set up to glorify the difficult but not desperate life of man. This ground is hallowed by the heroes of defeat.

I see the indifferent pass before my friend's last resting place; pause, with a shrug of pity, marveling that so rich an argosy had sunk. A pity, now that he is done with suffering,—a pity most uncalled for, and an ignorant wonder. Before those who loved him, his memory shines like a reproach; they honor him for silent lessons; they cherish his example; and in what remains before them of their toil, fear to be unworthy of the dead. For this proud man was one of those who prospered in the valley of humiliation;—of whom Bunyan wrote that, "Though Christian had the hard hap to meet in the valley with Apollyon, yet I must tell you that in former times men have met with angels here; have found pearls here; and have in this place found the words of life."

Complete. From «Memories and Portraits.»

BALFOUR STEWART

(1828–1887)

ALFOUR STEWART, a noted essayist on scientific subjects, was born at Edinburgh, Scotland, November 1st, 1828. After studying at St. Andrews and Edinburgh Universities, he went to Australia, remaining there seven years and returning in 1853. In 1858 he published his work on "Radiant Heat," and in 1859 became director of Kew Observatory. In 1870 he was appointed professor of Physics at Owens College, Manchester, and in the next three years published "Elementary Lessons in Physics," "An Elementary Treatise on Heat," "Physics Primer," and "The Conservation of Energy." The latter work, no doubt the most important of his life, appeared in 1873. He was joint author with Prof. Tait of "The Unseen Universe," which was published in 1875. He died December 19th, 1887, near Drogheda, Ireland.

THE CONSERVATION OF ENERGY

MATHEMATICIANS inform us that if matter consists of atoms or small parts, which are actuated by forces depending only upon the distances between these parts, and not upon the velocity, then it may be demonstrated that the law of conservation of energy will hold good. Thus we see that conceptions regarding atoms and their forces are allied to conceptions regarding energy. A medium of some sort pervading space seems also necessary to our theory. In fine, a universe composed of atoms, with some sort of medium between them, is to be regarded as the machine, and the laws of energy as the laws of working of this machine. It may be that a theory of atoms of this sort, with a medium between them, is not, after all, the simplest, but we are probably not yet prepared for any more general hypothesis. Now, we have only to look to our own solar system, in order to see on a large scale an illustration of this conception, for there we have the various heavenly bodies attracting one another, with forces depending only on the distances between them, and independent of the velocities; and we have likewise a medium of some sort, in virtue of which radiant energy is conveyed from the sun to the earth. Perhaps we shall not greatly err if we regard a molecule as representing on a small scale something analogous to the solar system, while the various atoms which constitute the molecule may be likened to the various bodies of the solar system. The short historical sketch which we are about to give will embrace, therefore, along with energy, the progress of thought and speculation with respect to atoms, and also with respect to a medium, inasmuch as these subjects are intimately connected with the doctrines of energy.

Heraclitus, who flourished at Ephesus, 500 B. C., declared that fire was the great cause, and that all things were in a perpetual flux. Such an expression will no doubt be regarded as very vague in these days of precise physical statements; and yet it seems clear that Heraclitus must have had a vivid conception of the innate restlessness and energy of the universe, a conception allied in character to and only less precise than that of modern philosophers, who regard matter as essentially dynamical.

Democritus, who was born 470 B. C., was the originator of the doctrine of atoms, a doctrine which, in the hands of John Dalton, has enabled the human mind to lay hold of the laws which regulate chemical changes, as well as to picture to itself what is there taking place. Perhaps there is no doctrine that has nowadays a more intimate connection with the industries of life than this of atoms, and it is probable that no intelligent director of chemical industry among civilized nations fails to picture to his own mind, by means of this doctrine, the inner nature of the changes which he sees with his eyes. Now, it is a curious circumstance that Bacon should have lighted upon this very doctrine of atoms, in order to point one of his philosophical morals.

"Nor is it less an evil," says he, "that in their philosophies and contemplations men spend their labor in investigating and treating of the first principles of things, and the extreme limits of nature, when all that is useful and of avail in operation is to be found in what is intermediate. Hence it happens that men continue to abstract Nature till they arrive at potential and unformed matter; and again they continue to divide Nature, until they have arrived at the atom; things which, even if true, can be of little use in helping on the fortunes of men."

Surely we ought to learn a lesson from these remarks of the great father of experimental science, and be very cautious before we dismiss any branch of knowledge or train of thought as essentially unprofitable.

As regards the existence of a medium, it is remarked by Whewell that the Ancients also caught a glimpse of the idea of a medium, by which the qualities of bodies, as colors and sounds, are perceived, and he quotes the following from Aristotle: "In a void there could be no difference of up and down; for, as in nothing there are no differences, so there are none in a privation or negation."

Upon this the historian of science remarks, "It is easily seen that such a mode of reasoning elevates the familiar forms of language, and the intellectual connections of terms, to a supremacy over facts."

Nevertheless, may it not be replied that our conceptions of matter are deduced from the familiar experience, that certain portions of space affect us in a certain manner; and, consequently, are we not entitled to say there must be something where we experience the difference of up or down? Is there, after all, a very great difference between this argument and that of modern physicists in favor of a plenum, who tell us that matter cannot act where it is not?

Aristotle seems also to have entertained the idea that light is not any body, or the emanation of any body (for that, he says, would be a kind of body), and that therefore light is an energy or act.

These quotations render it evident that the Ancients had, in some way, grasped the idea of the essential unrest and energy of things. They had also the idea of small particles or atoms, and, finally, of a medium of some sort. And yet these ideas were not prolific — they gave rise to nothing new.

Now, while the historian of science is unquestionably right in his criticism of the Ancients, that their ideas were not distinct and appropriate to the facts, yet we have seen that they were not wholly ignorant of the most profound and deeply-seated principles of the material universe. In the great hymn chanted by Nature, the fundamental notes were early heard, but yet it required long centuries of patient waiting for the practiced ear of the skilled musician to appreciate the mighty harmony aright. Or, perhaps, the attempts of the Ancients were as the sketches of a child who just contrives to exhibit, in a rude way, the leading outlines of a building; while the conceptions of the practiced physicist are more allied to those of the architect, or at least, of one who has realized, to some extent, the architect's views.

The Ancients possessed great genius and intellectual power, but they were deficient in physical conceptions, and, in consequence, their ideas were not prolific. It cannot indeed be said that we of the present age are deficient in such conceptions; nevertheless, it may be questioned whether there is not a tendency to rush into the opposite extreme, and to work physical conceptions to an excess. Let us be cautious that in avoiding Scylla we do not rush into Charybdis. For the universe has more than one point of view, and there are possibly regions which will not yield their treasures to the most determined physicists, armed only with kilograms and metres and standard clocks.

In modern times Descartes, author of the vertical hypothesis, necessarily presupposed the existence of a medium in interplanetary spaces, but, on the other hand, he was one of the originators of that idea which regards light as a series of particles shot out from a luminous body. Newton likewise conceived the existence of a medium, although he became an advocate of the theory of emission. It is to Huyghens that the credit belongs of having first conceived the undulatory theory of light with sufficient distinctness to account for double refraction. After him, Young, Fresnel, and their followers, have greatly developed the theory, enabling it to account for the most complicated and wonderful phenomena.

With regard to the nature of heat, Bacon, whatever may be thought of his arguments, seems clearly to have recognized it as a species of motion. He says, "From these instances, viewed together and individually, the nature of which heat is the limitation seems to be motion"; and again he says, "But when we say of motion that it stands in the place of a genus to heat, we mean to convey, not that heat generates motion or motion heat (although even both may be true in some cases), but that essential heat is motion and nothing else."

Nevertheless it required nearly three centuries before the true theory of heat was sufficiently rooted to develop into a productive hypothesis.

In a previous chapter we have already detailed the labors in respect of heat of Davy, Rumford, and Joule. Galileo and Newton, if they did not grasp the dynamical nature of heat, had yet a clear conception of the functions of a machine. The former saw that what we gain in power we lose in space; while the latter went further, and saw that a machine, if left to itself, is strictly limited in the amount of work which it can accomplish, although its energy may vary from that of motion to that of position, and back again, according to the geometric laws of the machine.

There can, we think, be no question that the great development of industrial operations in the present age has indirectly furthered our conceptions regarding work. Humanity invariably strives to escape as much as possible from hard work. In the days of old those who had the power got slaves to work for them; but even then the master had to give some kind of equivalent for the work done. For at the very lowest a slave is a machine, and must be fed, and is moreover apt to prove a very troublesome machine if not properly dealt with. The great improvements in the steam engine, introduced by Watt, have done as much, perhaps, as the abolition of slavery to benefit the workingman. The hard work of the world has been put upon iron shoulders, that do not smart; and, in consequence, we have had an immense extension of industry, and a great amelioration in the position of the lower classes of mankind. But if we have transferred our hard work to machines, it is necessary to know how to question a machine — how to say to it, At what rate can you labor? How much work can you turn out in a day? It is necessary, in fact, to have the clearest possible idea of what work is.

Our readers will see from all this that men are not likely to err in their method of measuring work. The principles of measurement have been stamped as it were with a brand into the very heart and brain of humanity. To the employer of machinery or of human labor, a false method of measuring work simply means ruin; he is likely, therefore, to take the greatest possible pains to arrive at accuracy in his determination.

Now, amid the crowd of workers smarting from the curse of labor, there rises up every now and then an enthusiast, who seeks to escape by means of an artifice from this insupportable tyranny of work. Why not construct a machine that will go on giving you work without limit, without the necessity of being fed in any way. Nature must have some weak point in her armor; there must surely be some way of getting round her; she is only tyrannous on the surface, and in order to stimulate our ingenuity, but will yield with pleasure to the persistence of genius.

Now, what can the man of science say to such an enthusiast? He cannot tell him that he is intimately acquainted with all the forces of Nature, and can prove that perpetual motion is impossible; for, in truth, he knows very little of these forces. But he does think that he has entered into the spirit and design of Nature, and therefore he denies at once the possibility of such a machine. But he denies it intelligently, and works out this denial of his into a theory which enables him to discover numerous and valuable relations between the properties of matter — produces, in fact, the laws of energy and the great principle of conservation.

We have thus endeavored to give a short sketch of the history of energy, including its allied problems, up to the dawn of the strictly scientific period. We have seen that the unfruitfulness of the earlier views was due to a want of scientific clearness in the conceptions entertained, and we have now to say a few words regarding the theory of conservation.

Here also the way was pointed out by two philosophers, namely, Grove in this country, and Mayer on the continent, who showed certain relations between the various forms of energy; the name of Seguin ought likewise to be mentioned. Nevertheless, to Joule belongs the honor of establishing the theory on an incontrovertible basis; for, indeed, this is pre-eminently a case where speculation has to be tested by unimpeachable experimental evidence. Here the magnitude of the principle is so vast, and its importance is so great, that it requires the strong fire of genius, joined to the patient labors of the scientific experimentalist, to forge the rough ore into a good weapon that will cleave its way through all obstacles into the very citadel of Nature, and into her most secret recesses.

Following closely upon the labors of Joule, we have those of William and James Thomson, Helmholtz, Rankine, Clausius, Tait, Andrews, Maxwell, who, along with many others, have advanced the subject; and while Joule gave his chief attention to the laws which regulate the transmutation of mechanical energy into heat, Thomson, Rankine, and Clausius gave theirs to the converse problem, or that which relates to the transmutation of heat into mechanical energy. Thomson, especially, has pushed forward so resolutely from this point of view that he has succeeded in grasping a principle scarcely inferior in importance to that of the conservation of energy itself, and of this principle it behooves us now to speak.

Joule, we have said, proved the law according to which work may be changed into heat; and Thomson and others, that according to which heat may be changed into work. Now, it occurred to Thomson that there was a very important and significant difference between these two laws, consisting in the fact that, while you can with the greatest ease transform work into heat, you can by no method in your power transform all the heat back again into work. In fact, the process is not a reversible one; and the consequence is that the mechanical energy of the universe is becoming every day more and more changed into heat.

It is easily seen that if the process were reversible, one form of a perpetual motion would not be impossible. For, without attempting to create energy by a machine, all that would be needed for a perpetual motion would be the means of utilizing the vast stores of heat that lie in all the substances around us, and converting them into work. The work would, no doubt, by means of friction and otherwise, be ultimately reconverted into heat; but if the process be reversible, the heat could again be converted into work, and so on forever. But the irreversibility of the process puts a stop to all this. In fact, I may convince myself by rubbing a metal button on a piece of wood how easily work can be converted into heat, while the mind completely fails to suggest any method by which this heat can be reconverted into work.

Now, if this process goes on, and always in one direction, there can be no doubt about the issue. The mechanical energy of the universe will be more and more transformed into universally diffused heat, until the universe will no longer be a fit abode for living beings. . . .

Although, therefore, in a strictly mechanical sense, there is a conservation of energy, yet, as regards usefulness or fitness for living beings, the energy of the universe is in process of deterioration. Universally diffused heat forms what we may call the great waste heap of the universe, and this is growing larger year by year. At present it does not sensibly obtrude itself, but who knows that the time may not arrive when we shall be practically conscious of its growing bigness?

It will be seen that we have regarded the universe, not as a collection of matter, but rather as an energetic agent,—in fact,

as a lamp.   Now, it has been well pointed out by Thomson, that,
looked at in this light, the universe is a system that had a beginning and must have an end; for a process of degradation cannot be eternal.   If we could view the universe as a candle not
lit, then it is perhaps conceivable to regard it as having been
always in existence; but if we regard it rather as a candle that
has been lit, we become absolutely certain that it cannot have
been burning from eternity, and that a time will come when it
will cease to burn.   We are led to look to a beginning in which
the particles of matter were in a diffuse chaotic state, but endowed with the power of gravitation, and we are led to look
to an end in which the whole universe will be one equally heated
inert mass, and from which everything like life or motion or
beauty will have utterly gone away.

From « The Conservation of Energy. »

SNORRE STURLESON

(c. 1179–1241)

NORRE STURLESON, the author of the "Heimskringla" and the "Younger," or "Prose Edda," is the best representative of the early prose literature native to Northern Europe. In his writings, and especially in the "Younger Edda," we see the first beginnings of the coherent development of the Teutonic prose essay as distinct from the Latin. In the change of form which takes place between the "Elder" and the "Younger Edda," we see how the essay originated as a vehicle for the traditional thought of primitive peoples. The "Elder Edda" stands for the expression of religious myth, or primitive science, philosophy, and ethics, in its natural form — the poetical. In the "Younger Edda," a later age translates the archaic poetical form into the first phase of the essay — a prose paraphrase of the verse, relieved by frequent quotations from the verse itself. Sometimes these quotations are exact; oftener they are paraphrased to please the taste of the later editor. We see in Persian literature the same phenomenon which is presented by the far North. The parallel is so close that if we were wholly ignorant of the laws of the parallel development of mind under pressure of related circumstances, we would be forced to the erroneous conclusion that the early Icelandic and the classical Persian writers had necessarily a common model, or were governed by some common tradition of style. The Homeric tradition undoubtedly influenced Iceland as it did Persia; but beyond the scope of its influence, we can see the effects of the natural laws of the mind working out in the literature of both countries. Comparisons of this kind have only to be made sufficiently comprehensive to force the conclusion that in all countries style itself is a product of natural causes, with an underlying unity governing in all its diversities.

Snorre (spelled also "Snorri," and "Snorro"; "Sturlason," "Sturleson," and "Sturluson") was born at Hvamm in Iceland in 1178 or 1179, He was a man of the highest Icelandic culture at a time when the literary culture of Iceland was the most remarkable native growth of Northern Europe. He visited Norway twice and was in favor at the Norwegian court. In his own country he served as "lawman," as well as the historian, poet, and prophet of his people. He met the usual reward of prophets at the last, for his great talents and his patriotism necessarily forced him into political leadership, and as he took sides against the Norwegian court influence, his assassination was instigated as a measure of court policy, and he was killed September 23d, 1241, by his own kinsman and friends. He is, in his own right, one of the greatest men produced by the primitive culture of Northern Europe. As a historian he has been compared to Thucydides, and in the "Younger Edda" he has left an immortal work of genius. His knowledge of poetical composition belongs to a time when the art of poetry was still consciously a part of the art of music, and what he has written on the subject has a high value as material for scientific investigation in the comparative study of the "Iliad," the "Odyssey," and the early poetry of Palestine and Persia. The most important philological discoveries of the twentieth century are likely to be made along lines of research which will show how great is the scientific importance of the unconsidered knowledge in which this thirteenth-century poet and philosopher was superior to the nineteenth.

                                                              W. V. B.

GEFJON'S PLOUGHING

KING GYLFI ruled over the land which is now called Svithiod (Sweden). It is related of him that he once gave a wayfaring woman, as a recompense for her having diverted him, as much land in his realm as she could plough with four oxen in a day and a night. This woman was, however, of the race of the Æsir, and was called Gefjon. She took four oxen from the North, out of Jotunheim (but they were the sons she had had with a giant), and set them before a plow. Now the plow made such deep furrows that it tore up the land, which the oxen drew westward out to sea until they came to a sound. There Gefjon fixed the land, and called it Saelund. And the place where the land had stood became water, and formed a lake which is now called "The Water" (Laugur), and the inlets of this lake correspond exactly with the headlands of Saelund. As Skald Bragi the Old saith:—

> "Gefjon drew from Gylfi,
>   Rich in stored-up treasure,
> The land she joined to Denmark.
>   Four heads and eight eyes bearing,
> While hot sweat trickled down them,
>   The oxen dragged the reft mass
> That formed this winsome island."

GYLFI'S JOURNEY TO ASGARD

K ING GYLFI was renowned for his wisdom and skill in magic. He beheld with astonishment that whatever the Æsir willed took place; and was at a loss whether to attribute their success to the superiority of their natural abilities, or to a power imparted to them by the mighty gods whom they worshiped. To be satisfied in this particular, he resolved to go to Asgard, and, taking upon himself the likeness of an old man, set out on his journey. But the Æsir, being too well skilled in divination not to foresee his design, prepared to receive him with various illusions. On entering the city Gylfi saw a very lofty mansion, the roof of which, as far as his eye could reach, was covered with golden shields. Thiodolf of Hvina thus alludes to Valhalla being roofed with shields.

> " Warriors all careworn,
> (Stones had poured upon them),
> On their backs let glisten
> Valhalla's golden shingles."

At the entrance of the mansion Gylfi saw a man who amused himself by tossing seven small swords in the air, and catching them as they fell, one after the other. This person having asked his name, Gylfi said that he was called Gangler, and that he came from a long journey, and begged for a night's lodging. He asked, in his turn, to whom this mansion belonged. The other told him that it belonged to their king, and added, " But I will lead thee to him, and thou shalt thyself ask him his name." So saying, he entered the hall, and as Gylfi followed the door banged to behind him. He there saw many stately rooms crowded with people, some playing, some drinking, and others fighting with various weapons. Gangler, seeing a multitude of things, the meaning of which he could not comprehend, softly pronounced the following verse (from the " Hava-mal ") : —

> " Scan every gate
> Ere thou go on,
> With greatest caution;
> For hard to say 'tis
> Where foes are sitting
> In this fair mansion."

He afterwards beheld three thrones raised one above another, with a man sitting on each of them. Upon his asking what the names of these lords might be, his guide answered: "He who sitteth on the lowest throne is a king; his name is Har (the High or Lofty One); the second is Jafnhar (*i. e.*, equal to the High); but he who sitteth on the high throne is called Thridi (the Third)." Har, perceiving the stranger, asked him what his errand was, adding that he should be welcome to eat and drink without cost, as were all those who remained in Hava Hall. Gangler said he desired first to ascertain whether there was any person present renowned for his wisdom.

"If thou art not the most knowing," replied Har, "I fear thou wilt hardly return safe. But go, stand there below, and propose thy questions; here sits one who will be able to answer them."

OF THE SUPREME DEITY

GANGLER thus began his discourse: — "Who is the first or eldest of the gods?"

"In our language," replied Har, "he is called Alfadir (All-Father, or the Father of All); but in the old Asgard he had twelve names."

"Where is this god?" said Gangler; "What is his power, and what hath he done to display his glory?"

"He liveth," replied Har, "from all ages, he governeth all realms, and swayeth all things great and small."

"He hath formed," added Jafnhar, "heaven and earth, and the air, and all things thereunto belonging."

"And what is more," continued Thridi, "he hath made man, and given him a soul which shall live and never perish though the body shall have moldered away, or have been burned to ashes. And all that are righteous shall dwell with him in the place called Gimli, or Vingolf; but the wicked shall go to Hel, and thence to Niflhel, which is below, in the ninth world."

"And where did this god remain before he made heaven and earth?" asked Gangler.

"He was then," replied Har, "with the Hrimthursar."

OF THE PRIMORDIAL STATE OF THE UNIVERSE

"B UT with what did he begin, or what was the beginning of things?" demanded Gangler.

"Hear," replied Har, "what is said in the 'Völuspá':—

> "''Twas time's first dawn,
> When naught yet was,
> Nor sand nor sea,
> Nor cooling wave;
> Earth was not there
> Nor heaven above.
> Naught save a void
> And yawning gulf.
> But verdure none.'"

"Many ages before the earth was made," added Jafnhar, "was Niflheim formed, in the middle of which lies the spring called Hvergelmir, from which flow twelve rivers, Gjoll being the nearest to the gate of the abode of Death."

"But, first of all," continued Thridi, "there was in the southern region (sphere) the world called Muspell. It is a world too luminous and glowing to be entered by those who are not indigenous there. He who sitteth on its borders (or the land's end) to guard it is named Surtur. In his hand he beareth a flaming falchion, and at the end of the world shall issue forth to combat, and shall vanquish all the gods, and consume the universe with fire. As it is said in the 'Völuspá':—

> "'Surtur from the south wends
> With seething fire
> The falchion of the mighty one
> A sunlight flameth.
> Mountains together dash,
> Giants headlong rush,
> Men tread the paths to Hel,
> And Heaven in twain is rent.'"

OF THE WAY THAT LEADS TO HEAVEN

"I MUST now ask," said Gangler, "which is the path leading from earth to heaven."

"That is a senseless question," replied Har, with a smile of derision. "Hast thou not been told that the gods made a bridge from earth to heaven, and called it Bifröst? Thou must surely have seen it; but, perhaps, thou callest it the rainbow. It is of three hues, and is constructed with more art than any other work. But, strong though it be, it will be broken to pieces when the sons of Muspell, after having traversed great rivers, shall ride over it."

"Methinks," said Gangler, "the gods could not have been in earnest to erect a bridge so liable to be broken down, since it is in their power to make whatever they please."

"The gods," replied Har, "are not to be blamed on that account; Bifröst is of itself a very good bridge, but there is nothing in nature that can hope to make resistance when the sons of Muspell sally forth to the great combat."

"What did All-Father do after Asgard was made?" demanded Gangler.

"In the beginning," answered Har, "he appointed rulers, and bade them judge with him the fate of men, and regulate the government of the celestial city. They met for this purpose in a place called Idavoll, which is in the centre of the divine abode. Their first work was to erect a court or hall wherein are twelve seats for themselves, besides the throne which is occupied by All-Father. This hall is the largest and most magnificent in the universe, being resplendent on all sides, both within and without, with the finest gold. Its name is Gladsheim. They also erected another hall for the sanctuary of the goddesses. It is a very fair structure, and called by men Vingolf. Lastly they built a smithy, and furnished it with hammers, tongs, and anvils, and with these made all the other requisite instruments, with which they worked in metal, stone, and wood, and composed so large a quantity of the metal called gold that they made all their movables of it. Hence that age was named the Golden Age. This was the age that lasted until the arrival of the women out of Jotunheim, who corrupted it.

"Then the gods, seating themselves upon their thrones, distributed justice, and bethought them how the dwarfs had been bred in the mold of the earth, just as worms are in a dead body. It was, in fact, in Ymir's flesh that the dwarf's were engendered, and began to move and live. At first they were only maggots, but by the will of the gods they at length partook both of human shape and understanding, although they always dwell in rocks and caverns.

"Modsognir and Durin are the principal ones. As it is said in the 'Völuspá':—

"'Then went the rulers there,
All gods most holy,
To their seats aloft,
And counsel together took,
Who should of dwarfs
The race then fashion
From the livid bones
And blood of the giant.
Modsognir, chief
Of the dwarfish race,
And Durin too
Were then created.
And like to men
Dwarfs in the earth
Were formed in numbers
As Durin ordered.'"

OF THE ASH YGGDRASILL, MIMIR'S WELL, AND THE NORNS OR DESTINIES

"WHERE," asked Gangler, "is the chief or holiest seat of the gods?"

"It is under the ash Yggdrasill," replied Har, "where the gods assemble every day in council."

"What is there remarkable in regard to that place?" said Gangler.

"That ash," answered Jafnhar, "is the greatest and best of all trees. Its branches spread over the whole world, and even reach above heaven. It has three roots very wide asunder. One of them extends to the Æsir, another to the Frost-giants in that very place where was formerly Ginnungagap, and the third stands over Niflheim, and under this root, which is constantly gnawed by Nidhogg, is Hvergelmir. But under the root that stretches out towards the Frost-giants there is Mimir's well, in which wisdom and wit lie hidden. The owner of this well is called Mimir. He is full of wisdom, because he drinks the waters of the well from the horn Gjoll every morning. One day All-Father came and begged a draught of this water, which he obtained, but was obliged to leave one of his eyes as a pledge for it. As it is said in the 'Völuspá':—

> "'All know I, Odin!
> How thou hiddest thine eye
> In Mimir's well-spring
> Of limpid water.
> Mead quaffs Mimir
> Each morn from the pledge
> Valfadir left him.
> Conceive ye this or not?'"

"The third root of the ash is in heaven, and under it is the holy Urdar-fount. 'Tis here that the gods sit in judgment. Every day they ride up hither on horseback over Bifröst, which is called the Æsir Bridge. These are the names of the horses of the Æsir. Sleipnir is the best of them; he has eight legs, and belongs to Odin. The others are Gladr, Gyllir, Glaer, Skeidbrimir, Silfrintoppr, Synir, Gils, Falhofnir, Gulltoppr, and Lettfeti. Baldur's horse was burned with his master's body. As for Thor, he goes on foot, and is obliged every day to wade the rivers called Kormt and Œrmt, and two others called Kerlaung.

"Through these shall Thor wade every day, as he fares to the doomstead under Yggdrasill's ash, else the Æsir Bridge would be in flames, and boiling hot would become the holy waters."

"But tell me," said Gangler, "does fire burn over Bifröst?"

"That," replied Har, "which thou seest red in the bow is burning fire; for the Frost-giants and the Mountain-giants would go up to heaven by that bridge if it were easy for every one to walk over it. There are in heaven many goodly homesteads, and none without a celestial ward. Near the fountain, which is under the ash, stands a very beauteous dwelling, out of which go three maidens, named Urd, Verandi, and Skuld. These maidens fix the lifetime of all men, and are called Norns. But there are, indeed, many other Norns, for, when a man is born, there is a Norn to determine his fate. Some are known to be of heavenly origin, but others belong to the races of the elves and dwarfs; as it is said:—

"'Methinks the Norns were born far asunder, for they are not of the same race. Some belong to the Æsir, some to the Elves, and some are Dvalin's daughters.'"

"But if these Norns dispense the destinies of men," said Gangler, "they are, methinks, very unequal in their distribution; for some men are fortunate and wealthy, others acquire neither riches nor honors, some live to a good old age, while others are cut off in their prime."

"The Norns," replied Har, "who are of a good origin are good themselves, and dispense good destinies. But those men to whom misfortunes happen ought to ascribe them to the evil Norns."

OF THE NORNS AND THE URDAR-FOUNT

"WHAT more wonders hast thou to tell me," said Gangler, "concerning the ash?"

"What I have further to say respecting it," replied Har, "is, that there is an eagle perched upon its branches who knows many things: between his eyes sits the hawk called Vedurfolnir. The squirrel named Ratatosk runs up and down the ash, and seeks to cause strife between the eagle and Nidhogg. Four harts run across the branches of the tree, and bite the buds. They are called Dainn, Dvalinn, Duneyr, and Durathror. But there are so many snakes with Nidhogg in Hvergelmir that no tongue can recount them. As it is said: —

> "'Yggdrasill's ash
> More hardship bears
> Than men imagine;
> The hart bites above,
> At the sides it rots,
> Below gnaws Nidhogg.'

'And again: —

> "'More serpents lie
> Under Yggdrasill's ash
> Than simpletons think of;
> Goinn and Moinn,
> The sons of Grafvitnir,
> Grabak and Grafjollud,
> Ofnir and Svafnir,
> Must for aye, methinks,
> Gnaw the roots of that tree.'

"It is also said that the Norns who dwell by the Urdar-fount draw every day water from the spring, and with it and the clay that lies around the fount sprinkle the ash, in order that its branches may not rot and wither away. This water is so holy that everything placed in the spring becomes as white as the film within an eggshell. As it is said in the 'Völuspá': —

> "'An ash know I standing,
> Named Yggdrasill,
> A stately tree sprinkled
> With water the purest;
> Thence come the dewdrops
> That fall in the dales;
> Ever blooming, it stands
> O'er the Urdar-fount.'

"The dew that falls thence on the earth men call honeydew. and it is the food of the bees. Two fowls are fed in the Urdar-fount; they are called swans, and from them are descended all the birds of this species."

OF LOKI AND HIS PROGENY

"THERE is another deity," continued Har, "reckoned in the number of the Æsir, whom some call the calumniator of the gods, the contriver of all fraud and mischief, and the disgrace of gods and men. His name is Loki or Loptur. He is the son of the giant Farbauti. His mother is Laufey or Nal; his brothers are Byleist and Helblindi. Loki is handsome and well made, but of a very fickle mood, and most evil disposition. He surpasses all beings in those arts called Cunning and Perfidy. Many a time has he exposed the gods to very great perils, and often extricated them again by his artifices. His wife is called Siguna, and their son Nari."

OF THE JOYS OF VALHALLA

"IF IT be as thou hast told me," said Gangler, "that all men who have fallen in fight since the beginning of the world are gone to Odin, in Valhalla, what has he to give them to eat, for methinks there must be a great crowd there?"

"What thou sayest is quite true," replied Har, "the crowd there is indeed great, but great though it be, it will still increase, and will be thought too little when the wolf cometh. But however great the band of men in Valhalla may be, the flesh of the boar Sæhrimnir will more than suffice for their sustenance. For although this boar is sodden every morning, he becomes whole again every night. But there are few, methinks, who are wise enough to give thee, in this respect, a satisfactory answer to thy question. The cook is called Andhrimnir, and the kettle Eldhrimnir. As it is said: 'Andhrimnir cooks in Eldhrimnir, Sæhrimnir.' 'Tis the best of flesh, though few know how much is required for the Einherjar."

"But has Odin," said Gangler, "the same food as the heroes?"

"Odin," replied Har, "gives the meat that is set before him to two wolves, called Geri and Freki, for he himself stands in no need of food. Wine is for him both meat and drink. As it is said:—

> "'Geri and Freki
> Feedeth the warfaring
> Famed Father of hosts,
> For 'tis with wine only
> That Odin, in arms renowned,
> Is nourished for aye.'

"Two ravens sit on Odin's shoulders and whisper in his ear the tidings and events they have heard and witnessed. They are called Hugin and Munin. He sends them out at dawn of day to fly over the whole world, and they return at eve towards mealtime. Hence it is that Odin knows so many things, and is called the Raven's God. As it is said:—

> "'Hugin and Munin
> Each dawn take their flight
> Earth's fields over.
> I fear me for Hugin,
> Lest he come not back,
> But much more for Munin.'"

All the foregoing are from Bishop Percy's translation of the "Younger Edda."

JONATHAN SWIFT

(1667–1745)

ONATHAN SWIFT, Dean of St. Patrick's, and the most remarkable of all satirists, was born at Dublin, November 30th, 1667. In 1688, after taking his degree *speciali gratia* at Trinity College, Dublin, he went to England and became secretary to Sir William Temple, serving in this position for about a year, after which he returned to Ireland. He did not remain very long, however, for in 1696, after taking a degree at Oxford and orders in the English Church, he returned to Sir William Temple's service and remained in it until January, 1699. It was during this period that he first became attached to Esther Johnson, the "Stella" to whom it is said that he was privately married in 1716. His "Tale of a Tub" and "Battle of the Books" both appeared in 1704. "Gulliver's Travels" his greatest work,—the greatest satire ever written,—did not appear until 1726, when a long list of essays, pamphlets, poems, and miscellanies of almost every conceivable description, including the celebrated Drapier letters, had already made him one of the foremost men of letters of his generation. All his other works are so far eclipsed by "Gulliver's Travels" that, full of his genius as they are, they might be completely forgotten without jeopardizing his place in literature. He was associated intimately with Steele, Addison, Pope, Congreve, Gay, and other noted writers of his day. All of them he surpassed in force, and had it not been impaired by bitterness, it would have made him the most effective prose writer of modern times. The same bitterness, however, which finally brought him insanity and death, shows in his best work to such an extent that he fails most in persuading where he succeeds best in compelling admiration. In his political affiliations from 1710 to his death (October 19th, 1745) he was ostensibly a Tory, but he was really the greatest Radical of his day. His "Argument against Abolishing Christianity" and the frightful irony of his proposal that the starving peasantry of Ireland should relieve the English government of embarrassment by eating their own children, suggest the "cruel indignation" which almost robbed him of his reason when he saw the enormous injustices to which the helpless classes of the eighteenth century were subjected. "*Ubi sæva indignatio ulterius cor lacerare nequit*" is part of the noble epitaph over the tomb in St. Patrick's Cathedral where his body was laid to rest in the same coffin with that of "Stella." He wrote the epitaph himself:—"Here lies the body of Jonathan Swift, S. T. P., Dean of this Cathedral — where cruel indignation can lacerate his heart no longer!" The lines are an autobiography. They tell more of the reality of his life than any one else can ever put into words.

THE ART OF POLITICAL LYING

I AM prevailed on, through the importunity of friends, to interrupt the scheme I had begun in my last paper, by an essay upon the Art of Political Lying. We are told the devil is the father of lies, and was a liar from the beginning; so that, beyond contradiction, the invention is old: and, which is more, his first essay of it was purely political, employed in undermining the authority of his prince, and seducing a third part of the subjects from their obedience: for which he was driven down from heaven, where (as Milton expresses it) he had been viceroy of a great western province; and forced to exercise his talent in inferior regions among other fallen spirits, poor or deluded men, whom he still daily tempts to his own sin, and will ever do so, till he be chained in the bottomless pit.

But although the devil be the father of lies, he seems, like other great inventors, to have lost much of his reputation, by the continual improvements that have been made upon him.

Who first reduced lying into an art, and adapted it to politics, is not so clear from history, although I have made some diligent inquiries. I shall therefore consider it only according to the modern system, as it has been cultivated these twenty years past in the southern part of our own island.

The poets tell us, that after the giants were overthrown by the gods, the earth in revenge produced her last offspring which was Fame. And the fable is thus interpreted: that when tumults and seditions are quieted, rumors and false reports are plentifully spread through a nation. So that, by this account, lying is the last relief of a routed, earth-born, rebellious party in a state. But here the Moderns have made great additions, applying this art to the gaining of power and preserving it, as well as revenging themselves after they have lost it; as the same instruments are made use of by animals to feed themselves when they are hungry, and to bite those that tread upon them.

But the same genealogy cannot always be admitted for political lying; I shall therefore desire to refine upon it, by adding some circumstances of its birth and parents. A political lie is sometimes born out of a discarded statesman's head, and thence delivered to be nursed and dandled by the rabble. Sometimes it is produced a monster, and licked into shape; at other times it comes into the world completely formed, and is spoiled in the licking. It is often born an infant in the regular way, and requires time to mature it; and often it sees the light in its full growth, but dwindles away by degrees. Sometimes it is of noble birth; and sometimes the spawn of a stockjobber. Here it screams aloud at the opening of the womb; and there it is delivered with a whisper. I know a lie that now disturbs half the kingdom with its noise, which, although too proud and great at present to own its parents, I can remember its whisperhood. To conclude the nativity of this monster; when it comes into the world without a sting, it is stillborn; and whenever it loses its sting, it dies.

No wonder if an infant so miraculous in its birth should be destined for great adventures; and accordingly we see it hath been the guardian spirit of a prevailing party for almost twenty years. It can conquer kingdoms without fighting, and sometimes with the loss of a battle. It gives and resumes employments; can sink a mountain to a molehill, and raise a molehill to a mountain; hath presided for many years at committees of elections; can wash a blackmoor white; make a saint of an atheist, and a patriot of a profligate; can furnish foreign ministers with intelligence and raise or let fall the credit of the nation. This goddess flies with a huge looking-glass in her hands, to dazzle the crowd, and make them see, according as she turns it, their ruin in their interest, and their interest in their ruin. In this glass you will behold your best friends, clad in coats powdered with fleurs-de-lis, and triple crowns; their girdles hung round with chains, and beads, and wooden shoes; and your worst enemies adorned with the ensigns of liberty, property, indulgence, moderation, and a cornucopia in their hands. Her large wings, like those of a flying fish, are of no use but while they are moist; she therefore dips them in mud, and soaring aloft scatters it in the eyes of the multitude, flying with great swiftness; but at every turn is forced to stoop in dirty ways for new supplies.

I have been sometimes thinking, if a man had the art of the second sight for seeing lies, as they have in Scotland for seeing spirits, how admirably he might entertain himself in this town, by observing the different shapes, sizes, and colors of those swarms of lies which buzz about the heads of some people, like flies about a horse's ears in summer; or those legions hovering every afternoon in Exchange alley, enough to darken the air; or over a club of discontented grandees, and thence sent down in cargoes to be scattered at elections.

There is one essential point wherein a political liar differs from others of the faculty, that he ought to have but a short memory, which is necessary, according to the various occasions he meets with every hour of differing from himself, and swearing to both sides of a contradiction, as he finds the persons disposed with whom he hath to deal. In describing the virtues and vices of mankind, it is convenient, upon every article, to have some eminent person in our eye, from whom we copy our description. I have strictly observed this rule, and my imagination this minute represents before me a certain great man famous for this talent, to the constant practice of which he owes his twenty years' reputation of the most skillful head in England, for the management of nice affairs. The superiority of his genius consists in nothing else but an inexhaustible fund of political lies, which he plentifully distributes every minute he speaks, and by an unparalleled generosity forgets, and consequently contradicts, the next half hour. He never yet considered whether any proposition were true or false, but whether it were convenient for the present minute or company to affirm or deny it; so that if you think fit to refine upon him, by interpreting everything he says, as we do dreams, by the contrary, you are still to seek, and will find yourself equally deceived whether you believe or not; the only remedy is to suppose that you have heard some inarticulate sounds, without any meaning at all; and besides, that will take off the horror you might be apt to conceive at the oaths, wherewith he perpetually tags both ends of every proposition; although, at the same time, I think he cannot with any justice be taxed with perjury, when he invokes God and Christ, because he hath often fairly given public notice to the world that he believes in neither.

Some people may think that such an accomplishment as this can be of no great use to the owner, or his party, after it has been often practiced, and is become notorious; but they are widely mistaken. Few lies carry the inventor's mark, and the most prostitute enemy to truth may spread a thousand, without being known for the author; besides, as the vilest writer hath his readers, so the greatest liar hath his believers, and it often happens that if a lie be believed only for an hour, it hath done its work, and there is no further occasion for it. Falsehood flies, and truth comes limping after it, so that when men come to be undeceived, it is too late; the jest is over, and the tale hath had its effect: like a man, who hath thought of a good repartee when the discourse is changed, or the company parted; or like a physician, who hath found out an infallible medicine, after the patient is dead.

From the Examiner.

A MEDITATION UPON A BROOMSTICK

(According to the style and manner of the Hon. Robert Boyle's meditations.)

THIS single stick, which you now behold ingloriously lying in that neglected corner, I once knew in a flourishing state in a forest. It was full of sap, full of leaves, and full of boughs; but now in vain does the busy art of man pretend to vie with nature, by tying that withered bundle of twigs to its sapless trunk; it is now at best but the reverse of what it was, a tree turned upside down, the branches on the earth, and the root in the air; it is now handled by every dirty wench, condemned to do her drudgery, and, by a capricious kind of fate, destined to make other things clean, and be nasty itself; at length, worn to the stumps in the service of the maids, it is either thrown out of doors, or condemned to the last use — of kindling a fire. When I beheld this I sighed, and said within myself, "Surely mortal man is a broomstick!" Nature sent him into the world strong and lusty, in a thriving condition, wearing his own hair on his head, the proper branches of this reasoning vegetable, till the ax of intemperance has lopped off his green boughs, and left him a withered trunk; he then flies to art, and puts on a periwig, valuing himself upon an unnatural bundle of hairs, all covered with powder, that never grew on his head; but now should this our broomstick pretend to enter the scene, proud of those birchen spoils it never bore, and all covered with dust, through the sweepings of the finest lady's chamber, we should be apt to ridicule and despise its vanity. Partial judges that we are of our own excellencies, and other men's defaults!

But a broomstick, perhaps you will say, is an emblem of a tree standing on its head; and pray what is a man but a topsy-turvy creature, his animal faculties perpetually mounted on his rational, his head where his heels should be, groveling on the earth? And yet, with all his faults, he sets up to be a universal reformer and corrector of abuses, a remover of grievances; rakes into every slut's corner of nature, bringing hidden corruptions to the light; and raises a mighty dust where there was none before, sharing deeply all the while in the very same pollutions he pretends to sweep away. His last days are spent in slavery to women, and generally the least deserving; till, worn to the stumps, like his brother besom, he is either kicked out of doors, or made use of to kindle flames for others to warm themselves by.

Complete.

THOUGHTS ON VARIOUS SUBJECTS

WE HAVE just enough religion to make us hate, but not enough to make us love one another.

Reflect on things past, as wars, negotiations, factions, etc. We enter so little into those interests, that we wonder how men could possibly be so busy and concerned for things so transitory; look on the present times, we find the same humor, yet wonder not at all.

A wise man endeavors, by considering all circumstances, to make conjectures and form conclusions; but the smallest accident intervening (and in the course of affairs it is impossible to foresee all) does often produce such turns and changes, that at last he is just as much in doubt of events as the most ignorant and inexperienced person.

Positiveness is a good quality for preachers and orators, because he that would obtrude his thoughts and reasons upon a multitude, will convince others the more, as he appears convinced himself.

How is it possible to expect that mankind will take advice, when they will not so much as take warning?

I forget whether Advice be among the lost things which Aristo says are to be found in the moon; that and Time ought to have been there.

No preacher is listened to but Time, which gives us the same train and turn of thought that elder people have tried in vain to put into our heads before.

When we desire or solicit anything, our minds run wholly on the good side or circumstances of it; when it is obtained, our minds run wholly on the bad ones.

In a glasshouse the workmen often fling in a small quantity of fresh coals, which seems to disturb the fire, but very much enlivens it. This seems to allude to a gentle stirring of the passions, that the mind may not languish.

Religion seems to have grown an infant with age, and requires miracles to nurse it, as it had in its infancy.

All fits of pleasure are balanced by an equal degree of pain or languor; it is like spending this year part of the next year's revenue.

The latter part of a wise man's life is taken up in curing the follies, prejudices, and false opinions he had contracted in the former.

Would a writer know how to behave himself with relation to posterity, let him consider in old books what he finds that he is glad to know, and what omissions he most laments.

Whatever the poets pretend, it is plain they give immortality to none but themselves; it is Homer and Virgil we reverence and admire, not Achilles or Æneas. With historians it is quite the contrary; our thoughts are taken up with the actions, persons, and events we read, and we little regard the authors.

When a true genius appears in the world you may know him by this sign, that the dunces are all in confederacy against him.

Men who possess all the advantages of life are in a state where there are many accidents to disorder and discompose, but few to please them.

It is unwise to punish cowards with ignominy, for if they had regarded that they would not have been cowards; death is their proper punishment, because they fear it most.

The greatest inventions were produced in the times of ignorance, as the use of the compass, gunpowder, and printing, and by the dullest nation, as the Germans.

One argument to prove that the common relations of ghosts and spectres are generally false may be drawn from the opinion held that spirits are never seen by more than one person at a time; that is to say, it seldom happens to above one person in a company to be possessed with any high degree of spleen or melancholy.

I am apt to think that, in the Day of Judgment, there will be small allowance given to the wise for their want of morals, nor to the ignorant for their want of faith, because both are without excuse. This renders the advantages equal of ignorance and knowledge. But some scruples in the wise and some vices in the ignorant will perhaps be forgiven upon the strength of temptation to each.

The value of several circumstances in story lessens very much by distance of time, though some minute circumstances are very valuable; and it requires great judgment in a writer to distinguish.

It is grown a word of course for writers to say, " This critical age," as divines say, " This sinful age."

It is pleasant to observe how free the present age is in laying taxes on the next. Future ages shall talk of this; this shall be famous to all posterity. Whereas their time and thoughts will be taken up about present things, as ours are now.

The chameleon, which is said to feed upon nothing but air, hath, of all animals, the nimblest tongue.

When a man is made a spiritual peer he loses his surname; when a temporal, his Christian name.

It is in disputes as in armies, where the weaker side sets up false lights, and makes a great noise, to make the enemy believe them more numerous and strong than they really are.

Some men, under the notions of weeding out prejudices, eradicate virtue, honesty, and religion.

In all well-instituted commonwealths care has been taken to limit men's possessions; which is done for many reasons, and among the rest, for one which perhaps is not often considered: that when bounds are set to men's desires, after they have acquired as much as the laws will permit them, their private interest is at an end, and they have nothing to do but to take care of the public.

There are but three ways for a man to revenge himself of the censure of the world: to despise it, to return the like, or to endeavor to live so as to avoid it. The first of these is usually pretended, the last is almost impossible; the universal practice is for the second.

I never heard a finer piece of satire against lawyers than that of astrologers, when they pretend by rules of art to tell when a suit will end, and whether to the advantage of the plaintiff or defendant; thus making the matter depend entirely upon the influence of the stars, without the least regard to the merits of the cause.

The expression in the Apocrypha about Tobit and his dog following him I have often heard ridiculed, yet Homer has the same words of Telemachus more than once; and Virgil says something like it of Evander. And I take the book of Tobit to be partly poetical.

I have known some men possessed of good qualities which were very serviceable to others, but useless to themselves; like a sundial on the front of a house, to inform the neighbors and passengers, but not the owner within.

If a man would register all his opinions upon love, politics, religion, learning, etc., beginning from his youth and so go on to old age, what a bundle of inconsistencies and contradictions would appear at last!

What they do in heaven we are ignorant of; what they do not we are told expressly: that they neither marry, nor are given in marriage.

It is a miserable thing to live in suspense; it is the life of a spider.

The stoical scheme of supplying our wants by lopping off our desires is like cutting off our feet when we want shoes.

Physicians ought not to give their judgment of religion, for the same reason that butchers are not admitted to be jurors upon life and death.

The reason why so few marriages are happy is because young ladies spend their time in making nets, not in making cages.

If a man will observe as he walks the streets, I believe he will find the merriest countenances in mourning coaches.

Nothing more unqualifies a man to act with prudence than a misfortune that is attended with shame and guilt.

The power of fortune is confessed only by the miserable; for the happy impute all their success to prudence or merit.

Ambition often puts men upon doing the meanest offices; so climbing is performed in the same posture with creeping.

Censure is the tax a man pays to the public for being eminent.

Although men are accused for not knowing their own weakness, yet perhaps as few know their own strength. It is in men as in soils, where sometimes there is a vein of gold which the owner knows not of.

Satire is reckoned the easiest of all wit, but I take it to be otherwise in very bad times; for it is as hard to satirize well a man of distinguished vices as to praise well a man of distinguished virtues. It is easy enough to do either to people of moderate characters.

Invention is the talent of youth, and judgment of age; so that our judgment grows harder to please, when we have fewer things to offer it. This goes through the whole commerce of life. When we are old, our friends find it difficult to please us, and are less concerned whether we be pleased or no.

No wise man ever wished to be younger.

An idle reason lessens the weight of the good ones you gave before.

The motives of the best actions will not bear too strict an inquiry. It is allowed that the cause of most actions, good or bad, may be resolved into the love of ourselves; but the self-love of some men inclines them to please others, and the self-love of others is wholly employed in pleasing themselves. This makes the great distinction between virtue and vice. Religion is the best motive of all actions, yet religion is allowed to be the highest instance of self-love.

Old men view best at a distance with the eyes of their understanding as well as with those of nature.

Some people take more care to hide their wisdom than their folly.

Anthony Henley's farmer, dying of an asthma, said, " Well, if I can get this breath once out, I'll take care it shall never get in again."

The humor of exploding many things under the name of trifles, fopperies, and only imaginary goods, is a very false proof either of wisdom or magnanimity, and a great check to virtuous actions. For instance, with regard to fame, there is in most people a reluctance and unwillingness to be forgotten. We observe, even among the vulgar, how fond they are to have an inscription over their grave. It requires but little philosophy to discover and observe that there is no intrinsic value in all this; however, if it be founded in our nature as an incitement to ̄irtue, it ought not to be ridiculed.

Complaint is the largest tribute heaven receives, and the sincerest part of our devotion.

The common fluency of speech in many men, and most women, is owing to a scarcity of matter, and a scarcity of words; for whoever is a master of language, and hath a mind full of ideas, will be apt, in speaking, to hesitate upon the choice of both; whereas common speakers have only one set of ideas, and one set of words to clothe them in, and these are always ready at the mouth. So people come faster out of a church when it is almost empty than when a crowd is at the door.

Few are qualified to shine in company; but it is in most men's power to be agreeable. The reason, therefore, why conversation runs so low at present is not the defect of understanding, but pride, vanity, ill nature, affectation, singularity, positiveness, or some other vice, the effect of a wrong education.

To be vain is rather a mark of humility than pride. Vain men delight in telling what honors have been done them, what great company they have kept, and the like, by which they plainly confess that these honors were more than their due, and such as their friends would not believe if they had not been told; whereas a man truly proud thinks the greatest honors below his merit, and consequently scorns to boast. I therefore deliver it as a maxim, that whoever desires the character of a proud man ought to conceal his vanity.

Law, in a free country, is, or ought to be, the determination of the majority of those who have property in land.

One argument used to the disadvantage of Providence I take to be a very strong one in its defense. It is objected that storms and tempests, unfruitful seasons, serpents, spiders, flies, and other noxious or troublesome animals, with many more instances of the like kind, discover an imperfection in nature, because human life would be much easier without them; but the design of Providence may clearly be perceived in this proceeding. The motions of the sun and moon — in short, the whole system of the universe, as far as philosophers have been able to discover and observe — are in the utmost degree of regularity and perfection; but wherever God hath left to man the power of interposing a remedy by thought or labor, there he hath placed things in a state of imperfection, on purpose to stir up human industry, without which life would stagnate, or, indeed, rather, could not subsist at all: *Curis accuunt mortalia corda.*

Praise is the daughter of present power.

How inconsistent is man with himself!

I have known several persons of great fame for wisdom in public affairs and counsels governed by foolish servants.

I have known great ministers, distinguished for wit and learning, who preferred none but dunces.

I have known men of great valor cowards to their wives.

I have known men of the greatest cunning perpetually cheated.

I knew three great ministers, who could exactly compute and settle the accounts of a kingdom, but were wholly ignorant of their own economy.

The preaching of divines helps to preserve well-inclined men in the course of virtue, but seldom or never reclaims the vicious.

Princes usually make wiser choices than the servants whom they trust for the disposal of places: I have known a prince, more than once, choose an able minister, but I never observed that minister to use his credit in the disposal of an employment to a person whom he thought the fittest for it. One of the greatest in this age owned and excused the matter from the violence of parties and the unreasonableness of friends.

Small causes are sufficient to make a man uneasy when great ones are not in the way. For want of a block he will stumble at a straw.

Dignity, high station, or great riches, are in some sort necessary to old men, in order to keep the younger at a distance, who are otherwise too apt to insult them upon the score of their age.

Every man desires to live long; but no man would be old.

Love of flattery in most men proceeds from the mean opinion they have of themselves; in women from the contrary.

If books and laws continue to increase as they have done for fifty years past, I am in some concern for future ages how any man will be learned, or any man a lawyer.

Kings are commonly said to have long hands; I wish they had as long ears.

Princes in their infancy, childhood, and youth are said to discover prodigious parts and wit, to speak things that surprise and astonish. Strange, so many hopeful princes, and so many shameful kings! If they happen to die young, they would have been prodigies of wisdom and virtue. If they live, they are often prodigies indeed, but of another sort.

Politics, as the word is commonly understood, are nothing but corruptions, and consequently of no use to a good king or a good ministry; for which reason courts are so overrun with politics.

A nice man is a man of nasty ideas.

Apollo was held the god of physic and sender of diseases. Both were originally the same trade, and still continue.

Old men and comets have been reverenced for the same reason: their long beards, and pretenses to foretell events.

A person was asked at court, what he thought of an embassador and his train, who were all embroidery and lace, full of bows, cringes, and gestures; he said it was Solomon's importation, gold and apes.

Most sorts of diversion in men, children, and other animals, is an imitation of fighting.

Augustus meeting an ass with a lucky name foretold himself good fortune. I meet many asses, but none of them have lucky names.

If a man makes me keep my distance, the comfort is, he keeps his at the same time.

Who can deny that all men are violent lovers of truth when we see them so positive in their errors, which they will maintain out of their zeal to truth, although they contradict themselves every day of their lives?

That was excellently observed say I, when I read a passage in an author, where his opinion agrees with mine. When we differ, there I pronounce him to be mistaken.

Very few men, properly speaking, live at present, but are providing to live another time.

Laws penned with the utmost care and exactness, and in the vulgar language, are often perverted to wrong meanings; then why should we wonder that the Bible is so?

Although men are accused for not knowing their weakness, yet perhaps as few know their own strength.

A man seeing a wasp creeping into a vial filled with honey, that was hung on a fruit tree, said thus: "Why, thou sottish animal, art thou mad to go into that vial, where you see many hundreds of your kind there dying in it before you?" "The reproach is just," answered the wasp, "but not from you men, who are so far from taking example by other people's follies, that you will not take warning by your own. If after falling several times into this vial, and escaping by chance, I should fall in again, I should then but resemble you."

An old miser kept a tame jackdaw, that used to steal pieces of money, and hide them in a hole, which the cat observing, asked why he would hoard up those round shining things that he could make no use of? "Why," said the jackdaw, "my master has a whole chest full, and makes no more use of them than I."

Men are content to be laughed at for their wit, but not for their folly.

If the men of wit and genius would resolve never to complain in their works of critics and detractors, the next age would not know that they ever had any.

After all the maxims and systems of trade and commerce, a stander-by would think the affairs of the world were most ridiculously contrived.

There are few countries which, if well cultivated, would not support double the number of their inhabitants, and yet fewer where one-third of the people are not extremely stinted even in the necessaries of life. I send out twenty barrels of corn, which would maintain a family in bread for a year, and I bring back in return a vessel of wine, which half a dozen good fellows would drink in less than a month, at the expense of their health and reason.

A man would have but few spectators, if he offered to show for threepence how he could thrust a red-hot iron into a barrel of gunpowder, and it should not take fire.

Complete.

AGAINST ABOLISHING CHRISTIANITY IN ENGLAND

I AM very sensible what a weakness and presumption it is to reason against the general humor and disposition of the world. I remember it was with great justice, and a due regard to the freedom, both of the public and the press, forbidden upon several penalties to write, or discourse, or lay wagers against the ——— even before it was confirmed by parliament; because that was looked upon as a design to oppose the current of the people, which, besides the folly of it, is a manifest breach of the fundamental law, that makes this majority of opinions the voice of God. In like manner, and for the very same reasons, it may perhaps be neither safe nor prudent to argue against the abolishing of Christianity, at a juncture when all parties seem so unanimously determined upon the point, as we cannot but allow from their actions, their discourses, and their writings. However, I know not how, whether from the affectation of singularity, or the perverseness of human nature, but so it unhappily falls out, that I cannot be entirely of this opinion. Nay, though I were sure an order were issued for my immediate prosecution by the Attorney-General, I should still confess that in the present posture of our affairs at home or abroad, I do not yet see the absolute necessity of extirpating the Christian religion from among us.

This perhaps may appear too great a paradox even for our wise and paradoxical age to endure; therefore I shall handle it with all tenderness, and with the utmost deference to that great and profound majority which is of another sentiment.

And yet the curious may please to observe how much the genius of a nation is liable to alter in half an age: I have heard it affirmed for certain by some very odd people, that the contrary opinion was even in their memories as much in vogue as the other is now; and that a project for the abolishing of Christianity would then have appeared as singular, and been thought as absurd, as it would be at this time to write or discourse in its defense.

Therefore I freely own that all appearances are against me. The system of the Gospel after the fate of other systems, is generally antiquated and exploded, and the mass or body of the common people, among whom it seems to have had its latest credit, are now grown as much ashamed of it as their betters; opinions, like fashions, always descending from those of quality to the middle sort, and thence to the vulgar, where at length they are dropped and vanish.

But here I would not be mistaken, and must therefore be so bold as to borrow a distinction from the writers on the other side, when they make a difference betwixt nominal and real Trinitarians. I hope no reader imagines me so weak to stand up in the defense of real Christianity, such as used in primitive times (if we may believe the authors of those ages) to have an influence upon men's belief and actions. To offer at the restoring of that would indeed be a wild project: it would be to dig up foundations; to destroy at one blow all the wit, and half the learning of the kingdom; to break the entire frame and constitution of things; to ruin trade, extinguish arts and sciences, with the professors of them; in short, to turn our courts, exchanges, and shops into deserts; and would be full as absurd as the proposal of Horace, where he advises the Romans all in a body to leave their city, and seek a new seat in some remote part of the world, by way of a cure for the corruption of their manners.

Therefore I think this caution was in itself altogether unnecessary (which I have inserted only to prevent all possibility of caviling), since every candid reader will easily understand my discourse to be intended only in defense of nominal Christianity, the other having been for some time wholly laid aside by general consent, as utterly inconsistent with all our present schemes of wealth and power.

But why we should therefore cast off the name and title of Christians, although the general opinion and resolution be so violent for it, I confess I cannot (with submission) apprehend the consequence necessary.

AGAINST BAD ENGLISH

FROM MY OWN APARTMENT, September 28th.

THE following letter has laid before me many great and manifest evils in the world of letters, which I had overlooked; but they open to me a very busy scene, and it will require no small care and application to amend errors which are become so universal. The affectation of politeness is exposed in this epistle with a great deal of wit and discernment; so that whatever discourses I may fall into hereafter upon the subjects the writer treats of, I shall at present lay the matter before the world, without the least alteration from the words of my correspondent.

To ISAAC BICKERSTAFF, ESQ.

Sir: —

There are some abuses among us of great consequence, the reformation of which is properly your province; though, as far as I have been conversant in your papers, you have not yet considered them. These are, the deplorable ignorance that for some years hath reigned among our English writers, the great depravity of our taste, and the continual corruption of our style. I say nothing here of those who handle particular sciences, divinity, law, physic, and the like; I mean the traders in history, politics, and the Belles-Lettres; together with those by whom books are not translated, but, as the common expressions are, done out of French, Latin, or other language, and made

English.   I cannot but observe to you that until of late years a Grub-Street book was always bound in sheepskin, with suitable print and paper, the price never above a shilling, and taken off wholly by common tradesmen or country peddlers; but now they appear in all sizes and shapes, and in all places.   They are handed about from lapfuls in every coffeehouse to persons of quality; are shown in Westminster Hall and the Court of Requests.   You may see them gilt, and in royal paper of five or six hundred pages, and rated accordingly.   I would engage to furnish you with a catalogue of English books, published within the compass of seven years past, which at the first hand would cost you a hundred pounds, wherein you shall not be able to find ten lines together of common grammar or common sense.

These two evils, ignorance and want of taste, have produced a third; I mean the continual corruption of our English tongue, which, without some timely remedy, will suffer more by the false refinements of twenty years past, than it hath been improved in the foregoing hundred.   And this is what I design chiefly to enlarge upon, leaving the former evils to your animadversion.

But instead of giving you a list of the late refinements crept into our language, I here send you the copy of a letter I received, some time ago, from a most accomplished person in this way of writing; upon which I shall make some remarks.   It is in these terms:—

Sir:—

I cou'd n't get the things you sent for all about town——I thôt to ha come down myself, and then I'd h' brôt 'um; but I ha'nt don't, and I believe I can't do't that's pozz——Tom begins to gi'mself airs, because he's going with the plenipo's——'Tis said the French king will bamboozl us agen, which causes many speculations.   The Jacks and others of that kidney are very uppish and alert upon't, as you may see by their phizz's——Will Hazard has got the hipps, having lost to the tune of five hund'rd pound, tho' he understands play very well, nobody better.   He has promis't me upon rep, to leave off play; but you know 'tis a weakness he's too apt to give into, tho' he has as much wit as any man, nobody more.   He has lain incog ever since—The mob's very quiet with us now——I believe you thôt I banter'd you in my last, like a country put——I shan't leave town this month, etc.

This letter is in every point an admirable pattern of the present polite way of writing; nor is it of less authority for being an epistle. You may gather every flower in it, with a thousand more of equal sweetness, from the books, pamphlets, and single papers offered us every day in the coffeehouses: and these are the beauties introduced to supply the want of wit, sense, humor, and learning, which formerly were looked upon as qualifications for a writer.   If a man of wit, who died forty years ago, were to rise from the grave on purpose, how would he be able to read this letter? and after he had got through that difficulty, how would he be able to understand it? The first thing that strikes your eye is the breaks at the end of almost every sentence; of which I know not the use, only that it is a refinement, and very frequently practiced. Then you will observe the abbreviations and elisions, by which consonants of most obdurate sound are joined together, without one softening vowel to intervene; and all this only to make one syllable of two, directly contrary to the example of the Greeks and Romans, altogether of the Gothic strain, and a natural tendency towards relapsing into barbarity, which delights in monosyllables, and uniting of mute consonants, as it is observable in all the Northern languages. And this is still more visible in the next refinement, which consists in pronouncing the first syllable in a word that has many, and dismissing the rest, such as phizz, hipps, mob, pozz, rep, and many more, when we are already overloaded with monosyllables, which are the disgrace of our language. Thus we cram one syllable, and cut off the rest, as the owl fattened her mice after she had bit off their legs to prevent them from running away; and if ours be the same reason for maiming our words, it will certainly answer the end; for I am sure no other nation will desire to borrow them. Some words are hitherto but fairly split, and therefore only in their way to perfection, as incog and plenipo; but in a short time, it is to be hoped, they will be further docked to inc and plen. This reflection has made me of late years very impatient for a peace, which I believe would save the lives of many brave words, as well as men. The war has introduced abundance of polysyllables, which will never be able to live many more campaigns: speculations, operations, preliminaries, embassadors, pallisadoes, communication, circumvallation, battalions; as numerous as they are, if they attack us too frequently in our coffeehouses, we shall certainly put them to flight, and cut off the rear.

The third refinement observable in the letter I send you, consists in the choice of certain words invented by some pretty fellows, such as banter, bamboozle, country put, and kidney, as it is there applied; some of which are now struggling for the vogue, and others are in possession of it. I have done my utmost for some years past to stop the progress of mob and banter, but have been plainly borne down by numbers, and betrayed by those who promised to assist me.

In the last place, you are to take notice of certain choice phrases scattered through the letter, some of them tolerable enough, until they were worn to rags by servile imitators. You might easily find them, though they were not in a different print, and therefore I need not disturb them.

These are the false refinements in our style which you ought to correct: first, by argument and fair means; but, if those fail, I think

you are to make use of your authority as Censor, and by an annual
Index Expurgatorius expunge all words and phrases that are offensive
to good sense, and condemn those barbarous mutilations of vowels
and syllables. In this last point the usual pretense is, that they spell
as they speak. A noble standard for language! to depend upon the
caprice of every coxcomb, who, because words are the clothing of our
thoughts, cuts them out and shapes them as he pleases, and changes
them oftener than his dress. I believe all reasonable people would
be content that such refiners were more sparing in their words, and
liberal in their syllables: and upon this head I should be glad you
would bestow some advice upon several young readers in our churches,
who, coming up from the university full fraught with admiration of
our town politeness, will needs correct the style of their prayer books.
In reading the Absolution, they are very careful to say pardons and
absolves; and in the prayer for the royal family, it must be endue'um,
enrich'um, prosper'um, and bring'um. Then in their sermons they
use all the modern terms of art, sham, banter, mob, bubble, bully,
cutting, shuffling, and palming; all which, and many more of the like
stamp, as I have heard them often in the pulpit from such young
sophisters, so I have read them in some of "those sermons that have
made most noise of late." The design, it seems, is to avoid the dreadful imputation of pedantry; to show us that they know the town,
understand men and manners, and have not been poring upon old,
unfashionable books in the university.

I should be glad to see you the instrument of introducing into
our style that simplicity which is the best and truest ornament of
most things in life, which the politer ages always aimed at in their
building and dress, *simplex munditiis*, as well as their productions of
wit. It is manifest that all new-affected modes of speech, whether
borrowed from the court, the town, or the theatre, are the first perish-
ing parts in any language; and, as I could prove by many hundred
instances, have been so in ours. The writings of Hooker, who was a
country clergyman, and of Parsons the Jesuit, both in the reign of
Queen Elizabeth, are in a style that, with very few allowances, would
not offend any present reader, and are much more clear and intelligible than those of Sir Harry Wooton, Sir Robert Naunton, Osborn,
Daniel the historian, and several others who writ later; but being men
of the court, and affecting the phrases then in fashion, they are often
either not to be understood, or appear perfectly ridiculous.

What remedies are to be applied to these evils I have not room
to consider, having, I fear, already taken up most of your paper.
Besides, I think it is our office only to represent abuses, and yours
to redress them. I am, with great respect, sir,   Yours, etc.

Complete. From the Tatler.

ALGERNON CHARLES SWINBURNE

(1837-)

LGERNON CHARLES SWINBURNE, a celebrated English poet and critic, was born in London, April 5th, 1837. His studies were begun in France and completed at Oxford, which he left without a degree in 1857. It is possible, however, that he did not leave a better Greek scholar behind him at the university, which failed to honor him. His love for Greek and French verse decided his career and his style. He became the most melodious versifier of his time. The English language as he employed it by joining Saxon alliteration to classical "staff rhyme" showed a capacity for melody before unsuspected. He employed this in his earlier poems and ballads (republished in America in 1866 as "Laus Veneris") to express a spirit of intense revolt against modern moral and social restrictions. This is more or less apparent throughout all his work, which in his later years shows an increasing tendency to prefer melody to meaning. In his youth he was a fierce Republican, a disciple of Landor and Hugo; but among his latest poems is a strongly patriotic ode in favor of crushing the Boers of the South African republics. He has published numerous essays, chiefly critical. Some of them have been collected in his "Prose Miscellanies," published in 1886.

W. V. B.

CHAUCER AND THE ITALIAN POETS

OF ALL whose names may claim anything like equality of rank on the roll of national poets — not even excepting Virgil — we may say that Chaucer borrowed most from abroad, and did most to improve whatever he borrowed. I believe it would be but accurate to admit that in all his poems of serious or tragic narrative we hear a French or Italian tongue speaking with a Teutonic accent through English lips. It has utterly unlearned the native tone and cadence of its natural inflections; it has perfectly put on the native tone and cadence of a stranger's; yet is it always what it was at first — *lingua romana in bocca tedesca*. It speaks not only with more vigor, but actually with more sweetness than the tongues of its teachers; but it speaks after its own fashion no other than the lesson they have taught. Chaucer was in the main a French or Italian poet, lined thoroughly and warmly throughout with the substance of an English humorist. And with this great gift of specially English humor he combined, naturally as it were and inevitably, the inseparable twinborn gift of peculiarly English pathos. In the figures of Arcite and Grisilde he has actually outdone Boccaccio's very self for pathos; as far almost as Keats was afterward to fall short of the same great model in the same great quality. And but for the instinctive distaste and congenital repugnance of his composed and comfortable genius from its accompanying horror, he might haply have come nearer than he has cared or dared to come even to the unapproachable pathos of Dante. But it was only in the world of one who stands far higher above Dante than even Dante can on the whole be justly held to stand above Chaucer, that figures as heavenly as the figures of Beatrice and Matilda could move unspotted and undegraded among figures as earthly as those of the Reve, the Miller, and the Wife of Bath; that a wider, if not keener, pathos than Ugolino's or Francesca's could alternate with a deeper, if not richer, humor than that of Absolon and Nicholas.

It is a notable dispensation of chance that the three great typical poets of the three great representative nations of Europe during the dark and lurid lapse of the Middle Ages should each afford as complete and profound a type of a different and alien class as of a different and alien people. Vast as are the diversities of their national and personal characters, these are yet less radical than the divergences between class and class which mark off each from either of his fellows in nothing but in fame. Dante represents, at its best and highest, the upper class of the Dark Ages not less than he represents their Italy; Chaucer represents their middle class at its best and wisest not less than he represents their England; Villon represents their lower class at its worst and its best alike even more than he represents their France. And of these three the English middle class, being incomparably the happiest and the wisest, is indisputably, considering the common circumstances of their successive times, the least likely to have left us the highest example of all poetry then possible to men. And of their three legacies, precious and wonderful as it is, the Englishman's is accordingly the least wonderful and the least precious. The poet of the sensible and prosperous middle class in England had less to suffer and to sing than the theosophic aristocrat of Italy, or the hunted and hungry vagabond who first found articulate voice for the dumb longing and the blind love, as well as for the reckless appetites and riotous agonies of the miserable and terrible multitude in whose darkness lay dormant, as in a cerecloth, which was also a chrysalis, the debased and disfigured godhead which was one day to exchange the degradation of the lowest populace for the revelation of the highest people — for the world-wide apocalypse of France. The golden-tongued gallows bird of Paris is distinguished from his two more dignified compeers by a deeper difference yet — a difference, we might say, of office and of mission no less than of genius and of gift. Dante and Chaucer are wholly and solely poets of the past or present — singers, indeed, for all time, but only singers of their own; Villon, in an equivocal and unconscious fashion, was a singer also of the future; he was the first modern and the last mediæval poet. He is of us in a sense in which it cannot be said that either Chaucer or Dante is of us, or even could have been; a man of a changing and self-transforming time, not utterly held fast, though still sorely struggling, in the jaws of hell and the ages of faith.

But in happy perfection of manhood the great and fortunate Englishman almost more exceeds his great and unfortunate fellow-singers than he is exceeded by them in depth of passion and height of rapture, in ardor and intensity of vision or of sense. With the single and sublimer exception of Sophocles, he seems to me the happiest of all great poets on record; their standing type and sovereign example of noble and manly happiness. As prosperous, indeed, in their several ages and lines of life were Petrarch and Ariosto, Horace and Virgil; but one only of these impresses us in every lineament of his work with the same masculine power of enjoyment. And when Ariosto threw across the windy sea of glittering legend and fluctuant romance the broad summer lightnings of his large and jocund genius, the Dark Ages had already returned into the outer darkness where there is weeping and gnashing of teeth — the tears of Dante Alighieri and the laughter of François Villon. But the wide warm harvest field of Chaucer's husbandry was all glorious with gold of ripening sunshine, while all the world beside lay in blackness and bonds, throughout all those ages of death called ages of faith by men who can believe in nothing beyond a building or a book, outside the codified creeds of a Bible or the ecumenical structures of a church.

From « Short Notes on English Poets.»

A POET'S HAUGHTY PATIENCE

I T IS the fashion of our day to look for the typical man or representative figure of the English commonwealth not so much in the poet who glorified as in the dictator who destroyed it. This is but natural and consistent in such historians as see nothing in the record of our short-lived republic worth admiration or regret but the triumph of a more harsh and earnest form of superstition over one somewhat less hellish in its cast of creed and greatly more graceful in its tone of life, accompanied by the substitution of a stern and steady system of dictatorial rule for the lax and trustless impulse of a treacherous and shifting tyranny; but those whose faith or feeling in the matter of historic patriotism lies deeper than a mere preference for competent over incompetent autocracy must perceive, or at least will believe, that the restoration which they admire as little as any military-minded Neo-Calvinist or Muscovitic imperialist of their time was not so much the doing of James Monk as the work of Oliver Cromwell: a consummation of catastrophe directly rather than indirectly due to the weakness and selfishness of the nominal and temporary protector, the actual and final destroyer of the commonwealth of England. For surely the dying hand which put into Richard Cromwell's the sceptre of its sway put by that act the crown of England into Monk's for delivery into Charles the Second's. And this, if we never have learned it from the evidence of Milton himself, we may learn with equal confidence from Landor's that Milton surely saw. "He had grown calmer at the close of life, and saw in Cromwell as a fault what he had seen before as a necessity or a virtue." And therefore is it rather in the loftier, purer, more loyal and more liberal virtue of its poet, than in the dubious and double-faced majesty of its august and imperious dictator, that we should salute the highest and most perfect type of the English republic; dragged down into his own grave by the fatal dead hand of Cromwell, yet surviving after a sort in the figure of the blind man "left upright"—in the phrase of a poet as glorious and a republican as faithful as himself—on the verge and in the shadow of her sepulchre.

In private matters, or such as belong to the range of ethics rather than of politics, the instinct of Milton seems to me as much truer and finer than the instinct of Dante as his judgment and his conscience were juster, sounder, purer than the conscience or the judgment of Cromwell. Only those disciples in whom congenital idolatry has passed into the stage of acute monomania can maintain that the quality of Dante's great work is never in any considerable degree impaired by the incessant invasion of merely personal polemics; that the reader is never or but rarely, fatigued and nauseated by the obtrusion and obsession of "verminous fellows," whom the higher muses at least should be content to leave in the native and natural shelter of that obscene obscurity which alone is proper to such animalcules as make the filth they feed on. There are others beside the "brothel lackeys" of a bastard empire who, as Victor Hugo said once, would desire us to shut our eyes, but compel us to stop our noses.

No matter what manner of offense may naturally be given by creatures whose very nature is offensive, a man who is duly and soberly conscious of any reason for self-respect will ultimately, as Milton did and Dante did not, determine that personal insolence, whether masked as Caliban or manifest as Thersites, shall draw down no further notice from his hand or foot. There are things unmentionable save by a too faithful pupil or too literal imitator of Swift, which, only for our own sake, we are careful not to spurn as we step over them. Upon such Milton did not hesitate to set his heel, when duly guarded by the thick-soled boot of prose; but, unlike Dante, he never permitted the too fetid contact of their feculence to befoul the sandal of his muse. The reddening knots of his controversial scourge fell only in cadences of prose, or at least but very rarely in brief reverberation of rhythmic numbers, on the noisome nudity exposed as in provocation of its lash by Saumaise or Du Moulin, the literary lackey of a princeling or the cryptonymous railer for his bread.

This high-souled and haughty respect for the dignity of his natural art should be duly borne in mind whenever we are tempted to dwell somewhat disapprovingly on Milton's indefatigable and fierce delight in "double-thonging" such equivocal sons of a dubious kennel; though it will not be denied that he spent more strength of arm than he need have wasted on the resonant reiteration of stripes from a deserved but superfluous dog whip, too constantly sent curling about their currish flanks.

It is certainly no very dignified amusement, no very profitable expenditure of energy or time, to indulge in the easy diversion of making such curs yelp, and watching them writhe under the chastisement which an insulted superior may condescend to inflict, till their foul mouths foam over in futile and furious response, reeking and rabid with virulent froth and exhalations of raging ribaldry. Yet when, like those that swarmed at the heels of Milton, the vermin venture on all possible extremes of personal insult and imputation to which dullness may give ear or malice may give tongue, a man cannot reasonably be held to derogate from the duty and the dignity of self-respect if he spurns or scourges them out of his way. To give these rascals rope is a needless waste of hemp; a spider's thread, spun from the inner impurity of his own venomous vitals, will suffice for such a creature to hang himself.

A ground more plausible may seem to exist for a graver charge against Milton than that of a ferocious condescension to take unmerciful notice of such leprous little malignants as these; for the charge of relentless and unmitigable savagery toward the dead, whose misdoings might seem — or to us may seem at this distance — to have been amply expiated by discomfiture and death. Cheap and not over-nice chivalry — the false Florimel who assumes and degrades the appearance of true knightliness of mind and sound nobility of spirit — is ever ready, when tyrants are fallen or when traitors are degraded, to remind us in the shrillest note of reproachful impertinence that "it is ill boasting over dead men." Ill indeed, and worse than ill, it is when those who could see nothing to blame in Nero, nothing to loathe in Judas, till the moment of ruin which reduced them to suicide, begin to cast stones at the carrion which had been found worthy of their adoration when a pontiff, of their adulation when an emperor. But ill it would also be, abominable and absurd, if the "piteous and unpitied end" of either were to be held as expiation sufficient to reverse the branding judgment or silence the damning voice of history or of poetry; to bid those now be silent out of pitiable pity and hypocritical high-mindedness who did not hesitate, while some among the posthumous revilers, as well as the posthumous champions of these wretches, were prone before the vilest of all idols on their knees like the courtier or on their bellies like the serpent, to call Judas by his name of Iscariot and Nero by his name of Bonaparte.

The self-confident and self-conscious majesty of Milton's devotion and dedication to their natural work of all the faculties assigned to him by nature has foolishly enough been objected against him as evidence of his poetic inferiority to Shakespeare. With that unapproachable name no rational man will assert the equality of Milton's; but if Shakespeare's claim to superiority rested only on the evidence of his intellectual self-effacement, his modest unconsciousness and humble-minded abnegation or ignorance of his right to put forward any claim whatever, it would be but too easy a task to convict him out of his own mouth, and prove by the avowal of his own pretensions that he can pretend to the credit of no such imbecility. No sandier foundation was ever discovered for a fallacy more futile than this. No man ever lived who had less title than Shakespeare to whatever blessing may be reserved for the poor in spirit. Not even Milton, not even Dante, had less right to say in appeal to God or man, " I am not high-minded." No man's writings bear witness more unquestionable that he worked and waited with the haughty patience of self-assured expectation for the inevitable homage of mankind in centuries to come.

From the Fortnightly Review.

JOHN ADDINGTON SYMONDS

(1840–1893)

JOHN ADDINGTON SYMONDS, an English writer, specially noted as an essayist and classical scholar, was born at Bristol, October 5th, 1840. He graduated at Oxford and won the Newdigate prize in 1860. In 1872 his «Introduction to the Study of Dante» laid the foundations of a reputation which he increased by his «Studies of the Greek Poets.» He has made many admirable translations from Greek, Latin, and Italian verse. «Italian By-Ways,» «Sketches of Study in Italy,» and a «Life of Michael Angelo» are among his more noted works. He died at Rome, April 19th, 1893.

MORNING RAMBLES IN VENICE

A STORY is told of Poussin, the French painter, that when he was asked why he would not stay in Venice, he replied, "If I stay here, I shall become a colorist!" A somewhat similar tale is reported of a fashionable English decorator. While on a visit to friends in Venice he avoided every building which contains a Tintoretto, averring that the sight of Tintoretto's pictures would injure his carefully trained taste. It is probable that neither anecdote is strictly true. Yet there is a certain epigrammatic point in both; and I have often speculated whether even Venice could have so warped the genius of Poussin as to shed one ray of splendor on his canvasses, or whether even Tintoretto could have so sublimed the prophet of Queen Anne as to make him add dramatic passion to a London drawing-room. Anyhow it is exceedingly difficult to escape from color in the air of Venice, or from Tintoretto in her buildings. Long, delightful mornings may be spent in the enjoyment of the one and the pursuit of the other by folk who have no classical or pseudo-mediæval theories to oppress them.

Tintoretto's house, though changed, can still be visited. It formed part of the Fondamenta dei Mori, so called from having been the quarter assigned to Moorish traders in Venice. A spirited carving of a turbaned Moor leading a camel charged with

merchandise remains above the water line of a neighboring building, and all about the crumbling walls sprout flowering weeds —
samphire and snapdragon and the spiked campanula, which shoots
a spire of sea-blue stars from chinks of Istrian stone.

The house stands opposite the Church of Santa Maria dell' Orto,
where Tintoretto was buried, and where four of his chief masterpieces are to be seen. This church, swept and garnished, is a triumph of modern Italian restoration. They have contrived to
make it as commonplace as human ingenuity could manage. Yet
no malice of ignorant industry can obscure the treasures it contains — the pictures of Cimabue, Giovanni Bellini, Palma, and the
four Tintorettos, which form its crowning glory. Here the master
may be studied in four of his chief moods: as the painter of
tragic passion and movement, in the huge "Last Judgment"; as
the painter of impossibilities, in the "Vision of Moses upon Sinai";
as the painter of purity and tranquil pathos, in the "Miracle of St.
Agnes"; as the painter of biblical history brought home to daily
life, in the "Presentation of the Virgin." Without leaving the "Madonna dell' Orto," a student can explore his genius in all its depth
and breadth; comprehend the enthusiasm he excites in those who
seek, as the essentials of art, imaginative boldness and sincerity;
understand what is meant by adversaries who maintain that, after
all, Tintoretto was but an inspired Gustave Doré. Between that
quiet canvas of the "Presentation," so modest in its cool grays and
subdued gold, and the tumult of flying, running, ascending figures
in the "Judgment," what an interval there is! How strangely the
white lamb-like maiden, kneeling beside her lamb in the picture
of "St. Agnes," contrasts with the dusky gorgeousness of the Hebrew women despoiling themselves of jewels for the golden calf!
Comparing these several manifestations of creative power, we feel
ourselves in the grasp of a painter who was essentially a poet,
one for whom his art was the medium for expressing before all
things thought and passion. Each picture is executed in the manner suited to its tone of feeling, the key of its conception.

Elsewhere than in the "Madonna dell' Orto" there are more
distinguished single examples of Tintoretto's realizing faculty. The
"Last Supper" in San Giorgio, for instance, and the "Adoration
of the Shepherds," in the Scuola di San Rocco, illustrate his
unique power of presenting sacred history in a novel, romantic
framework of familiar things. The most commonplace circumstances of ordinary life have been employed to portray in the one

case a lyric of mysterious splendor; in the other an idyl of infinite sweetness. Divinity shines through the rafters of that upper
chamber, where round the low large table the Apostles are assembled in a group translated from the social customs of the
painter's days. Divinity is shed upon the straw-spread manger,
where Christ lies sleeping in the loft, with shepherds crowding
through the room beneath.

A studied contrast between the simplicity and repose of the
central figure and the tumult of passions in the multitude around
may be observed in the "Miracle of St. Agnes." It is this which
gives dramatic vigor to the composition. But the same effect is
carried to its highest fulfillment, with even a loftier beauty, in
the episode of Christ before the judgment seat of Pilate, at San
Rocco. Of all Tintoretto's religious pictures that is the most
profoundly felt, the most majestic. No other artist succeeded as
he has here succeeded in presenting to us God incarnate. For
this Christ is not merely the just man, innocent, silent before his
accusers. The stationary, white-draped figure raised high above
the agitated crowd, with tranquil forehead slightly bent, facing
his perplexed and fussy judge, is more than man. We cannot
say perhaps precisely why he is divine. But Tintoretto has made
us feel that he is. In other words, his treatment of the high
theme chosen by him has been adequate.

We must seek the Scuola di San Rocco for examples of Tintoretto's liveliest imagination. Without ceasing to be Italian in
his attention to harmony and grace, he far exceeded the masters
of his nation in the power of suggesting what is weird, mysterious, upon the borderland of the grotesque. And of this quality
there are three remarkable instances in the Scuola. No one but
Tintoretto could have evoked the fiend in his "Temptation of
Christ." It is an indescribable hermaphroditic genius, the genius
of carnal fascination, with outspread downy rose-plumed wings,
and flaming bracelets on the full, plump arms, who kneels and
lifts aloft great stones, smiling entreatingly to the sad, gray Christ
seated beneath a rugged penthouse of the desert. No one again
but Tintoretto could have dashed the hot lights of that fiery sunset
in such quivering flakes upon the golden flesh of Eve, half hidden
among laurels, as she stretches forth the fruit of the Fall to
shrinking Adam. No one but Tintoretto, till we come to Blake,
could have imagined yonder Jonah, summoned by the beck of
God from the whale's belly. The monstrous fish rolls over in the

ocean, blowing portentous vapor from his trump-shaped nostril. The prophet's beard descends upon his naked breast in hoary ringlets to the girdle. He has forgotten the past peril of the deep, although the whale's jaws yawn around him. Between him and the outstretched finger of Jehovah calling him again to life there runs a spark of unseen spiritual electricity.

To comprehend Tintoretto's touch upon the pastoral idyl we must turn our steps to San Giorgio again, and pace those meadows by the running river in company with his Manna-Gatherers. Or we may seek the Accademia, and notice how he here has varied the "Temptation of Adam by Eve," choosing a less tragic motive of seduction than the one so powerfully rendered at San Rocco. Or in the Ducal Palace we may take our station, hour by hour, before the "Marriage of Bacchus and Ariadne." It is well to leave the very highest achievements of art, untouched by criticism, undescribed. And in this picture we have the most perfect of all modern attempts to realize an antique myth — more perfect than Raphael's "Galatea" or Titian's "Meeting of Bacchus with Ariadne," or Botticelli's "Birth of Venus from the Sea." It may suffice to marvel at the slight effect which melodies so powerful and so direct as these produce upon the ordinary public. Sitting, as is my wont, one Sunday morning, opposite the "Bacchus," four Germans with a cicerone sauntered by. The subject was explained to them. They waited an appreciable space of time. Then the youngest opened his lips and spake: "*Bacchus war der Weingott.*" And they all moved heavily away. *Bos locutus est.* "Bacchus was the wine god!" This, apparently, is what a picture tells to one man. To another it presents divine harmonies, perceptible indeed in nature, but here by the painter poet for the first time brought together and cadenced in a work of art. For another it is perhaps the hieroglyph of pent-up passions and desired impossibilities. For yet another it may only mean the unapproachable inimitable triumph of consummate craft.

Tintoretto, to be rightly understood, must be sought all over Venice — in the church as well as the Scuola di San Rocco; in the "Temptation of St. Anthony" at St. Trovaso no less than in the "Temptations" of Eve and Christ; in the decorative pomp of the Sala del Senato, and in the paradisal vision of the Sala del Gran Consiglio. Yet, after all, there is one of his most characteristic moods, to appreciate which fully we return to the "Madonna dell' Orto." I have called him "the painter of impossibilities." At rare moments he rendered them possible by sheer imaginative force. If we wish to realize this phase of his creative power, and to measure our own subordination to his genius in its most hazardous enterprise, we must spend much time in the choir of this church. Lovers of art who mistrust this play of the audacious fancy — aiming at sublimity in supersensual regions, sometimes attaining to it by stupendous effort or authentic revelation, not seldom sinking to the verge of bathos, and demanding the assistance of interpretative sympathy in the spectator — such men will not take the point of view required of them by Tintoretto in his boldest flights, in the "Worship of the Golden Calf" and in the "Destruction of the World by Water." It is for them to ponder well the flying archangel with the scales of judgment in his hand, and the seraph-charioted Jehovah enveloping Moses upon Sinai in lightnings.

The gondola has had a long rest. Were Francesco but a little more impatient, he might be wondering what had become of the padrone. I bid him turn, and we are soon gliding into the Sacca della Misericordia. This is a protected float, where the wood which comes from Cadore and the hills of the Ampezzo is stored in spring. Yonder square white house, standing out to sea, fronting Murano and the Alps, they call the Casa degli Spiriti. No one cares to inhabit it; for here, in old days, it was the wont of the Venetians to lay their dead for a night's rest before their final journey to the graveyard of San Michele. So many generations of dead folk had made that house their inn, that it is now no fitting home for living men. San Michele is the island close before Murano, where the Lombardi built one of their most romantically graceful churches of pale Istrian stone, and where the Campo Santo has for centuries received the dead into its oozy clay. The cemetery is at present undergoing restoration. Its state of squalor and abandonment to cynical disorder makes one feel how fitting for Italians would be the custom of cremation. An island in the lagoons devoted to funeral pyres is a solemn and ennobling conception. This graveyard, with its ruinous walls, its mangy riot of unwholesome weeds, its corpses festering in slime beneath neglected slabs in hollow chambers, and the mephitic wash of poisoned waters that surround it, inspires the horror of disgust.

The morning has not lost its freshness. Antelao and Tofana, guarding the vale above Cortina, show faint streaks of snow upon their amethyst. Little clouds hang in the still autumn sky. There are men dredging for shrimps and crabs through shoals uncovered by the ebb. Nothing can be lovelier, more resting to eyes tired with pictures than this tranquil, sunny expanse of the lagoon. As we round the point of the Bersaglio new landscapes of island and Alp and low-lying mainland move into sight at every slow stroke of the oar. A luggage train comes lumbering along the railway bridge, puffing white smoke into the placid blue. Then we strike down Cannaregio, and I muse upon processions of kings and generals and noble strangers, entering Venice by this water path from Mestre, before the Austrians built their causeway for the trains. Some of the rare scraps of fresco upon house fronts, still to be seen in Venice, are left in Cannaregio. They are chiaroscuro allegories in a bold bravura manner of the sixteenth century. From these and from a few rosy fragments on the Fondaco dei Tedeschi, the Fabbriche Nuove, and precious fading figures in a certain courtyard near San Stefano, we form some notion how Venice looked when all her palaces were painted. Pictures by Gentile Bellini, Mansueti, and Carpaccio help the fancy in this work of restoration. And here and there, in black canals, we come across colored sections of old buildings, capped by true Venetian chimneys, which for a moment seem to realize our dream.

A morning with Tintoretto might well be followed by a morning with Carpaccio or Bellini. But space is wanting in these pages. Nor would it suit the manner of this medley to hunt the Lombardi through palaces and churches, pointing out their singularities of violet and yellow pannelings in marble, the dignity of their wide-opened arches, or the delicacy of their shallow chiseled traceries in cream-white Istrian stone. It is enough to indicate the goal of many a pleasant pilgrimage; warrior angels of Vivarini and Basaiti, hidden in a dark chapel of the Frari; Fra Francesco's fantastic orchard of fruits and flowers in distant S. Francesco della Vigna; the golden Gian Bellini in San Zaccaria; Palma's majestic San Barbara in San Maria Formosa; San Giobbe's wealth of sculptured frieze and floral scroll; the Ponte di Paradiso, with its Gothic arch; the painted plates in the Museo Civico; and palace after palace, loved for some quaint piece of tracery, some molding full of mediæval symbolism, some fierce impossible Renaissance freak of fancy.

Complete. From "A Venetian Medley."